HENRY WARD BEECHER
The Indiana Years, 1837-1847

Henry Ward Beecher as a young man

HENRY WARD BEECHER

The Indiana Years, 1837-1847

Jane Shaffer Elsmere

INDIANAPOLIS
Indiana Historical Society
1973

Contents

Illustrations

Preface

WHILE SEARCHING THROUGH THE STACKS OF A LIBRARY FOR AN INTER-
esting biography, I came upon Paxton Hibben's *Henry Ward Beecher:
An American Portrait*. Familiar with the major events of Beecher's later
career, I had never read an account of his life. I glanced at the table of
contents; two names, Lawrenceburgh and Indianapolis, caught my
attention. In skimming the chapters I discovered that Beecher began
his ministry in Indiana where he spent ten years as a Presbyterian
clergyman. I was intrigued and wanted to learn about his experiences
in my native state.

Hibben's disappointing biography of Beecher left questions unanswered. Other biographies about the colorful clergyman were, for
the most part, equally unsatisfactory in their treatment of this formative
period in Beecher's life. It was during these years between 1837 and
1847 that he was a missionary, married, became a father, endured
poverty and humiliation, persevered, survived denominational controversy, obtained the pastorate of a new and fashionable church in the
state capital, bore suffering and tragedy, became a noted revivalist,
horticulturist, and journalist, was active in social reforms on the city
and state levels, and achieved a degree of national prominence. Neglect
of this important phase of his life seemed unwarranted. I wanted to
know the daily circumstances of his life and the people he encountered;
the ways in which he reacted to the challenges, responsibilities, disap-

pointments, and successes which came his way; and what contributions, if any, he made to Indiana.

Staffs of the following institutions replied to written queries and generously opened their archives and libraries to me during my research: Amherst College; Amistad Research Center at Fisk University; Ball State University; Boston Public Library; Butler University; Chicago Theological Seminary; Cincinnati Historical Society; Cincinnati Public Library; Cornell University; Columbia University; First Presbyterian Church, Huntington, Indiana; Forbes Library, Northampton, Massachusetts; Fort Wayne Public Library; Hanover College; Harvard University; the Hayes Memorial Library, Fremont, Ohio; Henry E. Huntington Library and Art Gallery, San Merino, California; Illinois College; Indianapolis Museum of Art; Indianapolis Public Library; Indiana Historical Society Library; Indiana State Library; Indiana University; Lawrenceburg Public Library; Library of Congress; Long Island Historical Society, Brooklyn, New York; Marine Historical Association Collections, Mystic, Connecticut; Miami University, Oxford, Ohio; Mount Holyoke College Library, South Hadley, Massachusetts; Museum of the City of New York; New-York Historical Society; New York Public Library; Presbyterian Historical Society, Philadelphia, Pennsylvania; Pierpont Morgan Library, New York, New York; Plymouth Church, Brooklyn, New York; Radcliffe College; Second Presbyterian Church, Indianapolis, Indiana; The Stowe-Day Foundation, Hartford, Connecticut; University of Cincinnati; University of Chicago; University of Georgia; Wabash College; Westminster Presbyterian Church, Fort Wayne, Indiana; Wooster College; and Yale University.

In preparing this study for publication it was found convenient to write HWB instead of Henry Ward Beecher in footnotes and explanatory references. His wife is referred to as Mrs. Henry Ward Beecher in footnotes rather than as Eunice Bullard Beecher, since it was the form she herself preferred to use in publications. Other women are identified by their Christian name, maiden surname, and married surname. Spelling of proper names varied in sources, and so the form which Beecher customarily used was selected. Conversations have been published as recalled by participants. It is recognized that some of these were written long after the event, but they have been included on the supposition that they relate the substance of what was said. Such conversations were substantiated with other evidence relevant to the event discussed. Punctuation of quotations has been altered slightly only when it aided clarity. The King James version of the Bible is used whenever reference to Biblical passages occur. No attempt has been made to analyze Beecher's theological development nor to criticize his sermons, as this was considered beyond the scope of this study.

I wish to express my gratitude to Caroline Dunn of the Indiana Historical Society Library for imparting a family reminiscence and locating manuscripts for me, to Lucia Ketcham for information about the Merrill-Ketcham families, to Gayle Thornbrough, Director of Publications of the Indiana Historical Society, who called my attention to pertinent material in the Calvin Fletcher letters, and to Donald L. Siefker, Head, Division of Information Sources and Reference at Ball State University Library, who was untiring in his efforts to obtain books for me. I am especially indebted to Maurice G. Baxter, Department of History, Indiana University, for his valuable comments and criticism of the manuscript, to the editorial staff of the Indiana Historical Society, and to my daughter Eva, husband, and parents for their encouragement.

JANE SHAFFER ELSMERE

North Manchester, Indiana

Symbols for Libraries and Manuscript Collections

CtHS-D—Beecher Family Papers, Stowe-Day Foundation, Hartford, Conn.

CtY   —Beecher Family Papers, Yale University, New Haven, Conn.

DLC   —Library of Congress, Washington, D.C.

In   —Indiana Division, Indiana State Library, Indianapolis, Ind.

InCW   —Wabash College, Crawfordsville, Ind.

InHan   —Hanover College, Hanover, Ind.

InHi   —Indiana Historical Society Library, Indianapolis, Ind.

InISPC —Archives of the Second Presbyterian Church, Indianapolis, Ind.

InU   —Hugh McCulloch Papers, Lilly Library, Indiana University, Bloomington, Ind.

MCR   —Beecher-Stowe Family Papers, Schlesinger Library, Radcliffe College, Cambridge, Mass.

OFH   —Beecher Family Miscellaneous Manuscripts, Hayes Memorial Library, Fremont, Ohio

HENRY WARD BEECHER
The Indiana Years, 1837-1847

Call to Lawrenceburgh

IN 1837 THE TOWN OF LAWRENCEBURGH LOCATED AT THE JUNCTION of the Ohio and Miami Rivers about twenty-two miles downstream from Cincinnati was a central point of communication between the interior of Indiana and the nation.[1] Over its wharves passed a steady flow of emigrants, travelers, merchandise, and raw goods bound to and from Indiana which was then considered to be little more than a frontier state in the Great West. Leading inland was the Manchester road which connected it with the capital of Indianapolis by way of Manchester, Napoleon, Greensburg, and Shelbyville. Just as steamboats and other river craft stopped regularly at the Lawrenceburgh landings so did stagecoaches pulled by four or six horses over the Manchester road maintain scheduled service between the town and the rest of the state.

Founded in 1802 by Revolutionary War veterans Benjamin Chambers, James Hamilton, and Samuel Vance, Lawrenceburgh within eight years so grew in significance that it was being seriously considered as the possible site of the second territorial capital of Indiana.[2] Although

1. The community's name was spelled Lawrenceburgh until the 1890s when it was changed to Lawrenceburg. Henry Ward Beecher (hereafter cited as HWB) used both endings as did others. See Ray C. Johnson and Jack R. Anderson (comps.), *History of Lawrenceburg, Indiana* (Lawrenceburg: Lawrenceburg Historical Society, Inc., 1953), pp. 4, 12, 30. In citing letters written from Lawrenceburgh the spelling used by the writer has been followed here.

2. R. Carlyle Buley, *The Old Northwest. Pioneer Period, 1815–1840* (2 volumes. Indianapolis: Indiana Historical Society, 1950), I, 61.

it did not receive this honor, the town continued to prosper. In 1833 its population was estimated to be one thousand. Lawrenceburgh contained a brick courthouse, a stone jail, a drugstore, two newspapers, two brick churches, three schools, three taverns, four physicians, eight lawyers, and nine stores.[3] In addition, it had industries to process the large quantities of wheat, corn, and hogs which were brought to its markets.

Much of Lawrenceburgh's prosperity was based on its catering to the needs of Indiana farmers who were handicapped in disposing of their crops by poor transportation facilities and lack of good markets near their homes. Some farmers who lived near streams would build flatboats on which they would float their produce to market when spring freshets deepened the normally shallow rivers and creeks. Others would feed grain to cattle and hogs and then drive the livestock overland to a market. Still other farmers would load their grain aboard huge, schooner-shaped wagons with covered tops and make the long trip to market in the fall when the roads were dry. If such men tried to sell their grain in Indianapolis, they would customarily receive ten cents a bushel for corn and thirty-seven-and-a-half-cents per bushel for wheat.[4] In Lawrenceburgh they could get more.

It was a common sight to see long-legged, long-snouted hogs being driven through the streets of Lawrenceburgh to slaughterhouses. Convoys of five or six wagons each laden with twenty-five bushels or so of grain would come creaking over the Manchester road into town where the grain would be sold to the mills and distilleries. From the proceeds the farmers would purchase items needed at home. Especially enterprising farmers would transport merchandise to merchants in Indianapolis and elsewhere in their wagons on the return journey and thus make the trip pay doubly. When the internal improvements craze

3. [John Scott], *The Indiana Gazetteer, or Topographical Dictionary* . . . (2d ed. Indianapolis: Douglass and Maguire, 1833), p. 104; *History of Dearborn and Ohio Counties, Indiana* (Chicago: F. E. Weakley & Co., Publishers, 1885), p. 258; Richard S. Fisher, *Indiana: In Relation to Its Geography, Statistics, Institutions* (New York: J. H. Colton, 1852), pp. 59–60.

4. Howard Johnson, *A Home in the Woods, Oliver Johnson's Reminiscences of Early Marion County* (Indiana Historical Society *Publications*, XVI, No. 2, Indianapolis, 1951), pp. 218, 222–24; Hugh McCulloch, *Men and Measures of Half A Century* (New York: Charles Scribner's Sons, 1888), p. 41.

reached the West, the residents of Lawrenceburgh were quick to see the possible benefits which a railroad and a canal might bring to them.

Plans for the Lawrenceburgh & Indianapolis Railroad received impetus in 1834 when the state legislature authorized surveys for the proposed routes. By 1837 several miles of the one selected for a right-of-way had been graded. Progress on the Whitewater Canal was even more rapid. Surveying was completed in 1835, and water was let into the first mile of the canal in late 1837. By the time the canal reached Brookville in 1839 there were periods when upwards of one thousand men might be employed upon its construction.[5] These companies and their crews looked to Lawrenceburgh for many necessities and provided the town with yet another source of income.

Though Lawrenceburgh's population would still be less than fifteen hundred in 1840, it was nevertheless considered to be one of the most important towns in the state. Its citizens took active roles in promoting internal improvements, in establishing and carrying on various types of business in other communities as well as their own, and in participating in government. These men, for the most part, came to Lawrenceburgh from Virginia, Kentucky, New York, and Delaware. There were few New Englanders among them.

Involved as they were in commerce and politics, they displayed little pride in their immediate surroundings; and there was a noticeable lack of interest in erecting beautiful houses such as graced the cities of Madison and Indianapolis. With the exception of the large house built for Samuel Vance in 1818 with its Federal and Palladian features there were few residences of note. A sprinkling of two-story houses existed, but most of the dwellings were insubstantial cottages only slightly superior to the log houses also still in evidence. The general impression was one of drabness.[6] Shade trees near a house were a rarity, and there were few yards worthy of the name. Most houses were built close to the

---

5. James M. Miller, "The Whitewater Canal," *Indiana Magazine of History*, III, No. 3 (September, 1907), pp. 108–12.

6. A Minister's Wife [Mrs. Henry Ward Beecher], *From Dawn to Daylight* (New York: Derby & Jackson, 1859), pp. 43–51; Wilbur D. Peat, *Indiana Houses of the Nineteenth Century* (Indianapolis: Indiana Historical Society, 1962), pp. 10–11; Lyman B. Stowe, *Saints, Sinners and Beechers* (Indianapolis: The Bobbs-Merrill Co., 1934), pp. 253–54. See Bibliographical Note, p. 304, below, for comment on *From Dawn to Daylight*.

unpaved streets upon which animals roamed at will. The business district was undistinguished although the residents were proud of the buildings which had been constructed since the founding of the town.

In spite of its commercial importance then, Lawrenceburgh was unprepossessing in appearance. When a future resident, Henry Ward Beecher, saw it in the spring of 1837, he thought it was a destitute hamlet.[7] Fresh from the cosmopolitan city of Cincinnati the twenty-four-year-old Beecher found little Lawrenceburgh a sharp contrast in size, appearance, and atmosphere.

Henry Ward Beecher was born on June 24, 1813, in Litchfield, Connecticut; and he was the seventh child of Lyman Beecher and Roxana Foote Beecher to reach maturity. His father was a nationally known revivalist, theologian, and educator who had served parishes respectively in East Hampton on Long Island; Litchfield, Connecticut; Boston, Massachusetts; and more recently as pastor of the Second Presbyterian Church in Cincinnati. He was also president of Lane Theological Seminary in nearby Walnut Hills, Ohio. Beecher's mother, Roxana Foote Beecher, was a descendant of the distinguished and numerous Foote family so prominent in New England's history.

Considering their relative youth, Beecher's older brothers and sisters were already a remarkable group. Catharine E. Beecher conducted the Western Female Institute, a school for young women in Cincinnati, and was a prolific writer on matters of concern to women. William Beecher, his eldest brother, was pastor of a church in Putnam, Ohio. Edward Beecher, a Congregational clergyman, was president of Illinois College in Jacksonville, Illinois. Mary Beecher, a former teacher, was the wife of Thomas Perkins and lived in Hartford, Connecticut. His favorite brother, George Beecher, was a clergyman in Batavia, Ohio; and his best-loved sister, Harriet Beecher, had been married recently to Calvin E. Stowe, a professor at Lane Theological Seminary. Charles Beecher, two years his junior, had also enrolled as a student at Lane. Three younger Beechers, children of Lyman Beecher and his second wife, the late Harriet Porter Beecher, resided with their father and his third wife, Lydia Jackson Beecher, in Walnut Hills. These were Isabella,

7. Reuben G. Thwaites, *Afloat on the Ohio* (New York: Doubleday & McClure, 1900), p. 186; HWB, Journal, May 4, 1837, CtY; Cincinnati *Commercial*, clipping, n.d., OFH.

Thomas, and James who were considerably younger than Henry. Thus, Henry Ward Beecher was a member of a large family with sisters and brothers whose ages in 1837 ranged from thirty-seven-year-old Catharine to nine-year-old James.

Henry Ward Beecher was generally considered to be one of the less promising Beecher children in regard to ability. His academic career was mediocre. He was regarded as a dull pupil in the little school he attended until the age of ten at Bethlehem, Connecticut. Next he was enrolled in the school for young ladies which his sister Catharine then operated in Hartford, Connecticut, in the hope that he would receive special attention to remove his educational inadequacies. Although intended from birth by his parents for the ministry as were his brothers, Henry expressed a desire to go to sea when he was thirteen. While Lyman Beecher encouraged the boy to enter Mount Pleasant Classical Institute ostensibly to study navigation in preparation for a naval career, the father hoped the prevailing religious climate at the institution might awaken responsive chords in the youth. His hopes were realized, and Henry began to prepare for the ministry as his father wished. He was graduated from Amherst College in 1834 and immediately entered Lane Theological Seminary where he underwent the rigorous three-year course thought desirable in the education of a Presbyterian clergyman.

In the spring of 1837 Henry Ward Beecher was invited to preach at the First Presbyterian Church in Lawrenceburgh, Indiana, with the expectation that a call to become minister of the church might ensue if the congregation was pleased with him. Beecher was looking for a pastorate, and he accepted the invitation to preach a trial sermon on Sunday, April 30. Ordinarily services at the First Presbyterian Church drew only about twenty people, but on this particular Sunday the number present was nearer one hundred.[8]

They came to see and hear a son of the controversial president of Lane Theological Seminary, Lyman Beecher. The father had been

8. Stowe, *Saints, Sinners and Beechers*, p. 253; William C. Beecher and Samuel Scoville, *A Biography of Henry Ward Beecher* (New York: C. L. Webster & Co., 1888), p. 157; [Mrs. Beecher], *From Dawn to Daylight*, pp. 32–36; John R. Howard, *Henry Ward Beecher* (New York: Fords, Howard & Hulbert, 1891), p. 26; Annie Beecher Scoville, Notes, n.d., CtY; HWB, *Yale Lectures on Preaching* (3 volumes in 1. Boston: The Pilgrim Press, 1902), I, 43.

charged with heresy in a trial before the Presbytery of Cincinnati in 1835 which attracted attention beyond denominational circles. In 1836 the senior Beecher received notoriety from a controversy which arose between the trustees of Lane and antislavery student activists led by Theodore Weld, the students contending that their academic freedom was being threatened. Although the charges of heresy were withdrawn and his part in the student unrest at the seminary had been minimal, Lyman Beecher was subjected to much publicity. He had the reputation of being one of the ablest preachers in the United States who was presently deeply engrossed in a factional dispute within the Presbyterian denomination.

The slim and boyish Henry Ward Beecher was tense when he began his sermon. He spoke against Universalism, a favorite topic of his father's, while clutching his Testament. It was not a good sermon, and his delivery of it was poor. Afterwards he placed the blame for his failure on the agitated state of his nerves. However, the congregation was not as aware of the sermon's deficiencies as was the young preacher and he was asked to return and preach again the next Sunday. Beecher recovered his poise and good spirits rapidly, but the memory of his ineptitude remained.[9] Later that day he was invited to tea along with others at the home of a physician in Lawrenceburgh. There the young man's charm, sincerity, and grasp of social amenities commended him to his fellow guests and host. Three members of the Walker family who heard him preach that morning observed his behavior at tea. It was their conclusion that "popularity rather than power would characterize his ministry."[10]

The First Presbyterian Church at Lawrenceburgh was one of 122 of the denomination in existence in Indiana. The oldest, the "Church of Indiana," had been organized in 1806 near Vincennes where it was attended by Governor William Henry Harrison and his wife. Since the founding of that first church seven Presbyteries (Salem, Vincennes,

9. Mrs. Henry W. Beecher, "Mr. Beecher as I Knew Him," *Ladies Home Journal*, December, 1891, p. 11; Beecher and Scoville, *A Biography of Henry Ward Beecher*, p. 157; James B. Walker, *Experiences of Pioneer Life* (Chicago: Sumner & Co., 1881), p. 186.

10. Walker, *Experiences of Pioneer Life*, p. 186. It is probable that this tea was given by Dr. Jeremiah H. Brower, who befriended HWB and in whose house the clergyman lived from July to October, 1837.

Madison, Crawfordsville, Indianapolis, Logansport, and a portion of Oxford) had been created and comprised sixty-nine ministers and 122 churches with an estimated membership of five thousand.[11]

In this expanding network the church at Lawrenceburgh in the beginning showed great promise. It was organized on September 27, 1829, with a charter membership of fourteen and was under the care of the Presbytery of Oxford after October 2, 1829. The minister was the Rev. Sylvester Scoville.[12] During his tenure the membership was increased by fifty-six and the church building on Short Street was erected. Thirty-seven additional members were added during the succeeding pastorates of Alexander McFarlane and Charles Sturdevant between the years 1832 and 1836. From the latter's departure until Beecher's arrival in 1837 a series of men supplied the pulpit and the average attendance at services fell to below twenty.[13]

The First Presbyterian Church was handicapped increasingly by the growth of the Methodist Episcopal Church which was locally considered to be the most prestigious denomination in Lawrenceburgh. The Methodists included in their membership the prominent and prosperous families of the town, while the Presbyterians drew their members mainly from laborers' wives, poor spinsters, and a few men. There were only two people who reportedly derived their incomes from sources other than their own labor when Beecher came.[14] Consequently, the Presbyterians had less to attract a superior minister than did the Methodists and this, in turn, contributed to the decline in the former's membership.

The deteriorating condition of the church caused anxiety to its

11. Hanford A. Edson, *Contributions to the Early History of the Presbyterian Church in Indiana* (Cincinnati: Winona Publishing Co., 1898), p. 41; E. H. Gillett, *History of the Presbyterian Church in the United States of America* (2 volumes. Philadelphia: Presbyterian Board of Publication and Sabbath School Work, 1864), II, 412.

12. A list of the charter members is included in John H. Thomas, *An Historical Sketch of the Presbyterian Church of Lawrenceburgh, Indiana* (Lawrenceburgh: Sam. Chapman, 1887), pp. 4–5; *History of Dearborn, Ohio and Switzerland Counties, Indiana* (Chicago: Weakley, Harraman & Co., Publishers, 1885), p. 272.

13. Thomas, *An Historical Sketch of the Presbyterian Church of Lawrenceburgh, Indiana*, pp. 5–7, 29.

14. Beecher and Scoville, *A Biography of Henry Ward Beecher*, p. 159; [Mrs. Beecher], *From Dawn to Daylight*, p. 56; New York *Times*, March 9, 1887; Joseph Tarkington, *Autobiography* (Cincinnati: Curts, 1899), pp. 134–35.

faithful members. One of these was a young woman about nineteen years of age named Martha Sawyer.[15] She began to seek a minister for the struggling church, and her quest led her to a hall in Covington, Kentucky, where Henry Ward Beecher was preaching for a few Sundays, as an attempt was being made in that city to establish a Presbyterian church. Such a task appealed to Beecher who was preparing for the ministry with the idea of serving in the West for a time as a missionary.

Martha Sawyer was favorably impressed by Beecher's sermon and bearing, and it was she who arranged for him to preach one Sunday at the First Presbyterian Church in Lawrenceburgh. About this time an unidentified woman from the Lawrenceburgh congregation journeyed to the office of the American Home Missionary Society in Cincinnati. She told Henry Little, secretary of the central board agency for the western states, that she was looking for a pastor for her church. Little was sympathetic. He was a good friend of the Beecher family and aware of Henry Ward Beecher's interest in securing a church. Little arranged to introduce Beecher to this woman, and amid a clutter of religious tracts, Bibles, and church papers Beecher received another invitation to preach at Lawrenceburgh.[16]

When Beecher returned to Walnut Hills after supplying the pulpit at Lawrenceburgh on April 30, 1837, he thought he might accept the pastorate of the First Presbyterian Church if the offer were made to him. The river town was close enough to Walnut Hills and Cincinnati that he could make the round trip without too much difficulty. This was desirable if he were to combine the role of missionary with another venture in which he was interested. He had received a taste of a second profession when the editor of the Cincinnati *Journal*, Thomas Brainerd,

15. Dr. Jeremiah H. Brower's second wife was Mary Ann Sawyer (1806–1882). Possibly it was a younger relative of Mrs. Brower's who was responsible for inviting HWB to Lawrenceburgh. See the Brower family tombstone, Greendale Cemetery, Greendale, Indiana.

16. Cincinnati *Commercial*, clipping, n.d., OFH; Beecher and Scoville, *A Biography of Henry Ward Beecher*, p. 157; Clifford M. Drury, *Presbyterian Panorama: One Hundred Fifty Years of National Missions History* (Philadelphia: Board of Christian Education, Presbyterian Church in the United States of America, 1952), pp. 181–82; Charles Cist, *Cincinnati in 1841: Its Early Annals* (Cincinnati, 1841), p. 99; Mrs. Henry Ward Beecher, Notes, n.d., CtY.

left to return to Philadelphia. Brainerd's duty on the Presbyterian periodical fell to Beecher who assumed the post on May 11, 1836. Beecher continued in the capacity for months and expected to receive permanent appointment as editor. In October of that year he understood that the coveted position with its salary of $40 a month was his, but various vicissitudes then affected the *Journal*. Beecher was given hope that he would be installed as editor sometime in the summer of 1837. With the prospect of this position before him Beecher wanted to find a church near Cincinnati. However, it was only to his fiancee, Eunice Bullard, that he confided his hope, and it proved to be a vain one.[17]

Henry Ward Beecher was not overly impressed with the residents of Lawrenceburgh who were members of the First Presbyterian Church. He was displeased, for example, by the lack of courtesy shown to visitors by members of the church. Little effort had been made to show these guests to seats or otherwise make them feel welcome.[18]

He became aware of the influential position held by the local Methodist Episcopal Church, and it was a circumstance he found difficult to comprehend. Fresh from the Presbyterian environment of his father's household and the halls of Lane, he had acquired that prejudice which viewed a Methodist as a worthy but lower member of society. In his Journal he cautioned himself to remember that "the cause of Christ requires a Methodist Church, for one class of people, Ergo, cut up by roots all disposition or wish to put this down."[19] Christian charity demanded as much, but the welfare of those who could be shown the superiority of the Presbyterian way should be given attention.

In Walnut Hills Beecher found waiting for him a letter from Eunice Bullard. Over their long separation of four years they wrote frankly of their hopes, worries, and dreams. Eunice had become alarmed that her letters might fall into strange hands, and she requested that he burn those in his possession. He complied; and, in so doing, he felt very close

17. HWB, Journal, May 11, 1836, CtY; HWB to William Beecher and Katharine Edes Beecher, Walnut Hills, October 4, 1836, Beecher-Stowe Family Papers, MCR; Mrs. Beecher, "Mr. Beecher as I Knew Him," *Ladies Home Journal*, July, 1892, p. 4; Cincinnati *Commercial*, clipping, n.d., OFH; HWB, Journal, May 4, 1837, CtY.

18. HWB, Journal, May 4, 1837, CtY.

19. *Ibid.*

in spirit to Eunice.[20] Perhaps if he were settled as pastor of a church and if the editorial post materialized they could be married soon.

The remainder of the month of May was a busy one for Beecher. His work at Lane was drawing to a close, he had sermons to prepare, and every Saturday he traveled to Lawrenceburgh in order to preach there on Sunday. Invited each week to return for the next Sunday's services Beecher heard nothing more about the hinted call. Beecher determined to convince the members of the First Presbyterian Church that he would make them a good minister. Choosing his sermon topics and text with care, he sought deliberately to impress the congregation with his orthodoxy. He prepared a sermon on regeneration using the texts John 3 and Revelations 22:11 for its basis. It was received well, and Beecher believed it removed many doubts concerning him.[21]

He tried to find out why the preceding ministers at the First Presbyterian Church had remained such a short time. From what he was able to discover and to infer, the inability of the congregation to support adequately a qualified minister tended to attract only incompetent men who could not secure better paid positions elsewhere. A few of them such as Alexander McFarlane had supplemented their salaries by holding other jobs and they generally left Lawrenceburgh to accept pastorates with a higher salary or else to pursue other work. The quality of the incumbents declined markedly in the years preceding Beecher's arrival. This was apparent to the congregation and disgust was expressed with their amateurish efforts in the pulpit.

Observing the western custom of sermons delivered without the use of notes, these latter ministers had concluded erroneously that they had only to stand up and inspiration would flow to them. Beecher pondered about this idea so prevalent in the West that a man could present an excellent sermon or speech without needing to prepare it in advance. It was a widely held belief that the prophets and disciples of Biblical times so spoke, and, therefore, it must be the desirable way for a man of God to proceed. Henry Ward Beecher could not accept this idea.[22]

20. HWB, Journal, May 4, 1837, CtY.
21. *Ibid.*, May 21, 1837.
22. *Ibid.*, May 23, 1837; Alexander F. Rankin to Charles Hall, Fort Wayne, January 22, 1839, American Home Missionary Society Papers, microfilm, In.

Since childhood he had been exposed to the thought and effort expended by men such as his father and his father's contemporaries before they gave sermons. During his years of formal schooling at the Mount Pleasant Classical Institute, Amherst College, and Lane Theological Seminary he had participated in discussions of complex theological issues. He would recall that when he was at home he would often be involved in similar discourses at the dinner table with members of the Beecher family and guests which might last two or three hours. Often the topics would arise from questions brought up by himself or others in class. The students enrolled at Lane took three years to complete their study of Biblical Literature, Sacred Rhetoric, Pastoral Theology, and Church History and Polity. The faculty was composed of Beecher's father, his brother-in-law Calvin E. Stowe, Baxter Dickenson, Darcia H. Allen, and T. J. Biggs. Each of these men impressed upon students the necessity of being well prepared for their chosen field.[23]

Since entering Amherst College, Beecher had practiced public speaking almost incessantly to overcome a speech impediment. He attributed this to a large palate but others diagnosed its cause as the result of enlarged tonsils.[24] At Amherst he was drilled by John Lovell in elocution and spent hours in practicing articulation, gestures, and correct posture. Later at Lane he continued this practice in company with his brother Charles and other students. The young men would enter the grove between the seminary and Lyman Beecher's house and there "make the night, and even the day, hideous with our voices, . . . exploding all the vowels, from the bottom to the very top of our voices."[25] By the time he was ready to graduate his speech was clear and

---

23. Cist, *Cincinnati in 1841: Its Early Annals*, p. 124; John R. Howard, *Henry Ward Beecher*, p. 19; Newell D. Hillis, "The Ruling Ideas of Henry Ward Beecher's Sermons," in *Henry Ward Beecher As His Friends Saw Him* (New York: The Pilgrim Press, 1904), p. 26; John P. Foote, *The Schools of Cincinnati and Its Vicinity* (Cincinnati: C. F. Bradley, 1855), pp. 214–18.

24. *Christian Union*, July 14, 1880, quoted in Lionel G. Crocker, *Henry Ward Beecher's Speaking Art* (New York: Fleming H. Revell Co., 1937), p. 10; Catharine E. Beecher, *Educational Reminiscences and Suggestions* (New York: J. B. Ford, 1874), pp. 55–58; Mrs. Beecher, "Mr. Beecher as I Knew Him," *Ladies Home Journal*, June, 1892, p. 1.

25. HWB, *Yale Lectures on Preaching*, I, 135; Crocker, *Henry Ward Beecher's Speaking Art*, pp. 49–50; "Mr. Beecher as a Social Force," *Scribner's Monthly*, IV (October, 1872), 753.

beginning to show promise of the effectiveness which would characterize it in later years.

As an aid to his professional development he decided to keep a record of the sermons he would give which would include the text, subject, and reasons for delivering them. He began his account with the sermon presented at Lawrenceburgh on Sunday, May 7, 1837. Recognizing the prejudice of many Westerners, he was careful to foster the impression that his sermons were more the result of inspiration than effort on his part.[26]

Beecher had an unsettling experience traveling to Lawrenceburgh on Saturday, May 20, 1837, when he was thrown into the Ohio River. It left him feeling shaken and ill, but he forced himself to speak at both services scheduled the next day. For the rest of the week he suffered from recurrent chills and fever and was unable to keep his promise to escort a bridesmaid at the wedding of his friend Miss Abbe Hall on Thursday, May 25.[27]

Still feeling weak, Beecher resumed his daily activities and considered his future. In conversation with Henry Little and Artemas Bullard he discussed the possibility of his preaching temporarily in Newport, Kentucky. Bullard was Eunice's brother and secretary of the American Board of Commissioners for Foreign Missions in the Mississippi Valley. The two officials assured Beecher that if he decided to go to Newport he would be paid for his work from missionary funds. He had not yet received a call from Lawrenceburgh and, as he needed the money, he agreed to go.[28]

His financial situation was precarious. Although he earned some money by teaching school for a time in Massachusetts, by giving lectures and sermons, and by editing the Cincinnati *Journal*, he was basically dependent upon his father for support. Living among and associating with Cincinnati's wealthy residents encouraged Beecher to

26. HWB, Journal, May 23, 1837, CtY.

27. *Ibid.*, May 23, 1837, and May 29, 1837; HWB to Miss Abbe Hall [Walnut Hills], May [?], 1837, CtHS-D.

28. HWB, Journal, May 29, 1837, and [June 5 ?], 1837, CtY; Z. M. Humphrey, "Biographical Sketches (New School Branch)," in *Presbyterian Reunion: A Memorial Volume, 1837–1871* (New York: De W. C. Lent & Co., 1870), pp. 237–38; William B. Sprague, *Annals of the American Pulpit* (9 volumes. New York: R. Carter & brothers, 1857–[69]), IV, 748–54.

spend more than his circumstances warranted, and he accumulated debts. The Beecher family belonged to the upper strata of society in Cincinnati. They were included as a matter of course in gatherings at Daniel Drake's Buckeye Hall and were members of the exclusive Semi-Colon Club. The New England heritage of the Beechers and their individual attainments recommended them to society in a city then dominated by that area's influence to the extent that a contemporary called it a "second edition of Boston."[29] Two of Beecher's uncles, Samuel E. Foote and John P. Foote, were successful entrepreneurs with diverse interests in Cincinnati. Henry Ward Beecher was a welcome guest, therefore, in the best homes of the city; and, in spite of the difference in wealth, he was tempted by the examples of his friends and cousins to live beyond his slender means.[30]

Beecher was not a spendthrift, but he gave little thought to what he owed until his creditors reminded him. Such a day of reckoning had occurred in the previous March, and it had precipitated a painful scene with his father which he did not care to repeat. Neither man had seemed aware of the irony of Lyman Beecher's lecturing his son for spending excessively when the elder Beecher was habitually "always before his salary in his expenses."[31] Henry Ward Beecher was rescued by his step-mother, Lydia Jackson Beecher, who told him she had received $100 from a friend for him. He thought it likely that either she or Judge [Isaac G. ?] Burnet was the friend and was grateful. In his Journal the young man wrote of the gift, "I thank God for it. I am resolved not again to get into debt for *any thing*. I will live within my means by living by my means & not upon credit."[32] Conceived in a contrite spirit the vow was sincere, but it did not allow for either Beecher's natural inclination to live comfortably or the effect on his character of spon-

29. McCulloch, *Men and Measures of Half A Century*, pp. 40–41; Charles F. Hoffman, *A Winter in the Far West* (2 volumes. London: R. Bentley, 1835), II, 127–28.

30. Harvey C. Minnich, *William Holmes McGuffey and the Peerless Pioneer McGuffey Readers* (Oxford, Ohio: Miami University, 1928), p. 9; Alice McG. Ruggles, *The Story of the McGuffeys* (New York: American Book Co., 1950), p. 78; Alvin F. Harlow, *The Serene Cincinnatians* (New York: E. P. Dutton & Co., 1950), pp. 120, 130; Abram W. Foote, *Foote Family* (2 volumes. Rutland, Vt., 1907; Burlington, Vt., 1943), I, 201–202.

31. HWB, Journal, [month ?] 24, 1836, CtY; Lyman Abbott, "Henry Ward Beecher," *Atlantic Monthly*, XCII, No. 552 (October, 1903), p. 541.

32. HWB, Journal, March 13, 1837, CtY.

taneous gifts from open-handed friends.[33] Such aid had been received by his father many times, and Henry had no reason to suppose that providence intended to treat him less well as witness his stepmother's assistance.

During his convalescence Beecher went to hear Daniel Webster speak in Cincinnati. The orator and politician had earlier paid a ceremonial call on William Henry Harrison at his home in North Bend, Ohio. Two days later Harrison introduced Webster who gave a speech on the currency question lasting almost two hours to a large audience in Cincinnati. Beecher listened carefully. He admired Webster's skill and style. The rant so common to western speakers was lacking; but "it shows one thing plainly," noted Beecher, "that is, a promiscuous western audience will listen *attentively* to plain sense and reasoning, and does not need the boisterous excitement, so prevalent and which it is said the people *must have*."[34] Beecher made no comment on the content of the speech.

Next day Beecher preached twice in Newport with about forty people in attendance each service. In the morning he repeated a sermon given previously at Lawrenceburgh on May 21, 1837.[35] It was his practice to refine a sermon and present it again when it seemed appropriate for a different congregation. Despite his youth Beecher was an experienced speaker. In boyhood while under the influence of a revival he preached a sermon to several classmates at Mount Pleasant Classical Institution. Later as a student at Amherst College he was a member of the debating society and participated in its activities. From 1831 through 1833 he taught school briefly at Northbridge and Hopkinton in Massachusetts, delivered lectures on temperance and phrenology, preached, and assisted with revivals. After entering Lane Theological Seminary he had supplied pulpits whenever the opportunity occurred. One such occasion was in 1835 during Beecher's visit to his brother, George Beecher, who was pastor of the First Presbyterian Church in

33. Beecher, *Educational Reminiscences and Suggestions*, p. 22; Barbara M. Cross (ed.), *The Autobiography of Lyman Beecher* (2 volumes. Cambridge: Belknap Press of Harvard University Press, 1961), II, 316–17.

34. HWB, Journal, June 3, 1837, CtY; George T. Curtis, *Life of Daniel Webster* (2 volumes. New York: D. Appleton & Co., 1870), I, 563.

35. HWB, Journal, June 5, 1837, CtY.

Batavia, Ohio. George Beecher could not preach at a service, and Henry was pressed to take his place by a member of the congregation, Judge Owen T. Fishback. His audience professed itself pleased by the younger Beecher's sermon, but he later recalled how inadequate he felt while filling the pulpit of his favorite brother.[36]

Beecher received the coveted call to become pastor of the First Presbyterian Church at Lawrenceburgh on June 15, 1837. He learned that at a meeting held three days earlier the nearly thirty members in attendance had voted unanimously to ask him. Beecher thought it "a very flattering call" which "did [his] heart good."[37]

Members of Beecher's family and circle of friends were less happy about it. They could not understand why a man with his ability and connections should be content to isolate himself in a little Indiana town as pastor of a church with such poor prospects. Beecher was not swayed by them as he had his own reason for wishing to remain near Cincinnati nor did he tell them of his hope for the editorship of the *Journal*. He let his family think that it was of little consequence to him where he located. The call from Lawrenceburgh was the first he received from any church, and he accepted it at once.[38]

The First Presbyterian Church was crowded on Sunday morning, June 18, 1837, when Beecher preached there for the first time in his capacity as its pastor. This cheered him and gave him confidence. Before returning to Walnut Hills he planned to discuss the details of his position with church officials.[39] He was to receive an annual salary of $250 guaranteed by the American Home Missionary Society. In keeping

36. Gilman C. Fisher, "Henry Ward Beecher at School, College and Seminary," *Education*, VII (May, 1887), 608–13; HWB to Edward W. Bok, Peekskill, New York, August 18, 1885, quoted in Thomas W. Handford, *Beecher: Christian Philosopher, Pulpit Orator, Patriot and Philanthropist* (Chicago, 1889), pp. 60–61; HWB, *Yale Lectures on Preaching*, I, 143–44; John R. Howard (ed.), *Patriotic Addresses in America and England, From 1850 to 1885* (New York, 1887), pp. 44–46; Thomas W. Knox, *Life and Work of Henry Ward Beecher* (Chicago: C. B. Beach & Co., 1887), pp. 71–72; newspaper clippings, n.d., CtY.

37. HWB, Journal, June 15, 1837, CtY.

38. Mrs. Beecher, "Mr. Beecher as I Knew Him," *Ladies Home Journal*, November, 1891, p. 9; Harriet Beecher Stowe, *Men of Our Times* (Hartford, Conn.: Hartford Publishing Co., 1868), p. 541; [Mrs. Beecher], *From Dawn to Daylight*, pp. 32–36.

39. HWB, Journal, June 19, 1837, CtY.

with the society's policy of encouraging a church to provide part of its minister's salary and thus enable him to earn at least $400 per year, the Lawrenceburgh congregation was expected to furnish an additional $150 in cash or provisions. If paid, Beecher could expect to receive a monthly salary of $33.25 for his first year's work as a missionary. In comparison, laborers on the Whitewater Canal construction crews earned $18 per month.[40]

Beecher would be one of 810 clergymen supported at least partially by the American Home Missionary Society, founded in 1826, which received most of its support from Presbyterian and Congregational sources. Though these missionaries were selected by and were responsible to church officials of their denomination, they were required to meet certain standards and to write quarterly reports of their activities for the society's records.[41]

The question of Beecher's place of residence arose. Since he was unmarried it seemed wisest for him to board with a Lawrenceburgh family. There was a suitable room available in the house of Dr. Jeremiah H. Brower, and the young clergyman made arrangements to occupy it. Beecher planned to commute weekly from Walnut Hills until after his graduation from Lane.[42]

He returned to Cincinnati aboard the steamboat *Dolphin*. On board he saw John Gibson Dunn who was enrolled in school at College Hill near Cincinnati. The boy's father, George H. Dunn, was probably the most important lawyer in Lawrenceburgh, a noted Whig in Indiana politics, and an organizer of the First Presbyterian Church. Dunn was a man whose acquaintance would be worth cultivating, and Beecher

40. *Ibid.*, June 15, 1837; John R. Howard, *Henry Ward Beecher*, p. 44; Beecher and Scoville, *A Biography of Henry Ward Beecher*, p. 159; Colin B. Goodykoontz, *Home Missions on the American Frontier* (Caldwell, Idaho: The Caxton printers, 1939), pp. 181–82, 243; Knox, *Life and Work of Henry Ward Beecher*, p. 212; Miller, "The Whitewater Canal," *Indiana Magazine of History*, III, 108–12.

41. Drury, *Presbyterian Panorama: One Hundred Fifty Years of National Missions History*, p. 117; Goodykoontz, *Home Missions on the American Frontier*, pp. 184–87; Beecher and Scoville, *A Biography of Henry Ward Beecher*, p. 159. The American Home Missionary Society Papers including the quarterly reports for the years 1836–1893 pertinent to Indiana do not include any written by HWB. See the American Home Missionary Society Papers, microfilm, In.

42. Archibald Shaw (ed.), *History of Dearborn County, Indiana* (Indianapolis: B. F. Bowen & Co., 1915), pp. 367–68; HWB, Journal, June 19, 1837, CtY.

considered the boy's presence on the *Dolphin* of sufficient interest to record in his Journal.[43]

Four days after Beecher's graduation from Lane Theological Seminary on July 4, 1837, he was settled in his small room at Dr. Brower's and ready to begin life as a missionary.[44] To his Journal he confided some plans for the future:

1. In different districts get men quietly to feel *themselves* responsible for progress of temperance or Sunday-schools.
2. Quietly to visit from house to house and secure congregations.
3. Secure a *large congregation*. Let this be the *first* thing. For this--
   1. Preach well uniformly.
   2. Visit widely and produce a personal attachment; also wife do same.
   3. Get the young to love me.
   4. See that the church have this presented as a *definite* thing, and set them to this work just as *directly* as I would to raising a fund, building, etc.[45]

These were good, sensible proposals for a minister establishing himself in a new church and community. Beecher did not have a wife, however, to carry out the role assigned to her. Would his fiancee, Eunice Bullard, consent to come immediately and share his life as a missionary in the West?

43. HWB, Journal, June 19, 1837, CtY; William T. Coggeshall, *The Poets and Poetry of the West* (Columbus, Ohio: Follett, Foster & Co., 1860), p. 537.

44. HWB, Journal, July 5, 1837, CtY.

45. *Ibid.*, July 10, 1837.

II

Courtship, Wedding, and Housekeeping

HENRY WARD BEECHER MET EUNICE WHITE BULLARD IN 1830 during Amherst's spring vacation when he visited the Bullard home in West Sutton, Massachusetts. One of her brothers, Ebenezer W. Bullard, was his classmate and close friend. The two young men and another college acquaintance walked to West Sutton to spend several days at the Bullard farm. Not quite seventeen, Beecher looked even younger and physically was not very attractive. His face was dominated by the prominent Foote nose inherited from his mother, Roxana Foote Beecher, and it drew attention away from Beecher's full eyebrows and large grayish-blue eyes and emphasized his slightly retreating forehead.[1] Though Eunice was charmed by his personality she thought he was "not an Apolo [sic] for beauty."[2]

Eunice Bullard was almost a year older than Beecher. Born on August 26, 1812, she was one of three daughters of Artemas Bullard, a physician and farmer, and Lucy White Bullard. Her father was a prominent member of the Congregational Church near his home on Bullard's Hill, and his children were active in its work. Three of Eunice's seven brothers were destined to be clergymen and a fourth

1. Lawrenceburg *Press*, September 22, 1921; Mrs. Henry Ward Beecher, Notes, n.d., CtY; John R. Howard, *Henry Ward Beecher*, p. 21; W. S. Searle, "Beecher's Personality," *North American Review*, CXLIV (May, 1887), 488–89; Mrs. Beecher, "Mr. Beecher as I Knew Him," *Ladies Home Journal*, October, 1891, p. 3.
2. Mrs. Henry Ward Beecher, Notes, n.d., CtY.

brother was superintendent of a Sunday School. One of her two sisters, Lucy Bullard Jones, was married to a minister; the other, Maria Bullard Barton, was the wife of a lawyer.[3]

Eunice was expected to do her full share of housework and farm chores, teach in a neighboring school, and attend church services regularly. Lightheartedness was not encouraged in the Bullard household. Artemas Bullard was a stern man who was close with his money, and all his children were educated to be thrifty. To Eunice, Beecher's zest for life and the sense of humor he displayed during his visit were rare qualities.[4]

Beecher was drawn to the quiet, auburn-haired girl who enjoyed his sallies and showed enough spirit to reply in kind. After the vacation ended he found reasons to return to West Sutton whenever he could. Eunice's parents liked him and were happy to have him as a guest. He won Mrs. Bullard's affection and never received a cross word from her, he recalled, in spite of his boyish pranks and teasing. After a time he managed to penetrate Dr. Bullard's reserve. Though Eunice's father was a physician of standing, he was a farmer by avocation. Beecher showed genuine interest in the operation of the Bullard farm and asked intelligent questions about its equipment, crops, and livestock. He gained Dr. Bullard's confidence and also learned much about good farming practices. Eunice's parents did not suspect Beecher, however, of having any romantic motive for his continued visits to their house.[5]

Young as he was, Beecher was having serious thoughts about his future and the possibility that Eunice Bullard might have a place in it. His father was considering going to the West where there was a need for clergymen and educators. Beecher would probably join him there after college and perhaps in time become a missionary. He felt that Eunice might be the right young woman to share his life's work. Several months later he asked Eunice to marry him. She would recall that his proposal was abrupt and seemed impetuous. She listened with favor,

3. New York *Tribune*, June 22, 1913; Knox, *Life and Work of Henry Ward Beecher*, pp. 68–69; Josephine C. Frost (comp.), *Ancestors of Henry Ward Beecher and His Wife Eunice White Bullard* (Brooklyn, N.Y., 1927), p. 15.

4. Knox, *Life and Work of Henry Ward Beecher*, p. 69; [Mrs. Beecher], *From Dawn to Daylight*, pp. 17–31.

5. HWB, Notes, n.d., CtY; Mrs. Henry Ward Beecher, Notes, n.d., CtY; [Mrs. Beecher], *From Dawn to Daylight*, pp. 1–16.

however, and told him he would have to discuss it with her father.
Beecher rode to West Sutton to speak to Dr. Bullard on the next Saturday. The physician and his wife were astonished. It had not occurred
to them that Beecher was interested in Eunice as his prospective wife;
indeed, they did not think him old enough for such a consideration.
Mrs. Bullard was unhappy about the proposed marriage although she
liked Beecher. Dr. Bullard became angry, possibly at his own failure to
perceive the young couple's interest in each other. Both felt that Beecher
was too young to be thinking of marriage since it might be seven years
until he would be able to support a wife. He must finish his work at
Amherst and receive theological training at a seminary if he entered the
ministry as planned. Eunice was eighteen and of an age to marry immediately. A long engagement would have its special peril for her. Neither
of Eunice's parents objected to Beecher as a person, but each had grave
doubts as to the wisdom of a lengthy engagement.[6]

The youthful couple prevailed, and the parents gave their reluctant
approval. Beecher presented to Eunice as an engagement gift a copy of
Richard Baxter's *The Saints' Everlasting Rest* which he purchased with
part of five dollars he had earned for delivering a temperance lecture.
Beecher inscribed in it:

> Take it as a gift of love
> That Seeks thy good alone
> Keep it for the giver's sake
> And read it for thine own.

Below this Eunice wrote "Given me on our engagement, January 2,
1831."[7] As another token of his love and their pledge Beecher presented
Eunice with a plain gold band which would serve as engagement ring
and wedding ring. It cost eighty-five cents. Beecher paid for it from ten
dollars which he received for giving still another lecture. Eunice would
remember that "nothing could be as precious as that" ring.[8] The en-

6. Mrs. Beecher, "Mr. Beecher as I Knew Him," *Ladies Home Journal*, October,
1891, p. 3.

7. This book is preserved in the Beecher Family Papers, CtY.

8. Mrs. Henry Ward Beecher, "In the Past," n.d., CtY. She stated in old age
that the money used to purchase her ring was earned by HWB for delivering a temperance lecture, but Fuess wrote that HWB received it for giving a lecture on
phrenology. See Mrs. Beecher, "Mr. Beecher as I Knew Him," *Ladies Home Journal*,
October, 1891, p. 3, and Claude M. Fuess, *Amherst* (Boston: Little, Brown & Co.,
1935), pp. 112–13; Lawrenceburg *Press*, September 22, 1921.

gagement so begun would last nearly seven years, and the couple would be apart almost the last four of those years.

Little wonder that by the spring of 1837 Beecher was eager to enter upon both his pastorate and marriage. His possessions were scarcely unpacked at Dr. Brower's before he was making plans to wed Eunice Bullard and bring her to Lawrenceburgh. Late in the month of July he wrote her a letter suggesting they be married in the autumn. He had a comfortable room at the Browers' where he was well treated, and perhaps Eunice and he could board there together. Somehow they would manage, he thought, to meet the additional expense of her support.

After posting the letter to Eunice, Beecher was seized with the thought that there was no reason to wait to marry. He hastened eastward and stopped only long enough in Ohio to borrow one of George Beecher's best suits for the anticipated wedding. His letter preceded him to West Sutton by hours where it arrived on Saturday morning, July 29, 1837. Eunice's joy in receiving it with its suggestion of an early wedding date was marred, however, by a brother's untactful remark about the length of her engagement. As an unmarried woman of twenty-five she was only too well aware of the prolonged absence of her fiance.[9]

Then Beecher himself arrived upon the scene. Scarcely taking time to greet the Bullard family, he made his proposal that the wedding should take place at once. It was decided to hold the ceremony at three o'clock on the following Thursday, August 3, and on Eunice fell much of the responsibility for the hurried wedding preparations. She would not have leisure to prepare a trousseau, but she did make some garments and in other ways readied her wardrobe for her journey to Indiana. Beecher and she together wrote invitations to those friends and relatives who lived near enough to come on such short notice. Eunice was surprised, pleased, and grateful at how well Beecher helped with everything entrusted to him. He beat the eggs and stoned the raisins for the wedding cake which Eunice made, and he performed many other homely tasks which she was unaccustomed to seeing men do. She

9. Beecher and Scoville, *A Biography of Henry Ward Beecher,* p. 170; Mrs. Beecher, "Mr. Beecher as I Knew Him," *Ladies Home Journal,* November, 1891, p. 9; [Mrs. Beecher], *From Dawn to Daylight,* pp. 32–36.

Henry Ward and Eunice Bullard Beecher

at the time of their marriage

would remember that his good humor and assistance eased the strain felt by the family in getting ready for the wedding.

By two o'clock on the afternoon of August 3, the clergyman, Mr. Joseph (?) Tracy, and the guests had assembled in the parlor of the Bullard home. A thunderstorm began and continued at the time appointed for the ceremony. Beecher and Eunice, dressed for the wedding, were in their rooms. When they were summoned to the parlor, Eunice refused to go. She had seen her sisters married during storms, and she was determined she would not be. Although some of the guests became restive with thoughts of chores awaiting them at home, Eunice was obstinate. She had waited nearly seven years to marry; they could wait a few minutes to please her. The storm began to abate, and Henry Ward Beecher in his borrowed suit and Eunice White Bullard wearing an India mull gown walked toward the company.[10]

"At four o'clock," recalled Eunice, "the clouds broke away and the sun appeared, and we were ushered into the parlor, Henry and I together. Just as we were entering the door (it was very warm, and doors and windows all open) a *rainbow,* the most brilliant I ever saw, and so remarked by all in the room, seemed through the open window to span the parlor, and the spectators said we walked under its arch to our places. In his prayer the clergyman spoke of the 'bow of peace and promise,' which he hoped was the beautiful symbol of what our lives were to be."[11]

Beecher and his bride left almost at once for Worcester, Massachusetts, where they were guests of Eunice's sister Maria and her husband, Ira M. Barton. The Bartons were very kind to the newlyweds and did much to put them at their ease. Though on his wedding trip, Beecher found time to deliver sermons at Worcester and later in Boston where he preached at the Bowdoin Church on Sunday morning and at the Park Street Church on the same evening.

10. Beecher and Scoville, *A Biography of Henry Ward Beecher,* pp. 170–71; Mrs. Beecher, "Mr. Beecher as I Knew Him," *Ladies Home Journal,* November, 1891, p. 9; HWB, Journal, August 3, 1837, CtY; Stowe, *Saints, Sinners and Beechers,* pp. 254–55; Gilbert H. Barnes and Dwight L. Dumond (eds.), *Letters of Theodore Weld, Angelina Grimke Weld and Sarah Grimke 1822–1844* (2 volumes. New York: D. Appleton Co., 1934), I, 196, note 4.

11. Mrs. Henry Ward Beecher quoted in Beecher and Scoville, *A Biography of Henry Ward Beecher,* pp. 170–71.

Eunice marred her stay in Boston by falling ill. Blaming her sickness on her eating too many leeks and cucumbers, she suffered great embarrassment and discomfort. Still unwell, Eunice left with Beecher for New York City where they were to stay at the home of a second sister, Lucy Jones. Eunice continued to feel ill, and it was feared she might have contracted the dreaded cholera morbus (probably gastroenteritis).[12] A physician prescribed some effective medication, however, and the distressing symptoms lessened and then disappeared. The Beechers remained several days in New York to give Eunice time to regain her strength before beginning the arduous trip westward.

Beecher wrote a proud and frank letter to Harriet Beecher Stowe. "This is to certify that, we are alive—safely & thoroughly married, coming, & *come* as far as N[ew] York," assured Beecher. "Oh Harriet how I long to see you—& *Calvin*. I shall soon show you my dear dear wife. I grow more & more proud of her every day. She is wonderfully fearful lest some of her new relatives should say that she *feigned* the cholera for sake of effect—& I believe she . . . evinced great *sincerity* in some parts of the attack *&* did works meet for the disease." To Beecher's letter Eunice attached a brief note written in pencil to her new sister-in-law. Calling her "Dear *Sister* Harriet," Eunice wrote that "this good husband of mine would gladly make you believe that he's detained by my sickness. I *am* a *leetle not well*—to be sure, but will you believe it—my Henry—wishes to stay & do up a little piece of *flirtation* —which he had no time to complete when he came to N[ew] E[ngland]."[13] "Dear Sister Harriet" with her quick perception must have read these letters with unusual interest.

Henry and Eunice Beecher proceeded to Lawrenceburgh by way of Pittsburgh and Walnut Hills. They traveled by rail, by canal, and by steamboat. Eunice was apprehensive on the railroad portion of their trip as it was the first time she had ever ridden on a train.[14] They had no misadventure and reached Walnut Hills toward the last of August. Eunice was warmly welcomed by her husband's relatives. Even Anna,

---

12. Samuel E. Morison and Henry S. Commager, *The Growth of the American Republic* (2 volumes. New York: Oxford University Press, 1962), I, 628.

13. HWB to Harriet Beecher Stowe, New York, N.Y., August 17, 1837, CtY; Mrs. Henry Ward Beecher to Harriet Beecher Stowe, *ibid.*; Beecher and Scoville, *A Biography of Henry Ward Beecher*, p. 171.

14. [Mrs. Beecher], *From Dawn to Daylight*, p. 45.

Harriet's crusty factotum, spontaneously plucked and put a rosebud into the bride's hair. Harriet wrote later to Eunice that "I thought you the most of a beauty of anybody we had ever seen."[15] The couple spent a few happy days at Walnut Hills and in Cincinnati during which Beecher proudly introduced his wife to his friends.

When it was time for them to go to Lawrenceburgh, they traveled on the steamboat of a friendly captain who had earlier given Beecher a free pass. It was fortunate they had it as the bridegroom had just eighteen cents with which to begin married life in the little river town. The Beechers were met at the wharf by Dr. Brower who escorted them to his house. The haphazard placement of buildings, the shabby houses and cabins, and the unpaved streets dismayed Eunice. Lawrenceburgh was so unlike the placid, well-ordered New England villages with which she was acquainted. She was relieved to discover that the Brower residence was a large two-story white house with an attractive verandah. It was set too close to the street to please Eunice, but it gave promise of providing clean and pleasant living quarters for the couple. The Beechers had the use of the small bedroom originally intended just for the occupancy of the minister. They took their meals with the Brower family, and Eunice had few household tasks to perform. For a time she busied herself unpacking trunks and arranging their possessions in their small room.

One of the first trials she had to face in Lawrenceburgh was the assault of mosquitoes which found their way to her through unscreened windows and doorways. Soon her face, throat, and arms were badly swollen. Told that a mosquito net about their bed might let Beecher and her sleep with less irritation from the pests, she tried to make one but had no real faith it would help. To this misery was added the knowledge that she must meet the members of Beecher's church. She would have been nervous about this under any circumstance, but knowing that her appearance was not at its best added deeply to her distress.[16]

15. Harriet Beecher Stowe to Mrs. Henry Ward Beecher, Walnut Hills, June 2, [no year], CtY.

16. Beecher and Scoville, *A Biography of Henry Ward Beecher*, p. 172; [Mrs. Beecher], *From Dawn to Daylight*, pp. 43–55.

Although Beecher professed to find it amusing, his wife was cha-
grined by an incident which occurred her first Sunday in Lawrenceburgh. She walked with her husband to the First Presbyterian Church
feeling very conscious of herself as the minister's bride. At the entrance
Beecher introduced Martha Sawyer to her. In spite of her sex and
youth Miss Sawyer was an important personage in the church who
served as its *de facto* clerk and treasurer. Eunice Beecher became flus-
tered and in responding to the other's greeting replied, "How do you do,
Mrs. Beecher!" Her husband laughed quietly and began speaking of
something else, but his wife felt extremely foolish and did not easily
regain her composure.[17]

The reception held for her to meet the members of the church and
people of the community was an ordeal. She dreaded this inspection.
People came alone, in couples, and in family groups. Determined to
make them like her, she tried to be pleasant and to act as she thought
a lady in her position should. As the reception continued she became
increasingly aware of the strangeness of dress and modes of speech of
the guests. Eunice Beecher was astonished by the grotesque combina-
tions of clothing which some of them wore. She had expected to hear
different accents, but she was unprepared for the odd and even crude
words which were spoken in her hearing. Asked several times if she had
a fever, Eunice realized her rosy cheeks were interpreted thusly rather
than as an indication of good health. She noticed that many of the
guests had an unhealthy appearance. They were, by her standards,
unusually sallow and pale. She did not observe a single person who
looked really well compared with the people she knew in Massachusetts.[18]

Several weeks after their arrival in Lawrenceburgh Beecher left
Eunice at the Browers' while he went to Cincinnati for a few days to
attend a meeting of Synod. Inopportunely for the newlyweds a relative
of the Browers' died and the surviving spouse planned to come and live
with the physician's family. The only room that would accommodate
him was that occupied by the Beechers. Dr. Brower gave them several

17. Indianapolis *Daily Sentinel*, May 28, 1882; Beecher and Scoville, *A Biography of Henry Ward Beecher*, p. 157.
18. [Mrs. Beecher], *From Dawn to Daylight*, pp. 51–55.

days to find new quarters, but Eunice had to meet the crisis alone.[19]

Her first thought was to rent a room in another boardinghouse, but she learned there was none available which would be at all suitable. Her next idea was to rent a house. This appealed to her homemaking instinct, but she knew they had little money and so she discussed with Dr. Brower how much of their income they could safely spend for rent and still have enough left for other necessities. After much figuring it was decided the Beechers could afford to pay thirty dollars a year for rent.[20]

For two exhausting days Eunice Beecher trudged up and down the dirty streets of Lawrenceburgh but could find no house which they could afford. Next she searched for four rooms. No success. A night's rest, and she looked for three rooms. Failure. Eunice became very tired as a result of her fruitless search, but as they had to have a place to live she kept looking.

At last she learned of two rooms which might be available over a store and livery stable near the bank of the Miami River. Formerly used for storage and briefly occupied by a hostler, the rooms were incredibly filthy. The owner of the building said the Beechers could have the use of the rooms in their existing condition for thirty dollars a year and conveyed the impression that he was doing a favor to the new minister and his wife. Eunice Beecher had explored, literally, every possible place to rent in Lawrenceburgh, and these dirty rooms were all she could find.

Telling the steamboat captain who was Beecher's friend of her plight, she secured his permission to bring back free of charge any household goods she could get in Walnut Hills and she was permitted to travel without payment to Cincinnati aboard his craft. She did not have a single penny. From the landing in Cincinnati she walked to Lyman Beecher's home in Walnut Hills where her husband was staying.

Her unexpected arrival and obvious fatigue alarmed the family, and she was greeted by cries of "What has brought you here? What is

19. Mrs. Henry Ward Beecher, Notes, n.d., CtY.
20. *Ibid.* In old age Eunice Beecher stated that HWB received $300 per year in Lawrenceburgh from which they paid $30 rent for their first home. In her book published in 1859, *From Dawn to Daylight*, she wrote that their fictional counterparts paid $40 per year. See [Mrs. Beecher], *From Dawn to Daylight*, pp. 62–68.

the matter?"[21] She refused to explain until she had rested a bit and then before a gathering composed of Lyman Beecher, Harriet Beecher Stowe, her brother Artemas Bullard, and Henry Ward Beecher, Eunice explained quietly what had occurred and her efforts to cope with the situation. When she finished she saw glances of surprise and concern exchanged. Beecher broke the silence, "Oh yes, of course, we can go to housekeeping easily. We have an abundance to begin with. Look!" and holding out his hand displayed less than a dollar in coins, "I have all of that toward it." Sarcastically he asked, "How much have you, my dear?"

Not to be intimidated by her husband's reaction, Eunice replied, "Not a penny." She explained that she thought they could manage since his salary was to be paid next week, and it would be coming in monthly.

Interrupted Beecher, "Oh, think of it, good friends! Next week we shall have twenty-five dollars to furnish the house and live on a whole month! Who says we can't go to housekeeping?" He asked, "How large is the house we are to furnish?"

Eunice Beecher said, "Two rooms!"[22]

Her answer, so unexpected, caused the listeners to burst into laughter, and the tension holding them all was released. Their mirth upset her more than had their initial response of alarm. She showed her dismay, and Lyman Beecher hushed them. Immediately they began to make plans to furnish the rooms. It did not seem such a big problem after contemplating equipping a house. On Sunday, October 8, 1837, Lyman Beecher delivered an eloquent sermon on the great importance of an educated ministry to the congregation of the Second Presbyterian Church. At its conclusion he asked for contributions of linens, carpets, and furniture for the use of students at Lane Theological Seminary to aid them in their pursuit of such an education. Lyman Beecher's request coincided with Eunice's hurried trip to Cincinnati. The Beechers returned to Lawrenceburgh laden with furniture and utensils. Among their more prized acquisitions were a cooking stove and lamps given

21. Mrs. Henry Ward Beecher, Notes, n.d., CtY; Indianapolis *Daily Sentinel*, May 28, 1882; Stowe, *Saints, Sinners and Beechers*, p. 255; Cist, *Cincinnati in 1841: Its Early Annals*, p. 118; Mrs. Beecher, "Mr. Beecher as I Knew Him," *Ladies Home Journal*, November, 1891, p. 9.

22. Mrs. Henry Ward Beecher, Notes, n.d., CtY.

them by George and Sarah Beecher, the furniture from Henry's room at Walnut Hills, a bed and strip of carpet from Lyman Beecher, linen from Lydia Jackson Beecher's scant supply, and a bureau, brass andirons, shovel, and tongs from Mrs. William Henry Harrison.[23]

Since the Beechers had to leave the Brower home within a week, they immediately fell to cleaning their future home. Eunice tried to reduce Henry's share of the work, but he would not permit it. He removed his jacket, rolled up his sleeves, and donned a big apron before doing most of the heavy scrubbing of the tobacco-stained walls and floors with soap, water, and sand. Eunice asked the owner of the building for permission to paint the floors, but he refused and said, "O, no! It would rot the wood!"[24] Some of the windows had to be scrubbed four times before it was possible to see through them clearly. When the rooms had been cleaned thoroughly, the Beechers arranged their possessions, and the clergyman made bookcases for his beloved books from the packing cases in which they had been shipped. Eunice sold a handsome cloak which her father had given her and from the $30 she received for it bought other necessities so they could begin housekeeping in modest comfort.[25]

The Beechers were settled in a home of their own, and they were content. Eunice would recall this week of working with Henry as one of the happiest of her life. Beecher went about town thinking, "Was there ever a man so happy as I am!" and in his Journal he wrote, "At Housekeeping with this same dear wife, Began Oct. 17, 1837."[26]

23. Indianapolis *Daily Sentinel*, May 28, 1882; Mrs. Beecher, "Mr. Beecher as I Knew Him," *Ladies Home Journal*, November, 1891, p. 9; Gamaliel Bailey to James G. Birney, Cincinnati, October 14, 1837, quoted in Dwight L. Dumond (ed.), *Letters of James Gillespie Birney, 1831–1857* (2 volumes. New York: D. Appleton Co., 1938), I, 427–28; James A. Green, *William Henry Harrison, His Life and Times* (Richmond, Va.: Garrett and Massie, Inc., 1941), p. 445; [Mrs. Beecher], *From Dawn to Daylight*, pp. 74–82.

24. Indianapolis *Daily Sentinel*, May 28, 1882; Mrs. Henry Ward Beecher, Notes, n.d., CtY.

25. Mrs. Beecher, "Mr. Beecher as I Knew Him," *Ladies Home Journal*, November, 1891, p. 9; Stowe, *Saints, Sinners and Beechers*, pp. 255–56. Mrs. Beecher left a touching account of locating and furnishing their first home in her *From Dawn to Daylight*, pp. 84–93.

26. Truman J. Ellinwood (ed.), *Autobiographical Reminiscences of Henry Ward Beecher* (New York: Frederick A. Stokes Co., [1898]), p. 153; HWB, Journal, October 23, 1837, CtY.

III

Missionary

T HE FIRST PRESBYTERIAN CHURCH OF LAWRENCEBURGH WAS
housed in a building probably erected in 1831 during the pastorate
of Sylvester Scoville. Located on a lot which cost seventy-five dollars,
it was on the west side of Short Street between William and Center
streets. It was a simple, rectangular brick building with one story and
a basement. To enter the church one climbed wooden steps, walked
across a small platform, and gained access to the sanctuary through
double doors. There was space for approximately one hundred fifty
worshipers in the unadorned church.[1]

Beecher performed the chores that would have fallen to a janitor
had there been money to pay one. The basement of the building was
used part of the time for a school taught by Mrs. Catherine Morehouse,
a member of the church, and Beecher was not responsible for its care.[2]
Every Saturday afternoon Beecher swept and dusted the church and
brought in kindling and wood in cold weather for the next day's fire.
He opened the church for services, lit the fire and tended it, and closed

1. Thomas, *An Historical Sketch of the Presbyterian Church of Lawrenceburgh,
Indiana,* p. 6; *History of Dearborn and Ohio Counties, Indiana,* p. 272; Johnson and
Anderson (comps.), *History of Lawrenceburg, Indiana,* p. [56]; New York *World,*
May 22, 1882; New York *Times,* March 9, 1887.

2. Lawrenceburg *Press,* September 22, 1921; Shaw (ed.), *History of Dearborn
County, Indiana,* p. 460; Beecher and Scoville, *A Biography of Henry Ward Beecher,*
pp. 159, 172.

First Presbyterian Church, Laurenceburgh

the building when the congregation left. Had there been a bell he said he would have rung it. The lack of lamps meant that evening services could not be held as the days shortened, and this troubled Beecher. He approached friends in Cincinnati with his problem and was given enough money to buy side lamps which he installed himself, kept filled with lard oil, and trimmed.[3]

Some of the men of Lawrenceburgh chaffed him about doing "woman's work" at the church, but Beecher refused to take offense or to point out that lack of financial support made it necessary for him to do the menial chores. Two young men, clerks in a local store, observed his efforts for several weeks and then offered to help with the tasks. Secretly pleased, Beecher declined their assistance, saying there was only enough work for one man. This intrigued them, and they told some of their friends what the preacher had said. It became a point of honor among the youths as to which could first persuade Beecher to accept his help. Aware of this rivalry the minister eventually agreed to let each young man help with the chores for a month in turn. "Having something to do in the church," recalled Beecher, "was a means of grace to them. It drew them to me and me to them. None of them were Christian young men; but I consulted them about various things, and by and by I brought a case to them. I said, 'Here is a young man who is in great danger of going the wrong way and losing his soul. What do you think is the best means of getting at him?' It made them rather sober and thoughtful to be talking about the salvation of that young man's soul, and the upshot was that they saved their own. They very soon afterward . . . were converted, and became good Christian men."[4] It was a success which deeply pleased Beecher.

The minister appreciated good music and could play the flute with some proficiency. During his student days at the Seminary he attended concerts and musicales in Cincinnati. He was distressed by the old practice of lining out—reading two lines of a hymn to the congrega-

3. Beecher and Scoville, *A Biography of Henry Ward Beecher*, pp. 159, 172. Mrs. Henry Ward Beecher states that she assisted her husband with this work, but in none of his later references to this period does he mention her aid. See Mrs. Henry Ward Beecher, Notes, n.d., CtY, and Beecher and Scoville, *A Biography of Henry Ward Beecher*, p. 172; HWB, *Yale Lectures on Preaching*, I, 144; New York *Times*, March 9, 1887.

4. HWB, *Yale Lectures on Preaching*, I, 144–45.

tion who sang them and then repeating the procedure with the next two lines—a custom of the First Presbyterian Church due to a lack of hymnals. To remedy this Beecher made another trip to Cincinnati where he again acquired enough money from friends to purchase hymnbooks. He gave much thought to the manner in which he should introduce them to his congregation. Since his first Sunday in Lawrenceburgh he had observed carefully the reactions of those attending the church. He noted in his Journal that "You can gain men easily if you get *round* their *prejudices* and put truth in their minds but *never* if you attack prejudice. Look well at this."[5] Having taken the measure of the people he concluded that they would be less apt to balk at an accomplished fact than if they were asked for an opinion first on the matter. Accordingly, he put the hymnals at intervals along the pews, and when the congregation assembled for the next service he noticed a few raised eyebrows and glances exchanged but nothing was said to him in criticism then or later. The hymnals were put into prompt use.[6]

With his household and church in order Beecher settled into a comfortable routine which included much time for reading. He loved books. Since childhood he had collected them; and when he was a student, a good share of his earnings from delivering sermons and lectures had been spent on their purchase. Often he walked long distances to give an address and applied the amount saved on transportation to buy one or more books he wanted. By the time he moved to Lawrenceburgh he owned approximately two hundred volumes. Most of them were theological works, but there was a sizable number of scientific books included. There were some novels, but Beecher did not particularly care for the form and read only those generally considered to be superior. So little interest did most novels have for him that he was quite capable of stopping in the middle of one and not picking it up again for days or maybe never.[7]

5. HWB, Journal, May 4, 1837, CtY.
6. HWB, *Yale Lectures on Preaching*, I, 144.
7. James C. Derby, *Fifty Years Among Authors, Books and Publishers* (New York: G. W. Carleton & Co., 1884), p. 468; HWB, Journal, December 2, 1835, CtY; Mrs. Henry Ward Beecher, Notes, n.d., CtY; Mrs. Beecher, "Mr. Beecher as I Knew Him," *Ladies Home Journal*, October, 1891, p. 3.

Considering himself a slow reader, Beecher carefully read for content and paid little attention to style. "I read for three things," he said, "—first, to know what the world has done in the last twenty-four hours, and is about to do to-day; second, for the knowledge which I especially want to use in my work; and thirdly, for what will bring my mind into a proper mood. . . . I gather my knowledge of current thought from books and periodicals and from conversation with men, from whom I get much that cannot be learned in any other way."[8] He turned frequently to his library for the second reason; he wanted to learn how other men had coped with the problems and questions which perplexed him.

In late October, 1837, he read a biography of John Wesley, the founder of Methodism. There were interesting parallels between Wesley's life and his own. Both were sons of noted clergymen and both had grown up in households where theological discussion was common. Wesley's mother, Susannah Annesley Wesley, was a deeply religious woman who educated her son with a view toward his entering the ministry. Beecher's mother, Roxana Foote Beecher, had expressed a desire that he as well as his brothers should become clergymen. Beecher was especially fascinated by Wesley's attempts to lead a spiritual life and compared his own progress at a similar age with that of the great English evangelist.[9]

Beecher was troubled that many of the residents of Lawrenceburgh habitually profaned the Sabbath. In his opinion there were five particular actions which detracted from worship and were prevalent: standing at street corners in conversation, visiting in private homes, reading light literature such as histories and novels, attending to correspondence and accounts, and traveling. He thought the last of these to be the most reprehensible.[10] His selection of these habits as being particularly offensive may have been influenced by his recognition that each held its attraction for him.

The Sunday morning service was the climax of Beecher's week,

8. Handford, *Beecher: Christian Philosopher, Pulpit Orator, Patriot and Philanthropist*, p. 39.
9. HWB, Journal, October 24, 1837, CtY.
10. *Ibid.*

and he endeavored to preach the best sermon he could prepare. Sometimes an idea for a sermon would come to him from a book. "I was a great reader," said Beecher, "of the old sermonizers. I read old Robert South through and through; . . . I formed much of my style and my handling of texts on his methods. I obtained a vast amount of instruction and assistance from others of those old sermonizers, who were as familiar to me as my own name. I read Barrow, Howe, Sherlock, Butler, and Edwards particularly. I preached a great many sermons while reading these old men, and upon their discourses I often founded the framework of my own."[11] He preached sermons on portions of Scripture and explained and interpreted them to his congregation. He liked to devote at least one service a week to this type of sermon but was seldom satisfied with his presentation.

Constantly aware that he was a son of Lyman Beecher, he thought that he was being compared with his celebrated father. He did not scruple, however, to select those sermons of his father's which pleased him and tailor them for delivery to his congregation in Lawrenceburgh just as he borrowed topics and whole sermons from the great preachers of the past.[12] That his own interpretation of a point might differ from his predecessors' did not bother him. "But I was learning," wrote Beecher, "and nobody ever tripped me up. I had no Board of Elders ready to bring me back to orthodoxy. [It was done] without damage to my people, for they knew too little to know whether I was orthodox or not. . . . They don't believe half that you say. The part that is nutritious they keep, and the rest they let alone."[13] Beecher could not satisfy himself so easily. He spent hours each week in deciding upon a topic and carried a notebook in which he jotted down ideas, read what others had written about his theme, and thought how best he could convey it to his congregation.

Since he made it a practice to deliver his sermons seemingly extemporaneously many in his congregation were unaware of the hours of

11. HWB, *Yale Lectures on Preaching*, I, 139, 146; John R. Howard, *Henry Ward Beecher*, p. 41.

12. HWB, *Yale Lectures on Preaching*, I, 139, 146, 204–205; John R. Howard, *Henry Ward Beecher*, p. 41; Stowe, *Saints, Sinners and Beechers*, p. 259; Towanda [Pa.] *Daily Review*, April 8, 1887.

13. HWB, *Yale Lectures on Preaching*, I, 146.

study he spent on each sermon or that he conscientiously wrote his sermons in full or else prepared copious notes.[14] Henry Ward Beecher did not trust his memory in the pulpit. "The fact is, I was cheated," said Beecher, "when I was born. Hattie Stowe and George took all the memory and left me without any. I do not dare to lead in the Lord's Prayer. I couldn't repeat correctly one commandment from beginning to end. I cannot repeat a verse of any hymn in the English language."[15] Probable exaggeration aside, it added greatly to Beecher's feeling of security to know that he was prepared to deliver a sermon and to have a reminder of what he planned to say. The notes which accompanied him to the pulpit were usually in outline form written on sheets of paper which fit inconspicuously into his Bible where they were accessible to him for reference but not readily visible to the congregation.

Beecher did not always preach the sermon he had so painstakingly prepared for a particular service. "Sometimes I would find," said the preacher, "that after working a subject up all the week, something else would take possession of me on Saturday, and I would have to preach it on Sunday to get rid of it. I felt ashamed and mortified, and began to fear I was on the way to superficiality."[16] On still other occasions the sight or absence of a member of the church might suggest to him the need for a change of emphasis in his sermon or lead him into preaching on another topic entirely. For a long time such was his concern over the nature, quality, and delivery of his sermons that he went regularly to bed with a headache on Sunday nights and considered quitting the ministry to become a farmer.[17]

Eunice Beecher was aware of her husband's feeling of inadequacy in the pulpit. Many times his mood was so low prior to giving a sermon that he asked her not to attend the service as he did not want her to hear him fail. For some time his gloomy predictions caused her deep

---

14. HWB, Notes, n.d., CtY; Mrs. Henry Ward Beecher, Notes, n.d., CtY; Hillis, "The Ruling Ideas of Henry Ward Beecher's Sermons," in *Henry Ward Beecher As His Friends Saw Him*, p. 24.

15. Derby, *Fifty Years Among Authors, Books and Publishers*, p. 451; Mrs. Beecher, "Mr. Beecher as I Knew Him," *Ladies Home Journal*, May, 1892, p. 5.

16. HWB, *Yale Lectures on Preaching*, I, 204–205.

17. *Ibid.*, I, 145; Mrs. Beecher, "Mr. Beecher as I Knew Him," *Ladies Home Journal*, May, 1892, p. 5.

anxiety. After months passed she noticed, however, that frequently he returned home after such foreboding to tell her that everything had gone well and that she should have been present. This eased her mind considerably, and when he expressed future doubts she tended to listen with a wifely grain of salt.[18]

The Beechers' lives in Lawrenceburgh were enlivened in the early spring of 1838 by a week's visit from George and Sarah Beecher. For several months the latter couple had been house guests of Lyman Beecher in Walnut Hills. Formerly pastor of a church at Batavia, Ohio, George Beecher had received calls to a church in Rochester, New York, and to one in New Albany, Indiana. He had decided to take the pastorate of the Rochester Brick Church, and the couple planned to leave soon for the East. The four young people enjoyed their good discussions which were an especial treat for Henry and Eunice who felt themselves to be intellectually isolated in Lawrenceburgh. George came to assist with the communion week at Henry's church and, quite possibly, to give his brother's morale a needed boost.

The Beecher brothers alternated preaching at the First Presbyterian Church. "When George preached the first sermon, I came home," recalled Henry, "and said to my wife: 'I never felt as much indisposition to go into the pulpit again as I do now.' But I struggled against it. The next night I preached, and George came home and said to his wife: 'Well, Sarah, since I have heard Henry preach I feel as if I had not been called to the ministry.' "[19] George Beecher was thought by the rest of his family to be the outstanding preacher among the Beecher sons. Born on May 6, 1809, he was Lyman Beecher's third son to enter the ministry and was already a rising luminary among Presbyterian clergy who listened to his advice and opinions with respect.

Attendance at the Lawrenceburgh church was relatively small and would not appreciably increase. Most of the congregation were women.

18. Mrs. Beecher, "Mr. Beecher as I Knew Him," *Ladies Home Journal*, December, 1891, p. 11; Indianapolis *Daily Sentinel*, May 28, 1882.

19. Derby, *Fifty Years Among Authors, Books and Publishers*, p. 450; James H. Hotchkin, *A History of the Purchase and Settlement of Western New York* (New York: M. W. Dodd, 1848), p. 489; [Mrs. Beecher], *From Dawn to Daylight*, pp. 94–95; Frost (comp.), *Ancestors of Henry Ward Beecher and His Wife Eunice White Bullard*, pp. 8–9; Gamaliel Bailey to James G. Birney, Cincinnati, December 19, 1837, in Dumond (ed.), *Letters of James Gillespie Birney, 1831–1857*, I, 434–35.

There was one man who was so disagreeable that Beecher fervently wished he would take his membership elsewhere; but the man, identity unknown, continued to attend.[20]

Of all the people they met in Lawrenceburgh, Beecher and his wife became fondest of Mrs. Elizabeth Rice, who had come to Indiana from Maine. "Mother" Rice had helped organize the first Sabbath School in Lawrenceburgh and also had been a charter member of the First Presbyterian Church.[21] Her personal life was unfortunate. Married to a drunken, retired shipmaster, John Rice, who swore at her and otherwise abused her, she was obliged to live in miserable rooms over a cooper's shop. The floors of her living quarters were simply loose boards which moved as she walked across them and through which she could see and be seen by the men at work below. Mrs. Rice worked at whatever she could find to do; and, all in all, she would seem to have been a natural object of charity herself.

Yet it was she who was known and loved throughout the community for her kindness and generosity to others. Mrs. Rice was a true Christian who visited the sick and comforted the distressed, and she helped at whatever task needed doing for any family in town. Beecher thought her to be "one of the sweetest, gentlest, and serenest of women," and he considered her "worth more than the whole church . . . and its minister put together." Beecher would cite Mrs. Rice as an example when he wanted to illustrate the nature of Christianity when practiced by an individual. His clinching statement to disbelievers was, "Don't you believe Mother Rice is a Christian?" He discovered that he seldom needed to say more.[22]

Beecher had an opportunity early in January to help a fellow clergyman when Adam Miller arrived in Lawrenceburgh to preach to German immigrants. The destitute Miller urgently needed clothing.

20. Surnames of people who attended or were members of the First Presbyterian Church during Beecher's pastorate include: Bengor, Boon, Bopet, Crooker, Cubbage, Dils, Dodson, Gage, Garrett, Gibson, Guard, Hanks, Hobbs, Hunt, John, Kyle, Lyon, Meechey, Moore, Morehouse, Morgan, Rice, Shepperd, Van Vorhis, and Wisner. See Lawrenceburg *Press*, September 22, 1921; HWB, *Yale Lectures on Preaching*, I, 143.

21. Lawrenceburgh *Political Beacon*, May 4, 1839.

22. HWB, *Yale Lectures on Preaching*, I, 151–52; HWB, *Sermons by Henry Ward Beecher. Plymouth Church. Brooklyn* (2 volumes. New York: Harper & Brothers, 1868), II, 160–61.

Beecher gave him a suit, a shirt, and some stockings. A woman presented the minister with three pairs of stockings; and Thomas Dodson, a member of Beecher's church, contributed two dollars to the newcomer. These gifts, with others, enabled the man to begin his work in decency, and he organized a German Methodist Episcopal Church on April 11, 1839, in Lawrenceburgh.[23]

Miller's poverty disturbed Beecher and may have been the reason he was led to reflect upon the sources of pauperism. After much thought Beecher concluded that poverty arose from the condition of society and from personal causes. The former was affected by the circumstances of a particular time or government, and the latter included indolence, intemperance, and misfortune resulting in a loss of capacity or a loss of property.[24] He did not indicate in his Journal his opinion as to the cause of Miller's difficulties.

A continuing disappointment to Beecher was his inability to bring on a revival in his church. Though he was licensed as an evangelist and had the status of a missionary his success in making conversions was quite limited. He was sincere in his efforts to encourage others to accept the teachings of Christ and to gain a sense of personal salvation. While a student at Lane he had himself experienced a revelation which had profoundly moved him. "The idea dawned upon me," recalled Beecher, "not that there had been a covenant formed between God and his Son, but that Christ revealed the nature of God, whose very soul was curative, and who brought himself and his living holiness to me, because I needed so much, and not because I was so deserving. That instant the clouds rose, and the whole heaven was radiant, and I exclaimed, 'I have found God.' It was the first time I had found him. *Good,* his name was; and I went like one crazed up and down through the fields, half crying, half laughing, singing and praying and shouting like a good Methodist."[25] He wished to share this concept with others and lead them, if he could, to a similar conviction.

Beecher had been brought up to regard the revival, or protracted

23. HWB, Journal, January 8, 1838, CtY; *History of Dearborn, Ohio and Switzerland Counties, Indiana*, pp. 267–68; Shaw (ed.), *History of Dearborn County, Indiana*, p. 402.

24. HWB, Journal, January 10, 1838, CtY.

25. Ellinwood (ed.), *Autobiographical Reminiscences of Henry Ward Beecher*, pp. 45–46.

meeting as it was sometimes called, as a leading means of bringing men and women into the church. Revivals promoted the spread of Christianity and increased membership rolls and church revenues. At Amherst College the revival had been a central feature of religious life.[26] His father was almost constantly engaged in conducting such meetings in the Cincinnati area. Beecher had imbibed these attitudes and expectations. He knew thoroughly his father's theory of the proper method of conducting a revival so as to gain the maximum number of conversions. "You will find a regular sequence," Beecher said, "in the process of conversion. I recollect hearing Dr. [Asahel?] Nettleton and my father talk of the method of bringing people into a regenerated condition. They said that first you must get the individual into a state of 'attention.' The state next to attention was 'interest.' That next to interest was 'conviction.' That next to conviction was a 'deep, rebellious condition.' And next to that was 'conversion.' These were the different stages that they deemed it necessary for the sinner to go through in order to become a Christian."[27]

In spite of his efforts Beecher could not bring enough members of his church to the first stage of attention which was the prerequisite for the beginning of a successful revival. Whether it was because their emotions could not be touched or, just as likely, because he had not developed the skill necessary to reach them, Beecher could not determine. He persevered, however, and gained the attention and interest of a few individuals.

One of these, David V. Culley, had a long conversation with Beecher on February 22, 1838. Formerly a co-publisher with Milton Gregg of the *Indiana Palladium,* Culley was appointed register of the Land Office in Indianapolis in March, 1838. The two men discussed aspects of Christianity and what it meant to be a Christian and a member of the church. Beecher deduced from Culley's remarks that he was not a real Christian but that he might be near the point of acknowledging his sinful heart. Though this was a hopeful sign Beecher was, nevertheless, disgusted that a person with so little intellectual ability

26. Timothy L. Smith, *Revivalism and Social Reform* (New York: Abingdon Press, 1957), pp. 50, 61.
27. HWB, *Lecture-Room Talks* (New York: J. B. Ford & Co., 1874), pp. 146–47.

should hold such a good opinion of himself. The conversation left Beecher feeling disgruntled.[28]

He was better pleased with several talks he had with old John Kyle. Beecher called upon the Revolutionary War veteran at his home where the two discussed what was involved in a man having a change of heart and making the decision to become a Christian. Beecher had learned from Thomas Dodson that Kyle was impressed by the change for the better in Dr. Elisha Morgan's conduct after the physician joined the First Presbyterian Church. Considered by many in the community as a "passionate and profane" man, Kyle's behavior improved noticeably following his conversations with Beecher. The minister "could not avoid the delightful conviction that [Kyle] had become a Sincere Christian." Continuing in his Journal, Beecher wrote, "May God speed the blessed work. Maybe by such instances multiplied many times, make me more faithful—more humble—more entirely consecrated to his Service."[29]

About this time Beecher began to keep another diary in which he recorded his observations and the substance of conversations with various members of the community. Believing that it was necessary for a clergyman to study the characters of men in order to "shape & direct the truth of the blessed Gospel of Christ," for their especial benefit, Beecher hoped "to condense the vague & general impressions wh[ich] men make upon me, into clear opinions & decisions." As if fearing scrutiny by others, Beecher wrote: "This book is a book Sacred from all intrusion of others—*Honor, & principle—Should hold back any who may chance to find it, from looking at that, which belongs strictly to the retirement & privacy of my own heart.*"[30]

Had Henry Ward Beecher recent cause to suspect that his papers were under scrutiny? Was it an adolescent response brought on by an imagined need to protect his secrets? He did not indicate the reason he thought it necessary to insert such a strong statement against prying by others.

28. HWB, Journal, February 22, 1838, CtY; D. J. Lake and B. N. Griffing, *Atlas of Dearborn County, Indiana* (Philadelphia: Lake, Griffing & Stevenson, 1875), p. 18.

29. HWB, Journal, February 22, 1838, CtY; *History of Dearborn, Ohio and Switzerland Counties, Indiana*, pp. 800–801.

30. HWB, Journal, March 9, 1838, Henry Ward Beecher Papers, DLC.

Two excerpts from this diary exemplify attitudes which Beecher encountered in his work in Lawrenceburgh.

> Called this morning on Mr. Hollister. His case is very dilatory. He for a long time clung to the excuse that he was as good as professors of Religion. He today showed that a remnant of it remained, by speaking of it again, but admitted immediately that, this was no excuse or palliation. He then said that he did not know that he sh[oul]d live any better if he should *join the church,* I an[swered] 'I know it. You w[oul]d be worse—you are not fit to join any church.' He seemed astonished.
>
> I then urged the duty of immediately resolving to live for [Christ] entirely. He obj[ected] that, one must support his *family* etc. I explained that reason why he sh[oul]d support them, was thereby to honor God.[31]

Another type of problem was posed by a man upon whom Beecher called at least three times. The man was:

> Distressed in mind . . . . He admitted that he c[oul]d do nothing to merit salvation—yet evidently relied on his *praying . . . God* into receiving him. I did not know how to manage him, exactly. But in prayer I was led to the true cause I believe.
>
> I intimated that I had given all advise I could prayed had done all—Bible could do no more for him—that in *his* case if Christ did not now work for him he *was gone,* it was hopeless.

Beecher thought he could frighten the man since he could not convince him otherwise. He continued, "Cases then wh[ich] *are* relying—tho' ignorantly on their own efforts or on advice . . . by alarming them—*giving them up.*" In this instance Beecher's intuition was correct, but the result may have caused him chagrin. The man in question joined the Methodist Episcopal Church three months later.[32]

This rival church was a continuing thorn in Beecher's side. Later in the summer he wrote to George and Sarah Beecher that "the Methodists held a ten days meeting here—about a fortnight ago & tho' they took in about 40 it is beyond doubt a decided failure—& demonstrates that one year of clearly preached truth has done a great deal. My meetings are fuller than before—& more of the intelligent of that church are gradually giving in, to right views & feelings."[33] The flavor of sour

31. *Ibid.,* March 12, 1838.
32. *Ibid.,* March 17 and June 20, 1838.
33. HWB to George and Sarah Buckingham Beecher, Lawrenceburgh, July 2, 1838, CtY.

grapes was strong in his description of a revival securing forty converts as a failure when he was unable even to begin such a meeting in his church.

Despite his envy the Methodist revival proved helpful to him since it sparked general interest in religion. Beecher used the circumstance to speak out boldly against the "excess & absurdity" exhibited by the Methodists in their attempts to win souls. Basing a sermon upon the text 1 Corinthians 15:58, he emphasized the themes that "1. God Never gives his joy to those who live half in world & half in religion" and "2. We see the mistake of those whose minds, being tender—& troubled —hope by some one act—joining church—partaking ordinances—to gain whole Ch[urc]h character & all its comforts."[34]

One whom Beecher considered to be among the more intelligent of the Methodists was a businessman in Lawrenceburgh named Thomas (?) Guard. When Beecher happened to walk past Guard's insurance office on June 20, 1838, Guard rapped on the window and motioned for him to enter. Guard "introduced the subject by Enquiring for our Confession of Faith—; then alluded to a conversation which I had with him last winter & said he had been thinking since then of the Subject of religion, & had concluded that it was his duty to join the Church & I enquired briefly of his leading feelings & appointed the Evening to converse with him." As they strolled later along the river bank, Beecher and Guard talked about religion. Beecher attributed Guard's remark that he would be happier if he joined the church to "the Methodist atmosphere in wh[ich] he had been raised." Asked for his views of sin and if he thought he could give up worldly temptations and pleasures for Christ, Guard answered satisfactorily. Guard told Beecher that if he did join the church he would endeavor "to grow in *grace* & *knowledge of God* & to avoid the finger of *scorn* for not living up to his profession."[35]

The interview with Guard was far more gratifying than one which Beecher was to have with another man in four days. This man was presumed to be on his death bed, a victim of consumption. Beecher visited him and "found him without feeling—from remorse—anxiety or anything else as to his future condition. Said he had read his Bible a

34. HWB, Sermons, June 17, 1838, CtY.
35. HWB, Diary, June 20, 1838, Henry Ward Beecher Papers, DLC.

great deal—but never had been awakened—& had not even been fearful as to end of life—& sh[oul]d probably die as he lived." Beecher was unable to bring forth a response from the sick man although he "tried to rouse his fear of future. . . . Set [Christ] before him, . . . prayed with him, . . . & left him as I found him, thinking what a place a death bed was for repentance." Beecher returned to preach at the First Presbyterian Church with the feeling that his call had been in vain.[36]

Beecher organized a Bible Class which met for the first time on October 29, 1838. Wanting to spark the interest of the men he deliberately chose a provocative topic based upon a text from the Acts of the Apostles as to the propriety of women speaking in church. Beecher did not question the ability of women to speak learnedly on religious topics. His father had praised his mother for her acumen in such discussions, and Beecher's sisters were all able to discuss theological subjects knowledgeably. This was not the issue. Because women were capable of speaking well on such matters did not mean they should do so in the sanctuary. To bolster the position he assumed Beecher referred the class to 1 Corinthians 14:34 which stated: "Let your women keep silence in the churches; for it is not permitted unto them to speak; but they are commanded to be under obedience, as also saith the law." Given the time, place, and prejudices of those present the outcome of the discussion was never in doubt; nevertheless, the members of the class enjoyed the meeting which had been Beecher's intention.[37]

On Sunday, November 4, 1838, Beecher visited Milton Gregg who was ill. Although Beecher usually established rapport rather easily with others, he found the sick man hostile. After much work he was able to elicit some response from Gregg in the form of terse answers to questions. The pastor discovered in Gregg "that he has tender and quick feelings, but concealed or repressed by a frigid indifference. I could scarcely converse," wrote Beecher, "his replies so cold—but just before praying veins on his forehead swelled—face flushed and after prayer he was bathed in tears." Beecher chose to believe that this reaction arose from Gregg's religious sensibilities.[38]

Early in November Beecher believed that the long-desired revival

36. *Ibid.*, June 24, 1838.
37. HWB, Journal, October 29, 1838, CtY; *Acts of the Apostles*, 1: 1–14.
38. HWB, Journal, November 4, 1838, CtY.

among his congregation might be stirring. There seemed to be a higher degree of religious interest evident among the members; and several of the women, including the Mesdames John, Brown, and Rice, supported the suggestion that prayer circles be established. "Mother" Rice was so enthusiastic about the idea her voice trembled with emotion when she spoke of it to Beecher.[39]

The religious state of mind of Elisha Morgan, a Lawrenceburgh physician, was brought to Beecher's attention. Morgan had grown lax in attending services and meetings at the church. Another member, James Darragh, and the physician had taken personally a sermon preached by Beecher on the topic "Neglect is Sin." The two men did not attend services for months as a result. Beecher had not delivered the sermon for their special benefit, but he surmised from their continued absence that they had guilty consciences.[40] On the morning of November 11, 1838, Morgan did attend the service at which Beecher preached on repentance. So affected was he by what he heard that Morgan called upon Beecher the next day. The physician spoke candidly of his worldliness, stupidity, and wish to live a better life. That same evening Beecher stopped at the Morgan home where he talked with Mrs. Morgan who also expressed her sense of unworthiness and neglect of Christian duty. "I endeavoured to impress upon her," wrote Beecher, "that hope or not *duty now* to go & surrender herself to Saviour—that Christ loved her,—that everyday she should have *close* communion with God in order hereafter to keep up resolutions—prayed with her. . . ."[41]

So passed Beecher's days in the late autumn and early winter of 1838 in Lawrenceburgh. He interspersed sermon preparation with church services, prayer meetings, pastoral calls, and other related duties. The revival did not materialize, however, and Beecher attributed it to the small number in the church who had reached the necessary degree of fervor and, humbly, from the "utter unpreparedness of my own heart."[42]

39. HWB, Journal, November 12, 1838, CtY.
40. *Ibid.*, September 27, 1838.
41. *Ibid.*, November 12, 1838.
42. *Ibid.*

When he visited his family in Walnut Hills, Beecher preached occasionally at the Second Presbyterian Church in Cincinnati of which his father was pastor. This church was located on Fourth Street between Vine and Race streets. Its congregation accorded Henry Ward Beecher praise as a preacher, and he appreciated the opportunity to speak before the larger and more sophisticated congregation than his own in Lawrenceburgh.[43]

To be accepted so well in Cincinnati made Beecher's position as minister of a church considered inferior to its local rival, the Methodist Episcopal Church, doubly humiliating. The Methodists in Lawrenceburgh worshiped in a brick building on Walnut Street. They had received a new pastor, Joseph Tarkington, in the winter of 1838, and he proved to be competent and energetic. Several successful revivals were held in Tarkington's church, and as a result of one of them 126 people were baptized.[44] It led Beecher to give much thought to such "Success in gaining over persons—otherwise sober. . . ." It seemed to the Presbyterian pastor that the Methodists relied upon:

> 1. *Influence of members.* 2. *Social influence.* 3. Doctrinal views are correct—so that preaching from pulpit has effect of Truth. 4. *Extraordinary zeal* of members, to increase their ranks. It is surprising to see what voracity they have. They leave no device untried. . . . 5. Character of meetings—Singing—the Solicitations of members. . . contagion of example.[45]

Beecher was determined "to break through this influence & secure for us a hearing & influence." To this end he formulated six means to reach the goal:

> 1. Make Singing regular and attractive. 2. Organize a female society which meets often. 3. More visitation, prayers of preparation first. 4. More spirited preaching. 5. Single out obnoxious actions. 6. Must cultivate own heart—Consecration—Solemnity—Fervor—Spirituality. His resolution concluded with "In doing the above let it be *done.*"[46]

43. John R. Howard, *Henry Ward Beecher*, pp. 45–46; Cist, *Cincinnati in 1841: Its Early Annals*, p. 96.

44. *History of Dearborn, Ohio and Switzerland Counties, Indiana*, pp. 267–68; Tarkington, *Autobiography*, pp. 9–11, 134–35, 163.

45. HWB, Journal, February 18, 1839, CtY.

46. *Ibid.*

Dismayed by Tarkington's success and discouraged by his comparative lack of achievement, Beecher wrote to his brother-in-law and former teacher, Calvin E. Stowe, and asked him to come to Lawrenceburgh and help him. But Stowe refused "for he thought it better for [HWB] to bear the yoke."[47] It was growing increasingly heavy.

47. HWB, *Yale Lectures on Preaching*, I, 10–11.

IV

Old School versus New School

LYMAN BEECHER AND HIS SON GEORGE BEECHER ATTENDED THE General Assembly of the Presbyterian Church which met in Philadelphia in 1838. Its meeting would be a momentous one for the denomination and for Henry Ward Beecher at home in Lawrenceburgh. After much discussion and juggling for advantage Old School and New School delegates agreed to form two separate Presbyterian churches. A struggle between the opposing factions had developed over preceding decades, and the action was not unexpected. The Beechers and their colleagues who favored the New School position were determined not to be placed at a disadvantage, so they "anticipated the course of the other side, kept a lawyer at their side, and, when the time for action came, were prompt and self-possessed, for they had looked ahead, and correct too, to the *letter of law,* for their counsel was at their ear."[1] At stake were church properties and funds as well as doctrinal differences and prejudices.

While the reasons for the division are seemingly endless in their ramifications, there were four major points of discord between those who were styled New School and those of the Old School. A student of the struggle categorized these issues as: "(1) the operation of the Plan

1. Charles Beecher (ed.), *Autobiography, Correspondence, Etc., of Lyman Beecher, D.D.* (2 volumes. New York: Harper & Brothers, 1864), II, 429–31.

51

of Union; (2) the conflict between the American Home Missionary Society and the Assembly's Board of Missions in attempting to work in the same field; (3) the doctrinal controversy; and (4) the question of slavery."[2]

The Plan of Union was an agreement made in 1801 by the General Assembly of the Presbyterian Church and the General Association of Connecticut representing Congregational churches in which they would co-operate to encourage the spread of religion in the West. At this time their theological differences were minor, and their mode of worship similar. Under the Plan of Union a Presbyterian or Congregational church could call an available pastor from either denomination to serve it. As it happened, Presbyterians of Scotch-Irish ancestry were foremost of the two in establishing new churches in the West. With the passage of years, however, men from New England reared in Congregational churches and schools migrated to the West where they joined existing Presbyterian congregations according to the terms of the Plan of Union. Soon these New Englanders began to assume leadership in the churches and introduce ideas which were changing the nature of Congregational thought in the East. Dissatisfaction grew among some Presbyterians who thought this imported "New Divinity" to be heretical.[3]

The Presbyterians who adhered to traditional Calvinistic theology and forms of church polity and custom became known as Old School men. Those who accepted the relatively more liberal theology advocated by Samuel Hopkins and Nathaniel W. Taylor were styled men of the New School. These latter men were responsible for introducing the "New Divinity" or "New Haven Divinity" concepts into clerical and lay circles where they were endlessly discussed, refined, and twisted to suit individual prejudices. The "New Divinity" differed basically from older Presbyterian theology in that it placed more emphasis upon man's responsibility for the fate of his soul. The two schools accepted

2. William W. Sweet, *The Presbyterians, 1783–1840* (New York: Harper & Brothers, Publishers, 1936), pp. 99–100.

3. *Ibid.*, pp. 100–101; Benjamin J. Lake, *The Story of the Presbyterian Church in the U.S.A.* (Philadelphia: Westminster Press, 1956), pp. 57–58, 64–66; William T. Hanzsche, *The Presbyterians, The Story of A Stanch and Sturdy People* (Philadelphia: Westminster Press, 1934), pp. 99–100; Lyman Abbott, *Henry Ward Beecher* (Boston: Houghton, Mifflin & Co., 1903), p. 608.

the same premises and consulted the same authorities but parted in their conclusions.[4]

So heated did the doctrinal controversy grow within the Presbyterian fold that by the 1830s a series of trials for heresy took place. Henry Ward Beecher's older brother, Edward Beecher, was one of three men brought before the Presbytery of Illinois in 1833 on charges that they had taught "New Divinity" doctrines at Illinois College. The men were acquitted on the grounds that their teaching was not substantially at odds with traditional Presbyterian thought. By far the most celebrated trial of the decade, however, was that of Lyman Beecher for heresy before the Presbytery of Cincinnati in 1835.[5]

Beecher was brought to trial largely at the instigation of Dr. Joshua L. Wilson who had been instrumental in bringing him to Lane Theological Seminary. Both were extremely able men. Wilson had been pastor of the influential First Presbyterian Church of Cincinnati for twenty-seven years. Beecher was pastor of the Second Presbyterian Church of Cincinnati in addition to being the president of the seminary. Wilson had approved earlier of Beecher's views but by 1835 was incensed by many of them which he thought heretical. He charged Beecher with various doctrinal errors and accused him further of slandering the denomination, of insulting Old School believers, of hypocrisy, and of dissimulation. The trial continued for days. At its conclusion the Presbytery of Cincinnati vindicated Lyman Beecher and resolved that the charges against him should not be sustained.[6] Henry Ward Beecher was an interested but disgusted observer of the proceedings.

4. George P. Hays, *Presbyterians* (New York: J. A. Hill & Co., 1892), pp. 175–76; C. Bruce Staiger, "Abolitionism and the Presbyterian Schism of 1837–1838," *Mississippi Valley Historical Review*, XXXVI, No. 3 (December, 1949), p. 393; McCulloch, *Men and Measures of Half A Century*, pp. 10–12; Sweet, *The Presbyterians, 1783–1840*, pp. 106–107.

5. Julian M. Sturtevant, Jr. (ed.), *An Autobiography* (New York: F. H. Revell Co., 1896), pp. 160–63, 183, 198–200; Robert E. Thompson, *A History of the Presbyterian Churches in the United States* (New York: The Christian Literature Co., 1895), pp. 108–109.

6. Hays, *Presbyterians*, pp. 185–86; Gillett, *History of the Presbyterian Church in the United States of America*, II, 463–65; Sprague, *Annals of the American Pulpit*, IV, 308–10; Robert Davidson, *History of the Presbyterian Church in the State of Kentucky; With a Preliminary Sketch of the Churches in the Valley of Virginia* (New York: Robert Carter, 1847), p. 365; Cincinnati *Commercial*, clipping, n.d., OFH.

Evidence of growing divergence could be noted also in the conduct of the mission program. From about 1801 until 1826 there were several missionary societies financed by both Congregational and Presbyterian sources. Perhaps the most prominent of these was the American Board of Commissioners for Foreign Missions, a Congregational-dominated body. In 1826 the American Home Missionary Society was organized which was supported by the two denominations among others but led primarily by Congregationalists. Irked by this circumstance some Presbyterians in Pittsburgh established the Western Foreign Missionary Society in 1831 which they intended to be supported by Presbyterian funds and operated according to Presbyterian principles. As the years passed the American Home Missionary Society was increasingly an organ of the New School faction, and the Western Foreign Missionary Society was Old School oriented.[7] In the field the two societies differed principally in their views of a missionary's work and of evangelism. The American Home Missionary Society favored settling a clergyman in a mission station as exemplified in Henry Ward Beecher's position at Lawrenceburgh whereas the Western Foreign Missionary Society preferred that its missionaries be circuit riders who visited stations in turn. The New School men gave more emphasis to personal evangelism and the revival as weapons in the struggle to gain souls for Christ than did the Old School followers who tended to discredit these means of reaching people and relied instead on pastoral visitation and regular services.[8]

An underlying difference of magnitude was the attitude toward slavery held by Old School and New School factions. Contemporary clergymen and commentators ignored or denied this in an unsuccessful attempt to reduce a source of friction, and the issue was not permitted to be debated in either of the crucial General Assemblies of 1837 or 1838. It was, nevertheless, a central point of discontent. Briefly, many of

---

7. Hanzsche, *The Presbyterians, The Story of a Stanch and Sturdy People*, pp. 101–102; Sweet, *The Presbyterians, 1783–1840*, p. 102; Goodykoontz, *Home Missions on the American Frontier*, pp. 179–80.

8. Julius Melton, *Presbyterian Worship in America, Changing Patterns Since 1787* (Richmond, Va.: John Knox Press, 1967), pp. 28–29, 43; Elwyn A. Smith, *The Presbyterian Ministry in American Culture* (Philadelphia: Westminster Press, 1962), p. 143; Drury, *Presbyterian Panorama: One Hundred Fifty Years of National Missions History*, pp. 30–31.

the Old School Presbyterians had family and commercial connections in the South. While they might personally abhor slavery, they did not believe it worthwhile to challenge the institution at the risk of dividing their denomination. According to their understanding of the Bible, slavery was permissible and a slave might use the circumstance of his condition as an aid in furthering his spiritual growth. The New School men, on the other hand, were predominantly of New England origin and viewed slavery as an evil which could not be condoned. There was not complete agreement among the New School as to how slavery should be ended. Some were content to state their dislike but perform no further action, the majority favored various schemes of abolishing slavery gradually, and a few advocated immediate emancipation.[9]

This simplified explanation of the differences between Old School and New School gives only a hint of what was actually a very complex situation. Each of these issues, and others, played a part in widening the gulf between the factions which resulted in the abrogation of the Plan of Union in 1837 and the division of the denomination in 1838. Though Henry Ward Beecher did not take an active part in events leading to the creation of the Presbyterian Church, N. S. (New School), his welfare was affected by the controversy and by his relationship to Lyman Beecher.

Henry Ward Beecher's first personal concern with the controversy dated from 1837 when he was still a student at Lane and residing in his father's home. Beecher had to obtain the approval of the Presbytery of Cincinnati in order to be licensed to preach within its boundaries. This same Presbytery had become increasingly Old School in sympathy since the time of Lyman Beecher's trial in 1835 and could be expected to show little favor to the son. Getting this license was crucial if Beecher hoped to preach near Cincinnati, and he was genuinely worried that it might be denied him. Adding to his anxiety was his realization that he could not accept completely the doctrinal views held by his father. To Eunice, Beecher wrote, "In a short time, now I shall have finished my studies at Lane, and must then apply for examination, and License.

9. Sweet, *The Presbyterians, 1783–1840*, pp. 111–19, 122–23; Frank H. Foster, *A Genetic History of the New England Theology* (New York: Russell & Russell, 1963), p. 431; Staiger, "Abolitionism and the Presbyterian Schism of 1837–1838," *Mississippi Valley Historical Review*, XXXVI, 391–92.

Shall I get it? Doubtful! I have always told you freely, how perplexed and troubled I have been, for a long time—about some of the *doctrines*. I shall, undoubtedly, be called upon to subscribe to—if I secure a license —and am ordained as an Evangelist. I can see that my father is troubled *for*—and in some degree, *with* me. For the last four years, we have talked very freely—going over the ground, in different lines, week after week. Each discussion, has but strengthened my repugnance to many points. But now as the time is coming so near we are *both very silent.*" Beecher told Eunice that he would never assent to some of the views held by certain members of Presbytery; and, even if the license were refused him, he continued "*Preach I will, licensed or not. On that point I am determined. If I can do no better I will go far out into the West—build a log cabin, among the lumber men—and trappers.*"[10] This last possibility had dismayed Eunice and her parents, but the need for such rash action never arose as Beecher did receive his license to preach. It is probable that it was granted without a struggle rather than precipitate a conflict between the Old School and New School forces when neither felt prepared for it. The suspense and anxiety had marked Beecher, though, and coupled with the remembered tension and acrimony surrounding his father's trial left him with a sense of distaste for sectarianism.

"Going into my work . . . [at Lawrenceburgh] I made up my mind," recalled Beecher, ". . . I would never engage in any religious contention. I remember riding through the woods . . . I sat in my saddle . . . perhaps half an hour, and there, all alone, in a great forest of Indiana, probably twenty miles from any house, prayed for that kingdom [of Christ], saying audibly, 'I will never be a sectary.' . . . Not that I would accept others' belief, not that I would embrace their theology . . . ; but whatever their instruments might be, if they were sincerely working for the kingdom of Christ I would never put a straw in their way and never strike a blow to their harm."[11]

Under normal circumstances Beecher should have been ordained a minister in the autumn of 1837 since he was a licentiate in good standing who had received and accepted a call to be pastor of a church, but

10. HWB to Eunice Bullard, n.p., n.d. (copy in Eunice Bullard's handwriting), Mrs. Henry Ward Beecher, Notes, CtY; Mrs. Beecher, "Mr. Beecher as I Knew Him," *Ladies Home Journal*, November, 1891, p. 9.

11. Beecher and Scoville, *A Biography of Henry Ward Beecher*, pp. 157, 167–68.

his position after the division of the church in 1838 was increasingly difficult. Though he was identified with the New School, his church in Lawrenceburgh was located in the Presbytery of Oxford which was dominated by Old School clergymen.[12] Still hoping to be ordained, Beecher applied for examination in September, 1838. He did not fear the questions that would be asked by the presumably hostile Presbytery, since he was confident of his ability to answer satisfactorily any doctrinal query which might be put to him. Presbytery was to meet near Eaton, Ohio, and Beecher departed from Lawrenceburgh on horseback to make the nearly sixty-mile trip. Preoccupied by the coming encounter, he was thrown from his horse into high water. He managed to rescue himself and his gear, but it was a nasty experience and added to his fear of water.[13]

Beecher produced his letter of dismissal from the Presbytery of Cincinnati and applied formally for examination prior to ordination. He learned that "Father" Archibald Craig was to be the presiding clergyman at his examination. Beecher had met Craig at his father's house and liked the tall, gaunt man in spite of Craig's "shrill, ringing voice." Beecher described the examination to which he was subjected: "I was a model to behold, and so were they! Elders opened their mouths, gave their noses a fresh blowing, fixed their spectacles, and hitched forward on their seats. The ministers clinched their confessions of faith with desperate fervor and looked a little nervous, not knowing how the youth would stand fire." Continuing in a sarcastic vein, Beecher stated, "There he sat, the young candidate begotten of a heretic, nursed at Lane; but, with such a name and parentage and education, what remarkable modesty, extraordinary meekness, and how deferential to the eminently acute questioners who sat gazing upon the prodigy! Certainly this was a bad beginning. Having predetermined that I should be hot and full of confidence, it was somewhat awkward, truly, to find such gentleness and teachableness." As the examination continued, Craig warmed to the young man and aided him whenever possible.[14]

12. Thomas, *An Historical Sketch of the Presbyterian Church of Lawrenceburgh, Indiana*, p. 9.

13. Beecher and Scoville, *A Biography of Henry Ward Beecher*, p. 165; John R. Howard, *Henry Ward Beecher*, p. 19.

14. HWB to [George Beecher?], Lawrenceburg, [September ?], 1838, CtY; Beecher and Scoville, *A Biography of Henry Ward Beecher*, p. 166.

Some of the questions Beecher disposed of rapidly and directly; others were answered by him with a degree of circumlocution if that seemed the wiser course. As the third and last hour of the ordeal neared, Beecher felt a friendly response growing among many who had been neutral or hostile to him earlier in the day. His examination was adjudged satisfactory, and the Presbytery extended to him the wish of the First Presbyterian Church at Lawrenceburgh that he should be ordained its pastor at a salary of $500 for the coming year. The date for his ordination was to be determined the next day.

Several Old School men present had second thoughts in the interval about ordaining Beecher. For all his apparent orthodoxy and knowledge he was still, in their opinion, a New School man and a Beecher. Accordingly, Professor John McArthur of Miami University, a member of Presbytery, moved successfully to postpone setting the time for Beecher's ordination in order that some resolutions might first be introduced and acted upon by Presbytery. The first of these resolutions stated that the Presbytery of Oxford adhered to the Old School division of the denomination and the second required that all candidates and licentiates under its care should be Old School in sympathy and allegiance. Those who could not accept the resolutions were not to be considered as under the care of the Presbytery of Oxford.

Beecher declined to acknowledge the authority of the Presbyterian Church, O.S. It would have constituted a betrayal of his father and many of his own beliefs. Craig was sympathetic to the young man and fully aware of McArthur's intent, so he offered Beecher six months to reflect upon the matter. During that period he might continue to preach at Lawrenceburgh. It was a generous gesture, but Beecher refused. Rather, he requested permission to withdraw his letter of dismissal from the Presbytery of Cincinnati, and he asked for a copy of the proceedings of the Presbytery of Oxford in regard to himself. Next he ascertained his status at Lawrenceburgh and was told that the pulpit of its First Presbyterian Church was vacant. It was "just what I wanted them to say, and, moreover," wrote Beecher in bravado, "just what I determined they should say."[15]

Beecher started immediately for Lawrenceburgh and arrived on

15. Beecher and Scoville, *A Biography of Henry Ward Beecher*, p. 166.

Saturday. The next morning he told his congregation what had taken place at Presbytery, discussed its implications, and said he could not continue as their minister if the church remained under the jurisdiction of the Presbytery of Oxford. At a meeting held the following Wednesday, September 26, 1838, the members of the First Presbyterian Church elected to withdraw from the Presbytery of Oxford and declared their church to be an Independent Presbyterian Church. Beecher noted in the Session records that the "resolutions were read and unanimously adopted."[16] It marked the end of Beecher's tenuous connection with the Old School.

The action of the Presbytery of Oxford and the subsequent withdrawal of the First Presbyterian Church aroused considerable interest in the West. The sequence of events emphasized the polarization of Old School and New School thought. Not all observers, however, believed it would be final. The respected president of Miami University, Robert H. Bishop, wrote, "It is no inconsiderable matter in these days that Dr. [Lyman] Beecher has at least one son, who, after a full and free examination before the Oxford Presbytery, has been pronounced to be orthodox and sound in the faith; and that, in order to exclude the son . . . *a new term* of ministerial communion had to be introduced." To Beecher, he continued, "I hope you will, as I do this morning, thank God and take courage. The Presbyterian Church, if it is to be saved, is to be saved by those who have not yet taken their stand with either Assembly, but have taken *new* and independent ground, anathematizing neither."[17] Beecher was pleased to receive Bishop's "affectionate hieroglyphics" and wrote to Harriet that he would translate them and send a copy to their father, her husband, and Baxter Dickenson.[18]

Having played so conspicuous a role at the meeting of the Presbytery of Oxford, Beecher was especially interested in the outcome of the

16. *Ibid.;* Lawrenceburgh *Political Beacon,* September 29, 1838. Thomas wrote that these resolutions "were attached to the book by wafers and have disappeared, perhaps torn out, perhaps soaked off in the waters of the Ohio in which the volume lay for some weeks during a flood." See Thomas, *An Historical Sketch of the Presbyterian Church of Lawrenceburgh, Indiana,* pp. 9–11; HWB to Harriet Beecher Stowe, Lawrenceburg, October 1, 1838, CtY.

17. Robert H. Bishop to HWB, Oxford, October [?], 1838, quoted in Charles Beecher (ed.), *Autobiography, Correspondence, Etc., of Lyman Beecher, D.D.,* II, 434.

18. HWB to Harriet Beecher Stowe, Lawrenceburg, October 1, 1838, CtY.

meeting of the Synod of Cincinnati. There was now a General Assembly, O.S., and a General Assembly, N.S., but the Synod had not as yet divided. Such division was predicted, and before Synod convened each faction tried to gain the advantage over the other. The first overt contest occurred when it was time to select a moderator. Beecher's brother-in-law, Calvin E. Stowe, and James(?) Coe were nominated, with the latter winning the election by a majority of twenty-three votes. Under Coe's leadership the dominance of the Old School was promoted as committee after committee was appointed with its men in the majority. An especially glaring instance of partisanship was the willingness shown to grant leaves of absence to New School men but not to Old School clergy. And so it continued throughout the meeting. "It is Tuesday morning," wrote Beecher, "and everybody is talking, planning, plotting—all bustle; heads together; knots at every corner; hands going up and down, and faces approaching earnestly or drawing back in doubt; one taking hold of the other's coat, leading off into one corner for a particular argument; elders receiving drill, some bolting the collar. Here, in my room, are father, George [Beecher ?], and Mr. [John] Rankin. They are looking over the ground, prognosticating, arranging for the onset."

Alternately amused or disgusted, Beecher continued, "I never saw so many faces of clergymen, and so few of them intellectual faces. . . . And the elders are just what forty or fifty common farmers would be supposed to be—except that for eldership the soberest men are chosen and as stupidity is usually graced with more gravity than great good sense, the body of elders are not quite so acute in look as the higher class of workingmen."[19] At last it became apparent to all that a reconciliation could not be effected between Old School and New School forces. John Rankin rose, and in his capacity as moderator of the previous Synod declared the present body dissolved. Each group, Old School and New School, assembled in separate Synods; and the parting was accomplished.

The Synod of Indiana, N.S., declared that the area formerly under the jurisdiction of the Presbytery of Oxford would henceforth be guided by the Presbytery of Cincinnati, N.S. The newly organized

---

19. HWB to [George Beecher?], Lawrenceburg, September [?], 1838, CtY.

Presbytery began its existence by arranging to ordain Henry Ward Beecher on November 9, 1838, as minister of an Independent Presbyterian Church.[20]

Beecher had few illusions about the division of the church. In a lengthy letter to his younger half brother, Thomas K. Beecher, he stated, "I agree with you intirely that division in our Church was uncalled for—that it was wicked. There was no doctrinal difference which called for it—& no corruption—& no innovation of new upon old usages—or any *necessity* of any kind except that which mad ambition & madder jealousy begets. Men are arrayed sternly against one another now, who, had they been left free from *extrinsic influences* would have lived—labored & died without dreaming that they differed." He was aware of the irony of his own position. Continuing, he wrote, "My case may Stand for many. A graduate of Lane (that Propaganda of heresy)—the son of the Arch Heretic—has received the *imprimatur* of Orthodox Oxford! The *same sentiments* are orthodox in me at Cincinnati & at *Oxford*. They are new school in Hamilton Co[unty] & Old school in Butler & Preble [counties]!"[21]

The Presbytery of Cincinnati, N.S., met at Lawrenceburgh on November 8 and 9 with several notable New School clergymen present. Before a large congregation Henry Ward Beecher was ordained. His father presided at the solemn service, Jonathan Blanchard charged the young clergyman, and Calvin E. Stowe charged the congregation.[22] Henry Ward Beecher was the fourth son of Lyman Beecher and Roxana Foote Beecher to be ordained a minister.

20. *Ibid.*; Beecher and Scoville, *A Biography of Henry Ward Beecher*, pp. 162–63; Thomas, *An Historical Sketch of the Presbyterian Church of Lawrenceburgh, Indiana*, p. 11.

21. HWB to Thomas K. Beecher, Lawrenceburg, October [?], 1838, copied in HWB, Journal, October [?], 1838, CtY.

22. Thomas, *An Historical Sketch of the Presbyterian Church of Lawrenceburgh, Indiana*, p. 11; HWB, Journal, November 10, 1838, CtY.

V

Growing Discontent

THE FIRST MONTHS OF MARRIAGE WERE DIFFICULT FOR EUNICE Beecher. Wed hurriedly after so many years of waiting, she had begun a new life among strangers whose values and priorities often differed from her own. Within quick succession she had to adjust to the roles of bride, minister's wife, housekeeper, and expectant mother. The infant's birth was expected to occur in May. The situation was enough to tax the fortitude of a more resilient woman than Eunice Beecher who had to face her problems and fears without the comfort and reassurance of nearby relatives and friends.

Beecher tried to ease her life in small ways. Upon occasion he would make a pot of coffee or, more rarely, prepare a steak for their dinner when Eunice was unwell. Once he finished mixing and baking a batch of bread which she had become too sick to complete; so pleased was Beecher with his prowess with the bread that he also baked some cookies at the same time. These were served to callers who dropped by that afternoon. Such activities helped give rise to an untrue rumor that Beecher did much of the housework. He did not do routine housecleaning, laundry, or dishes. Such tasks he said could be put off to a more convenient time when Eunice was well enough to do them.[1]

The burden of household chores fell upon Eunice since they could

1. Mrs. Henry Ward Beecher, Notes, n.d., CtY; Mrs. Beecher, "Mr. Beecher as I Knew Him," *Ladies Home Journal*, December, 1891, p. 11.

not afford to hire a servant. Every drop of water used in cooking, cleaning, and washing had to be carried up the flight of steep steps to their rooms from a well in the yard at the rear of the building. Wood used in the stove for heating and cooking was carried up those same stairs and the ashes taken down them. As her figure thickened from pregnancy such work became increasingly hard and awkward for Eunice.

She was an expert seamstress and in an effort to augment their income which was proving inadequate she began to take in sewing. When she could get enough such work to do, she might be able to earn nearly two dollars a week by working several hours each day. The money was welcome since they were beginning to accumulate debts in the town.[2] As a result of her sewing and malaise from pregnancy there were days when their rooms were not in order. Such lapses became known in the community as visitors afterwards commented upon the cluttered state of the Beecher home. It was the consensus among Lawrenceburgh matrons that Eunice Beecher was a poor housekeeper.[3]

Harriet Beecher Stowe and Beecher's stepmother, Lydia Jackson Beecher, were aware of Eunice's poor health and fear of her approaching confinement. The latter traveled to Lawrenceburgh to comfort Eunice, and Harriet urged her sister-in-law to tell the older woman, "all your difficulties & trials & that you will find her advice an assistance to you." Harriet advised Eunice not to "do so much active work. If you can make money," she continued, "by sewing & it hurts you to wash & iron & do those things why not hire the latter with the avails of the former?" This was advice which Harriet herself followed—she wrote instead of sewed—but it was impractical for Eunice. Still every cent that she could earn was needed. Harriet promised generously to give Eunice a rocking chair or a wrapper similar to one of her own which Eunice had admired. She thought the rocker would be best "for it really grieved me to think that with your aching back you had nothing to rest yourself in when tired with work." The letter mentioned baby clothes which

2. Mrs. Beecher, "Mr. Beecher as I Knew Him," *Ladies Home Journal*, November, 1891, p. 9; Mrs. Henry Ward Beecher to Harriet Beecher Stowe, Lawrenceburg, October 1, 1838, CtY; [Mrs. Beecher], *From Dawn to Daylight*, p. 73.

3. Miss Caroline Dunn, Librarian at the Indiana Historical Society Library, recalls hearing her mother, Mrs. Jacob P. Dunn, Jr., relate that Eunice Beecher was considered a poor housekeeper by Mrs. Jacob P. Dunn, Sr., and her contemporaries who resided in Lawrenceburgh in 1837.

Harriet was collecting for Eunice's expected infant and, in general, was warm and comforting.[4] By dint of such encouragement Eunice managed to get through the last weeks of waiting without succumbing to the breakdown which the family feared.

Harriet Eliza Beecher was born on May 16, 1838, at about eight o'clock in the morning. Her proud father wrote an informative letter about the event to the anxious grandmother in Massachusetts.

> After an illness of eight hours Eunice presented us with . . . a nice plump child weighing somewhat more than *Eight Pounds*. She [Eunice] is now quite comfortable & there seems to be nothing to hinder her getting up soon in good health. She has had no fever—& has had as yet no need of any medicine. . . . For *three weeks*, she had false labor pains which led the doctor . . . & others to expect a confinement *hourly*. But after suffering thus from day to day—on Tuesday night at about 12 she was happily taken with true labor.

Henry Ward Beecher knew the details which would interest a mother and grandmother. He continued,

> The child was presented wrong, its hands being on its head & it was *two hours* before it could be remedied—which so exhausted the child that we thought at first that it was dead—but after a few moments it shot forth from its mouth very satisfactory evidence of breath & breath well used.

A member of Beecher's church, probably Mrs. Rice, nursed Eunice through her ordeal and stayed to care for the mother and child. Neither she nor the physician charged for their services, and clothing for the baby had been given to the Beechers by relatives and friends. Beecher reassured Mrs. Bullard that "The babe is in fine health, perfectly formed in limb & feature, & looks more like a child a month old, than a new born,—having nothing of that appearance commonly seen, at first. Its a real *Beecher* baby, & I shall be much mistaken if everybody does not say '*Oh how exactly like its father!*' As yet we have had no drawback to our pleasure in this Event."[5] He included a complete list of the baby's layette so that her grandmother could share in that important item.

The name Harriet Eliza was selected as a compliment to Beecher's

4. Harriet Beecher Stowe to Mrs. Henry Ward Beecher, [Walnut Hills, 1838], CtY.

5. HWB to Lucy White Bullard, Lawrenceburg, May 17, 1838, CtY.

sister and to Eliza Tyler Stowe, Calvin's first wife who had befriended Beecher. The baby, quickly nicknamed Hatty, thus bore the names of her twin cousins, Harriet and Eliza, the toddlers of Calvin and Harriet Beecher Stowe. The only immediate problem that Hatty, a quiet baby, caused her inexperienced parents was her difficulty in learning to nurse. This feat was not mastered successfully until almost a week after her birth.[6]

Beecher's joy in the child was not shared fully by his wife. At moments during her pregnancy she "had felt that it would be no great trial to me—& release me from a load of responsibility, which I felt unfit to sustain, should the babe be stillborn."[7] She grew to love her daughter and was pleased that Beecher was fond of the child, but she retained "a wee bit of jealous fear, lest he should love *me less* as he loves his babe more. Jealous of my own daughter!"[8] After waiting seven years to claim Beecher's affection and attention as his wife she found it hard to share him so soon with a child.

As it was, Eunice Beecher resented the amount of leisure time her husband spent away from her in the company of the men and boys of Lawrenceburgh. Irritated and hurt, she remonstrated with him and expressed "a wish . . . for a share of his society, or at least a *small portion* of his hours of relaxation." His response was calculated to make her appear "exacting . . . [and] unkind."[9] It was the custom for the males of the community to meet for long conversations in one of the local stores. This period of casual fellowship, or "loafing," was the social event of a man's day in Lawrenceburgh. Beecher fell readily into the pattern and could generally be found in the midst of such a group. In spite of Eunice's displeasure Beecher continued to "loaf" with the men, and on fine days could often be found lounging and talking on the river bank with others who gathered there to fish or rest. After a rain Beecher would throw lines into the water to secure driftwood. This wood he sawed into lengths suitable for use in the family stove with a saw he purchased in the general store operated by Levin B. Lewis.[10]

6. *Ibid.*; Cross (ed.), *The Autobiography of Lyman Beecher*, I, 38.
7. Mrs. Henry Ward Beecher to George Beecher and Sarah Buckingham Beecher, Lawrenceburg, June 15, 1838, CtY.
8. *Ibid.*
9. [Mrs. Beecher], *From Dawn to Daylight*, pp. 39–42.
10. Lawrenceburg *Press*, September 22, 1921.

Beecher assumed that most of the people in the community were familiar with his family background but such was not actually the case. Accustomed to the ill-educated men who were fairly common among pioneer clergymen, Lewis once asked Beecher, "Why is it that you use such good English and have such facility in the use of the language?"

"That is no secret," replied Beecher, "My father and mother were both educated. We heard nothing but the very best language, for father and mother used it all the time."[11]

It irked Eunice Beecher that many people in Lawrenceburgh did not recognize her husband as superior and give him the respect which she thought he deserved. She had grown up in a New England village in which clergymen had high status, and she had listened to Beecher preach in the leading churches of Boston and Cincinnati. To her it was incomprehensible that residents of an insignificant Indiana town should treat him with what she could only view as undue familiarity bordering on contempt. The western view that a man should be judged by what he accomplished and earned rather than by his position or family was basically foreign to her. An individual preacher might gain liking and respect; but, in general, the members of the clerical profession did not automatically enjoy high esteem in frontier Indiana where contributions to their salaries were considered to be acts of charity.[12] It was a galling lesson for Eunice to learn that being the wife of a minister and a Beecher counted for very little in Lawrenceburgh, Indiana.

The Beechers sought larger living quarters and, hopefully, a boarder or two. The classic Beecher family solution to financial distress was to take in boarders; and, in view of their own earlier failure to find a suitable place to room in Lawrenceburgh, it seemed reasonable to assume they could find someone willing to pay them for such accommodation. Less than two weeks after the baby's birth they learned that the house which they wanted had been vacated. They rented it, and Beecher employed men to make needed repairs. He put down new carpeting and in other ways prepared the house for his family. While Beecher was busy with the house, Eunice and the baby were cared for

11. Lawrenceburg *Press*, September 22, 1921.
12. Goodykoontz, *Home Missions on the American Frontier*, p. 220; [Mrs. Beecher], *From Dawn to Daylight*, p. 59; Stowe, *Men of Our Times*, pp. 547–48.

by the nurse who remained one more week. Eunice was still too weak to take an active part in the preparations to move. A servant girl and a boarder were expected to take up residence with the Beecher family on June 16, 1838, and somehow Beecher got the house ready and moved their possessions into it in time.[13]

The early summer of 1838 was a relatively happy one for Henry Ward Beecher. The baby had been born safely, Eunice was recovering her health and spirits, and they at last had room to entertain properly the relatives who came to see them. Margaret Jackson, Beecher's step-sister, came first and stayed to help nurse Eunice and the baby. A while later the Beechers were pleased to have as guests Harriet Beecher Stowe and her small son, Henry. Harriet enjoyed herself tremendously. "How many good times we had in Lawrenceberg [*sic*] when . . . [Henry Stowe and Harriet Eliza Beecher] were both babies lying on the carpet & we drank spruce beer which flew in our face & all over us to Henry's unbounded delight," she wrote.[14] Having house guests and a boarder imposed extra work on Eunice Beecher, but it was offset by having a servant to do the harder labor.

The Beechers' financial situation looked promising. The church was making an effort to rent the house for them for a period of five years, and this seemed tacit approval of Beecher's ministry. It appeared likely that the American Home Missionary Society might pay the clergyman's accumulated debts. Beecher thought the Lawrenceburgh church would probably offer him a salary of $500 per year and might even go to $600. Nearly the former amount was pledged.[15] With such prospects and a little money coming to them from the boarder the Beechers could begin to live more comfortably than in the preceding year.

With the approach of the Fourth of July the publisher of the

13. Mrs. Henry Ward Beecher to George Beecher and Sarah Buckingham Beecher, Lawrenceburg, June 15 and July 2, 1838, CtY; Mrs. Henry Ward Beecher, Notes, n.d., CtY; [Mrs. Beecher], *From Dawn to Daylight*, pp. 125–29.

14. Harriet Beecher Stowe to Mrs. Henry Ward Beecher, Walnut Hills, June 2, [no year], CtY.

15. Mrs. Henry Ward Beecher, Notes, n.d., CtY; [Mrs. Beecher], *From Dawn to Daylight*, pp. 125–30; HWB to George Beecher and Sarah Buckingham Beecher, Lawrenceburg, July 2, 1838, CtY.

Lawrenceburgh newspaper, Milton Gregg, began a campaign to have the holiday commemorated in the community with a program designed to promote and benefit the American Colonization Society. On June 16, 1838, he featured an article favoring colonization on the front page of his newspaper, and a week later he suggested that his fellow citizens assemble in a local church where they would listen to a reading of the Declaration of Independence and an address on the cause of colonization.[16] Beecher was quick to offer the use of the Presbyterian Church for the occasion.

Shortly before eleven o'clock on the morning of July 4th the bell of the Baptist Church rang out calling Lawrenceburgh residents to the program at the Presbyterian Church. It was an exceptionally fine day, and the church seats were soon filled. Arthur St. Clair took the chair and spoke briefly, a prayer was given by Ezra Ferris, and the Declaration of Independence was read by Jeremiah H. Brower. Four resolutions were then offered by Philip Spooner favoring colonization and contributions to that cause. Henry Ward Beecher rose to second and sustain the resolutions.[17]

Beecher advocated the support of the colonization movement as an acceptable means of "freeing us from the pest of slavery."[18] He asserted that the white and Negro races could never merge successfully. Contending it was historical fact, he said that the two races could not live side by side without one becoming the ruler and the other the ruled. To prevent resulting evils it was wisest that the races should be separated. Under present circumstances, Beecher continued, it was advisable that the Negroes should be removed to another land; and, therefore, it was desirable for responsible citizens to support colonization. Beecher stressed that colonization was not synonymous with abolitionism as some people erroneously claimed. In his view the doctrines of each were irreconcilable, and he stated his belief that the best way to destroy abolitionism was to promote colonization.[19] At the conclusion of Beecher's address a collection was taken which yielded almost $20 for the American Colonization Society. This speech was the first for

16. Lawrenceburgh *Political Beacon*, June 16, 23, 1838.
17. *Ibid.*, June 30, July 7, 1838.
18. HWB, Journal, January 2, 1839, CtY.
19. Lawrenceburgh *Political Beacon*, July 7, 1838.

which Henry Ward Beecher received notice beyond the boundaries of Lawrenceburgh.[20]

Beecher's antislavery position mirrored many of his father's convictions on the subject rather than having been the result of independent reasoning. Far from being an abolitionist in the early 1830s, Lyman Beecher deplored the divisive effects upon church and society which proponents of abolitionism were creating; and he favored colonization as a means of ridding the nation of problems created by the institution of slavery. In February, 1834, he reluctantly gave approval for a series of debates about slavery to take place at Lane Theological Seminary. A group of mature students led by Theodore Weld, also an agent of the American Anti-Slavery Society, had made preparations for the event over a period of nine months; and the president of the seminary finally acceded to their pleas for permission to hold the so-called debates. Actually, the eighteen evening meetings devoted to them had more the aspect of a revival than a traditional debate. At the conclusion of the series the students formed an antislavery society "devoted to immediate emancipation to be achieved by approaching slaveholders with the truth, in the spirit of the Gospel."[21]

20. *Ibid.*; Forrest Wilson, *Crusader in Crinoline* (New York: J. B. Lippincott Co., 1941), p. 206.

21. In their enthusiasm the students began at once to implement their goal by lecturing, writing, and working among the Negroes in the Cincinnati area. This upset race-conscious white residents of the city, including the trustees of Lane. Lyman Beecher tried ineffectually to curb the zeal of the students and abate the anger of the trustees, and, on October 10, 1834, while he was away, the trustees voted to abolish antislavery and colonization societies on the campus. Less than a week later twenty-eight students withdrew from the seminary.

After an interim of five months, during which these students attempted to carry on their education as best they could in a building loaned to them at nearby Cumminsville, they were offered $5,000 to purchase a building and promised a professorship by Arthur Tappan of New York if they would establish a school under antislavery principles and influences. The Reverend Asa Mahan, pastor of the Sixth Street Presbyterian Church (Cincinnati) and a trustee of Lane who had resigned in objection to the so-called "gag law," plus John J. Shipherd, a faculty member at Oberlin College, devised a plan incorporating Tappan's offered donation to add a Theological Department to Oberlin. This took place after months of negotiation, and the former Lane students took up residence at Oberlin in 1835. See James H. Fairchild, *Oberlin: The Colony and the College, 1833–1883* (Oberlin: E. J. Goodrich, 1883), pp. 50–66, and Robert S. Fletcher, *A History of Oberlin College* (2 volumes. Oberlin: Oberlin College, 1943), I, 150–66.

Hoping to provide an acceptable alternative to radical abolitionist societies and perhaps channel constructively, in his opinion, the antislavery proclivities of Weld and the other students, Lyman Beecher organized the American Union for the Relief and Improvement of the Colored Race in 1834. He intended it to be a moderate antislavery society which would attract both abolitionists and colonizationists, but the latters' differences were too great and the organization failed in 1836.[22]

Lyman Beecher's adult sons followed closely the debates at Lane and seem to have been influenced by them in varying degrees. Over the decade each of the three eldest gradually moved away from the mild antislavery position shared at first with Lyman Beecher to one approaching or embracing abolitionism. Edward Beecher, president of Illinois College, was an organizer of the Illinois State Anti-Slavery Society in October, 1837. George Beecher joined the Ohio State Anti-Slavery Society in 1836, gave lectures in its behalf, and drafted a memorial urging discipline of slaveholders among Presbyterians by the denomination's General Assembly. In 1837, George Beecher converted his eldest brother, William, to the cause of abolitionism at a meeting in Putnam, Ohio.[23]

Of them all, Henry Ward Beecher was the son who remained closest in viewpoint to his father concerning antislavery and abolitionism. As a boy and young man the former accepted the concept that self-interest and colonization were the most efficacious means of ridding the nation of the evils of slavery. At Amherst on July 10, 1833, he had presided over a debate, "Is the Colonization or the Antislavery Society more worthy of patronage?" The supporters of the colonizationist posi-

---

22. Barnes and Dumond (eds.), *Letters of Theodore Weld, Angelina Grimke Weld, and Sarah Grimke 1822–1844*, I, 12, note 7.

23. Andrew E. Murray, *Presbyterians and the Negro—A History* (Philadelphia: Presbyterian Historical Society, 1966), p. 95; A. L. Bowen, "Anti-Slavery Convention Held in Alton, Illinois, October 26–28, 1837," *Journal of the Illinois State Historical Society*, XX, No. 3 (October, 1927), pp. 336–48; Frank J. Heinl, "Congregationalism in Jacksonville and Early Illinois," *Journal of the Illinois State Historical Society*, XXVII, No. 4 (January, 1935), p. 451; James G. Birney to Lewis Tappan, Cincinnati, September 26, 1836, quoted in Dumond (ed.), *Letters of James Gillespie Birney, 1831–1857*, I, 360; Elizur Wright, Jr., to Theodore Weld, New York, November 4, 1836, quoted in Barnes and Dumond (eds.), *Letters of Theodore Weld, Angelina Grimke Weld, and Sarah Grimke 1822–1844*, I, 348.

tion won the debate. Two years later Beecher wrote approvingly of colonization as a solution to the problem of slavery, and his opinion did not alter substantially in the years preceding his Fourth of July address in 1838.[24]

In the fall of 1838 Beecher gave further thought to the plight of the Negro slave in the United States. He contemplated preaching a sermon based on the captivity of the Israelites in Egypt, and he believed there were analogies which could be developed. As he studied the subject he began to question his earlier ideas in regard to slavery and the race problem. He wondered if it might be God's plan to unite races eventually rather than permit them to remain separated by color. He considered the mingling of the darker Ethiopians with those of lighter color which he thought had contributed to the rise of the famed Egyptian civilization. Beecher reflected that intermingling of whites and blacks had already occurred extensively in the United States and elsewhere and would presumably continue. His aunt, Mary Foote Hubbard, when a girl of eighteen had married a West Indian planter and had been shocked to discover that her husband was the father of mulatto children who lived on his plantation. She returned to Connecticut to make her home with Lyman and Roxana Beecher until her death from consumption. Beecher was familiar with his aunt's history and knew the effect its narration had produced in his family.[25]

While some whites experienced a profound revulsion when forced to associate with Negroes, others mingled freely with them to the extent that a large number of mulattoes were born each year. Beecher reasoned that if these latter married darker Negroes the resulting offspring would, in time, be lighter. This in turn should lessen the dislike of the whites for blacks. Finally, he had come to think it physically and financially impracticable to remove all Negroes to Africa. He concluded that perhaps the eventual integration of the races was the solution to the festering problem. Beecher did not worry about the consistency of his ideas or the accuracy of the evidence upon which he based them.

24. Fuess, *Amherst*, p. 110; Clifford E. Clark, Jr., "Henry Ward Beecher: Revivalist and Antislavery Leader, 1813–1867." (Ph.D. thesis, Harvard University, 1968), pp. 37–38, 50; HWB, Sermons, December 16, 1835, CtY.

25. Stowe, *Saints, Sinners and Beechers*, pp. 170, 173; Charles Beecher (ed.), *Autobiography, Correspondence, Etc., of Lyman Beecher, D.D.*, I, 136–37; Foote, *Foote Family*, I, 89–93.

His musings were confined to his Journal, for he was shrewd enough to realize that few people in Indiana were ready to listen with equanimity to them.[26]

The latter months of the year 1838 were distressing ones for Henry Ward Beecher and his wife. They were concerned about the effects of the denominational controversy upon his future in the ministry; and they experienced financial problems, domestic annoyances, and criticism. The Beechers, like so many others, became victims of the Panic of 1837, one of the severest depressions ever to afflict the economy of the United States. Indiana was involved in an extensive internal improvements program with turnpikes, canals, and railroads planned or at varying stages of construction. Despite the general contraction of credit enough resources were available to keep many of these ventures afloat throughout much of 1839. Beecher happened to be among those, however, who began to feel the effects of the depression in 1838. Farmers and laborers who lived in or near Lawrenceburgh were affected as the price for crops and wages paid declined more rapidly than did the cost of staples. Due to the scarcity of money such men often were forced to barter their crops or services for necessities at a poor rate of exchange. Hugh McCulloch wrote that "money was as scarce as prices were low. The dollar had great purchasing power, but the dollar was difficult to get."[27]

As autumn's chilly nights gave hint of the coming winter the Beechers would have agreed wholeheartedly with McCulloch's statement. On the strength of what had seemed favorable prospects in the spring Beecher had gone further into debt to repair the rented house and purchase furniture for it. His expectations had not been fulfilled. It was his misfortune that the members of his church could not contribute as much toward his salary as had been promised. The American Home Missionary Society upon which Beecher depended for part of his salary had been able to meet its commitment earlier, but its collections had dropped and it could not provide the expected amounts to

26. HWB, Journal, January 2, 1839, CtY.
27. Shaw (ed.), *History of Dearborn County, Indiana*, p. 243; Robert D. Clark, *The Life of Matthew Simpson* (New York: The Macmillan Company, 1956), p. 99; McCulloch, *Men and Measures of Half A Century*, p. 57.

its men in the field. Beecher's income for the year 1838 would be less than $300, plus contributions such as potatoes and corn.[28]

The keeping of a boarder proved to be yet another disappointment and was given up. They had been unable to find a reliable servant. Of their last experience, Eunice wrote "that after hunting for help in every nook & corner & working myself most sick—a stout good looking girl came to us last Tuesday. . . . after working about *three hours*— she went to bed very sick with disentary [*sic*] & has continued so ever since. So instead of help I have had her to wait upon & I never saw any one require more attention. But never mind—I'm not dead yet. The Dr. thinks she will be able to go home soon."[29] It was the Beechers' last attempt to employ a servant in Lawrenceburgh.

Many people in the community knew of their troubles. One of these, Thomas Dodson, chided Beecher and told him that his "*credit too freely exercised*" caused much adverse comment; but Dodson, a member of the church, made no mention of the fact that it was the failure to pay Beecher his promised salary which was at the root of many of the debts. Beecher was depressed by his conversation with Dodson. He talked it over with Eunice, and they decided to ask Ira M. Barton for a loan of $200 to be repaid in two years. The borrowed money would be used to pay their most pressing obligations and lift immediate worry from them. Barton was the most promising relative to approach for a loan. Beecher's family was in little better financial condition than Henry and Eunice, and the Bullards were unlikely to lend money even if they could do so. Eunice's father was noted for his parsimony. To Eunice was left the task of writing the letter requesting the loan. Beecher was upset by the necessity and wrote in his Journal, "Let me trust now in God & humble myself. I was becoming too much elated, & too independent. Tho' painful I can truly say it has done me good. It has given me *Experience*. It will be my fault if I am not a better man, & do not preach better for it, than before." He

28. Henry Little to Milton Badger, Cincinnati, December 1, 1837, American Home Missionary Society Papers, microfilm, In; Joseph Howard, Jr., *Life of Henry Ward Beecher* (Philadelphia: Hubbard Bros., 1887), p. 63; Goodykoontz, *Home Missions on the American Frontier*, pp. 243–44.

29. Mrs. Henry Ward Beecher to Harriet Beecher Stowe, Lawrenceburg, October 1, 1838, CtY.

promised himself that he would "1. Take vigorous measures to liquidate all my debts" and "2. I am *determined*, never again to have credit or regular bills, at stores in my affairs."[30]

The Beechers had to wait a month for Barton's reply. When it came it brought disappointment, since Barton could not lend them the money. Beecher chose to see in his brother-in-law's refusal "a severe chastisment from the hand of God to lead me to him & to detatch me entirely from self & from the world." He cautioned himself not to let worry about his debts prevent him from preaching better sermons and making more pastoral calls than in the past.[31]

The painful conversation with Dodson about his alleged faults coincided with the breaking of the Old School connection and the creation of the Independent Presbyterian Church. It is possible that Dodson saw this as an appropriate time to chide Beecher for past errors and to encourage him to do better in the future. Besides his debts Dodson also mentioned Beecher's neglect of his ministerial duties in recent weeks. Though the young minister strove constantly to improve the quality of his sermons, he had become lax in visiting members of his congregation regularly. He did not like to call on the seriously ill or those involved in trouble which he could not ameliorate, since he "was easily affected by sorrow, sickness, or death."[32]

Beecher resolved to do better. "I shall begin to visit more & labor more abundantly," he wrote. "[I shall] strive to exercise a meek, forgiving softened spirit toward all." He interpreted Dodson's remarks as a warning. "*See to it*, that these things," wrote Beecher, "by the above course do not break me up from here at present—To Church—to our cause at West & to my own Character it would be eminently disasterous [*sic*]." He considered it essential to diminish his self-esteem, to spend more time on church duties, to reduce his debts, and to "abate my desire for *fine living*."[33] With his resolutions he indicates the nature of many of Dodson's charges against himself and Eunice.

Eunice Beecher was not popular with many people in Lawrenceburgh who looked askance at her New England ways. It was resented

30. HWB, Journal, September 27, 1838, CtY.
31. *Ibid.*, October 22, 1838.
32. Knox, *Life and Work of Henry Ward Beecher*, pp. 475–76.
33. HWB, Journal, September 27, 1838, CtY.

by many matrons, for example, that she insisted upon serving every meal upon a tablecloth. This was not customary in Lawrenceburgh households. By continuing to follow the practices of her childhood home in this and other small details she emphasized the gulf that lay between her and her neighbors. In such manner she unwittingly added to her husband's troubles with his congregation. Beecher did not always defend her when one of her actions was questioned or remarked upon publicly, and this omission hurt Eunice. With reference to his silence she would write that when "the husband, either through misjudged, or unguarded friendships, or through fear of his people, is ever tempted to listen to these petty words of censure or complaint from others, then woe be to that wife! It is an evil which creeps upon a man insidiously."[34]

Henry Ward Beecher became ill during the last week of November and had to curtail work. After a partial recovery his first sermon was based on a verse from John 14:27—"Peace I leave with you, my peace I give unto you: not as the world giveth, give I unto you. Let not your heart be troubled, neither let it be afraid." He spoke of how to bear troubles, sickness, perplexity, and blasted hopes. Eunice and he had experienced each of these tribulations within the preceding year. Beecher affirmed that with God's help it was possible to keep one's perspective about events in life which might otherwise appear as insurmountable obstacles and problems. It was a touching statement of trust and, perhaps, a plea for divine aid.[35]

34. [Mrs. Beecher], *From Dawn to Daylight*, pp. 99–100.
35. HWB, Sermons, December 2, 1838, CtY.

VI

Beecher Goes to Indianapolis

W HILE HENRY WARD BEECHER WAS GROWING INCREASINGLY
discouraged in Lawrenceburgh, events were taking place in the
state capital which would affect his future. Scarcely recovered from the
shock of losing several members who withdrew in 1837 to form an
Episcopal church, the First Presbyterian Church of Indianapolis was
troubled by the controversy between Old School and New School
supporters within its membership. A majority of the approximately one
hundred thirty members and the pastor, James W. McKennan, held Old
School views. A small minority were inclined to the New School position. McKennan was "a useful if not a brilliant preacher" who felt it to
be his duty to strike against what he considered were New School
heresies.[1]

The clergyman's sharp words brought criticism and censure upon
his head. Remonstrating with McKennan, Samuel Merrill, a leading
citizen of the community, wrote, "I have understood though in this I
may be misinformed, that you rather took pains to treat [those with
New School views] with disrespect. . . . I considered it [McKennan's
action] to arise from prejudice which would not acknowledge as
brothers, persons who should differ from you in certain matters usually

1. *The Second Presbyterian Church of Indianapolis. One Hundred Years,
1838–1938* (Indianapolis: The Second Presbyterian Church, 1939), pp. 22–23, 27;
Centennial Memorial. First Presbyterian Church. Indianapolis, Indiana (Greenfield,
Ind.: Wm. Mitchell Printing Co., 1925), pp. 190–91.

supposed to be of minor importance. It is this feeling which is contributing largely," continued Merrill, "to produce the present division in the Pres[byterian] Ch[urch]. Numbers amongst whom I am one, have never specially studied the points in dispute. Yet they take sides perhaps, with warmth because persons whom they know to be good and great are excommunicated without a hearing on charges which they positively deny."[2] Merrill was not a member of the First Presbyterian Church, but many of his family were and he was active in its concerns. He was included among those who believed it advisable for a New School church to be established in Indianapolis.

Plans had been laid for such a church at least as early as the summer of 1838. In July of that year Merrill had written to his brother, the Reverend David Merrill, inviting him to accept the pastorate of the proposed church.[3] David Merrill hesitated to leave his position as minister of a church in Urbana, Ohio, and he responded with a temporizing reply asking for more information. Samuel Merrill assured his brother that the committee in charge of finding a pastor wanted him to accept the post and were "strongly of opinion that you ought to come and that you could be well sustained here. . . . it seems to me that so far as this place is concerned the time was never more favorable. Forty one members of the Pres[byterian] Ch[urch] in town without counting some 20 or 30 more from the country, it is understood are willing to . . . form a church at once and they prefer on the whole that it should be called 2 Presbyterian." Almost as an afterthought Samuel Merrill included the vital information that the minister for the new church would receive a salary sufficient for him to "live like the rest of us."[4] The brothers exchanged many letters touching on the subject. David Merrill was tempted to remove to Indianapolis, but he decided finally not to do so. In November he wrote a definite refusal to his brother and the committee.[5]

2. Samuel Merrill to James McKennan, Indianapolis, December 22, 1838, Samuel Merrill Papers, InHi. Merrill, formerly state treasurer, was president of the State Bank of Indiana.

3. Samuel Merrill to David Merrill, Indianapolis, July 7, 1838, Samuel Merrill Papers.

4. Same to same, August 24, 1838, Samuel Merrill Papers.

5. Same to same, July 7, September 1, 8, October 2, and November 10, 1838, Samuel Merrill Papers; Samuel Merrill to James Merrill, Indianapolis, September 8, 1838, Samuel Merrill Papers.

The Second Presbyterian Church of Indianapolis was organized on November 19, 1838, in the lecture room of the Marion County Seminary. In charge of the meeting were the Reverend James H. Johnston and the Reverend John M. Dickey from the Presbytery of Madison, N.S. Two elders were elected, Daniel Yandes and Bethuel F. Morris, and a third, Luke Munsell, would be chosen the next day. A call was sent to the Reverend Sylvester Holmes of New Bedford, Massachusetts, offering the pastorate to him.[6] Most important was the consideration of the letter requesting withdrawal from the First Presbyterian Church and affixing signatures to it. Dated November 19, 1838, the letter stated in part:

> The undersigned being members of your Communion in regular standing, so far as they know, respectfully ask for a dismission from the same for the purpose of forming a separate worshipping congregation in this place. In taking this step, they trust they are influenced by no other motive than that of the glory of God. . . . we earnestly desire that in all our intercourse with each other, both as Christian brethren, fellow citizens, & neighbors, those charities may be exercised & those friendly and fraternal feelings . . . which ought ever to characterize those who hold the same relation to the Great Head of the Church.[7]

The fifteen charter members were far fewer in number than Merrill had predicted optimistically the preceding August.

A dramatic feature of the meeting was the baptism of Samuel Merrill by the Reverend Mr. Johnston. Merrill had attended the First Presbyterian Church for years and had served as a superintendent of the local Sabbath School for a time. He had delayed making a profession of faith, however, and it seemed fitting that he should be baptized into the church he was helping to found.[8]

6. Records of the Second Presbyterian Church, pp. 1–7, InISPC.

7. The charter members of the Second Presbyterian Church were Sidney Bates, A. H. T. Davidson, William Eckert, James F. Holt, Margaret R. Holt, William S. Hubbard, Jane Ketcham, John L. Ketcham, Catharine Merrill, Robert Mitchell, Bethuel F. Morris, Luke Munsell, Lawrence M. Vance, Mary Jane Vance, and Daniel Yandes. Records of the Second Presbyterian Church, pp. 1–2, InISPC; "Beecher's Indianapolis Church," *Indiana Magazine of History*, I, No. 4 (1905), p. 210.

8. George M. Maxwell, *A Discourse on the Death of Samuel Merrill. Delivered at Indianapolis, Aug. 25, 1855* (Indianapolis: Indianapolis Journal Co., 1855), p. 13; William R. Holloway, *Indianapolis* (Indianapolis: Indianapolis Journal Print., 1870), p. 67.

On December 13, 1838, the Session of the First Presbyterian Church agreed to dismiss the members who wished to withdraw and made an affirmation of good will toward them. A committee consisting of Isaac Coe and James M. Ray was appointed to work with Samuel Merrill and Daniel Yandes to effect an equitable division of church property. A "just basis of action was readily agreed upon, and the transaction completed to the satisfaction of both parties in a fraternal and Christian manner."[9]

Sylvester Holmes declined the call extended to him. This irked Merrill and the others who had assumed he would accept it in view of his comments made to them earlier. Altogether six men (David Merrill, a Mr. Smalley, Darcia H. Allen, Sylvester Holmes, John C. Young, and Elihu Baldwin) refused the proffered pastorate. Several other clergymen were canvassed informally with the same result.[10] Though the church was organized, included wealthy and prominent members, and appeared to possess good prospects, its pulpit apparently was not regarded as particularly desirable. Contemporary accounts do not make the reason for this clear.

In its continuing search for a minister, the committee listened with interest when Samuel Merrill mentioned the name of Henry Ward Beecher whom he had heard preach. He attended Beecher's church in Lawrenceburgh when he made his periodic inspections of the branch of the State Bank of Indiana in his capacity as president of the state institution. On one such trip Merrill suffered a broken leg when a box of coins fell on it as the stagecoach in which he was riding entered Lawrenceburgh. Forced to remain in the river town for six weeks, Merrill became acquainted with Beecher who called on him regularly. Merrill received the impression that Beecher was content in Lawrenceburgh, and for this reason he had not suggested Beecher's name earlier to the committee. That body, repeatedly frustrated in its efforts to find a pastor, decided to ask Beecher to preach a trial sermon. Thus, Samuel

9. *Centennial Memorial. First Presbyterian Church. Indianapolis, Indiana,* pp. 50, 190–91; Records of the Second Presbyterian Church, pp. 3–6, InISPC.

10. Samuel Merrill to David Merrill, Indianapolis, July 7, September 1, 1838, and January 17, 1839, Samuel Merrill Papers, InHi; Records of the Second Presbyterian Church, p. 9, InISPC; Ambrose Y. Moore, *History of the Presbytery of Indianapolis* (Indianapolis: J. G. Doughty, Printer, 1876), pp. 50–51; Sprague, *Annals of the American Pulpit,* IV, 572–81.

Merrill was the man most responsible for bringing Henry Ward Beecher to Indianapolis.[11]

Though in his middle twenties, Beecher still appeared boyish to the congregation of the Second Presbyterian Church when he preached before it for the first time. His initial sermon was satisfactory, and he was invited to return and preach again. The Merrill family was so pleased by his sermon and manner that it was ready to call him at once.[12] Beecher preached several sermons before the congregation prior to May 13, 1839, when the call came. He wrote to his father in April that he was "well advanced toward a decision of removing [to] Indianapolis—a thing which will surprise you considering the tenor of my first letter to you from there that morning after I arrived."[13]

It is not surprising that Henry Ward Beecher was unimpressed with some aspects of the Hoosier capital when he first saw it. Settled in 1821, Indianapolis was situated near the center of the state on the east bank of the west fork of the White River. In 1839 the area surrounding it was covered largely by a dense forest of maple, walnut, oak, and ash trees for a distance of approximately forty miles. Roads leading into the town were poor. A contemporary of Beecher's gave this description of them: "There wasn't many roads leadin out of Indianapolis. For the Ohio River towns you had your choice of the Madison Road or the Brookville Road. About all you could say was that they was roads in name only; jist a lane cut through the woods, with trees and stumps purty well cleared out of the right-of-way, but mighty little gradin

11. Contrary to later beliefs HWB's speech at the Fourth of July celebration in 1838 in Lawrenceburgh was not a factor in his receiving a call to the Indianapolis church. For an expression of this erroneous idea see Wilson, *Crusader in Crinoline*, p. 206. David V. Culley is given much credit for bringing Beecher to Indianapolis in *The Second Presbyterian Church of Indianapolis. One Hundred Years, 1838–1938*, pp. 130–31. See also Katharine Merrill Graydon, "A Pioneer Tale, The Life of Samuel Merrill," pp. 13–14, MS, In; Samuel Merrill to Hazen Merrill, Indianapolis, May 14, 1839, Samuel Merrill Papers, InHi; Jane Merrill Ketcham, "Presbyterian (Marion County) History of 2nd Presbyterian Church of Indianapolis," pp. 4–5, photostat of MS, In; McCulloch, *Men and Measures of Half A Century*, pp. 140–41; Jane Merrill Ketcham," Early Memories of the Second Presbyterian Church of Indianapolis, Indiana," MS, InISPC.

12. Ketcham, "Presbyterian (Marion County) History of 2nd Presbyterian Church of Indianapolis," pp. 4–5, In; Jane Merrill Ketcham, "Reminiscences of Jane Merrill Ketcham," p. 69, MS, In; Stowe, *Saints, Sinners and Beechers*, p. 17.

13. HWB to Lyman Beecher, Cincinnati, April [?], 1839, MCR.

done. Swampy places had been corduroyed by rollin logs in side by side until the bog was spanned. Mighty little dirt was put on the logs. A wagon would go thump, thump, thump over them, shakin the daylights out of you. They was only wide enough for one way travel."[14] The National Road, extending east and west, was little better than the roads described, and completed portions of it alternated with sections under construction or scarcely begun.

In Indianapolis only Washington Street, the principal thoroughfare and a part of the National Road, and two or three other streets were free from stumps. There were no sidewalks; and, as in Lawrenceburgh, pigs and other domestic animals roamed freely. There were pastures within sight of the public buildings, and there was no railroad to provide passenger or freight service to other cities. Becoming the state capital in 1825 with the attendant public business gave Indianapolis claim to its only distinction as a city. With its population of less than four thousand it was not appreciably larger than Lawrenceburgh.[15]

Beecher's conduct after learning that he might be called to the Second Presbyterian Church was designed to prevent embarrassment for himself should the invitation not be extended. He was aware that other men had been offered the Indianapolis pastorate and had declined. If he appeared too eager and was not called, he would be in a humiliating position among his peers. If he gave an impression of indifference, however, the committee might think it not worthwhile to send him a call. For several weeks, therefore, Beecher strove to appear interested in the Indianapolis position while seemingly reluctant to leave his church in Lawrenceburgh.

There was more at stake than simply Beecher's personal advancement. The Beechers, father and sons, had worked for years to bring religion to the West. Indeed, Lyman Beecher believed that "to plant Christianity in the West" was as "grand an undertaking as to plant it

14. Johnson, *A Home in the Woods, Oliver Johnson's Reminiscences of Early Marion County*, p. 219.
15. Fisher, *Indiana: in Relation to Its Geography, Statistics, Institutions*, pp. 78–81; Graydon, "A Pioneer Tale, The Life of Samuel Merrill," pp. 16–17, In; HWB, Reminiscences, n.d., CtY; Alexander C. Howard, *A. C. Howard's Directory, for the City of Indianapolis* (Indianapolis: A. C. Howard, publisher, 1857), p. 41; Holloway, *Indianapolis*, p. 4; Kate M. Rabb, *No Mean City* (Indianapolis: L. S. Ayres & Co., 1922), p. 15.

in the Roman empire, with unspeakably greater permanence and power."[16] He, himself, filled a dual role as educator and pastor in Walnut Hills and Cincinnati; his son George was pastor of an influential church in Rochester, New York; his son William was minister of a church in Putnam, Ohio; and a third son, Edward, was president of Illinois College. In Henry Ward Beecher's opinion Indianapolis was the key to Indiana. Once a New School church was firmly established there, he believed, it could serve as a center for spreading correct views across the state. Beecher saw himself as a man who could lead such a church into a position of usefulness and thereby further denominational and family aims. It did not trouble him that he would have to give up his congregation in Lawrenceburgh. "It is *much easier,*" wrote Beecher, "*to get one* [a minister] *suited for Lawrenceburgh than one suited for Indianapolis.*"[17] He believed his duty would be fulfilled if he secured a visiting preacher to supply the Lawrenceburgh pulpit until the church chose to call another minister.

Beecher permitted the members of the Independent Presbyterian Church to think that he had received a call from the Indianapolis church in April when the possibility of it only had been mentioned to him. A few days later he told people in Lawrenceburgh that he had declined a second call to the church in the capital city. No such call had yet been extended to him. When he believed that an invitation was really in the offing, he arranged to have the matter discussed at the next meeting of the Presbytery of Cincinnati, N.S. This step, recommended to him by experienced clerical friends, had the advantage of placing responsibility for his decision to remain at Lawrenceburgh or go to Indianapolis on Presbytery and thereby transferred from Beecher's shoulders any possible criticism. Presbytery's response was predictable as its members were as eager as the Beechers to see a strong New School church in Indianapolis.[18]

Beecher waited in suspense. In Indianapolis the organization of the Second Presbyterian Church continued. On April 24, 1839, three trustees were elected: Samuel Merrill, Edwin J. Peck, and Daniel

---

16. Charles Beecher (ed.), *Autobiography, Correspondence, Etc., of Lyman Beecher, D.D.,* II, 477–79.
17. HWB to Lyman Beecher, Cincinnati, April [?], 1839, MCR.
18. *Ibid.;* Stowe, *Saints, Sinners and Beechers,* p. 260.

Yandes. They were expected to hold office for one year or until successors were elected. Beecher was acquainted with Merrill. Peck was thirty-three years old, a native of Connecticut, and actively making a mark for himself as a leading contractor. He supervised the construction of branch buildings of the State Bank of Indiana at Lafayette, Madison, South Bend, and Terre Haute. Peck was a Presbyterian who held intense religious convictions and would be generous in his support of the new church.[19]

The third trustee, Daniel Yandes, had been elected an elder of the church at the meeting on November 19, 1838. Although a Lutheran by inheritance, he allied himself with the Presbyterians in Indianapolis. Born in Fayette County, Pennsylvania, in 1793, Yandes served under General William Henry Harrison in the War of 1812, and came to Indianapolis in 1821. He had extensive business interests throughout the state, was the first treasurer of Marion County, and was known as a man of integrity who held firm convictions. Beecher would learn to respect Yandes, but he would at times be exasperated by the man's tactlessness and stubbornness.[20]

Expected in Indianapolis to preach at a service on May 4, Beecher left Lawrenceburgh to make the long trip over the "horrible, abominable, outrageous roads."[21] Scarcely had he started on his journey when his dear friend, Mrs. Elizabeth Rice, died in the river town; thus was severed his closest tie with that community.[22] Beecher arrived in Indianapolis late on May 3, 1839. Tired, dirty, hungry, and unaware of his friend's fate he spent the evening resting at Browning's hotel, Washington Hall. Lawrence M. Vance called on him and invited him to go

19. Records of the Second Presbyterian Church, pp. 9–10, InISPC; Berry R. Sulgrove, *History of Indianapolis and Marion County, Indiana* (Philadelphia: L. H. Everts & Co., 1884), pp. 156–57; James I. Osborne and Theodore G. Gronert, *Wabash College, The First Hundred Years, 1832–1932* (Crawfordsville, Ind.: R. E. Banta, 1932), pp. 14–15.

20. Sulgrove, *History of Indianapolis and Marion County, Indiana*, pp. 100–103; *Seventy-Fifth Anniversary, Second Presbyterian Church, Indianapolis, Indiana, 1838–1913* (n.p., n.d.), pp. 5–6; Annabelle Robinson *et al.* (comps.), *Daniel Yandes and His Family* (Crawfordsville, Ind.: R. E. Banta, 1936), pp. 1–10; *Centennial Memorial. First Presbyterian Church. Indianapolis, Indiana*, pp. 415–16.

21. HWB, Journal, May 4, 1839, CtY; Fisher, *Indiana: In Relation to Its Geography, Statistics, Institutions*, p. 50.

22. Lawrenceburgh *Political Beacon*, May 4, 1839.

visit Judge Bethuel F. Morris, but the fatigued preacher declined. They arranged, however, for Beecher to have breakfast at the Vance home next morning. Vance and his wife, Mary Jane, were among the original members of the Second Presbyterian Church. Born in Cincinnati in 1816, Vance was a partner of his father-in-law, Hervey Bates, and a successful merchant with connections in his birthplace and in Lawrence-burgh. The latter town was named in honor of his mother, Mary Morris Lawrence, who was a granddaughter of General Arthur St. Clair.

Beecher awoke to an unseasonably cold morning. The crust of the ground was frozen to a depth of half an inch in places, and it was sur-mised that the frost had destroyed the greater part of the fruit crop. The breakfast at Vance's was a festive affair with other guests present. Beecher thought his hostess was an attractive woman. Following the meal, he spent the morning acquainting himself with Indianapolis and its residents.[23]

Beecher's host at dinner was Judge Bethuel F. Morris. Stocky and of medium height, Morris was a quiet, temperate man who often read a sermon to the congregation of the Second Presbyterian Church when a minister was not present. Beecher admired Mrs. Morris who he thought had a "seemingly plain, affectionate sound head and heart," and he paid her the compliment of stating that she "set a fine table."[24] Beecher preferred simple dishes and customarily ate moderately, but this did not prevent him from recognizing and enjoying superior cook-ing whenever he encountered it.[25]

After the noonday meal Beecher sauntered out into the brisk air to indulge himself in more sightseeing and visiting. It was Saturday, the

23. John H. B. Nowland, *Sketches of Prominent Citizens of 1876* (Indianapolis: Tilford & Carlon, Printers, 1877), pp. 187–88; *Seventy-Fifth Anniversary, Second Presbyterian Church, Indianapolis, Indiana,* pp. 7–8; Sulgrove, *History of Indianapolis and Marion County, Indiana,* p. 153.

24. HWB, Journal, May 4, 1839, CtY; Calvin Fletcher Diary, May 4, 1839, Fletcher Papers, InHi; Sulgrove, *History of Indianapolis and Marion County, Indiana,* p. 153.

25. HWB, Journal, May 4, 1839, CtY; *The Second Presbyterian Church of Indianapolis. One Hundred Years, 1838–1938,* pp. 129–30; Mrs. Henry Ward Beecher, Notes, n.d., CtY; Knox, *Life and Work of Henry Ward Beecher,* p. 439; Mrs. Beecher, "Mr. Beecher as I Knew Him," *Ladies Home Journal,* March, 1892, p. 4.

day of the week that he spent habitually in some pleasant activity.[26] He discovered that the city of Indianapolis had been planned on a generous and imaginative scale. The yellow brick Governor's Mansion with its mansard roof and "widow's walk" was situated in the center of the Governor's Circle which in turn was centered on four blocks known as the Governor's Square. This was the heart of the city, and from it streets branched out at angles. These were named Indiana, Kentucky, Massachusetts, and Virginia. The width of the streets varied from ninety to one hundred twenty feet. There were open spaces around the public buildings, and some of the latter were enclosed with rail fences. Beecher was particularly interested in the stucco exterior of the State House as he had heard derogatory comments about it. He found it to be more attractive than he had been led to expect, but he thought the building might better have been erected on higher ground.[27] The principal businesses faced Washington Street which ran east and west. Most of the buildings were constructed of wood and were two stories in height. It seemed to Beecher that the upper floors were all windows and the lower consisted of doors. Two hotels, or taverns, built of brick were the Mansion House which was a meeting place for Democrats and Washington Hall which served as headquarters for Whig activities in Indiana.[28]

The more he explored Indianapolis the more Beecher chose to be pleased with it. "Residences are very fine," he wrote, "with large yards and gardens on sides and fronts. Houses not crowded as if they had run together for fear of the indians—but separated and dispersed over much ground." There were indeed some distinguished houses in and near the city. One that captured Beecher's fancy was a "cottage with wings—fine grounds filled with trees—and everflowing clear brook running behind

26. Searle, "Beecher's Personality," *North American Review*, CXLIV, 490.

27. HWB, Journal, May 4, 1839, CtY; Kate M. Rabb (ed.), *A Tour Through Indiana in 1840* (New York: Robert M. McBride & Co., 1920), p. 144; McCulloch, *Men and Measures of Half A Century*, pp. 70–71; Lew Wallace, *An Autobiography* (2 volumes. New York: Harper & Brothers, 1906), I, 47–48; Ernestine B. Rose, *The Circle* (Indiana Historical Society *Publications*, XVIII, No. 4, Indianapolis, 1957), p. 360.

28. Lee Burns, *The National Road in Indiana* (Indiana Historical Society *Publications*, VII, No. 4, Indianapolis, 1919), p. 232; HWB, Journal, May 4, 1839, CtY.

and by the side of," the house which belonged to ex-Governor Noah Noble.[29]

Beecher preached to the congregation of the Second Presbyterian Church on May 4 and again on May 9. Three days later he presided at the baptism of the eighth and ninth children, the twins George and Margaret, of Daniel and Anna Yandes. The baptism of the year-old infants was the first such rite Beecher performed in Indianapolis. Further marking the service as one of exceptional importance was the presence of Edmund O. Hovey, a professor at Wabash College, who delivered the sermon.[30] Hovey was New School in sympathy and used his considerable influence to propagate its views throughout the state.

At a meeting next day, May 13, 1839, a unanimous call was extended to Henry Ward Beecher to become pastor of the Second Presbyterian Church. Beecher was promised a salary of $600 per year, and he and his family were expected to be in residence in Indianapolis by July 31.[31] So skillfully had Beecher managed the feat of balancing interest and hesitation that Samuel Merrill could write, "We have now some expectations of getting a son of Dr. Beecher for our pastor. . . . he is personally disposed to come though the wishes of his Presbytery and his own Ch[urch] may prevent."[32]

Henry Ward Beecher wanted to go to Indianapolis. It would be personally advantageous, and the challenge of building a strong New School church appealed to him. He was pleased, too, with the prospect of being pastor to many of the important men in Indiana. Most of all, he wanted to leave Lawrenceburgh. He was sick of never having enough money to live in comfort, he felt stifled in an atmosphere so alien to his

29. HWB, Journal, May 4, 1839, CtY.

30. HWB, Sermons, May 4 and 9, 1839, CtY; Robinson et al. (comps.), *Daniel Yandes and His Family*, pp. 1–10, 14–15; *The Second Presbyterian Church of Indianapolis. One Hundred Years, 1838–1938*, p. 37; Records of the Second Presbyterian Church, p. 11, InISPC.

31. John H. Barrows, *Henry Ward Beecher, the Shakespeare of the Pulpit* (New York: Funk & Wagnalls Co., 1893), p. 78; Stowe, *Saints, Sinners and Beechers*, p. 260; *The Second Presbyterian Church of Indianapolis. One Hundred Years, 1838–1938*, p. 38. The Second Presbyterian Church of Indianapolis does not possess a record of the salary paid to HWB during his pastorate.

32. Samuel Merrill to Hazen Merrill, Indianapolis, May 14, 1839, Samuel Merrill Papers, InHi.

upbringing, and he was discouraged by his lack of success. In the time he resided in Lawrenceburgh twenty-seven people joined his church, but he was unable to bring about a single revival. By the standard maintained by his father and by that of his local rival, Joseph Tarkington, this was dismal failure. "While there I was very much discontented. I had been discontented," wrote Beecher, "for two years. I had expected that there would be a general public interest."[33] It had not developed in spite of his earnest efforts.

Beecher was given credit by his congregation in Lawrenceburgh for his preaching ability, but in other ways he was thought by many to be an ineffective pastor. It was sensed that he cared little for his duties outside the pulpit. Beecher preferred to talk casually with all sorts of people, for example, rather than to limit himself to formal calls in which he discussed only religious topics. He was "kindly, genial and free with all classes," but this counted for little in the estimation of the more influential of the members of the Independent Presbyterian Church.[34]

In the interval between accepting the call to the Indianapolis church and preparing to leave Lawrenceburgh, Beecher answered an urgent summons of his father to come and assist him with a revival he was conducting on the campus of Miami University at Oxford, Ohio. "I know he [HWB] will come if he can, he has felt so deeply ... & is so willing to work—& likeminded with his father," wrote Lyman Beecher.[35] It was a fine compliment for Henry Ward Beecher. The young man hurried to Oxford, and there on May 31, 1839, he preached the sermon based on Hebrews 1:2–3 that he had delivered three weeks earlier in Indianapolis on the nature of God's law and man's law.[36]

Beecher returned to Lawrenceburgh in time to deliver the principal speech at the Fourth of July commemoration. His topic is not known, but the editor of the *Political Beacon* proclaimed the address to be "a

33. HWB, *Yale Lectures on Preaching*, I, 10–11; HWB, *Lecture-Room Talks*, p. 147; Thomas, *An Historical Sketch of the Presbyterian Church of Lawrenceburgh, Indiana*, p. 29.

34. Thomas, *An Historical Sketch of the Presbyterian Church of Lawrenceburgh, Indiana*, p. 8; Lawrenceburg *Press*, September 22, 1921.

35. Lyman Beecher to Lydia Jackson Beecher, Oxford, May 26, 1839, CtHS-D.

36. HWB, Sermons, May 31, 1839, CtY.

rich treat."[37] When asked for a copy of it to be printed in a later issue of the newspaper Beecher declined on the grounds that it would take more time to write it from his meager notes than he could conveniently spare.

There was talk that Lyman Beecher would come to Lawrenceburgh during the second week of July to assist his son with a protracted meeting at the latter's church, and a notice to that effect appeared in the local paper.[38] Presumably the revival did not occur, however, for no further mention of it was made in the *Political Beacon* nor in Beecher's papers.

The Beechers had their household goods transported to Indianapolis by wagon in two separate shipments. The first sent in early July included two boxes, one large barrel, one-half barrel, one stove, one oil can, one sack of coffee containing approximately forty pounds, and ten brooms. The rest of their possessions, except for hand luggage, weighed about one thousand pounds and was shipped several days later.[39]

Beecher and his wife expected to leave Lawrenceburgh about one week before he was due to begin work in Indianapolis. Having given up their house, they spent their last few days in the town as guests of a local merchant and his family. This invitation represented a personal triumph for Beecher who recalled that their host had "lived over on the other side of the street in Lawrenceburgh . . . , a very profane man, who was counted ugly. I understood," said HWB, "that he had said some very bitter things of me. I went right over to his store, and sat down on the counter to talk with him. I happened in often, —day in and day out. My errand was to make him like me. I did make him like me,—and all the children too."[40]

The ill health of Hatty delayed the Beechers' journey to Indianapolis. The little girl was having a miserable time teething in the intense heat of an Indiana summer. She was fretful, had poor color, and was obviously losing weight. Exposing the child to the rigors of the hot, dusty trip to Indianapolis must have caused her parents great anxiety. Beecher did inform Judge Morris, however, that they would try to leave

37. Lawrenceburgh *Political Beacon*, July 13, 1839.

38. *Ibid.*, July 6, 1839.

39. HWB to Lawrence M. Vance for David I. Beatty, Lawrenceburgh, July 10, 1839, Vance Collection, InHi.

40. HWB, *Yale Lectures on Preaching*, II, 153.

Lawrenceburgh for Indianapolis no later than July 29. He preached his final sermon to the congregation of the Independent Presbyterian Church on July 28.[41]

The trip to the capital city was made easier by Samuel Merrill who fortuitously arrived in Lawrenceburgh on one of his bank inspection tours accompanied by his young daughter, Julia Dumont Merrill. They called on the Beecher family and were shocked at the state in which they found them. Merrill had been unaware that Beecher was so hard pressed financially. The minister was almost penniless, and his wardrobe was depleted to the extent that he had to wear some ill-fitting cast-off clothing given to him by a local judge. The appearance of Eunice Beecher and her daughter gave additional evidence of the little family's distress. Making a typically generous gesture, Merrill left Julia to assist Eunice with the baby on the trip to Indianapolis in the Merrill carriage while the banker continued on his tour by public coach.[42]

Julia Merrill, twelve years of age, was experienced in child care and housekeeping. She was a real help to Eunice and relieved her of many tiresome tasks. The girl's assistance and cheerfulness encouraged the Beechers, and soon the party was on its way to Indianapolis. Julia was delighted with the Beechers and enjoyed talking with them on the long ride. They were touched by her father's thoughtfulness and her good nature. Proceeding leisurely, they stopped along the way to pick some blackberries which they saw growing near the road. Eating all they wanted, they also gave some to the baby. The child ate the fruit and seemed to feel better. Beecher attributed the beginning of Hatty's recovery to the refreshing effect of the berries. In any event her lessened discomfort and complaining improved the trip for the other three.[43]

---

41. Mary Jane Vance to Lawrence M. Vance, Indianapolis, July 14, 1839, Vance Collection, InHi; [Mrs. Beecher], *From Dawn to Daylight,* pp. 130–33; Barrows, *Henry Ward Beecher, the Shakespeare of the Pulpit,* p. 84.

42. New York *Times,* March 9, 1887; Joseph Howard, Jr., *Life of Henry Ward Beecher,* pp. 114–15; Stowe, *Saints, Sinners and Beechers,* p. 256; "Reminiscences of Jane Merrill Ketcham," p. 69, In; Barrows, *Henry Ward Beecher, the Shakespeare of the Pulpit,* p. 84; Susan M. Fletcher Notebook, II, 69–71, John L. Ketcham Family Papers, InHi.

43. Joseph Howard, Jr., *Life of Henry Ward Beecher,* pp. 114–15; "Reminiscences of Jane Merrill Ketcham," p. 69, In; [Mrs. Beecher], *From Dawn to Daylight,* pp. 134–39; HWB to [?], n.d., quoted in Graydon, "A Pioneer Tale, The Life of Samuel Merrill," p. 16, In.

The Beechers were invited to stay at the Merrills' until they could locate a suitable house. On reaching the city they drove to the imposing Merrill residence which was set on ground extending from New Jersey to Delaware streets and from McCarty to South Street. Built in 1836 it was reminiscent of houses in Vermont where Merrill spent his boyhood. Entering the house the Beechers saw a large central hall, a prominent staircase, carved woodwork, and a high ceiling. From this hall opened spacious rooms. It was considered to be one of the finer houses of the city, and Merrill enjoyed asking guests to stay for indefinite visits. Although the Merrills employed two servants from time to time, much of the actual housework was done by Julia and her sister Catharine. There were other children, older and younger, but these girls were their mother's chief aides in 1839. Jane Anderson Merrill was a semi-invalid who could not overcome the ill effects of frequent childbearing, malaria, and consumption.[44]

Julia Merrill took her new friends to greet her mother and other family members who happened to be at home. Eunice Beecher's first impression of Mrs. Merrill was that she was much prettier than Julia or Catharine. The meeting between the two women was spoiled, however, when the overwrought Eunice reacted audibly to the scene which met her gaze. She observed that Mrs. Merrill was encased in blankets, two small children were ill on a bed, and an older girl was shaking visibly. Eunice burst into tears and said, "Oh, Henry, they are all sick with 'chills,' and you were told no one ever had them here!"

"You must be mistaken, Mrs. Beecher," said Mrs. Merrill, "everyone has 'chills and fever' more or less constantly."

"No!" said Beecher, "we were emphatically told that it never came here."[45] The atmosphere became unpleasantly tense during the interchange, and with little further conversation the Beechers were shown to the pleasant, comfortable room they were to occupy during their stay.

44. Katharine Merrill Graydon (comp.), *Catharine Merrill, Life and Letters* (Greenfield, Ind.: Mitchell Co., 1934), pp. 23, 32.

45. Mrs. Henry Ward Beecher, Notes, n.d., CtY; Mrs. Beecher, "Mr. Beecher as I Knew Him," *Ladies Home Journal*, December, 1891, p. 11; [Mrs. Beecher], *From Dawn to Daylight*, pp. 140–43.

Eunice Beecher was familiar with the effect that malaria produced on its victims. Reared in New England she could not accept as a normal occurrence the severe attacks of "chills and fever" which most Westerners looked upon so calmly, and her major concern in the contemplated move to Indianapolis had been whether the city was free from malaria. Beecher had assured her that the climate of the Hoosier capital was unusually healthy. She was dismayed, naturally, to find her hostess ill with the affliction and indicating it was common.

Considering the number of times Beecher had been in Indianapolis during the spring and summer of 1839 it is difficult to believe he was unaware of the true situation. After the outburst downstairs the Beechers did not refer to its cause immediately. "I was astonished," Eunice wrote later, "that he said no more; . . . his perfect silence and power of self-control, under what he felt was a wrong done to himself, but which he saw it was too late to prevent. No reproaches, no comments."[46] Another member of his family, Harriet Beecher Stowe, wrote of this quality in Beecher: "I have . . . seen him [HWB] under very trying circumstances. . . . When he is angry he doesn't say anything; he shuts his mouth and sits still."[47] A biographer of Beecher's who did not have such a charitable view of the preacher's character, wrote, "[HWB] could be silent; no man more utterly so. And at times, when pursued by questions that he did not wish to answer, he would pass into silence, not only, but an impassibility of countenance that gave no more sign of understanding or of response than the face of the Sphinx."[48]

Indianapolis in the 1830s was notorious for the malaria which plagued its residents from about the first of July until the first killing frost of autumn,[49] and it must be concluded that Beecher's reasons for accepting the call to Indianapolis outweighed, in his opinion, Eunice's dread of malaria, and he could not bring himself to tell her the truth. This, too, was in character; for Beecher's "courage never failed, except when it was necessary to do something that would displease or grieve

46. Mrs. Henry Ward Beecher, Notes, n.d., CtY; Mrs. Beecher, "Mr. Beecher as I Knew Him," *Ladies Home Journal*, December, 1891, p. 11.
47. Derby, *Fifty Years Among Authors, Books and Publishers*, p. 456.
48. John R. Howard, *Henry Ward Beecher*, p. 134.
49. L. H. Scott to Charles White, Terre Haute, July 25, 1842, Hovey Letters #3, Archives, InCW; Holloway, *Indianapolis*, p. 63.

or afflict a friend; and then he was cowardly—there is no other word for it."[50]

The scene in the Merrill parlor was unfortunate for Beecher. In the eyes of his wife and of Mrs. Merrill he appeared to be either a dupe or a liar. It was not an auspicious beginning, but Beecher did not permit it to dampen his elation in his new position.

50. John R. Howard, *Henry Ward Beecher*, p. 147.

VII

The Proud Pastor

A VERY PROUD HENRY WARD BEECHER PREACHED HIS FIRST SER-
mon as minister of the Second Presbyterian Church of Indianapolis in the lecture room of the Marion County Seminary located on
the northeast corner of Meridian and New York streets. The two-
story brick building, still unfinished in 1839, was used as a school, lecture hall, and scene of religious services.[1]

To reach the room on the second floor where services were held
it was necessary to ascend the stairs from the lobby at the east end of
the building.[2] So rural was Indianapolis that people "climbed up the
open crooked stairway underneath which a lot of stray sheep gathered
for rest. On hearing the steps of the ascending congregation," recalled Jane Merrill Ketcham, "these same sheep either from surprise
or native politeness rose and walked out one by one. This continued
for a few times but on becoming accustomed to the sound of footsteps
and regarding politeness troublesome they slept on without disturbing
themselves."[3] Imaginative members of the congregation saw charm in

1. Landon, *Kings of the Platform and Pulpit*, p. 127; New York *Times*, March
9, 1887; *The Second Presbyterian Church of Indianapolis. One Hundred Years,
1838–1938*, pp. 35–36; Sulgrove, *History of Indianapolis and Marion County, Indiana*, pp. 418–19.
2. Sulgrove, *History of Indianapolis and Marion County, Indiana*, pp. 418–19.
3. Ketcham, "Presbyterian (Marion County) History of 2nd Presbyterian
Church of Indianapolis," pp. 4–5, In.

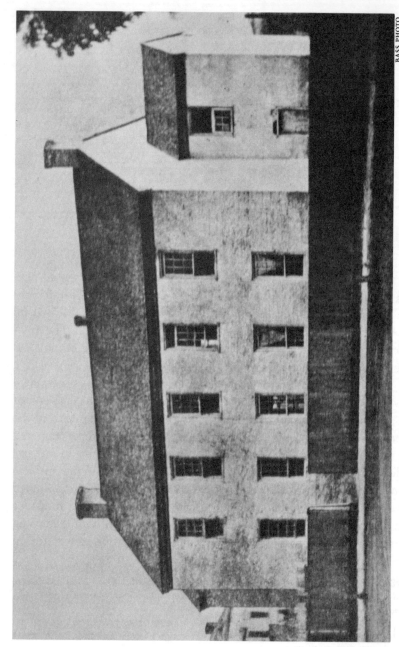

Marion County Seminary, Indianapolis, where the Second Presbyterian Church held services its first year

the presence of the sheep. They reminded at least one woman of Biblical scenes and the "Upper Room" in which Christ met with his disciples. The lecture room which could seat perhaps a hundred people was low and broad, and candles provided illumination for evening meetings. Beecher's presence enhanced the services for his congregation who thought his movements purposeful, his demeanor earnest, and his personality magnetic.[4]

Beecher was sensitive to the atmosphere and happenings at the first services. "The persons present," he wrote, "the transient expressions which the faces wore during the exercises, their dress, and the little incidents,—as where an old man put his cane, the knocking over a pile of hats, the crying of a child."[5] Nor was he the only one conscious of others. Mrs. Ketcham recalled that "We were not . . . people of fashion, although Ladies were self-duped. They all had handsome silk gowns and there were many elegant wraps. The one annual . . . bonnet that each wore trimmed by the town milliner was plain but becoming. While we were still in the Seminary, a jolly stage Contractor brought his pretty wife to town. She attended service in the lecture room. Her Leghorn bonnet with its flaring front and . . . The ostrich feathers and ribbons appropriate, exceeding anything we had ever seen. It was said to have cost forty dollars!"[6] Beecher's salary was fifty dollars per month.

The Second Presbyterian Church had a membership of thirty-two people including the fifteen charter members when Henry Ward Beecher became its minister. He enrolled his wife's name on the membership list as of July 31, 1839, thus making her the first addition to the church after his pastorate began. Encouragingly, four more people were received into the church less than three weeks after Beecher began his work. These were Mary Harman, Eliza Black, Orlando Chester, and Susan Chester. They became members on August 17, 1839.[7]

4. *Ibid.*; "Mr. Beecher as a Social Force," *Scribner's Monthly*, IV, 753; McCulloch, *Men and Measures of Half A Century*, p. 142; HWB, *Eyes and Ears* (Boston: Ticknor and Fields, 1862), pp. 109–10.

5. HWB, *Eyes and Ears*, pp. 109–10.

6. Ketcham, "Presbyterian (Marion County) History of 2nd Presbyterian Church of Indianapolis," p. 8, In.

7. Jacob P. Dunn, *Greater Indianapolis* (2 volumes. Chicago: The Lewis Pub-

The initial listing of Beecher's name in an Indianapolis newspaper occurred on August 3, 1839, when an announcement appeared which read, "The Rev. Henry W. Beecher will hold Divine Service on Sabbath next in the Second Presbyterian Church, commencing at half past 10 o'clock, A.M."[8] He would be "Henry," never "Henry Ward," to those who would become his friends in Indianapolis just as he was called by his first name among members of his family.[9]

Beecher took an immediate lead in helping to organize a Second Presbyterian "Sunday School and School Society." The group met each Sunday in the small library of the Seminary where its members studied reading, writing, and the Bible. At first the class was composed of boys but soon classes for girls were begun. After its formation in August, the "Sunday School and School Society" had an enrollment of fifty with approximately thirty-one children attending each session. The Sunday School movement had existed in various forms in Indianapolis for nearly two decades, but the leaders of the Second Presbyterian Church believed it desirable to sponsor their own organization.[10]

After suffering a severe attack of malaria followed by congestive fever in August, Beecher reflected upon the state of his spiritual welfare as he had done in Lawrenceburgh subsequent to personal adversity. "In looking back on my past life," wrote Beecher, "I find it wholly wrong—a wonderful deficiency of right feeling & particularly I am . . . astonished how as a minister I have been able to do anything as a minister." He outlined a plan which he felt would aid his spiritual advancement. First, he would try to observe the Sabbath more strictly than in the past by devoting more time to prayer, contemplation, and reading. Second, he would conscientiously allot a portion of each day to private devotions. In the course of these devotions he would read

lishing Co., 1910), I, 582; List of Members of the Second Presbyterian Church, CtY; List of Members, Records of the Second Presbyterian Church, InISPC.

8. Indianapolis *Indiana Journal*, August 3, 1839.

9. Stowe, *Men of Our Times*, p. 546; Hanford A. Edson, *The Church God's Building. A Historical Discourse Delivered December 22, 1867* (Indianapolis: Douglass & Conner, 1868), p. 7.

10. *The Second Presbyterian Church of Indianapolis. One Hundred Years, 1838–1938*, pp. 231–33; *Centennial Memorial. First Presbyterian Church. Indianapolis, Indiana*, p. 213.

some appropriate sermon or memoir, read a hymn, study a Biblical subject, and "After these [he trusted his] mind will be in . . . proper frame to pray, without doing it lightly, or formally, or hurriedly." To these good intentions Beecher added a revealing one: "I think I may now, at my *age & judgement* [*sic*] venture upon a *private journal*. In early youth I regard them, *generally,* as either *warm delusion* or half-conscious hypocrisies. But now I *know* more of my feelings . . . from having seen."[11] No mention was made of the journal kept for his eyes only during the period of his residence in Lawrenceburgh.

Beecher established the pattern of preaching which he would follow throughout his career in Indianapolis. He delivered two sermons on Sunday and an average of five sermons in the city or elsewhere during the week. On September 22, 1839, he preached in Indianapolis on the wilfulness of men which prevented their salvation. This sermon was repeated at Putnamville, on October 12, and at Greencastle, on October 13. As he became better known throughout the state he received increasing numbers of invitations to preach at distant churches. The records do not show that he sought or was granted permission by the Second Presbyterian Church to accept these invitations. If a request would require him to be absent from Indianapolis for a number of days or was of special significance, he usually discussed it with one or more of the church officials before agreeing to go. Other than this he was free to conduct his schedule as circumstances warranted and his own wishes dictated.[12]

Beecher was following Presbyterian policy when he preached in as many different churches as he could. There were more calls for ministers than there were qualified men, and congregations with settled pastors were expected to share them with less fortunate churches. Such men, in effect, were itinerant missionaries during a good share of the year. Trips to churches outside of Indianapolis were arduous, tedious, and often unpleasant to a man of Beecher's temperament. As a traveler he might have a choice of staying overnight in a private dwelling, in a hotel or tavern, in a barn, or out in the open. Given a choice between a hotel or barn, Beecher would usually elect to sleep

11. HWB, Journal, September 15, 1839, CtY.
12. Stowe, *Men of Our Times,* p. 542; HWB, Sermons, September 22, October 12 and 13, 1839, CtY; Records of the Second Presbyterian Church, InISPC.

in the barn. It was customary for travelers staying at a hotel to sleep in the same room and often in the same bed with one or more strangers. Lack of personal hygiene, the presence of bugs, and the questionable morals and honesty of other travelers all deterred Beecher from staying in hotels if he could avoid it. Sleeping on a pile of fresh straw seemed preferable.[13]

Securing a clean bed in a private home was possible but not at all predictable. Often Beecher would ride many miles beyond the place at which he had planned to stop because no suitable place presented itself. If he could not stay with acquaintances whose housekeeping habits he already knew and approved, he "always looked for flowers. If there were no trees for shade, no patch of flowers in the yard, we were suspicious of the place. But, no matter how rude the cabin or rough the surroundings, if we saw that the window held a little trough for flowers, and that some vines twined about strings let down from the eaves, we were confident that there was some taste and carefulness in the log-cabin. . . . We were seldom misled. A patch of flowers came to signify kind people, clean beds, and good bread."[14] The usual charge made for overnight hospitality to passersby was twenty-five cents for a bed and the same amount for each meal which might be served. Householders along heavily traveled roads sometimes were forced into erecting signs proclaiming their houses as taverns to protect themselves from travelers who would otherwise expect to be guests of the family with no remuneration paid for service or food.[15]

Henry Ward Beecher had to cope with mud in its season or ruts and bumps which could cause his horse to throw him or even lame the animal. Rivers and creeks usually had to be forded as bridges were few and far between. Beecher hated fords. "I had a peculiar fear of them," he wrote, "arising from an early experience in which I was twice swept away, and came near losing my life. I was courageous in most things, but I dreaded fords because they seemed so dark and

13. Hanzsche, *The Presbyterians, The Story of A Stanch and Sturdy People,* pp. 126–27; HWB, *Sermons by Henry Ward Beecher. Plymouth Church. Brooklyn,* II, 414; Goodykoontz, *Home Missions on the American Frontier,* p. 219.

14. HWB, *Eyes and Ears,* p. 154.

15. Burns, *The National Road in Indiana,* p. 229.

pokerish. In the mud rivers of the West one never knew when the ground might shift, nor what condition a certain ford would be in when he got to it. In going from place to place the thought of the fords that I would have to cross was a perpetual torment to me. For instance, I would go through White River all right, and Blue River would be back of me, but there would be Eel River to come, and I could not get there till five or six o'clock in the afternoon. That was the worst ford. The next one was always the worst. . . . Then I would be mad because it was not deep, after I had been fretting all day about it! . . . I never got any wiser. I was always afraid of a ford."[16] Having to combat such obstacles, a rider was thought to have done well if he could cover twenty-five miles between dawn and dark.[17]

Beecher had his share of vexations on his journeys. On one occasion when fording the Miami River he was unseated and dunked. The story made the rounds in Indianapolis and was heard by a friendly rival, a Baptist preacher. Shortly afterwards Beecher entered a store where were gathered many of the clergy of the city. There he encountered the Baptist who said, "Oh, ho, Beecher, glad to see you! I thought you'd have to come into our ways at last! You've been immersed at last; you are as good as any of us now." The sally was followed by bursts of laughter from the other men present.

"Poh, poh," replied Beecher, "my immersion was a different thing from that of your converts. You see, I was immersed by a *horse*, not by an ass." The mirth at his response was louder than before.[18]

Beecher traveled to Greencastle, to attend Synod which met there on October 10, 1839. It was an eventful meeting, and he took a large part in its deliberations. He was appointed to a committee with John M. Dickey and Samuel K. Sneed to prepare a report on the subject of doctrine, and he was also asked to serve on another committee with Dickey and James Thomson to investigate the feasibility of establishing a religious periodical in co-operation with the Synod of Cincinnati.

The Presbytery of Madison to which the Second Presbyterian Church of Indianapolis belonged was divided the next day, and the

---

16. Ellinwood (ed.), *Autobiographical Reminiscences of Henry Ward Beecher,* pp. 145–46.

17. Mrs. Henry Ward Beecher, Notes, n.d., CtY.

18. Stowe, *Men of Our Times,* pp. 549–50.

Presbytery of Indianapolis came into being. The latter included churches in the counties of Hamilton, Hancock, Hendricks, Henry, Johnson, Madison, Marion (Indianapolis), Morgan, Rush, and Shelby. It was ordered that the Presbytery of Indianapolis, N.S., meet for the first time on Thursday, March 26, 1840. The last day of Synod found Beecher and fellow committee members reporting on the state of doctrine. So well was the report received that it was decided to publish and distribute two thousand copies of it to members of the New School congregations within the bounds of the Synod of Indiana. Beecher, Daniel Yandes, and Bethuel F. Morris were appointed to superintend the details of printing and distribution.[19]

Henry Ward Beecher enjoyed the weekly prayer meetings in which devotion, study, and fellowship were present. Since the group could not use the Seminary room, members of the church took turns in having it meet in their homes. For a time in November, for example, it was held alternately in the candlelit homes of Bethuel F. Morris and Daniel Yandes. Morris had been host to Beecher in the preceding May and was the elder who accompanied him to Greencastle in October. Yandes, an elder and trustee of the church, was a devout man whose custom it was to read the book of his namesake, Daniel, in the Bible every Sunday. The Yandes' home on North Pennsylvania Street was a year newer than Samuel Merrill's house. A row of evergreen trees was planted on each side of the walk which led to the front door of the large brick dwelling, and the house possessed one of the first door bells ever to reach Indianapolis. Either the parlor or sitting room on the ground floor was large enough to accommodate the prayer meeting comfortably.[20]

After the group assembled Beecher would read the hymn for the evening and give its history. At times his account would bring tears to

19. Records of the Synod of Indiana, I, 262–72, Archives, InHan; Moore, *History of the Presbytery of Indianapolis*, pp. 51–52. The report was published under the title: *Circular Letter to the Churches of Indiana in Connection with the Constitutional General Assembly; Charging Them on the Subject of Doctrine.* By the Synod of Indiana (Indianapolis: Douglass & Noel printers, 1839).

20. Ketcham, "Presbyterian (Marion County) History of 2nd Presbyterian Church of Indianapolis," pp. 6–7, In; *The Second Presbyterian Church of Indianapolis. One Hundred Years, 1838–1938*, pp. 35–36; Robinson *et al.* (comps.), *Daniel Yandes and His Family*, pp. 9–11.

the eyes of the softer hearted. A portion of Scripture would be read, and the pastor or another man would expound on it a bit and then a discussion would follow. The meeting would conclude with prayer. And then, in Beecher's opinion, the real meeting might begin. "The best prayer meetings I ever had," Beecher would recall, "were those that came along after I had got through with the main one. That is, when we had finished the regulation prayer-meeting, and there was something that interested the folks, and we got around the stove, a dozen or fifteen of us, and fell to talking about something. Some of those who were not so much interested stood off on the edge, and were looking over the hymn-book and humming a tune. Then we all joined, and sang the tune, and thus we had a meeting."[21] These were among the good times in Indianapolis for Beecher.

He was working hard and beginning to see positive results. News of his efforts and successes trickled back to his family in Walnut Hills and in the East. "I think in *one year* my brother Henry will make his influence felt," wrote his sister Catharine, "all over the state of Indiana. . . . I have never seen persons improve as fast *morally & intellectually* as my brothers since they commenced the duties of their mission."[22] His half sister Isabella was just as enthusiastic. "Brother Henry . . . is working with all his might—he feels much encouraged—& writes to father in great haste, once in a while of what he is doing —his hopes & fears. I think," continued Isabella, "he is going somewhat in father's track & will perhaps one day come somewhere near him in eminence."[23]

Beecher's first real test in Indianapolis came in his attempt to convert Elijah S. Alvord. Told that the banker was seriously contemplating changing his way of life, Beecher went at once to see him. Their conversation was interrupted, but Alvord returned his call later the same day. Beecher recorded the gist of their talk:

> He [Alvord] says he is conscious that it is time to change his course of life; He is determined to *give his life* to the work. I explained to him

21. HWB, *Yale Lectures on Preaching*, II, 108; Stephen M. Griswold, *Sixty Years With Plymouth Church* (New York: Fleming H. Revell Co., 1907), p. 42.

22. Catharine E. Beecher to John P. Hooker, Walnut Hills, November 27, 1839, CtHS-D.

23. Isabella Beecher to John P. Hooker, Walnut Hills, December 2, 1839, CtHS-D.

as well as I could what he has to do, *to repent*. I advised him to *read and pray morning and evening* daily, break off from light companions. This he promised to do. Oh how ignorant I feel when attempting to guide a soul to Christ. Lord, if it is thy work begun O let it be guarded and perfected by thee. I cast my care and burdens upon thee—sustain thou it![24]

Alvord was received by examination into the church on December 13, 1839. It left Beecher feeling humble. "If God will give me grace," wrote the youthful pastor, "I will preach faithfully all parts of the Gospel necessary for conversion of men & perfecting them in holiness. . . . I will give my life to bringing all Christians to work of spreading the true power of Gospel—the love of Christ."[25]

The year 1840 was scarcely underway when his Lawrenceburgh acquaintance, David V. Culley, joined the Second Presbyterian Church. Culley had moved to Indianapolis following his appointment as Register of the Land Office there. Although described by another as "plain, neat" and possessing "native dignity," Beecher still considered Culley to be slow of wit and possessing unwarranted self-esteem. His name swelled the membership list, however, and the possibility existed that his wife and daughter could also be brought into the church.[26]

The newly formed Presbytery of Indianapolis met in Franklin, on March 26, 1840, at eleven o'clock in the morning. The sermon was delivered by Moody Chase who was later chosen moderator of the meeting. An item of business which concerned Beecher dealt with the failure of his church to send records of its Session meetings between November 4, 1839, and March 26, 1840, for the customary examination by a committee of Presbytery. Beecher was chosen temporary clerk and later Stated Clerk of Presbytery, a position he would hold for several years. He seemed to be fulfilling the prophecy of his father who had written to George that "Henry, though so recently estab-

24. HWB, Journal, November [?], 1839, CtY; Dunn, *Greater Indianapolis,* I, 343.

25. HWB, Journal, December [?], 1839, CtY.

26. List of Members, Records of the Second Presbyterian Church, InISPC; Dunn, *Greater Indianapolis,* I, 13; Sulgrove, *History of Indianapolis and Marion County, Indiana,* pp. 236–37; Nowland, *Sketches of Prominent Citizens of 1876,* pp. 450–52; HWB, Journal, February 22, 1838, CtY.

lished at Indianapolis, is beginning to be felt not only at home in the power of the Holy Spirit which attends his labors, but abroad as a man of piety, talents, and power, in the churches and in the capital of his state."[27]

It was unseasonably cold when Beecher left Franklin for his return journey to Indianapolis, and by morning a heavy frost covered the ground. "I remember once riding from Franklin, Indiana, on a cold night," wrote Beecher. "I was chilled. It was so cold that I almost feared I should freeze. After a while I came across a blacksmith's shop. I saw a bright shining light on the forge. Logs were burning and smouldering there, and sending up their red flame. So cold was I that, to tell you the truth, I cried. I wanted to get off from my horse and warm myself, but I was so numb that I was afraid that if I did I could not get on again. So I sat and looked at the fire a moment. Then I said, 'Well, I feel better just for looking at you,' and rode on."[28]

Much of Beecher's time and energy were consumed by attending to details involved in the construction of the building to house the Second Presbyterian Church. It was erected on a lot purchased for $1000 from the State of Indiana in May, 1839, located on the northwest corner of Market Street and the Governor's Circle. Ephraim Colestock built the church for the sum of $8,800. The "Pepper-box Church," as it was nicknamed because of the shape of its cupola, was in style similar to many churches in New England. To reach the sanctuary on the second floor the congregation walked up a flight of steps and across a covered porch. The church could seat approximately three hundred people. The pulpit, centered at the front, was made according to Beecher's design. It was of black walnut, unusually low, and massive in effect. Beecher preferred to be near his listeners, and he wanted his pulpit to be placed to aid this effect. Before the building was completely finished the congregation began meeting in it, and it was dedicated on October 4, 1840.[29]

27. Lyman Beecher to George Beecher, Cincinnati, January 6, 1840, quoted in Cross (ed.), *The Autobiography of Lyman Beecher*, II, 336; Records of the Presbytery of Indianapolis, March 26 and 27, 1840, pp. 1–4, InHan; Moore, *History of the Presbytery of Indianapolis*, pp. 51–52.

28. Ellinwood (ed.), *Autobiographical Reminiscences of Henry Ward Beecher*, pp. 3–4; Calvin Fletcher Diary, March 27, 1840, InHi.

29. Indianapolis *Times*, November 16, 1963; "Beecher's Indianapolis Church,"

Second Presbyterian Church, Indianapolis

The activities of the Sunday School and School Society expanded rapidly under the guidance of Samuel Merrill who had been elected superintendent in 1839. More classes were begun for both older and younger members, and these were taught by those who had especial interest in the work. The Bible was the text studied by all classes from those for the youngest children to the most elderly adults.[30]

Henry Ward Beecher was not present at the meeting of Presbytery in Greenwood, on October 5 and 6, 1840. Since he was Stated Clerk, this caused real inconvenience and he was rebuked: "It being ascertained that the Stated Clerk of Presbytery [HWB] had not only failed to forward the Records, but even to have them put into Such a condition as is necessary for the use of Presbytery:—therefore resolved that Presbytery very much regret the *Seeming* negligence of the Stated Clerk in this matter as it is very much to the predjudice [sic] of the transaction of the business of the Presbytery." Despite the scolding administered to Beecher, he was appointed *in absentia* to a committee consisting of P. S. Cleland and himself to prepare by-laws for the regulation of the Presbytery.[31] Perhaps it was hoped it would encourage him to obey rules if he helped formulate them.

From Greenwood many members of Presbytery went directly to Indianapolis to attend Synod which convened on Thursday, October 8, at the new Second Presbyterian Church. "Father" Martin M. Post of Logansport gave the opening sermon. Beecher took an active part in the three-day meeting. He was made a member of the Committee of Bills and Overtures, and he was appointed to preach the Missionary Sermon at the next Synod. An issue which was causing irritation and misunderstandings was called to the attention of Synod on Saturday. Because of the effects of the depression the various charities, educational institutions, and missionary societies were pressed for operating funds. Their agents were busy within the bounds of Synod soliciting

---

Indiana Magazine of History, I, 210; Knox, *Life and Work of Henry Ward Beecher,* p. 455; *The Second Presbyterian Church of Indianapolis. One Hundred Years, 1838–1938,* pp. 42–43; Rose, *The Circle,* p. 388. HWB's pulpit may be seen in the present Second Presbyterian Church.

30. *The Second Presbyterian Church of Indianapolis. One Hundred Years, 1838–1938,* pp. 231–33.

31. Records of the Presbytery of Indianapolis, October 5 and 6, 1840, pp. 5–7, InHan.

financial support. Too often these men arrived at a church in numbers and were embarrassingly competitive. They were making nuisances of themselves and alienating many ministers and congregations. The Synod urged that the agents restrict their pleas to certain months so that less conflict would occur. In the Presbytery of Indianapolis, for example, they were asked to abide by the following schedule:

January–February	Tract Cause
March–April	Foreign Missions
May–June	Sabbath School
July–August	Education Cause
September–October	Bible Society
November–December	Home Missions

Synod adjourned on Saturday, but many of the clergymen planned to remain over Sunday so as to avoid travel on that day and also so they could hear Beecher preach.[32] Henry Ward Beecher was rapidly acquiring a reputation as an outstanding speaker. Many listeners became so engrossed in his sermons that they reacted audibly to them. At one such incident Beecher spoke about

> nature with its varied seasons. . . . He likened it to man's existence on earth. Finally closed, held his hand above his head in a dramatic pause after his climax. Everyone was spellbound. An old man sat in front of me, [one who was present recalled] with face intent on Beecher. Finally he came to and brought his fist down on the back of the seat in front of him and said, under his breath, "Now damn them, let 'em beat that if they can!"[33]

Beecher had served his apprenticeship well as a speaker in Lawrenceburgh, and when he arrived in Indianapolis he was technically proficient but still unsatisfied with the response his sermons drew. It dawned upon him that

> the sermon was the *end* and not the *means*. [He] had a vague idea that truth was to be preached, and that then it was to be left to do its work under God's blessing as best it might. The results were not satisfying. Why should not preaching do now what it did in the Apostles' days?[34]

32. Records of the Synod of Indiana, I, 273–83, InHan.
33. John Bradshaw, Reminiscences, May 25, 1902, in George S. Cottman's Indiana Scrapbook Collection, VIII, 44, In.
34. HWB, *Eyes and Ears,* pp. 109–10; Lyman Abbott and S. B. Halliday,

He decided to study carefully examples of the Apostles' preaching. "I took every single instance," stated Beecher,

> In the Record [Acts of the Apostles], where I could find one of their sermons, and analyzed it . . . and I studied the sermons until I got this idea: That the Apostles were accustomed first to feel for a ground on which the people and they stood together; a common ground where they could meet. Then they heaped up a large number of the particulars of knowledge that belonged to everybody; . . . then they brought it to bear upon them with all their excited heart and feeling.[35]

When Beecher felt ready to preach a sermon prepared with his new concept in mind, he based it upon the presumed needs of members of his congregation. It was successful.

> Preaching was a definite and practical thing. Our people needed certain moral changes. Preaching was only a method of enforcing truths, not for the sake of the truths themselves, but for the results to be sought in *men*. *Man* was the thing. Henceforth our business was to work upon *man;* to study him, to stimulate and educate him. A sermon was good that had power on the heart, and was good for nothing, no matter how good, that had no moral power on *man*.[36]

Since his first days at Lawrenceburgh, Beecher had observed others and analyzed their motives and actions. He had tended to build his sermons, however, on the foundations erected by early theologians and his father's contemporaries. He still attempted to foster the impression that his carefully prepared sermons were given extemporaneously and were more the result of inspiration than perspiration, and now he began to shape sermons which were uniquely designed to reach the particular individuals facing him at a service. So successful was he that the Second Presbyterian Church became a mecca for visitors to Indianapolis who were curious to hear the new kind of sermon preached by its minister. Residents of the city who were not members of Beecher's church fell into the habit of visiting the Second Presbyterian Church to hear Beecher, and the Sunday evening service at-

---

Henry Ward Beecher: A Sketch of His Career (Hartford, Conn.: American Publishing Co., 1887), p. 609.

35. HWB, *Yale Lectures on Preaching*, I, 11–12; H. R. Haweis, "Henry Ward Beecher," *Littell's Living Age*, CXIII, No. 1455 (April 27, 1872), p. 201.

36. HWB, *Eyes and Ears*, p. 110.

tracted large numbers of them each week.[37] A frequent visitor was Charles Dewey, judge of the state Supreme Court, who thought Beecher affected when he folded his arms across his chest prior to expressing himself forcefully from the pulpit. Dewey also interpreted this to mean that the preacher was saying, "There, damn you, beat that."[38]

From the number of churches in the city of Indianapolis and in the immediate vicinity of the Second Presbyterian Church it would appear that the Devil would have had much opposition in the Hoosier capital. In 1841 there were five churches in or adjacent to the Governor's Circle: First Presbyterian, Second Presbyterian, Wesley Chapel (Methodist), Christ (Episcopal), and English Lutheran. Beecher found a ready audience for a series of sermons dealing with Old Lucifer's methods, and he delivered at least three of them in February, 1841. Stressing fallacies, superstition, and potential harm to the young from misinformation, Beecher presented "a rational and scriptural understanding of the subject of fallen spirits." It was an exciting topic and one which helped dispel the boredom of Indiana's long winter nights. The sermons attracted much attention and were discussed at an unusual length in a local newspaper.[39]

Despite Beecher's efforts the Devil did lay a hand on some members of the Second Presbyterian Church. At the Session meeting on March 12, 1841, Beecher in his role as moderator discussed with the elders, Daniel Yandes, Bethuel F. Morris, and Luke Munsell, the behavior of one member who reportedly was guilty of unspecified im-

37. A roster of those who attended the Second Presbyterian Church as visitors included such notable Hoosiers as Charles Dewey, Jeremiah Sullivan, Isaac Blackford, Gen. Tilghman A. Howard, Joseph G. Marshall, Amos Lane, James H. Lane, Michael G. Bright, Jesse D. Bright, George H. Dunn, James Whitcomb, Joseph A. Wright, Oliver P. Morton, Hugh McCulloch, Schuyler Colfax, Jacob P. Chapman, Alexander F. Morrison, Hugh O'Neal, and John B. Dillon. See *The Second Presbyterian Church of Indianapolis. One Hundred Years, 1838–1938*, pp. 44–45; Stowe, *Men of Our Times*, pp. 542–43; McCulloch, *Men and Measures of Half A Century*, pp. 141, 146; "A Morning at the Church of the Pilgrims," *The United States Democratic Review*, VI (January, 1856), 53; *Henry Ward Beecher As His Friends Saw Him*, p. 113.

38. Charles W. Taylor, *Biographical Sketches and Review of the Bench and Bar of Indiana* (Indianapolis: Bench & Bar Publishing Co., 1895), p. 39.

39. Indianapolis *Indiana Democrat*, February 12, 1841.

moral conduct. When taxed with the charge the accused admitted its truth. Since one purpose of the Session was to discipline any erring member of the church, it was resolved that he should be suspended from the privileges and ordinances of the church until he exhibited signs of true repentance.[40] It was the first of several disciplinary actions which Beecher would initiate or participate in during his pastorate in Indianapolis.

40. Records of the Second Presbyterian Church, pp. 15, 20, InISPC; Joel Parker and T. Ralston Smith, *The Presbyterian's Hand-Book of the Church* (New York, 1861), pp. 11–16.

VIII

Family and Friends

WITHIN A FEW WEEKS OF THEIR ARRIVAL IN INDIANAPOLIS IN 1839 Beecher and his wife who was again pregnant were taken ill with the "chills and fever" so feared by Eunice. The onset was attended by "yawnings and stretching, a feeling of lassitude, blueness of the fingernails, then little cold sensations which increased until the victim's teeth chattered in his jaws. . . . After an hour or so warmth returned, then gradually merged into raging heat with racking head pains and aching back. The spell ended with copious sweating and a return to normal."[1] So common was the disease that many people viewed it as an unavoidable hardship of frontier life. It made its appearance with climbing summer temperatures and continued until a killing frost occurred in the fall. Known by various names such as "dumb ague," "shaking ague," "chills and fever," "intermittent," "remittent," "autumnal fever," "agur," and malaria it was expressed in predictable rhythms. Some attacks might occur daily, others on alternate days or once every three days, and occasionally every fourth day. Usually an individual was subject to attacks on a fairly regular schedule and could plan his business and social life accordingly.[2] Various theories were current as to

1. Madge Pickard and R. Carlyle Buley, *The Midwest Pioneer, His Ills, Cures and Doctors* (Crawfordsville, Ind.: R. E. Banta, 1945), p. 16; Mrs. Beecher, "Mr. Beecher as I Knew Him," *Ladies Home Journal*, December, 1891, p. 11.
2. Pickard and Buley, *The Midwest Pioneer, His Ills, Cures and Doctors*, pp. 16,

the cause of the disease. One of Beecher's contemporaries said its "cause . . . was the dense damp woods and the rotten logs and leaves."[3] Another idea was that the disease originated "in the numerous swamps that gave rise to a subtle malarial poison. The theory was tenable that this effluvia arose from stagnant pools of water and hovered about, especially at night—this 'night-air' thus acquired a questionable reputation."[4] The mosquito was not called to account.

After the attack of malaria the Beechers contracted an ailment which was diagnosed as congestive fever. They became so ill that they were unaware when a friend took Hatty away from the Merrill house to her own home where the child remained several weeks. Alarmed at the condition of Eunice and Henry, Merrill sent for Lyman Beecher to come to Indianapolis. The couple recovered but afterwards were subject to recurrent attacks of malaria in a milder form. While Beecher tended to regard his illness as a visitation from God to encourage him to mend his ways, Eunice could not accept the malaria so philosophically. She blamed Indianapolis residents for encouraging Beecher to move there under false pretenses, and her dissatisfaction with the town and its people grew apace with the illnesses suffered by the Beecher family.

Partially recovered and with their child once more at their side, the Beechers began to look for a place of their own. For nine weeks they had lived as guests in the Merrill home and then as residents in the house of the Merrills' son-in-law and daughter Jane—the John L. Ketchams—when the Ketchams were away. They then moved into a furnished house on Delaware Street. When its owners returned earlier to the city than expected, the Beechers moved into a second house which proved quite unsatisfactory. They may have moved one or two more times during the fall and winter of 1839. Finally, Beecher learned of a house for sale which might be suitable. The price is not known, but Beecher discussed its purchase with some church members who were willing to advance him the money for it if he would agree to repay

---

18; Johnson, *A Home in the Woods, Oliver Johnson's Reminiscences of Early Marion County*, pp. 171–72.

3. Johnson, *A Home in the Woods, Oliver Johnson's Reminiscences of Early Marion County*, pp. 171–72.

4. Jacob P. Dunn, *Indiana and Indianans* (5 volumes. Chicago: The American Historical Society, 1919), II, 797.

them $100 annually from his salary of $600 until the full amount was discharged. Tired of frequent moving and wanting a home of his own, Beecher accepted these terms and bought the dwelling which was located on East Market Street.[5]

The house was a one-story frame structure just ten feet wide. "One room was to serve for entrance into the house, for parlor, study, and bedroom; the other to be dining and workroom. The bedroom was so small that I was obliged to make the bed on one side first," recalled Eunice Beecher, "then go out on the veranda, raise a window, reach in and make the bed on the other side. . . . The little kitchen—partitioned off from the veranda—was just large enough to allow a passage between the cooking table and the stove into the dining-room without burning my dress; and my kitchen table was only divided from Mr. Beecher's study table by the partition."[6] The Beechers moved into their diminutive residence before the end of January, 1840.[7]

Eunice Beecher's health was unusually poor. Nearing the end of her second pregnancy, she again experienced false labor pains over a period of three weeks culminating in real labor which began on the morning of March 10, 1840. Through the cold day with its threat of snow Eunice experienced "a horribly protracted labor . . . [and] brought forth a dead son. She was very quiet & easy afterward," wrote Beecher.[8] She was exhausted. She was worn down by privation, overwork, and worry in Lawrenceburgh, and she had become pregnant shortly before removing to Indianapolis. She had subsequently suffered a severe attack of malaria, uprooted her household several times, and

5. "Reminiscences of Jane Merrill Ketcham," p. 69, In; Graydon (comp.), *Catharine Merrill, Life and Letters*, p. 23; [Mrs. Beecher], *From Dawn to Daylight*, pp. 138, 160–61; Kate M. Rabb and William Herschell, *An Account of Indianapolis and Marion County* (Volumes III and IV of Logan Esarey, *History of Indiana* . . . [Dayton, Ohio: Dayton Historical Publishing Co., 1924]), III, 51; Barrows, *Henry Ward Beecher, the Shakespeare of the Pulpit*, p. 93; Mrs. Beecher, "Mr. Beecher as I Knew Him," *Ladies Home Journal*, December, 1891, p. 11; Beecher Family Circular Letter [begun] December 28, 1839, OFH; Susan M. Fletcher, Notebook, II, 69–71, John L. Ketcham Family Papers, InHi.

6. Mrs. Beecher, "Mr. Beecher as I Knew Him," *Ladies Home Journal*, December, 1891, p. 11.

7. Beecher Family Circular Letter [begun] December 28, 1839, OFH.

8. HWB, Journal, March 10, 1840, CtY; Calvin Fletcher Diary, March 10, 1840, InHi.

cared for an active toddler in addition to performing housework. Eunice did not attend the burial of her stillborn son, and Luke Munsell accompanied Beecher with the baby's body to the cemetery. The two men buried the little boy a day after his birth. No one else was present. Little apparent emotion was felt by either parent at the infant's death, but Beecher did write later, "At the last day, May not this little spirit, give triumph to its body, above hundreds who lie beside it—cut down in manhood?"[9]

Beecher attributed the boy's death to the unskillfulness of the attending physician. His sister Harriet wrote consolingly, "It often seems as if his [God's] dealings with his children were so severe as to threaten to consume instead of refining the gold, but after awhile we begin to see that He has not been careless or inattentive & that he has done only exactly what was necessary & so I trust you will find it in the end. It is a hard thing to get us to Heaven. I feel it every day. The world seems as empty & worthless as a world need to be & yet how like a slave the soul stoops to it, how instinctively & with what a death grasp it holds on to it." Married to the eccentric Calvin E. Stowe, she had to cope with his peculiarities, her frequent pregnancies, and real poverty which she alleviated by her earnings from writing. In many respects Harriet Beecher Stowe's lot was far harder than Eunice's, but the former possessed an inner serenity which Beecher's wife had not attained. Harriet was Eunice's chief confidant in the West and gave her comfort, advice, and what practical aid was in her power. Her letter continued, "I cannot on the whole regret that Providence saw fit to deny the gift of life to another little one at a time when your [Eunice's] extremely reduced & enfeebled health must have made the charge of it an extremely trying & laborious if not dangerous one—& I hope that since you have begun to gain strength that God will grant you a season of rest & ease, to recover the tone of better body & mind." Harriet also told her brother that she was tempted to visit them in Indianapolis if she could travel free of charge as "we have no *Mammon*."[10] It was a common circumstance in her household.

9. HWB, Journal, March 11, 1840, CtY.
10. Harriet Beecher Stowe to HWB and Mrs. Henry Ward Beecher, Walnut Hills, April 15, [1840], and Harriet Beecher Stowe to HWB, Walnut Hills, April 15, [1840], CtY.

About this time a letter filled with Beecher family news and comments arrived in Indianapolis on its circuit. By such means the wide-scattered clan kept in almost constant communication. One member would begin a letter on a large folio sheet and mail it to the brother or sister nearest him who would add his own news and send it on. Eventually the letter would be returned to the original correspondent. The length of time it took to reach all the family depended mainly upon the promptness it was added to and mailed. One letter begun on December 28, 1839, by Mary Beecher Perkins in Connecticut, for example, was continued by Charles Beecher in New Orleans on March 18, 1840, after having passed through several hands. Charles Beecher, the family's prodigal son, wrote that he was doing well in the southern city. Somewhat facetiously he penned "times is not quite so hard with me as they used to was. I am paying out say $35 per month or call it $40. Have just cleared $100 by a Singing School, & recieve [sic] $71 per month. With a fair prospect of an income next year say $150 per month." Charles was an assistant teacher in a school in which Eunice's brother, Talbut Bullard, was principal. Bragging a bit, he wrote, "Two or three years hence we may be something in the world."

Thomas K. Beecher, Henry's younger half brother, was attending Illinois College and boarding with brother Edward in Jacksonville. Young Tom wrote for the Beecher contingent in Illinois with a cheerful account saying, "we all are well—just got our back parlour papered & painted—looks spruce as a pin." Always playful, he ended his portion of the letter "I remain yours until spirits shall cease to hover miscellaneously through space."

Henry Ward Beecher's contribution was dated April 10, 1840. Expecting his sister Catharine to visit him in Indianapolis he asked her to bring some seeds and four or five slips of the so-called Tree of Heaven. "There are *none in this region*," wrote Beecher, "& if these grow I wish to set them out with alternating *Locusts*. . . . Affairs stand as usuall with me. . . . Eunice yesterday walked out & made two or three calls—the first time for six months." He mentioned that he had "been shaking & burning alternately with remarkable vehemence. Between both operations a man is left well nigh stultified."

Harriet Beecher Stowe wrote that "all well in this region [Walnut

Hills] & middling happy" on April 17, 1840. Catharine E. Beecher in her portion referred to an earlier letter received from George and Sarah Beecher in which they had mentioned a domestic concern and asked that they would excuse her "for not better appreciating your trials—but as I never had children myself—& as so much of the sufferings of my brothers and sisters has come either from poverty or from having children my mind did not so much understand the sorrow you have experienced 'Every heart knoweth its own bitterness.' " Catharine E. Beecher had a tart tongue, and sometimes it was difficult to separate her sincerity from her sarcasm. This circular letter was typical of those which passed from one Beecher to another.[11] If a family member had private business or news, however, he wrote directly to the person concerned.

In totting up his accounts in the spring of 1840 Beecher listed seventeen individuals or firms to whom he owed money. These were in addition to the $100 per year he had agreed to pay on the house debt. He owed $140.95 to Daniel Yandes, $175.73 to Lawrence M. Vance, $43.00 to Espy & Sloan, $11.69 to Seibert & Buehler, $9.50 to a man named Wilson, $2.50 to someone named Porter, and undisclosed amounts to the remainder. It was a heavy debt for a man whose only income was a promised salary of $600 per year.[12] In her semifictional account mirroring their life in Indiana Eunice Beecher wrote: "[He] is, as usual, sure it 'will all come out right.' He is ever more sanguine about matters *coming right* than I am; but the worst of it is, I am sorry to say, that in *money matters* my view of our affairs is generally the most correct."[13]

In some manner Eunice succeeded in accommodating William S. Hubbard as a paying guest in the tiny Beecher house. Still a bachelor, the affable Hubbard had come to Indianapolis in 1837 at the age of twenty-one to be clerk to the Board of State Fund Commissioners. It was said that out of his first year's salary of $500 he managed to save

11. Beecher Family Circular Letter [begun] December 28, 1839, OFH; Charles Beecher (ed.), *Autobiography, Correspondence, Etc., of Lyman Beecher, D.D.*, II, 410; Annie Beecher Scoville, Notes, n.d., CtY.

12. HWB, Journal, n.d., [probably late March, 1840], CtY.

13. [Mrs. Beecher], *From Dawn to Daylight*, p. 139.

$250, and in time the energetic Hubbard would amass a fortune in real estate in Indiana.[14] As it was, the small amount he paid for his board and room at the Beechers' helped them greatly.

An honor came to Henry Ward Beecher in May when he was asked to officiate at the wedding of a member of his congregation, Alexander H. T. Davidson, to Catherine Noble, daughter of ex-Governor Noah Noble. The ceremony took place at seven o'clock on the evening of May 19, 1840, in the large parlor of the Noble home on East Market Street. Nearly two hundred guests crowded the parlor, front hall, and lawn hoping to witness the ceremony. Enough light came through the windows to illuminate the bridal setting, and the candles were not lit till later in the evening. It was an elaborate wedding. The bride wore a dress of heavy white satin with rows of shell trimming, white kid satin gloves edged in blonde (a type of lace), and shoes of light kid which appeared white in the dim light. Her hair was plaited in back with a single white rose tucked into it and there were mock orange blossoms in the Grecian curls over her forehead. A pocket handkerchief trimmed with wide lace and a chain and watch completed her costume. The bride's attendants were Elizabeth L. Browning, Mary Yandes, and Jane Rings; and the groom was attended by Hugh O'Neal, John S. Bobbs, and William S. Hubbard.

The bridal party faced Beecher whose back was to a fireplace. Honored guests sat on sofas and chairs in the room while others peered in from the outside as best they could. Beecher gave a "quite long *beautiful appropriate* [prayer]." Feeling unwell, he did not linger over the ceremony and at its conclusion kissed both the bride and groom. He told the company it was *"done now"* and then had to be carried into another room where he rested on a bed. Presumably he was unable to enjoy the lavish refreshments which were served to the guests between eight and nine o'clock. The bride's cake sat in solitary splendor on a mahogany candle stand which had been covered with a white tablecloth. The guests were served jelly cake, other kinds of cakes in fruit

14. Nowland, *Sketches of Prominent Citizens of 1876*, pp. 186–87; *The Second Presbyterian Church of Indianapolis. One Hundred Years, 1838–1938*, pp. 136–37; Rabb (ed.), *A Tour Through Indiana in 1840*, pp. 156–57; [Mrs. Beecher], *From Dawn to Daylight*, pp. 276–77.

baskets, ice cream, and tea and coffee. As a courtesy and to atone for his illness at their wedding, Beecher invited the newlyweds to dine with him a few weeks later.[15]

The political contest between William Henry Harrison and Martin Van Buren for the Presidency captured the attention of the residents of Indianapolis during the summer of 1840. Beecher who was a mild Whig was especially interested in the progress of the campaign because of his acquaintance with the old warrior from North Bend, Ohio. He passed almost daily the cabin constructed of buckeye logs which had been erected to honor General Harrison at the corner of Illinois and Washington streets. Barrels of cider sometimes mixed with whiskey were readily accessible to the thirsty when Whig meetings were scheduled. Parades, or processions as they were termed, took place frequently, the participants singing about "Tippecanoe and Tyler too" and "little Van . . . a used-up man." On one occasion a banner painted by Jacob Cox, Beecher's artist friend, was carried at the head of the "Wild Oats of Indianapolis" delegation to a Whig rally for Harrison at the Tippecanoe Battleground. The banner portrayed an adult raccoon surrounded by little raccoons, and the "Wild Oats" were quite proud of it.[16]

Calvin E. Stowe visited the Beechers in Indianapolis early in July and preached on two occasions at the Second Presbyterian Church.[17] In view of Stowe's earlier refusal to preach at Beecher's church in Lawrenceburgh because he felt the younger man must learn to make his own way in the ministry, his willingness to preach in Indianapolis was an indication of his respect for Henry Ward Beecher's success in his new pastorate.

Harriet Eliza Beecher was two years old in 1840, and her relatives in the East had never seen her. Eunice wanted to show the child to her

15. "A Pioneer Wedding," *Indiana Magazine of History*, XVI, No. 4 (December, 1920), pp. 303–307; *Seventy-Fifth Anniversary, Second Presbyterian Church, Indianapolis, Indiana*, p. 8.

16. Indianapolis *News*, February 14, 1879; Mary Q. Burnet, *Art and Artists of Indiana* (New York: The Century Co., 1921), pp. 79–80; Wilbur D. Peat, *Pioneer Painters of Indiana* (Chicago: Lakeside Press, 1954), pp. 152–53; McCulloch, *Men and Measures of Half A Century*, pp. 54–55; Holloway, *Indianapolis*, p. 71.

17. Records of the Second Presbyterian Church, p. 17, InISPC.

Grandmother Bullard and tentative plans were made to make the trip. Beecher was to escort his wife and daughter to West Sutton where they would remain for a long visit while Beecher would return to Indianapolis. As the departure date approached, however, Eunice's health was so poor that it was thought unwise for her to attempt the journey. Instead, Beecher took her and Hatty to Walnut Hills for a few days.[18]

In September Henry Ward Beecher was invited to Indiana Asbury (now DcPauw) University at Greencastle to address the Philological and Platonean Literary societies on the combined occasion of Commencement and the inauguration of the school's new president, Matthew Simpson. The Methodist-affiliated institution had been established recently in part to combat the influence of the Presbyterians in the field of higher education in Indiana who dominated the faculties of Hanover College (O.S.), Wabash College (N.S.), and Indiana University. It was surprising, therefore, for a Presbyterian minister to be invited to speak before the most important student organizations on such a special event.

An escort from Indiana Asbury arrived in Indianapolis to conduct Beecher in an open buggy to the campus at Greencastle. On this trip Beecher and the students discussed denominational differences and attitudes. At one point he said that "he had great respect for the Methodist Church for the good it had done by way of preaching in the destitute regions, but he feared that in turning their attention to educational matters they were entering a field in which they were not likely to be so successful. However, what help he could render them should be afforded cheerfully."[19] The reply of the students is unknown.

Henry Ward Beecher approved of Matthew Simpson's inaugural address. Lasting two hours, the speech was well received, and Beecher was among those who paid it the compliment of suggesting that it be printed and distributed. Simpson had first prepared to become a physician and later decided to enter the ministry. He was received on trial into the Pittsburgh Conference of the Methodist Episcopal Church in 1834, and three years later he became professor of natural science at

18. HWB, Journal, July 17, 1840, CtY.
19. New York *Times*, June 5, 1882; William W. Sweet, *Indiana Asbury-DePauw University, 1837–1937* (New York: The Abingdon Press, 1937), pp. 51–52, 75; Clark, *The Life of Matthew Simpson*, pp. 79–84.

Allegheny College. He came to Indiana as the result of being suggested by the president of Allegheny as a possible successor to Indiana Asbury's acting president, Cyrus McNutt.

Beecher spoke to the literary societies on the evening of September 15, 1840. The audience thought so highly of his speech which stressed the evils of avarice that it was printed in its entirety.[20] Calvin Fletcher, an Indianapolis acquaintance and a trustee of Indiana Asbury, read it a month later and wrote, "It is good—I hope to profit by it."[21] It was the first time a speech of Beecher's was published in pamphlet form.

Beecher's influence in the inner councils of the Presbyterian Church, N.S., grew rapidly in 1840. A pressing problem arose with the death of Elihu Baldwin, president of Wabash College. On October 22, 1840, Beecher received a letter from Professor Edmund O. Hovey of the college asking him to recommend a suitable man to succeed Baldwin. The deceased had declined a call to the pastorate of the Second Presbyterian Church in 1838, and he was the father of Julia C. Ackley, the church's leading soprano. Touring Indiana in the preceding summer with James Hanna on a mission which combined preaching and fund raising, Baldwin became ill after eating some poisonous berries which he had mistakenly thought were whortleberries. He recovered only to succumb to bilious fever from which he died on October 15, 1840. Baldwin had contributed his considerable talents to Wabash College, and his death was felt to be a blow to the school. Hovey was as tireless as Baldwin in working for the institution's welfare, and he assumed the lead in securing a worthy successor for the dead man.[22]

Beecher was in a particularly good position to recommend suitable men because of his ties with both East and West and the connections of his father and Calvin E. Stowe. The Indianapolis clergyman wrote to Hovey that he would preach a sermon which "will give me an opportunity to introduce your college, . . . and to excite as far as possible, deep sympathy & partiality in y[ou]r behalf. . . . I have written to

20. HWB, *An Address, Delivered Before the Platonean Society of the Indiana Asbury University, September 15, 1840* (Indianapolis: Printed by William Stacy, 1840). 28 p. Simpson's address was likewise printed by William Stacy.

21. Calvin Fletcher Diary, October 15, 1840, InHi.

22. Sprague, *Annals of the American Pulpit,* IV, 572–81; Osborne and Gronert, *Wabash College, The First Hundred Years, 1832–1932,* p. 50; HWB to Edmund O. Hovey, Indianapolis, October 22, 1840, CtHS-D.

father & prof. Stowe & . . . requested thier opinion & such . . . names as they might suggest. If you send for an Eastern man, they will cooperate with you & write in your behalf, as embarked in common cause."[23] Beecher and Hovey were convinced of the need to find a man who could raise funds for the struggling college in Crawfordsville. Such a person with an eastern background would be more apt to appeal successfully to the wealthier Presbyterians of that region where money was relatively abundant for philanthropic and educational purposes.

Beecher's thoughts were turned eastward in another regard in the fall of 1840, for Eunice was again pregnant and fearful for her life if she remained in Indianapolis' malarial climate. In November Beecher escorted his wife and daughter to West Sutton where the two would remain until the following September. It was a bittersweet homecoming for Eunice Beecher who had not seen her parents since her wedding in 1837. Walking alone into her old home, she met her mother who said, "You want to see the Doctor? The Doctor is out, but will be in soon. Won't you sit down?" Lucy Bullard did not at first recognize her daughter in the tired, faded woman facing her.

The blow to Eunice's pride was compounded when her father returned. He said, "Good morning Madam; do you wish to see me? You look as if you needed a Doctor. What can I do for you?"

Eunice replied, "Well, I should think you might kiss me!"

Shocked, the good doctor spread out his hands and said, "Madam; what a proposition!" With that, Mrs. Bullard laughed and told her husband that it was Eunice.[24]

Beecher had informed his congregation that he would return to Indianapolis in a month or so, but there was some speculation as to whether or not he would do so. "Mr. Beecher left us on Monday," wrote Samuel Merrill, "to take his wife to New England who is in very bad health and who is strongly suspected here to be as *ill disposed* as indisposed. Mr. Beecher is still popular but his wife is a great weight on him whether from mere ill health or something else I cannot say." Merrill commented further, "I fear the usefulness of Mr. B. will be much impaired wherever he may be by the difficulties alluded to and some of

23. HWB to Edmund O. Hovey, Indianapolis, October 22, 1840, CtHS-D.
24. Indianapolis *Daily Sentinel*, May 28, 1882.

our Ch[urch] fear that he will not return to stay."[25] Eunice's dislike of Indianapolis was common knowledge, and her attitude of occasional hostility toward members of her husband's church did not help him. She resented what she considered had been deliberate deception of her husband in regard to the prevalence of malaria in the city. She resented the fact that the leading families in the church spent more on entertaining than her family had to live on a year; and she resented that she, as well or better born than they, had to scrimp and contrive to stretch Beecher's income while others had luxuries. She felt, as in Lawrenceburgh, that the congregation regarded the salary paid to Beecher as charity, and this hurt her pride.[26]

In turn, Eunice Beecher was held in little regard by many of her acquaintances in Indianapolis. They noticed her frequent absences from church services which the charitable ascribed to her ill health or family responsibilities. "I had never yet seen such a woman; she [Eunice] could be as beautiful as a princess, and as plain and homely as possible," recalled Jane Merrill Ketcham who knew her well. "So she could be sparklingly bright and bitterly sarcastic."[27] This latter quality and an alleged tendency to stretch the truth did not endear Eunice Beecher to her husband's congregation. She had too sharp a tongue for their comfort.

Samuel Merrill was not upset at the prospect of Beecher's possibly resigning and removing to the East. The banker still wished to see his brother, David Merrill, installed as pastor of the Second Presbyterian Church. While Beecher was gone his pulpit was filled by visiting clergymen including P. S. Cleland and John Fairchild. However, having no intention yet of resigning the pastorate of the Second Presbyterian Church, Henry Ward Beecher was back in Indianapolis well within the period he had said he would return.[28]

He welcomed Horace and Amanda Bassett who were received by

25. Samuel Merrill to David Merrill, Indianapolis, November 14, 1840, Samuel Merrill Papers, InHi.

26. [Mrs. Beecher], *From Dawn to Daylight*, pp. 161–62.

27. "Reminiscences of Jane Merrill Ketcham," p. 69, In.

28. Samuel Merrill to David Merrill, Indianapolis, November 14 and 26, 1840, Samuel Merrill Papers, InHi; John Fairchild to John N. Bishop, Marinette, Wisconsin, May 25, 1880, quoted in the *Covington* [Ind.] *Journal*, clipping, n.d., E. O. Hovey Papers, InCW.

letter into the Second Presbyterian Church. Bassett had been an elder in Beecher's church at Lawrenceburgh, and after becoming clerk of the United States Court in Indianapolis he began attending the Second Presbyterian Church. From the original fifteen members in 1838 the roll now numbered seventy-seven. While the increase was not spectacular it was respectable.[29]

The affairs of Wabash College assumed more importance for Beecher on April 2, 1841, when Samuel Merrill and he were elected trustees of that institution along with Israel Williams and Samuel G. Lowrie.[30] The major business facing the officers was the selection of a president to succeed the deceased Elihu Baldwin. Edmund O. Hovey's choice for the post was his brother-in-law, Charles White. Six years older than Hovey, White had been pastor at a church in Owego, New York, in the Presbytery of Tioga since 1832. His wife, Martha, was a sister of Hovey's wife, Mary. The Hoveys wanted the Whites to move to Crawfordsville and wrote numerous letters encouraging them to do so. A typical letter was that written on March 2, 1841, in which Hovey assured White that both Lyman Beecher and Calvin E. Stowe stressed the importance of Wabash College to the church, that the renowned Henry Little was convinced of the College's worth, and that the Synod of Indiana strongly supported it. He told White that the promised salary was $1,200 a year and that it was possible to travel from New York City to Crawfordsville for about sixty dollars per person. After much vacillation White agreed to accept the presidency of the small New School college in Indiana. He was elected the second President of Wabash College on April 6, 1841, and he was to be styled President and Professor of Moral and Intellectual Philosophy and Political Economy.[31]

Beecher traveled to Danville which was located a few miles west

29. *The Second Presbyterian Church of Indianapolis. One Hundred Years, 1838–1938,* p. 132; Records of the Second Presbyterian Church, InISPC.

30. Theodore H. Ristine, *A Digest of the Minutes of the Board of Trustees of Wabash College, 1832–1922* (n.p., 1922), pp. 10–14; Osborne and Gronert, *Wabash College, the First Hundred Years, 1832–1932,* pp. 80–81.

31. Osborne and Gronert, *Wabash College, the First Hundred Years, 1832–1932,* pp. 19–21, 54–57; Hotchkin, *A History of the Purchase and Settlement of Western New York,* pp. 439–40; Edmund O. Hovey to Charles White, Crawfordsville, March 2, 1841, typed copy, Hovey Letters #7, InCW; *A Catalogue of the Officers and Students of Wabash College* (Indianapolis: Printed by Cutler & Chamberlain, 1841), p. 2.

of Indianapolis on April 8, 1841, to attend a meeting of the Presbytery of Indianapolis. As the second day's session began he was honored by being requested to give the opening prayer. Embarrassingly, it was his duty as Stated Clerk of Presbytery to prepare a statement chiding the Session of his Second Presbyterian Church for failing to send the record of its meetings for examination by a committee of Presbytery.[32]

On April 13 word reached Indianapolis of the death of President William Henry Harrison. For the old hero to die so soon after his inauguration was considered especially tragic by his fellow Whigs in Indiana. Harrison had ridden down Pennsylvania Avenue bareheaded and without overcoat in a chilly northeast wind to his outdoor inauguration and probably contracted the severe cold which led to his death a month later. A committee of leading citizens of Indianapolis was formed to make arrangements to show proper respect to the memory of the commander-in-chief. So closely allied was Harrison with Indiana's history that he seemed to be one of her own, and his passing would be commemorated with every possible display of esteem. On the Saturday designated for the memorial service all houses in Indianapolis were requested to present an appearance of being closed and all business was suspended for the day. At ten o'clock in the morning a procession was formed on the Courthouse square; and, under the direction of a marshal, it proceeded to the State Capitol where the service was to take place. The major addresses were delivered by Governor Samuel Bigger and the Reverend Henry Ward Beecher. The selection of Beecher was due to his acquaintance with the dead President as well as to his own Whig sympathies and the connection of Harrison with the Presbyterian denomination.[33]

The month of May held irritations for Beecher. A female member of the Second Presbyterian Church had behaved so badly as to make a hearing on her misdeed necessary at the meeting of Session on May 6th. The situation was complicated further as she had removed to Bloom-

32. Records of the Presbytery of Indianapolis, pp. 8–9, InHan.

33. Jeannette Nolan, *Hoosier City* (New York: Julian Messner, Inc., 1943), p. 111; Holloway, *Indianapolis*, p. 73; Indianapolis *Indiana Journal*, April 13 and 24, 1841. Green was in error when he wrote, "Then, although he [HWB] was not on the program, Henry Ward Beecher jumped to his feet . . . [and spoke at the memorial service for Harrison.]" See Green, *William Henry Harrison, His Life and Times,* p. 445.

ington, and while technically she was still a church member in Indianapolis she was no longer attending its services. The members of Session decided that the woman was guilty of breaking the seventh commandment and so excommunicated her.[34]

Beecher felt it necessary to interfere in a budding romance of which he disapproved involving a member of his congregation and a Methodist. He was displeased that Mary Yandes, a daughter of Daniel Yandes and one of the outstanding young women of Indianapolis, was interested seriously in John Wheeler. The young woman was unusually well-educated, a student of Latin and Greek, loved music, and had received local acclaim for her poetry. Beecher thought Wheeler was unworthy of the affection of such a superior girl. A native of Portsmouth, England, Wheeler graduated from Indiana Asbury in 1840, and came to Indianapolis. He taught school, lectured on natural philosophy, published a meteorological journal, and otherwise tried to make a place for himself in the city. In the limited society of the capital he soon became acquainted with Mary Yandes. Beecher observed their growing friendship and believed it his duty to warn Mary's father about the relationship. It upset Daniel Yandes so much that he wrote to Matthew Simpson to inquire about young Wheeler. Simpson replied that Wheeler was a fine man with whom he was well acquainted and who had lived for a time with the Simpson family. As Wheeler conducted himself well in Indianapolis and Yandes learned nothing to his discredit the courtship was permitted to continue.[35]

In Massachusetts, Eunice Beecher gave birth to a son, Henry Barton, on July 8, 1841.[36] The father planned to leave about the 19th of the

34. HWB, Journal, May [?], 1841, CtY. The woman's name and those of others subsequently disciplined for immoral conduct may be found in the Records of the Second Presbyterian Church, p. 21, InISPC; Records of the Presbytery of Indianapolis, pp. 30–31, InHan.

35. Robinson et al. (comps.), *Daniel Yandes and His Family*, p. 125; Clark, *The Life of Matthew Simpson*, pp. 92–93; George B. Manhart, *DePauw Through the Years* (2 volumes. Greencastle, Ind.: De Pauw University Press, 1962), I, 34–35; Indianapolis *Indiana Journal*, February 1 and April 20, 1842; Holloway, *Indianapolis*, p. 61; Eleanore A. Cammack (ed.), "Cyrus Nutt Becomes A Hoosier," *Indiana Magazine of History*, LIII, No. 2 (March, 1957), p. 68.

36. Miscellaneous Records, CtY; Frost stated erroneously that Henry Barton Beecher was born in Indianapolis. See Frost (comp.), *Ancestors of Henry Ward Beecher and His Wife Eunice White Bullard*, p. 10.

month to make the trip East to bring back his wife and their children. He had intended to stop briefly for a visit in Walnut Hills, but his plans were altered when he agreed to escort the Samuel Merrills' daughter Julia and the Hervey Bates's daughter Elizabeth on their journey to visit relatives in New England. Julia's health had not been good, and her father hoped the trip with her best friend would restore it and her spirits. Beecher knew the girls well. He had taught them for a time, had lived in the Merrill home, and was currently boarding with the Bates family.[37]

Beecher abandoned his plan to stop at Walnut Hills. Instead, the trio took a more direct route and were in Batavia, New York, by July 25. Julia Merrill sent several letters to members of her family which described the events of their trip and her impressions. In Ohio, between Dayton and Cleveland, "a woman asked Mr. Beecher where we were going and he told her home. At Dayton we met with Mr. Mason of Cincinnati brother to Lowell Mason. Mr. Beecher was acquainted with him; and he is going to Boston so we will have his company all the way; he is a kind and pleasant travelling companion." Julia expressed surprise with the degrees of rudeness and kindness encountered on the trip from strangers. The worst roads they encountered on their entire journey were between Columbus and Cleveland. Leaving Cleveland, they boarded the *Buffalo* and "staid all night on the Boat and came off in the morning and stopped at the Hotel in Buffalo and started for Niagara on the Railroad and arrived there in two hours. Took dinner there everything was new to me changing the plates often." Julia was thrilled with Niagara Falls and quoted Beecher as saying that the water "was in such a tremendous hurry to get over but the fall is so much worse than it expected that it is perfectly satisfied, and then moves off slowly and solemnly as if nothing had happened." Possibly to reassure her parents, she continued, "Mr. Beecher has been very kind to us as kind as any person could be, correcting us when used words wrong. . . . I have had no signs of headache."[38]

---

37. HWB, *Eyes and Ears*, pp. 113–14; Samuel Merrill to David Merrill, Indianapolis, July 9, 1841, Samuel Merrill Papers, InHi; HWB, Journal, July 17, 1841, CtY.

38. Julia D. Merrill to her mother, Jane Anderson Merrill, Batavia, New York, July 25, 1841, Julia Merrill Moores Papers, InHi.

They visited William Beecher's family in Batavia, and from that city they traveled by train to West Sutton. Of this portion of their trip, Julia wrote "we came very near having a dreadful accident. It was night and we were on a part of the road that was very narrow going pretty fast when we came suddenly on a stick of wood that had been fixed firmly in the ground by some wicked person on purpose to throw the train off the track. But the engine passed by it and it hit the ashpan and tore it all to pieces passed on to the first car struck it in the middle tore up a board the whole length. Mr. Beecher said that if it had struck a beam or something that was strong enough to hold it up, it would have thrown the train off the track and no one knows how many would have been killed." The small party arrived safely in West Sutton, however, where the girls felt at ease with the Bullard family.

They rested for a few days and sampled New England fare. "I am too much of a hoosier yet," wrote Julia, "to love Brown bread or Huckleberries, . . . sickening taste about them I do not like."[39] From West Sutton, Beecher escorted the girls to Franklin and Nashua, New Hampshire, where he left them in the care of their relatives and returned alone to Massachusetts. The money entrusted to him for their expenses had not been sufficient as Julia had been required to pay the adult fare most of the way. Beecher wrote to Samuel Merrill that he would need more money which he would obtain in New York City by means of a draft on the account of Noah Noble, the pre-arranged solution for just such a contingency.[40]

Henry Ward Beecher had been unable to start a revival in his Indianapolis church during the first three years of his pastorate, although he worked steadily toward such a goal. It was ironic then that no sooner did he leave on the trip to Massachusetts in July, 1841, than a wave of interest in religion spread among many members of the Second Presbyterian Church. It was a phenomenon which affected all Protestant churches in Indianapolis. The Methodists led the way with a successful camp meeting and this was followed by a revival held at the First Presbyterian Church. The Methodists were said to have added

39. Julia D. Merrill to Priscilla and Catharine Merrill, West Sutton, Massachusetts, July 31, 1841, Julia Merrill Moores Papers.
40. HWB to Samuel Merrill, attached to *ibid.*; Julia D. Merrill to Jane Merrill Ketcham, Boston, August 21, 1841, Samuel Merrill Papers, InHi.

nearly one hundred new members, and the Old School church gained twenty or thirty. Disgruntled that their pastor should be absent at such a stirring time, some members of Beecher's church wrote to his father and explained the situation.[41]

It was a call to which Lyman Beecher responded at once. He lived "every moment under the impression that he had a great work to do for God and man, which must be done at once, not a minute to be lost. He was all absorbed in his work, he lived for nothing else, he thought of nothing else.[42] Lyman Beecher was as familiar with the art of the revival as any clergyman in the United States. He was acquainted with members of the Second Presbyterian Church and knew what to expect in Indianapolis. On his journey to the Hoosier capital he planned a campaign which he hoped would be successful. Deciding he would need help as the work would require "more preaching talking visiting & effort to embody an influence around us in Henries Church than I alone can safely put forth," he asked Darcia H. Allen, a faculty member at Lane Theological Seminary, to come to Indianapolis to assist him. "I have no doubt," wrote Lyman Beecher, "that Mr. Allen & Myself can commence a course of operations that God will smile upon & save the church from injury and save in a great measure the results of Henrys past labors."[43]

The senior Beecher began the rigorous schedule of holding a prayer meeting each morning, calling on possible converts until noon, delivering a sermon in the afternoon, more calling and personal contacts, preaching another sermon at night, and then, if interest existed as it usually did, conducting a meeting with interested people for discussion and counseling after the close of the evening service. It was physically and mentally demanding work. Years later Henry Ward Beecher may have been thinking of his father's efforts in Indianapolis in 1841 when he wrote, "Although a prudent man would scarcely undertake to lead a church into a revival in the midst of

41. Samuel Merrill to David Merrill, Indianapolis, August 30, 1841, Samuel Merrill Papers.

42. Stowe, "Sketches and Recollections of Dr. Lyman Beecher," *Congregational Quarterly*, VI, 221–22.

43. Lyman Beecher to Lydia Jackson Beecher, Madison, Indiana, August 17, 1841, CtY.

summer . . . , yet the summer is a time when men who have a heart to work, . . . can do things that they can never do so well at any other time."[44]

Beecher and Allen dined with clergymen and laymen during their stay in Indianapolis. Since a woman's worth and her husband's status were often judged by the quality and quantity of food served to guests, the revivalists were subjected to huge meals two and three times a day. Beecher complained humorously to his wife that he was expected to eat more than was good for him or else hurt his hostess's feelings. His one stomach upset, he thought, was caused by his injudicious sampling of a watermelon, and he cautioned his wife against such a danger.

Lyman Beecher made it a special point to call at the Hervey Bates's residence where Henry Ward Beecher lived during Eunice's absence. The elder Beecher thought Mrs. Bates was "a neat woman [with an] agreeable family." He took pleasure in walking through Henry's garden and noted its profusion of corn, cabbages, tomatoes, pumpkins, turnips, celery, and other vegetables. When he needed a quiet moment by himself, he went to Henry's house and seated at his son's writing table meditated, read, and penned, "I am now writing in his [HWB's] Study grateful for the good providence of God—which has opened me to . . . him so many children whom he condescends to accept & bless & render useful—a favor in which we both sympathize in respect to our children."[45] When Lyman Beecher left Indianapolis in ten days it was thought his efforts would result in ten to thirteen people joining the Second Presbyterian Church.

Henry Ward Beecher returned early in September with Eunice, Hatty, the new baby, Julia Merrill, and Elizabeth Bates. Julia's father was pleased with the apparent improvement in his daughter's health and received the impression that the girls had enjoyed their visit to the East.[46]

44. HWB, *Lecture-Room Talks*, p. 28.

45. Lyman Beecher to Lydia Jackson Beecher, Indianapolis, August 23, 1841, CtHS-D; Calvin Fletcher Diary, August 21 and 22, 1841, InHi; Samuel Merrill to David Merrill, Indianapolis, August 30, 1841, Samuel Merrill Papers, InHi.

46. Samuel Merrill to Hazen Merrill, Indianapolis, November 13, 1841, Samuel Merrill Papers.

IX

Horticultural Interests

THE ONLY REALLY ATTRACTIVE FEATURE OF THE TINY BEECHER HOME on East Market Street was the large lot on which it stood. There were several fruit trees, rose bushes, shrubs, and space for a garden. Beecher deeply loved gardening, and it was believed by his family that he had inherited his feeling for it from his mother who had spent much time working with her flowers prior to his birth. As a boy at his father's home in Litchfield, Connecticut, Beecher had had his own garden and contributed its produce to the family table. When he was a pupil at Mount Pleasant he had impressed the school's gardener with his genuine interest and been given his own small plot to tend. The gardener supplied him with seeds and good advice. As Beecher matured his interest in growing things was maintained. Another asset of the property on East Market Street was the proximity of a ten-acre pasture on which Beecher could keep livestock. Over the years the Beecher family would have one or more cows, pigs, and a horse.[1]

Eager to begin his gardening, Beecher planted rose bushes, starts of honeysuckle, and a willow tree in the early spring of 1840. On the day that his stillborn son was buried, March 11, Beecher placed onion sets

---

1. Mrs. Beecher, "Mr. Beecher as I Knew Him," *Ladies Home Journal*, December, 1891, p. 11; Knox, *Life and Work of Henry Ward Beecher*, pp. 42, 348; John R. Howard, *Henry Ward Beecher*, p. 50; HWB, *Eyes and Ears*, pp. 113–14; Stowe, *Men of Our Times*, pp. 541–42.

near the water spout on the house, planted cabbage seed behind the pigpen, and started cauliflower in a bed next to a fence. He would be credited with growing the first cauliflower in Indianapolis. Beecher planted more onions, radishes, lettuce, and peas on the following day. Later he planted four varieties of radishes. He also set hyacinth, jonquil, and tulip bulbs around the house. For the remainder of the spring and summer much of his attention would be centered upon his garden and its progress.[2]

Largely due to his enthusiasm and conversations with gardening devotees and nurserymen Beecher was instrumental in creating interest in a proposed organization dedicated to horticulture. In an announcement appearing in the *Indiana Democrat* like-minded people were invited to meet at the State House on August 22, 1840, to consider founding such a society. The venture would not be new to Indianapolis and the rest of Indiana. In 1835 a Marion County Agricultural Society was organized and under its auspices the first fair in Marion County was held on October 30 and 31, 1835, at which prizes were awarded for outstanding examples of farm produce. A State Agricultural Society was also organized in 1835. Each failed within a few years probably due to the state's small population, inadequate communications, and poor transportation.[3]

James Blake was appointed chairman of the group which met at the State House on August 22, 1840, to organize the Indiana Horticultural Society. Its purpose was to promote the science of horticulture in the state and to provide a focus for interest in the subject. Blake appointed Jacob S. Willets, editor of the *Indiana Farmer*; Calvin Fletcher, banker and farmer; Henry P. Coburn, businessman; and Aaron Aldridge, a nurseryman, to a committee to prepare a constitution for the

2. HWB, Journal, March 11 and 12, 1840, CtY; Rabb and Herschell, *An Account of Indianapolis and Marion County*, III, 51; Rose, *The Circle*, p. 389.
3. Sulgrove, *History of Indianapolis and Marion County, Indiana*, p. 117; Gayle Thornbrough (ed.), *The Diary of Calvin Fletcher* . . . (volume I–, Indianapolis: Indiana Historical Society, 1972–), I, 259, 361; W. H. Ragan, "The First Indiana Horticultural Society," *Indiana Magazine of History*, IV, No. 2 (June, 1908), p. 71; Indianapolis *Indiana Democrat*, August 14, 1840; Johnson, *A Home in the Woods, Oliver Johnson's Reminiscences of Early Marion County*, p. 214; Holloway, *Indianapolis*, p. 49.

society. People had been invited to exhibit fruits and vegetables, and many specimens were brought. A committee consisting of Beecher, William J. Brown, Sherman Day, and William Wright reported upon the exhibits, but no prizes were given. After hearing an address by Willets, the audience amused itself inspecting the displays. Of particular interest to the nurserymen was the exhibit of a Williams Bon Chretien, or Bartlett, pear by Joshua Lindley. So far as anyone knew it was the first of its type to be grown in Indiana, and at the close of the meeting the sample was presented to Willets. While Beecher did not play a conspicuous role at the organizational meeting of the Indiana Horticultural Society, he would be one of its most loyal supporters.[4]

Beecher addressed the society on January 6, 1841, at two o'clock in the afternoon in the hall of the House of Representatives. Although the day was rainy with a hint of thawing in the air a large audience assembled to hear him. Standing among house plants and baskets of fruit brought for exhibition and decorative purposes, the clergyman used anecdotes and humor to illustrate his topic that "most of the improvements in fruits including rootes [sic] are of modern growth & perfection from the wild parent stock."[5] The speech was described as eloquent by the Whig newspaper and as beautiful and interesting in the rival Democratic sheet which called it "an intellectual treat of no ordinary character."[6] At the conclusion of the meeting the fresh fruit brought for exhibit was distributed to those present.

Henry Ward Beecher was not satisfied for long with the amount of space available for gardening around his home, and he looked for more land which he could rent. Deciding that two lots owned by Calvin Fletcher would serve his purpose, he called upon the banker on the evening of January 11, 1841, and asked to rent them for the coming year. Fletcher liked the young minister and agreed to his suggested

4. Ragan, "The First Indiana Horticultural Society," *Indiana Magazine of History*, IV, 72; Indianapolis *Indiana Journal*, September 12, 1840; Ignatius Brown, "History of Indianapolis," in *Logan's History of Indianapolis From 1818* (Indianapolis: Logan & Co., 1868), p. 42.

5. Calvin Fletcher Diary, January 6, 1841, InHi; Indianapolis *Indiana Democrat*, January 9, 1841.

6. Indianapolis *Indiana Journal*, January 16, 1841; Indianapolis *Indiana Democrat*, January 9, 1841.

terms. In his dry but penetrating New England way Fletcher joked with Beecher and told him that "it was a dangerous matter for him [HWB] to engage in this business [gardening] as he had just been commenting with severity on Sluggards in his horticultural address."[7]

There may have been a tenuous tie linking Beecher and Fletcher, but they were probably unaware of it. When Fletcher, a native of Ludlow, Vermont, was about nineteen years old he left his home and made his way to Ohio. On his journey he was aided by a man named Foote who may have been one of Beecher's uncles, either Samuel or John P. Foote.[8] From Ohio, Fletcher had gone to Indianapolis where he became a lawyer, banker, and farmer. He joined the Methodist Episcopal Church in 1829, but he enjoyed visiting other churches and contributed generously to their support. His eleven children in adulthood could be found scattered among four denominations. Fletcher would become and remain a good friend to Beecher and his family.

Contrary to the adage that corn should be "a foot high by the Fourth of July," Beecher's sweet corn was mature enough for him to savor the "first mess" of it on July 17, 1840, and the following year it was ready to eat on June 7.[9] Raising more vegetables than could conveniently be used, Beecher began to sell the surplus as a means of adding to his income. It became a common sight to see the clergyman pushing a wheelbarrow loaded with vegetables to the city market located just north of the Courthouse where he was permitted to sell them on the market days of Wednesdays and Saturdays. Under the eye of the market master, Jeremiah Wormegan, all who wished to buy and sell could do so for two hours after dawn. Beecher's rhubarb, or pieplant, was his specialty; and the housewives of Indianapolis would purchase enough for their cooking and baking needs during its short season in the spring. Henry Ward Beecher apparently saw nothing incongruous in his selling vegetables in a market and often drew an

7. Calvin Fletcher Diary, January 12, 1841, InHi; Dunn, *Indiana and Indianans,* III, 1425; William W. Woollen, *Biographical and Historical Sketches of Early Indiana* (Indianapolis: Hammond & Co., 1883), p. 474; William B. Trask, "The Honorable Calvin Fletcher," *New-England Historical and Genealogical Register,* XXIII (October, 1869), 384.

8. Calvin Fletcher to his parents, Urbana, Ohio, June 27, 1817, Thornbrough (ed.), *The Diary of Calvin Fletcher,* I, 9.

9. HWB, Journal, July 17, 1840, and June 7, 1841, CtY.

audience around his stall as he bantered with his customers and passers-by.[10]

With the onset of spring and summer the activities of the Indiana Horticultural Society slipped into high gear. The executive committee decided in June that weekly meetings should be held on Saturdays at three o'clock in the afternoon to exhibit the results of gardening. All were invited to display their prize specimens of fruits, vegetables, and flowers.[11] Soon residents of the city and surrounding countryside were competing as to who could bring the best samples. Democracy reigned; neither a gardener's sex nor his social status mattered, only his ability and good fortune with his plants and trees.

In the middle of July Beecher contracted to buy for $500 the two lots he was renting from Calvin Fletcher. The lots were more valuable than the price agreed upon, thought Fletcher, but it was worth "something to have him in the neighborhood of my other property." The clergyman was to pay one fifth, or $100, to Fletcher as a down payment and to pay $100 annually with 10 per cent interest till the full amount due was paid. Since Beecher lacked the down payment, he borrowed it at 6 per cent interest from a brother of Fletcher's, Stoughton A. Fletcher, a private banker, and arranged to repay this when it was convenient for him to do so. Beecher took the title bond for Lots 1 and 2 of Square 42 and gave it for safekeeping into the hands of a third banker, Hervey Bates, who was a member of his church and his host while Eunice was in Massachusetts. Beecher had his lots, but he had increased his debts disproportionately to his income.[12]

Henry Ward Beecher owed $100 a year upon his house, he owed an additional $100 yearly upon the two lots plus the $100 due Stoughton A. Fletcher plus the sizable interest upon all three principal payments in addition to substantial amounts which were due to various individuals and firms in Indianapolis. His financial position was extremely precarious. No record exists of Beecher's conversation with

10. Knox, *Life and Work of Henry Ward Beecher*, p. 456; Dunn, *Greater Indianapolis*, I, 113, 120.

11. Indianapolis *Indiana Journal*, June 12, 1841.

12. Calvin Fletcher Diary, July 17, 1841, InHi; HWB, Journal, July 17, 1841, CtY. According to the Marion County Deed Records Fletcher and his wife conveyed to Beecher the West ⅔ds of lots 1, 2, and 3 in square 42, the frontage lying on the north side of East Ohio Street and west of New Jersey.

Calvin Fletcher upon the occasion of the lot purchase, but it is possible that it was at this time that Fletcher said to him: "If I do business with any man and he gets angry at me, or does not act right, it is my fault. My business is to see that everybody with whom I do business shall do right; I charge myself with that responsibility."[13] Whether it was a statement of philosophy, a warning, or both, it made a deep impression upon Beecher.

Immediately after making his purchase Beecher left for the East. Upon his return in September he began to prepare for the second annual fair of the Indiana Horticultural Society which would be held at the Courthouse on October 20 and 21, 1841. At the fair Beecher was much in evidence as a member of the committee charged with reporting upon the flowers, fruits, and vegetables brought in for exhibit. Among the items which Beecher described were apples, pears, quinces, grapes, an orange tree, dahlias, geraniums, and thirty-five different kinds of vegetables. Someone must have looked after his garden while he was away, for his own contribution to the exhibit was impressive: two marrow squashes, one acorn squash, a Canada crook-neck squash, citron squash, Savoy cabbage, cauliflower, white and yellow carrots, long blood beets, Rohan potatoes, Chinese tree corn, rice corn, and two other varieties of corn. His marrow squashes were judged to be the best of their variety displayed at the fair. After the main speaker, Jacob S. Willets, had concluded his address and the other business was ended, a motion was made and carried that the produce displayed be sold at auction and the results paid to the treasurer for the benefit of the society. The owners were given the right, of course, to reserve any specimens from sale if they so wished. The auction was held, and a substantial sum was added to the capital of the society.[14]

With the approach of spring in 1842 Henry Ward Beecher spent much time in his enlarged garden. The lack of fences in Indianapolis and resulting roaming livestock gave rise to a problem which tried Beecher's patience. He was particularly annoyed by a "cunning old sow, who every day or two would get into the field, in spite of all nails and string, latches or hinges. . . . One midnight I heard her eating and

13. HWB, *Yale Lectures on Preaching*, I, 258.
14. Indianapolis *Indiana Journal*, October 29, 1841.

crunching vigorously among my corn, salads, strawberries and I could endure it no longer. Springing from my bed," he recalled, "[I] seized my gun and dashed out after her. Away she scampered down the garden and away went I down the central path to be ready for her return. She stopped and so did I. The night was dark. I could see nothing . . . hear nothing . . . and it began to strike me that I had rather the worst of it and only needed a spectator to appear decidedly ludicrous. Just then . . . she dashed by me on the left." Beecher fired successive shots in the sow's direction, and at each one she squealed. To his knowledge she never returned.[15]

The audacity of the animal infuriated Beecher whenever he thought of it and caused him to declare that she was a "lineal descendant of the old sow who refused to drown in the sea when the whole herd ran, violently driven, down the steep plane under the influence of the devils, and that she was a living proof of the transmissibility of total depravity."[16] Much of the problem was his own fault. The marauding pigs probably were descended from a pair given to him two years earlier which he had permitted to range freely. These pigs' depredations had irritated his neighbors for months; it was not until Beecher's own garden was endangered, however, that he took action. Upset by the incident he had all the swine which presumably belonged to him rounded up and driven to the Bradshaw farm north of Indianapolis.[17] The episode confirmed in Beecher a dislike of pigs so intense that, according to Charles Beecher, "Henry would go a square out of his direct road to kick a pig at any time."[18]

The opening of the third annual fair of the Indiana Horticultural Society at the State House on Friday, October 7, 1842, found exhibited the largest collection of fruits, vegetables, and flowers yet seen in the state. At the initial session Beecher was appointed to a committee with his friends Calvin Fletcher and Henry P. Coburn to examine the seedling fruit trees and to decide which was worthy to receive the single prize to be awarded at the fair. The committee made the award, a set

15. HWB, Reminiscences, n.d., CtY.

16. New York *Times*, June 5, 1882.

17. John Bradshaw, Reminiscences, May 25, 1902, clipping in George S. Cottman's Indiana Scrapbook Collection, VIII, 44, In.

18. New York *Times*, June 5, 1882.

of six silver teaspoons, that evening to Reuben Ragan of Putnam County. The favored seedling was an apple tree, as yet unnamed. In presenting the award Beecher suggested that the seedling should be called "Osceola" in honor of the Seminole Indian who reportedly behaved so bravely under great stress, and so the tree was named.

On the second day of the fair Calvin Fletcher spoke at ten o'clock in the morning. Realizing he was not an orator, Fletcher talked to the audience rather than presenting a memorized address. His plan worked well, and he was complimented. Other speakers included Governor Samuel Bigger, Henry P. Coburn, and Henry Ward Beecher. The fruit on display was sold in the evening at an auction reminiscent of the one held a year previously. All brought good prices, but the pears were sold for the highest amounts. People paid twelve and a half cents, twenty-five cents, and even fifty cents for a single pear. A specimen from a Duchesse d'Angouleme pear tree which was believed to be the first one of its variety grown in the state brought the most spirited bidding. Beecher was determined to have it. He gained the pear finally after a bid of sixty-two and a half cents. "I am afraid I should have doubled the bid," he wrote, "rather than have lost her ladyship. . . . I need not say I was 'somewhat filled' with her company."[19] It was a steep price to pay for a single piece of fruit when semiskilled laborers worked long and hard for a wage of seventy-five cents per day. It was a dear price to pay for a man as deeply in debt as was Beecher in 1842. The owner of the pear was so flattered by the attention it received, however, that he gave Beecher a seedling tree and also one of the Beurre d'Aremberg trees.[20]

Henry Ward Beecher continued to be one of the most active members of the Indiana Horticultural Society in the years that followed. A meeting of the organization on Saturday, March 30, 1844, held particular interest for him. W. Thompson Hatch, editor of the *Western Cultivator,* had received a selection of rare garden seeds from the Hon. Henry L. Ellsworth, commissioner of the United States Patent Office in

19. "Indianapolis in 1843—A Henry Ward Beecher Letter," *Indiana Magazine of History,* III, No. 4 (December, 1907), pp. 189–90; *Illustrated Historical Atlas of the State of Indiana* (Chicago: Baskin, Forster & Co., 1876), p. 222.

20. Calvin Fletcher Diary, October 7 and 8, 1842, InHi; Ragan, "The First Indiana Horticultural Society," *Indiana Magazine of History,* IV, 72–73; Charles J. Worden, *Historical Sketches Concerning the First Presbyterian Church, Fort Wayne, Indiana* (Fort Wayne, Ind.: The First Presbyterian Church Foundation, 1945), p. 9.

Washington, D.C. Hatch presented the seeds to the society with the wish that some of its members would plant them. Included were more than twenty varieties of vegetable and grain seeds, and many of them had never been grown in the United States. The seeds were left at the store of Dr. Abner Pope where members could obtain those with which they wished to experiment. The opportunity presented a rare challenge to those men and women who took real delight and pride in their gardens, and Beecher moved that Hatch be thanked for his contribution.[21]

Beecher had succeeded Jacob S. Willets as the favorite speaker of the Indiana Horticultural Society, and late in 1844 the clergyman gave an address on the causes of fire blight which was praised highly by the society's members. It was published subsequently in the January, 1845, issue of *Hovey's Magazine*, and it was the first article of Beecher's on a horticultural topic to appear in print. In an effort to be just he wrote later in the *Indiana Farmer and Gardener* that the ideas for it had originated with Reuben Ragan.[22]

The success of the speech and article gave Beecher confidence to pursue a project that interested him. He began to collect information from leading farmers of the state as to prevailing agricultural conditions in their areas. One of these men was James Perry who lived near Richmond, Indiana. Perry supplied Beecher with details related to: (1) qualities of soil, (2) quantity of production per acre, (3) number of apple trees on each quarter section of land, (4) quality of sheep, (5) varieties of hogs, and (6) quality and variety of cattle.[23] If Henry Ward Beecher could assemble similar statistics for each county he would have an invaluable view of agriculture in Indiana. More and more his time and attention were being focused on his horticultural interests; however, at the same time he was able to improve as a preacher and revivalist. It was his pastoral obligations which were neglected.

21. Indianapolis *Indiana State Journal*, April 6, 1844.

22. *Indiana Farmer and Gardener*, I, No. 2 (February 8, 1845), pp. 26–29. For Beecher's association with this publication, see Chapter XIII, below.

23. James Perry to HWB, Richmond, December 31, 1844, quoted in *Indiana Farmer and Gardener*, I, No. 1 (February 1, 1845), p. 2.

X

Revivalist

A PERIOD OF INTENSE ACTIVITY WAS ABOUT TO COMMENCE FOR HENRY Ward Beecher. Called to Terre Haute to assist with a revival early in January, 1842, he left his family in Indianapolis and reached the Vigo County seat on January 14. There he found the revival in progress with twenty-eight converts to its credit. Merrick A. Jewett invited Beecher to help with the protracted meeting at his church which was Congregational in spirit though not at the time in affiliation. Such an invitation was possible because of the close co-operation still existing between Congregational clergymen and New School Presbyterians in the West.[1]

Jewett's church had prospered since its beginning less than a decade earlier. The village of Terre Haute lacked a settled Protestant minister when young Jewett, a native of Baltimore, Maryland, stopped overnight in 1834 on his way farther West. Learning that he was a preacher some residents asked him to give a sermon which he delivered at the Courthouse. Jewett was requested to stay, and money was pledged for his salary. He accepted, and on December 30, 1834, organized a church with a charter membership of eleven. Within three years his congregation was able to build a substantial brick church, and it

---

1. Samuel Merrill to David Merrill, Indianapolis, February 11, 1842, Samuel Merrill Papers, InHi; Lyman Abbott, "Reminiscences," *Outlook*, CVIII (September 23, 1914), 206.

was from this structure located at the corner of Sixth and Cherry streets that Jewett and Beecher led the series of revival meetings.[2]

This was the first revival in Indiana in which Beecher took a leading part, and he prayed and worked "until [his] heart was on fire."[3] He would recall that he "used to get up early in the morning, and, immediately after breakfast, take a horse, and ride from house to house, and converse with people. I worked in that way till ten o'clock. Between ten and eleven I attended the daily prayer-meeting that was held there [Terre Haute]. Then I rode with the pastor till dinner-time. After dinner I rested till evening, when I attended another meeting."[4] Ten people joined the church while Beecher was in Terre Haute, and another seventeen were converted shortly after he returned to Indianapolis. Upwards of 120 people joined Jewett's church during the year, and Beecher's work was recognized as contributing to the increase in membership.[5]

Henry Ward Beecher was elated by his success in Terre Haute. "I came home," he said, "full of fire and zeal, praying all the way. There was a prayer that began in Terre Haute and ended in Indianapolis."[6] He devoted his next sermon on January 30 to an account of the revival in Terre Haute which he described "in a masterly manner." He spoke of the halting believer who hesitated as compared with the individual who proceeded purposefully with his business and the results each could expect to achieve. Calvin Fletcher approved Beecher's analogy and thought it "a fine illustration of practical life."[7] Beecher ended his sermon with an announcement that a revival would commence the next evening at the Second Presbyterian Church.

Beecher's enthusiasm was not shared immediately by his congregation. The initial meeting was held on a stormy evening and the lecture room of the church was only about two-thirds full. Beecher did not

---

2. Abbott, "Reminiscences," *Outlook*, CVIII, 204–206; H. C. Bradsby, *History of Vigo County, Indiana* (Chicago: S. B. Nelson & Co., 1891), pp. 591–92.

3. HWB, *Yale Lectures on Preaching*, I, 46–48.

4. HWB, *Lecture-Room Talks*, pp. 76–77.

5. Samuel Merrill to David Merrill, Indianapolis, February 11, 1842, Samuel Merrill Papers, InHi; Bradsby, *History of Vigo County, Indiana*, pp. 591–92; Abbott, "Reminiscences," *Outlook*, CVIII, 207.

6. Landon, *Kings of the Platform and Pulpit*, p. 127.

7. Calvin Fletcher Diary, January 30 and 31, 1842, InHi.

create much response in his listeners. After the service on the second night of the revival, another rainy evening, the minister called for those who would like to talk further with him to remain, but no one did. To himself Beecher said, "It makes no difference; if the Lord wishes it to be so, I do!"[8] He preached ardently and persuasively on the third night. Once more he watched, however, as the congregation filed out of the room at the close of service. This time one person stayed behind to talk with him. Two accounts by Beecher survive of what occurred. In one he stated that "one poor little thin servant-girl stopped! She smelt of the kitchen and looked kitchen all over. . . . my first feeling . . . as I went toward her, was one of disappointment. I said to myself that after so much work it was too bad. It was just a glance, an arrow which the Devil shot at me, but which went past. The next minute I had an over-whelming revulsion in my soul; and I said to myself, 'If God pleases, I will work for the poorest of his creatures.' "[9]

In a second version Beecher was quoted, "I made a strong appeal, but only one person—a poor German servant-girl—stopped. All the children of my friends, the young people that I knew very well, got up and went out . . . . I remember that there shot through me a spasm of rebellion. I had a sort of feeling, 'For what was all this precious oint-ment spilled? Such a sermon as I had preached, such an appeal as I had made, with no result but this!' " Beecher continued, "In a second, how-ever, almost quicker than a flash . . . there opened to me a profound sense of the value of any child of the Lord Jesus Christ. . . . My pride was all gone, my vanity was all gone, and I was caught up into a blessed sense of the love of God to men, and of my relation to Christ; and I thought it to be an unspeakable privilege to unloose the shoe-latchets from the poorest of Christ's disciples."[10] It was the turning point. Beecher believed the experience had been designed to bring about just such a result and that God "paid me the next night, for two of my sweetest children [Julia Merrill and Elizabeth Bates ?]—not my own, but they were like my own to me—stopped on the next night, and after that the work went on."[11] After Wednesday evening, February 4, interest

8. HWB, *Yale Lectures on Preaching*, I, 46–48.
9. *Ibid.*
10. Landon, *Kings of the Platform and Pulpit*, p. 127.
11. HWB, *Yale Lectures on Preaching*, I, 46–48.

quickened in the congregation, and Beecher was plunged into exhilarating and satisfying work.

Henry Ward Beecher modeled himself upon his father as a revivalist. Using the tools of reason, persuasion, and argument he attempted to bring men to an understanding of the nature of their sinfulness and to give them hope and inspiration that they could improve and enter Christ's kingdom. He disdained the practice of urging people to follow the pathway to Heaven by attempting to scare the hell out of them first. To Beecher, this was "not Christianity; it is the worst form of paganism."[12] In Lawrenceburgh he had resorted to it in his desperate attempts to rouse a response from his apathetic congregation, and he had been disgusted and disillusioned by the result.[13] Beecher preached upon topics relevant to the lives and concerns of his listeners. Complex theological discourses and historical narratives found little place in his sermons. He talked about problems common to all men and suggested alternatives and acceptable solutions which, he said, were simple and obvious if the precepts of Christ were applied. Indeed, his revival sermons differed mainly from his ones for regular services chiefly in their more pronounced emphasis upon salvation. In either, Beecher spoke understandably and pointedly and gave his hearers the impression he was speaking directly to them as individuals.[14]

Sermon followed sermon in almost dizzying succession. Buoyed up by coffee and perhaps some toast before preaching, Beecher guided brilliantly the services which continued week after week with no perceptible lessening of interest. Afterwards he would eat a cold meat supper before going to bed. Each afternoon he would try to take a short nap; and, indeed, he trained himself to fall asleep quickly and soundly in the midst of household noise.[15]

12. HWB, "Thoughts By the Way," *Christian Union*, XXXV (April 21, 1887), 19.

13. *Ibid.*; Hillis, "The Ruling Ideas of Henry Ward Beecher's Sermons," in *Henry Ward Beecher As His Friends Saw Him*, pp. 11–12; HWB, *Lecture-Room Talks*, p. 147.

14. Sidney E. Mead, *The Lively Experiment* (New York: Harper & Row, 1963), pp. 123–25; Winthrop S. Hudson, *The Great Tradition of the American Churches* (New York: Harper & Brothers, 1953), p. 170.

15. James B. Pond, *Eccentricities of Genius* (New York: G. W. Dillingham Co., 1900), p. 51; Searle, "Beecher's Personality," *North American Review*, CXLIV, 489–90; Knox, *Life and Work of Henry Ward Beecher*, pp. 436–39.

Henry Ward Beecher carried the major responsibility for the revival, but he occasionally invited a fellow clergyman to preach a sermon or two. Jewett of Terre Haute came to assist; and Charles White, president of Wabash College, was another who spoke to the congregation of the Second Presbyterian Church. White preached on February 16, 1842, and his sermon was adjudged very good by that connoisseur, Calvin Fletcher. The efforts of Beecher and his peers bore fruit. Among the first to be converted were Harriet and Julia Bassett, Elizabeth Bates, Julia Merrill, Mary Biles, Hannah A. Culley, Louisa Vandegrift, and Catherine and Lafayette Yandes. Julia Bullard, a cousin of Eunice's who had come some weeks previously to Indianapolis to make her home with the Beechers, was also included in the number.[16]

The revival spirit was not confined to the Second Presbyterian Church. Several of the local churches were conducting similar meetings or else were experiencing renewed interest in their regular services. The editor of the *Indiana Journal* commented: "Since this season of daily preaching, prayer, and supplication at a Throne of Grace became so . . . in the Churches, in the families, and in . . . hearts of our citizens, a great change has been . . . in this community. Between one and two hundred persons have already united themselves with . . . Church, and a great many others are earnestly . . . [seeking] the way of eternal salvation."[17] Sometimes the community was surprised to learn of the conversion of a person of whom it was unexpected. Such an instance occurred in Beecher's church when Cary H. Boatright and his wife were received into the Second Presbyterian Church by examination on March 22 and April 5, respectively. Beecher "gathered good people together," recalled William N. Jackson, "but he got some as rough as could be, among them Cary Boatright, whom he afterwards baptized."[18]

The revival continued. Beecher presided at a prayer meeting from eight to nine o'clock every morning. Between the close of prayer meeting and the evening service, he visited members of the congregation and others. He talked with those who were troubled, and he encouraged

16. Calvin Fletcher Diary, February 16, 1842, InHi; List of Members, Records of the Second Presbyterian Church, InISPC.
17. Indianapolis *Indiana Journal*, March 16, 1842.
18. William N. Jackson, "Reminiscences," n.d., clipping, CtY.

them to accept Christ. "Young and old were happy in believing. Nothing was thought of but these meetings. There were no *parties* as receptions were then termed," wrote Jane Merrill Ketcham. "Everyone who could went to Church." Beecher throve on this hectic schedule. "I can see him still," continued Mrs. Ketcham, "in his rough brown overcoat, his trousers tucked in his heavy boots, flying about full of zeal and inspiration."[19]

In his efforts to reach people, however, Beecher sometimes encountered hostility. "I had a man in my [Indianapolis] parish," said Beecher,

> . . .who was a very ugly fellow. He had a wife and daughter who were awakened during the revival. . . and, while visiting others who needed instruction, I went to see and talk with them. He heard that I had been in his house, and shortly afterwards I passed down the street in which he lived. He was sitting on the fence; and of all the filth that was ever emptied on a young minister's head, I received my share. He. . . said everything that was calculated to harrow my pride. I was very wholesomely indignant for a young man. I said to myself, "Look here, I will be revenged on you yet." He told me I should never darken his door again, to which I responded that I never would until I had his invitation to do so.

When Beecher's anger cooled and he reflected upon the situation, he decided to change the man's attitude toward him. The minister told no one of the heated exchange, nodded or spoke pleasantly to the man when their paths crossed, and advocated the fellow's candidacy when the latter was up for election to a local office. Continued Beecher, "I never saw a man so utterly perplexed as he was. . . . He came to me one day, awkward and stumbling, and undertook to 'make up' . . . . He said he would be very glad to have me call and see him. . . . from that time forth I never had a faster friend in the world than he was."[20]

During the course of the revival meetings in the city a controversy arose as to the correct mode of baptism. The denomination referred to as the Disciples of Christ or Campbellites insisted that immersion was necessary while the Methodists and Presbyterians contended that sprinkling was preferable. Beecher was brought publicly into the dis-

19. Ketcham, "Presbyterian (Marion County) History of 2nd Presbyterian Church of Indianapolis," pp. 10–11, In.
20. HWB, *Yale Lectures on Preaching*, I, 252–53.

pute when John O'Kane, a clergyman of the Disciples, challenged him to a debate on the topic. Beecher declined. He was not permitted to avoid the issue, however, for some people who planned to join the Second Presbyterian Church indicated a preference for baptism by immersion. One of these was Thomas A. Morris, a graduate of West Point and chief engineer on the construction of the Madison and Indianapolis Railroad. Believing that such baptism was unusual in the Presbyterian Church, Morris asked Beecher if he could be immersed as he felt he would be a more contented Christian as a result. Beecher reassured Morris that there was no objection to the procedure and that he would gladly baptize him that way. For his tolerant attitude Henry Ward Beecher received sharp criticism from those who felt strongly upon the subject of baptism, but he did not retract his promise to Morris.[21]

As a result of the revivals in their churches the pastors of the Baptist, Methodist, and Second Presbyterian churches had several people awaiting baptism. They decided to hold a union ceremony on Sunday, April 10, 1842. Each clergyman would baptize those who were joining his church. An estimated two thousand to three thousand people turned out to witness the unusual service which took place on the bank of the White River near the New Bridge. Beecher and his people awaited their turn in the sunny, warm weather under the shade of a towering sycamore. When it was time for Beecher to proceed with his part in the ceremony, he baptized Charles Williams by affusion; next, he baptized by immersion Elliott Davis, Daniel Foutz, Sarah L. Morris, and Thomas A. Morris; and he baptized Esther Vandegrift and her infant daughter, Frances Matilda,[22] by sprinkling. The banks of White River were lined with huge trees, and some small boys climbed them to

21. Knox, *Life and Work of Henry Ward Beecher*, pp. 91–92; Sulgrove, *History of Indianapolis and Marion County, Indiana*, p. 301; Margaret M. Scott, "Local Woman Tells of Early Indianapolis and of Mr. McGuffy's [sic] 'Select School' for Young Ladies in Ky.," pp. 4–5, MS, In; Anna Nicholas, *The Story of Crown Hill* (Indianapolis: Crown Hill Assoc., 1928), pp. 76–77.

22. Frances Matilda Vandegrift Osbourne (1840–1914) married the Scottish poet and novelist, Robert Louis Stevenson, on May 19, 1880, in San Francisco, California. For the record of her baptism see Records of the Second Presbyterian Church, pp. 33–34, InISPC; Ketcham, "Presbyterian (Marion County) History of 2nd Presbyterian Church of Indianapolis," pp. 11–12, In.

gain a higher perch from which to watch. They observed that when it was Morris's turn to be baptized, his head did not go wholly under water. When adults learned of this, they wondered if Morris's penchant for thoroughness would make him insist upon another baptism. It did not.[23]

Beecher tethered his horse conveniently near the site, and as soon as his part was completed he was seen to hurry in his wet clothes toward the animal, jump on, and speed down the road. A person who noticed his leave-taking was amused that the jolting gallop of the horse caused drops of water to fall like rain from both sides of Beecher's departing figure. The union baptism was the climax of the revival. Interest slackened, and people began to direct their thoughts to accustomed entertainments and diversions.

For Beecher's sake it was just as well. The minister was visibly fatigued. The revival which began the first week in February had continued into April. In all those weeks Beecher had carried almost the entire burden of it. His efforts were rewarded, however, and twenty-eight were admitted to the church in February, forty more joined in March, and an additional twenty-two were added in the first week of April. Of these, some twenty-five or thirty had been attending the Sabbath School but had not been church members, and the rest were drawn from the community. The Second Presbyterian Church added more to its roll than all the other denominations combined had been able to do. It was a triumph for Henry Ward Beecher.[24]

After his successful revivals in Terre Haute and Indianapolis, Beecher received ever-increasing numbers of invitations to preach in outlying communities. In accord with the policy of his church he accepted as many as he could. One of these took him on a journey of seventy miles over rough, dusty roads through a heavily timbered and

---

23. Nicholas, *The Story of Crown Hill*, pp. 76–77; Calvin Fletcher Diary, April 10, 1842. Fletcher recorded: "The children went to the river to see the Revd. Good of the methodist Beecher of the new school presbyterians & Chandler of the baptists immerse several."

24. Scott, "Local Woman Tells of Early Indianapolis and of Mr. McGuffy's [sic] 'Select School' for Young Ladies in Ky.," pp. 4–5, In; Samuel Merrill to David Merrill, Indianapolis, April 1 and 29, 1842, Samuel Merrill Papers, InHi; Landon, *Kings of the Platform and Pulpit*, p. 127.

relatively unimproved area of the state northward to Logansport. The county seat of Cass County, it was a thriving town which was the commercial and agricultural center for the surrounding region largely due to the presence of the Wabash and Erie Canal and the emptying of the Eel River at that point into the Wabash River.

Beecher was asked to preach by his friend, Martin M. Post, who had helped organize the Second Presbyterian Church of Logansport in 1831 and who had served it as pastor ever since. Beecher spoke from a pulpit in the six-year-old frame church building located on the south side of Broadway. The sanctuary was 26 by 36 feet and was reputedly the largest room in Logansport. Beecher's major sermon, however, was delivered at a camp meeting in progress on the outskirts of the town. Attending the latter was a new experience for Beecher who had little previous contact with such gatherings. Most Presbyterian clergy of the New School disapproved of them because of the excesses which too often marred their assemblies and the lack of personal contact between clergy and converted. The first Presbyterian camp meeting in the West had taken place in Logan County, Kentucky, in July, 1800, and it had become the prototype for succeeding gatherings. People had come from as far away as one hundred miles to attend. Placing their tents and wagons to form a hollow square, the people assembled in the center where they sat on rows of logs around a rude platform; and it was from this temporary pulpit that the worship services originated.[25]

When Henry Ward Beecher approached the pulpit at the Logansport camp meeting on a Sunday in 1842 he noted that all sorts of people were present, but he could see no law officers among them. This troubled him, for it was customary to have a patrol on duty to control the unruly who used the camp meeting as a pretext to gather for bouts of drinking, gambling, fighting, and fornicating. To the audience, Beecher said, "Friends, there are five thousand of you here to-day; it is very hot and dusty, there is very little water, the children will be fretful, mothers may be tired, it is feared that there may be trouble. Now we haven't a single watchman or policeman on this ground. If there is good order

25. Jehu Z. Powell (ed.), *History of Cass County, Indiana* (2 volumes. Chicago: Lewis Publishing Co., 1913), I, 424; Davidson, *History of the Presbyterian Church in the State of Kentucky; With a Preliminary Sketch of the Churches in the Valley of Virginia*, pp. 134–35.

here to-day, you will have to keep it."[26] Miraculously, order was kept and the day passed without an unpleasant incident.

Soon Beecher was riding across the rugged, picturesque terrain of southern Indiana to attend Synod at Madison, on the bank of the Ohio River. Madison was easily the most sophisticated and beautiful city in the state. Beecher was present for the convening of Synod on Thursday, September 1, 1842, at the Second Presbyterian Church which fronted on one of Madison's busiest streets. In attendance with him was David V. Culley. Beecher was appointed to the powerful judicial committee, and worship services and business meetings followed in stately succession. Lyman Beecher arrived from Walnut Hills to be present for the business meeting on Saturday and was invited by Synod to take a seat as a corresponding member. He came to report on the nature of theological preparation followed at Lane Theological Seminary. Father and son had a long visit before it was time for Lyman Beecher to return to Ohio.[27]

Henry Ward Beecher remained in Madison to begin his third revival of the year. His father had preached several times in Madison's Second Presbyterian Church, and the two men discussed the situation that would face Henry. After the revival was underway the younger Beecher wrote to his father that the church was not *"Sitting on the edge of the Red Sea Smoking Cigars,"* a figure of speech indicating the presence of activity. Between sixty and seventy people were soon attending morning services, and in the evenings the number rose to between three hundred and four hundred. Beecher was pleased that Mrs. William McKee Dunn, a daughter of the noted James F. D. Lanier, showed signs of being truly converted. He wrote to Lyman Beecher that there were ten to fifteen hopeful conversions and another thirty to forty people making inquiries.[28]

Samuel Merrill chanced to be in Madison on business and attended many of the services. The banker was impressed by the silence and attention which Beecher's sermons commanded. Feeling he needed

26. HWB, *Yale Lectures on Preaching*, II, 110.
27. Records of the Synod of Indiana, I, 293–303, InHan.
28. HWB to Lyman Beecher, Madison, September 12, 1842, MCR; Blanche G. Garber, "The Lanier Family and the Lanier Home," *Indiana Magazine of History*, XXII, No. 3 (September, 1926), p. 277.

more time to complete his work in Madison, Beecher asked Merrill's advice and was told to remain longer. Merrill hoped that Beecher would return to Indianapolis as fired with enthusiasm as he had from the revival in Terre Haute.[29] Upon his return home, however, Beecher did not attempt to begin another revival.

Within five months Beecher was called to assist with another revival gathering momentum in a New School church. The residents of Lafayette were flocking to services held at churches in the city, with the Presbyterians and Methodists drawing the greatest numbers. "Lafayette has been about the vilest place in the state," wrote Samuel Merrill, "and now [as result of revivals] it is said to be almost entirely reformed."[30] Beecher learned something of the history of the Presbyterian church from its pastor, the Reverend Joseph Wilson. About three years earlier eight people had organized a New School church, and services were held at first in a farm house and later in a rented grocery. There had been an increase in membership until there were nearly fifty on the roll when the church building was erected. It had been an achievement for Wilson to gain so large a congregation, for Lafayette was reputedly antireligious. The Sabbath was not kept as it was in better regulated communities such as Indianapolis, and the churches were bypassed if an amusing entertainment were available. Wilson worked hard to overcome the apathy he encountered and made progress.

Earlier in the year Wilson had gone to nearby Peru, Indiana, to assist with a revival. He returned home at a time when the religious fervor sweeping the state had made Lafayette's residents aware of their shortcomings and began a revival. Feeling unequal to the task of conducting the revival alone, he appealed to Beecher for assistance.

Henry Ward Beecher followed the course of revivals in the state with professional interest. In his notes he jotted down the names of communities in Indiana which had experienced revivals in the preceding three years: Madison, Brownstown, Greenfield, Fort Wayne, Wabash town [sic], Peru, Logansport, Delphi, Monticello area, Dayton, Oxford, Attica, Newton [Newtown ?], Rockville, and Terre Haute. He com-

29. Samuel Merrill to Jane Anderson Merrill, Madison, September 14, 1842, Samuel Merrill Papers, InHi.

30. Samuel Merrill to David and Jesse Merrill, Indianapolis, March 22, 1843, Samuel Merrill Papers.

menced his work at Lafayette with his accustomed enthusiasm and planning. "Any person who enters upon a Revival," he wrote, "—who arranges the meeting—*preaches,* directs the church—if he is fit to be a pastor, ought to have some idea of what is to be done. Some plan. Not machinery, none in it. But what the end to be gained is. What means to be used shall be." He continued, "The plan of labor proposed & prosecuted at Lafayette fr[om] beginning to end, was to develope the character of *Christ* & to as great an Eternal; or was possible to bring church up to that State, that *Love* should be the *Working Principle."* Beecher's days were divided into his usual revival schedule of morning services, visits, evening services, and inquiry meetings.

Beecher was gratified with the effect which a morning service produced upon its hearers.

> At times, it rose above anything I had ever witnessed. It seemed as if all utterances were forbidden except *smiles & tears.* . . when meeting was dismissed *none moved. One spoke*—sung again—none moved—all still—silent—tender. . . . *This meeting,* by far the most profitable. Each narrated religious feelings. . . . Enquirers who came here soon found the Redeemer, *& my opinion is that to awaken men, or lead them to Christ, nothing on Earth so powerful as manifestation of tender deep love among Christ* [Christians].[31]

He attempted to visit daily all those who had remained after the preceding evening's services. These calls he kept short so as not to intrude and also to enable him to see more people. In addition, he held informal conferences. At each evening service in Lafayette he preached an evangelistic sermon. Designed to persuade the members of the congregation to accept Christ as a personal Saviour, each was constructed to lead the listeners toward a desire for salvation. At a sermon's close he asked earnestly: "Are any willing to *begin tonight* [?] *We are ready!* God is ready, *Are You?"*[32] In his plea he put every bit of vocal artistry he could command. Shaken by the dramatic plea usually between twenty-five and fifty people would stay behind for the inquiry meeting.

Henry Ward Beecher worked in Lafayette a little over two weeks. Just before he left, Merrick A. Jewett came to carry on the revival which was still attracting intense response. There were between sixty

31. HWB, Notes on Lafayette Revival, March 12, 1843, CtY.
32. *Ibid.*

and seventy conversions in the Presbyterian church during Beecher's stay in Lafayette and even more, he heard, after he returned home. "So *pure,* & unexceptionable a work I never witnessed," he wrote to his father.[33]

Returning home, Beecher discovered the way prepared for a revival at his own church. Interest in religion was at a high pitch in the capital city, and other denominations were also involved in conducting protracted meetings. Beecher began at once to preach, visit, and confer. The results of his efforts were again highly gratifying, and he wrote jubilantly, "On my return [from Lafayette], I found my church much prepared. They had been praying—God was with them—I began at once. . . . [There is] clearness & strength of Christian feeling, visible among my people."[34] Among those who subsequently joined the Second Presbyterian Church at this time were Calvin Fletcher, Jr., and his uncle, Stoughton A. Fletcher. The two Fletchers were received into the church on an extremely cold Sunday morning, and a light snow fell prior to the service. Calvin Fletcher, Sr., a Methodist, reflected that his son's joining the Second Presbyterian Church was a "fearful gratification to me." [35] It mattered little to him which church a child of his selected so long as evidence of conversion and a choice was made.

It would be two years until Beecher would lead another revival at the Second Presbyterian Church. In February, 1845, he was in the mood to start one, and he let the members of the church know of his intention. If one did not materialize in Indianapolis he would travel to Lafayette or Delphi where the prospects for successful revivals were reported to be bright. It was a time of year well suited to begin a revival, for there was very little to distract a congregation and community bored from the long nights of winter and the pervading cold which kept them indoors. A revival brought them an opportunity to inject a little drama, personal or vicarious, into their lives at this dreary season. At the prayer meeting on February 12 Beecher led the forty or so people present toward expressing a desire for a revival in the church. They asked for a second prayer meeting that week in spite of the extremely

33. HWB to Lyman Beecher, Indianapolis, March 18, 1843, CtY.
34. *Ibid.*
35. Calvin Fletcher Diary, March 26, 1843, InHi.

bad weather which reduced their number, and the familiar routine began.[36]

When involved in leading revivals Beecher paid little attention to the state of his clothing. To the consternation of some of his congregation he appeared for a Sunday evening service still wearing the muddied overcoat and spattered green baize leggings which had protected him from the weather while he traveled to and from a special service at Southport that afternoon. Arriving too late in Indianapolis to change and have supper, he dismounted in front of the church and entered. Striding down the aisle he removed his coat, shook himself a little, told the congregation of his mission that day, and proceeded with the service.[37] While successful, the revival held at the Second Presbyterian Church in 1845 did not create the intense response to Beecher's efforts that had happened earlier among his congregation. Beecher would continue to conduct revivals in Indianapolis and throughout the state for the remainder of his pastorate in Indiana, but as their novelty faded, they held a decreasing interest for him.

36. Samuel Merrill to Jane Anderson Merrill, Indianapolis, February 13, 1845, Samuel Merrill Papers, InHi; Charles Beecher (ed.), *Autobiography, Correspondence, Etc., of Lyman Beecher, D.D.*, II, 486.
37. New York *Times*, June 5, 1882.

XI

Life in Indianapolis

THE TEMPO OF HENRY WARD BEECHER'S ACTIVITIES ACCELERATED over the years between 1842 and 1845. Keyed up at the end of each day he relaxed by reading about some phase of gardening. Beecher's personal library was relatively large, but it was heavily weighted with theological works. His friends, Samuel Merrill, Calvin Fletcher, and James Blake all had extensive private libraries which were open to him. The State Library, containing slightly more than two thousand volumes, had titles of particular interest to Beecher, and he borrowed works on horticulture from it which he read "not only every line, but much of it many times over."[1] He recalled that "there was a charm in reading even the names of the plants in the catalogues, although there was nothing very stimulating in it. . . . In that way, I let myself down quietly, and then I could go to sleep."[2]

Located in the State House, the State Library's west windows let in light filtered by seldom-disturbed spider webs. It was so gloomy in the mornings that it was difficult to locate a given title rapidly. The carpeted room was lined with shelving so high that the uppermost rows could be reached only by use of a stepladder. This ladder was the personal property of the librarian, and library patrons were supposed to be

1. *Henry Ward Beecher As His Friends Saw Him*, p. 58.
2. HWB, *Yale Lectures on Preaching*, I, 202.

aware of the privilege of its use. Beecher borrowed repeatedly such books as Loudon's works on horticulture, architecture, and agriculture; Lindley's *Horticulture;* and Gray's *Structural Botany.* From these and similar books he gained a superior knowledge of plant culture. During this period a friend gave Beecher a subscription to the *London Gardener's Chronicle,* a gift which he treasured.[3]

The Beecher family circle in Indianapolis was enlarged when Charles Beecher brought his wife and infant son to live there. The school in which Charles had taught with Talbut Bullard in New Orleans failed to prosper, and the younger Beecher brought his family north in late 1841 to visit the Beecher clan in Ohio and then to Jacksonville, Illinois, for a time to see his wife's kinsmen as well as Edward Beecher and his family. From Illinois they came to Indianapolis. Soon they were established in a small house near and almost identical with that occupied by the Henry Ward Beechers.[4]

From the first, Charles Beecher was a favorite with the members of the Second Presbyterian Church. Henry was regarded as plain and undistinguished in appearance, but Charles was thought to be "in face and form an Apollo."[5] Taller than Henry, Charles had regular features and seemed to radiate a melancholy and mysterious air which intrigued women. The congregation of the church received its first glimpse of Charles Beecher in the sanctuary prior to a service. "He was sitting," wrote Mrs. Ketcham, "on one of the seats near the platform on which the Elder sat. He was singing alone—'Do not I love thee, Oh, my Lord.' Never can I forget how his countenance shown with that love."[6] Rumors of his supposedly romantic past had reached Indianapolis. His walk from Cincinnati to New Orleans with only his violin for company in his search for faith took on the aspect of a holy quest. Educated for

3. Jacob P. Dunn, *The Libraries of Indiana* (Indianapolis: W. B. Burford, 1893), p. 9; Wallace, *An Autobiography,* I, 52–53; HWB, *Plain and Pleasant Talk About Fruits, Flowers and Farming* (New York: Derby & Jackson, 1859), pp. iv–v.

4. Lyman Beecher to Lydia Jackson Beecher, Indianapolis, August 23, 1841, CtHS-D; Stowe, *Men of Our Times,* p. 546; Ketcham, "Presbyterian (Marion County) History of 2nd Presbyterian Church of Indianapolis," pp. 8–9, In.

5. Ketcham, "Presbyterian (Marion County) History of 2nd Presbyterian Church of Indianapolis," pp. 9–10, In.

6. *Ibid.*

the ministry, Charles Beecher had forsaken it because of doubts and skepticism. His efforts to overcome his lack of faith were understandable and seemed admirable to the ladies of Indianapolis.[7]

Charles Beecher was soon caught up in the work of the Second Presbyterian Church. He assumed, unofficially, the duties attached to the superintendency of the Sunday School and otherwise assisted Henry. An extremely skilled and talented musician, he became the first organist of the church. "There was never any failure at the organ," recalled Mrs. Ketcham. "The whole soul of our organist was in his music. As he touched the keys the listener was thrilled."[8] Both Beechers agreed upon the importance of music to a worship service. While Charles Beecher was content, however, to regard the presence of music as justified by its beauty alone, Henry Ward Beecher viewed it as a means of imparting spiritual truths. "Any tune or hymn which excites or gives expression to true devout feeling is worthy of use," contended the elder brother who said further that "there is more sound instruction given to a congregation by [proper use of music] than by almost any other [means]."[9]

The younger Beecher directed the choir of the Second Presbyterian Church which quickly gained an enviable reputation in the city and throughout the state. It customarily sang twice at each church service, and it would occasionally present a public concert. On these latter times it used as its theme song, *Man the Lifeboat, Brother*. Charles Beecher might present a solo on his violin or on the organ as well as accompany the choir. In late December the choir and soloists presented selections from a wide range of composers including Mozart, Naumann, and Haydn in a concert thought to be the first of its scope ever presented in the state. Henry Ward Beecher sang with the choir when it offered Mozart's *Twelfth Mass* and may have accompanied it upon

7. Stowe, *Men of Our Times*, p. 546.
8. Ketcham, "Presbyterian (Marion County) History of 2nd Presbyterian Church of Indianapolis," pp. 13–15, In.
9. HWB, "The Importance of Music in the Church," *Etude*, XLI, No. 8 (August, 1923), pp. 560–61; Oliver H. Smith, *Early Indiana Trials and Sketches* (Cincinnati: Moore, Wilstach, Keys & Co., 1858), pp. 93–94; Wilson, *Crusader in Crinoline*, p. 148.

his flute during other selections. Despite the wintry weather a sizable audience came to the event.[10]

The choir of the Second Presbyterian Church was deprived of the services of a boy singer on one occasion because of his father's distrust of the effect Beecher's sermons might have upon him. Ezra Meeker, a newsboy for the *Indiana Journal*, had a good alto voice which was brought to the attention of some choir members. Although his parents were members of the local Campbellite church, Ezra was asked to join the choir of the Second Presbyterian Church. His mother would not permit it saying that he did not have suitable clothes. When someone promised to buy a suit for him, and the choir offered to pay a small salary to him, his father refused to let him accept. The senior Meeker, a miller by trade, feared the pernicious effect which Beecher's sermons might produce on Ezra and insisted that the boy should hear only those preached by the Campbellite pastor.[11]

Beecher attended fairly assiduously to his pastoral duties. In company with an elder of the church he visited members of his congregation and called upon others in the city. In this way he came to know the family of Lazarus B. Wilson, the surveyor of the Wabash and Erie Canal. Wilson was prosperous and lived well, and Beecher dined frequently at the Wilson table where he was a welcome guest. The surveyor and his family lived in a magnificent new house which was located on the southeast corner of Tennessee and Maryland streets. Built in 1842 the house rivaled those erected a few years earlier by Samuel Merrill and Daniel Yandes. The Wilson house had twelve rooms and was two stories high. Its walls were twelve inches thick, and its beams measured twelve inches by three inches. Every piece of wood

10. Ketcham, "Presbyterian (Marion County) History of 2nd Presbyterian Church of Indianapolis," pp. 13–15, In; Martha F. Bellinger, "Music in Indianapolis, 1821–1900," *Indiana Magazine of History*, XLI, No. 4 (December, 1945), p. 346; Smith, *Early Indiana Trials and Sketches*, pp. 93–94; Indianapolis *Indiana Journal*, December 28 and 30, 1842; clipping from Towanda [Pa.] *Daily Review*, March 8, 1887, CtY.

11. C. B. Galbreath, "Ezra Meeker, Ohio's Illustrious Pioneer," Ohio Archaeological and Historical *Publications*, XXXVI, No. 1 (January, 1927), pp. 6–7; Ezra Meeker, *The Busy Life of Eighty-Five Years of Ezra Meeker* (Seattle: Published by the author, 1916), pp. 6–7, 12.

in the structure was black walnut. There were double parlors on the right of a center hall; and on the left was a sitting room, a dining room, and to the rear was a two-story porch. The furniture was all handmade of mahogany or black walnut.[12]

Illness and sorrow came to this home, however, as it did to less impressive ones. Henry Ward Beecher spent hour after hour sitting by the bedside of the Wilson's six-year-old daughter who was mortally ill. In an attempt to amuse and cheer the child Beecher "would hold her hand, tell her pretty stories, pet her, talking in a way that would bring a smile to the child's face and comfort to [a] mother's heart. At the close of the last afternoon," recalled a sister, "when he arose and started to leave the room, he paused at the foot of the bed and after looking into the sweet face of the little one, turned and said to mother, 'Mrs. Wilson, she has the most beautiful eyes I have ever seen in any human head. It is the gazelle eye, the asking eye.' " The girl died early next morning, and the parents asked Beecher to conduct the funeral service. Standing beside the casket and holding his worn pocket Testament, Beecher spoke of the little girl and tried to comfort those who grieved her passing.[13]

Washington Street was busy with local traffic and with travelers passing through. A constant stream of individuals and families traveling westward to new lives moved along it. Some walked with all their worldly goods in their arms and on their backs, others pushed carts containing their possessions and maybe a child or two, small families might ride in relative comfort on a wagon pulled by one or two horses, and the wealthier emigrants had "road-wagons" pulled by fine horses. Always could be heard the tinkling of bells tied to the necks of animals, the shouts and cries of travelers calling to one another or to straying animals, and the creaks of the carts and wagons which were too often overloaded with goods and people.

The day's event which Beecher looked forward to was the arrival of the mail coach. When the sound of the bugle announcing its approach was heard, the postmaster would hurry out with the bag of

12. Scott, "Local Woman Tells of Early Indianapolis and of Mr. McGuffy's [sic] 'Select School' for Young Ladies in Ky.," pp. 1–4, In.

13. *Ibid.*, p. 5; "The Anecdotal Side of Mr. Beecher," *Ladies Home Journal*, March, 1900, p. 3.

mail ready to be taken away and to await the sack intended for Indianapolis. These mail coaches were driven by men chosen for their strength, skill, and daring; the coaches were drawn by teams of four horses and on extraordinary occasions relays of additional horses would be provided at shorter intervals to speed the passage of the bulky vehicles. The mail coach did not linger, and small boys were warned to stay out of its way. It was the single most important link with the rest of the world in a city to which a railroad had not yet penetrated.

The aristocrat of the National Road, however, was the stagecoach designed primarily for passenger service. Usually kept freshly painted, it was drawn by four matched horses which were harnessed luxuriously. The stagecoach was the most comfortable means of traveling for those who had to make a long journey. It, too, had its arrival in a town or city announced by a bugle flourish. For this elegance and attention its passengers paid an average rate of five cents a mile and could expect to cover eight miles an hour in good weather. While on many routes a coach would stop for the night after traveling sixty miles, it was customary for those coaches passing through Indianapolis on the National Road to go one hundred fifty miles every twenty-four hours with no overnight stop.[14]

It was in such a stagecoach that Martin Van Buren entered Indianapolis on June 11, 1842, while touring the West. Staying at the Palmer House, Van Buren was visited by leading citizens of Indianapolis and invited to be guest of honor at a banquet. The prospect of seeing an ex-President of the United States proved alluring to Democrats and Whigs alike, and the hall was crowded with people eager to see Van Buren. Toward the end of the dinner waiters passed plates upon which those present put money for their meals. Van Buren's demeanor and words did much to dispel the hostility toward him engendered by the recent political campaign.[15]

When it became known that Van Buren would attend church services at the Methodist chapel and at the Second Presbyterian

---

14. Burns, *The National Road in Indiana*, pp. 227–29; W. Swift Wright, *Pastime Sketches* ([Logansport, Ind.], 1907), p. 31.

15. Ruggles, *The Story of the McGuffeys*, p. 77; Holloway, *Indianapolis*, p. 74; Johnson, *A Home in the Woods, Oliver Johnson's Reminiscences of Early Marion County*, pp. 227–28.

Church, men scurried to tell the respective pastors. Told of Van Buren's intention, Beecher responded, "He is certainly welcome. There is plenty of room there [Second Presbyterian Church]."

"We thought, possibly, you might like to know it as it might make some difference," one of the informants said.

"Oh, no," replied Beecher, "no difference. I should preach to him just as I would to any other sinner."[16]

Henry Ward Beecher had had his first glimpse of Martin Van Buren years earlier when both were aboard a train on the route between Albany and Schenectady. They were seated in the same car, and Beecher could not help overhearing the conversation of strangers who were discussing means of securing the election of one of them to the Presidency. He learned later that this fellow passenger had been Martin Van Buren.[17] The ex-President did attend service at the Second Presbyterian Church. Later Beecher was laughingly told, "Perhaps you would like to hear what the Ex-President had to say about your sermon. He said he thought your trousers didn't set too well!"[18]

The remark about the fit of Beecher's trousers may not have been kind, but it was apt. Even allowing for the minister's perennial straitened circumstances his dress was seldom in keeping with his station. It was his habit to rise early, dress rapidly, and sit down immediately at his writing table where he would work until called for breakfast. Often he donned garments which he had discarded in a heap the night before. He detested wearing gloves and did so only to protect his hands from severe cold. He was not observed to wear a dress coat during his residence in Indianapolis and may not have owned one. The knees of his trousers might be stained and soiled during the gardening season. Perhaps his most noticeable departure from the correct contemporary dress for a clergyman was his habit of wearing a soft felt hat or, in hot weather, a straw hat. Beecher could, and did, appear meticulously groomed for special occasions; but such occasions were very few.

16. Derby, *Fifty Years Among Authors, Books and Publishers*, p. 467.
17. Cincinnati *Commercial*, clipping, n.d., OFH; HWB, *Eyes and Ears*, p. 96; Brown, "History of Indianapolis," in *Logan's Indianapolis Directory*, 1868, p. 43.
18. Derby, *Fifty Years Among Authors, Books and Publishers*, p. 467.

His behavior did not contribute to his appearance or the well-being of his clothes. At twenty-eight years of age Henry Ward Beecher still had much of the unrestrained adolescent in his personality. Near the Second Presbyterian Church was a board fence which enclosed the Governor's Circle, and people tied their horses to it when attending service or on business. Usually keyed up after preaching, Beecher quite frequently would challenge Charles or other young men to jump the fence with him as a test of comparative fitness. Sometimes the minister cleared the fence, and sometimes he missed. On the latter occasions Eunice would have extra mending, and Beecher's clothing would show evidence of his athletic shortcomings.[19]

Henry Ward Beecher's small house in Indianapolis was packed to overflowing in the summer of 1842, with his family, a boarder, the artist Thomas W. Whittredge, and relatives. Eunice's cousin Julia Bullard came for a visit and Henry's half brother, Tom, was spending the summer in Indianapolis before returning in the fall to Illinois College for his senior year. Henry and Tom's father, Lyman Beecher, came to stay a few days with his children before proceeding with the former to attend the inauguration of Charles White as president of Wabash College. Lyman Beecher was pleased with the progress made by his sons, especially Henry's, in Indianapolis. "Meeting with children," he wrote, "[is] a great Happiness never perhaps greater—Henrys sweep . . . as a preacher & in revivals . . . in this place—& since among his own people has afforded me great satisfaction."[20] Charles was living near Henry, and their father thought the latter's proximity and influence were having a good effect upon the younger brother. He saw signs that Charles's spiritual state was better than it had been for some time, and he had hopes his spiritual doubts might eventually be resolved. The family would continue to pray, though, for Charles.[21]

19. Knox, *Life and Work of Henry Ward Beecher*, p. 470; Stowe, *Saints, Sinners and Beechers*, p. 270; Mrs. Beecher, "Mr. Beecher as I Knew Him," *Ladies Home Journal*, July, 1892, p. 4; New York *Times*, June 5, 1882.

20. Lyman Beecher to Lydia Jackson Beecher, Terre Haute, Indiana, July 23, 1842, CtHS-D.

21. *The Second Presbyterian Church of Indianapolis. One Hundred Years, 1838–1938*, pp. 231–33; Charles Beecher (ed.), *Autobiography, Correspondence, Etc., of Lyman Beecher, D.D.*, II, 461–68.

Tom Beecher seemed also to be benefiting from the presence of Henry. The youth had for many months been undergoing that period of religious questioning which afflicted the Beecher offspring in youth. Though he was intended for the ministry as were all his brothers, Tom had serious qualms as to his fitness for the vocation. In the preceding January he had written a disturbing letter to Lyman Beecher in which he suggested as an alternative that he might enter West Point. Since coming to Indianapolis, however, Tom had been caught up in the activities and work at Henry's church and seemed more at ease in his mind about religion. The lad had a high regard for Henry and wrote, "of all my brothers . . . I think I like Henry best. He is the most like father of all his sons—& as a speaker & writer far surpasses any divine I have ever heard." He was already planning to return to spend the following summer with Henry and Eunice in Indianapolis.[22] A still younger half brother, James Beecher, remained at home in Walnut Hills, and Lyman Beecher decided that the boy should also make a long visit to Indianapolis for exposure to Henry's faith and optimism.[23]

Lyman Beecher and Henry Ward Beecher left for the ceremonies at Crawfordsville after an early dinner on Monday, July 18. It would take them approximately sixteen hours of travel, and they broke their journey by an overnight stop at Mount Meridian, which Henry Ward Beecher described as a "small, poverty-stricken little town . . . [with] shackly houses, huts and hovels, pale faces and ragged children." Accustomed to such settlements in central Indiana in which ignorance and shiftlessness too often seemed to be the predominant characteristics of the inhabitants, he was surprised to discover at the rear of the village's most imposing tavern a "well standing in the middle of a very beautiful little flower garden—neat beds full of flowers, cleaned walks, trimmed borders. I could hardly trust my eyes," recalled Beecher. "From the rear of the grounds I could almost throw a stone into the primeval forests . . . . Opening a rude wicket gate, I entered a spot of nearly an acre, well laid out and filled with the choicest vegetables, growing with the most vigorous health." Delighted with the garden, Beecher learned that it

---

22. Thomas K. Beecher to Isabella Beecher Hooker, Jacksonville, Illinois, October 4, 1842, CtHS-D.

23. Thomas K. Beecher to Lyman Beecher, Jacksonville, January 4, 1842, OFH; Lyman Beecher to Lydia Jackson Beecher, Terre Haute, July 23, 1842, CtHS-D.

was tended by a poor, elderly man who had created and maintained the oasis of beauty in such unpromising surroundings.[24]

The Beechers arrived in Crawfordsville about noon on Tuesday, then proceeded to the Center Presbyterian Church, N.S., where the inaugural ceremony was to take place. The event was as impressive as it could be made. All the faculty and as many of the trustees as could be accommodated sat on the platform at the front of the church. Henry Ward Beecher opened the service with a prayer which was followed by a reading of Scripture and a hymn. Tall, distinguished-looking General Tilghman A. Howard delivered the charge to the new president and invested him with the insignia of his office. Considered to be the greatest Democratic orator in Indiana, Howard with his black hair and sparkling dark eyes was listened to critically and appreciatively. The audience then was interested to hear how well White would compare with the magnetic Beecher and eloquent Howard.[25]

The listeners were not disappointed. Charles White, robed in a handsome black silk gown, spoke on "Religion as an Essential Part of All Education." His sister-in-law, Mary Carter Hovey, praised his speech, and among those agreeing with her evaluation was Lyman Beecher who paid White the compliment of calling him the "Dwight of the West."[26] The elder Beecher thought that White's address exhibited "Talent tact & Scholarship in a high degree. I had no conception," he wrote, "that there was such a man East to be out West. I rejoiced in him—& his prospective influence."[27]

The commencement exercises began at four o'clock on Wednesday afternoon. Lyman Beecher delivered the principal address, but neither he nor his hearers were pleased by his discourse attacking

24. "Indianapolis in 1843– A Henry Ward Beecher Letter," *Indiana Magazine of History*, III, 191.

25. Osborne and Gronert, *Wabash College, The First Hundred Years, 1832–1932*, pp. 57, 86; Lyman Beecher to Lydia Jackson Beecher, Terre Haute, July 23, 1842, CtHS-D; Taylor, *Biographical Sketches and Review of the Bench and Bar of Indiana*, pp. 64–65.

26. Timothy Dwight (1752–1817), a renowned clergyman and educator in Connecticut. Mary Carter Hovey to Emily Carter Foord, Crawfordsville, September 1, 1842, Hovey Letters #4, InCW; Osborne and Gronert, *Wabash College, The First Hundred Years, 1832–1932*, p. 57.

27. Lyman Beecher to Lydia Jackson Beecher, Terre Haute, July 23, 1842, CtHS-D.

Catholics in the United States. Suffering indigestion probably caused by consuming too much coffee and green tea, Beecher felt wretched when he began to speak. He wrote to his wife that he had to content himself with making a "pretty Strong impression" on the audience, but he was too optimistic. Samuel Merrill dismissed it as being an anti-Catholic speech, and Mrs. Hovey mentioned it briefly in a noncommittal fashion while praising other speeches at length.[28]

Entertainment of the important guests fell mainly on the shoulders of the sisters, Martha Carter White and Mary Carter Hovey. The former gave dinner parties on Monday and Tuesday evenings and following the commencement on Wednesday the Hoveys gave a dinner party for the prominent guests in their small frame house adjacent to the campus while Mrs. White finished preparations for the culminating event, the President's Levee, which took place later that evening at the White residence. The levee was an ambitious undertaking for nearly two hundred guests were expected. Fortunately, the weather was pleasant, and the guests mingled on the piazza and lawn as well as in the small parlor of the president's house. Mrs. Hovey wrote later to another sister that the "entertainments [were] good and abundant."[29]

The chief diversion of the evening party was an exchange between Henry Ward Beecher and Edward A. Hannegan, lawyer and Democratic state representative and later congressman and United States Senator, whose home was in Covington. The short, blue-eyed Hannegan was "ardent, impulsive and undaunted, thinking, acting and speaking with the utmost freedom."[30] The preacher and the politician were the acknowledged stars of the evening, and they drew others to listen as their conversation gained momentum. "The two seemed . . . to have exchanged places," wrote an observer. "The preacher's . . . wit

28. *Ibid.*; Samuel Merrill to David Merrill, Indianapolis, August 1, 1842, Samuel Merrill Papers, InHi; Mary Carter Hovey to Emily Carter Foord, Crawfordsville, September 1, 1842, Hovey Letters #4, InCW.

29. Mary Carter Hovey to Emily Carter Foord, Crawfordsville, September 1, 1842, Hovey Letters #4, InCW.

30. Taylor, *Biographical Sketches and Review of the Bench and Bar of Indiana*, p. 66; *History of the United States and State of Indiana* (Chicago: Union Publishing Co., 1896), pp. 254–55.

fell swift and thick . . . which the politician in a voice that was melody itself [responded in a fascinating manner]. . . . These two . . . were thoroughly conscious that their display of intellectual pyrotechnics were brilliant and all-satisfying."[31]

Mrs. White was dismayed. While she wanted her guests to enjoy themselves, she was worried that the coffee which was ready to serve might be ruined by further delay. Preparing good coffee in sufficient quantity to serve two hundred people with the equipment available to her had taken all her ingenuity. She knew she could not do it again that evening. Distressed and "worried into a fever of impatience," Mrs. White, "laid her hands on the preacher's shoulder [so] that he ceased talking. 'Mr. Beecher, you and Mr. Hannegan must be weary after so much argument and my coffee is spoiling,' she said. It was a drawn battle and Hannegan arose and taking the preacher's hand, said: 'Well, Brother Beecher, you certainly promise to achieve fame as a minister of the gospel, but if you had been bred to politics, you would have captured the country.' 'And you, Brother Hannegan,' replied the preacher, 'with the grace of God implanted in your heart, and a pulpit at your command, would have captured more souls for Christ than ever I hope to be my lot.' "[32]

The Beechers left Crawfordsville the next morning en route for Rockville where Lyman Beecher preached Thursday evening. They stayed two nights at the home of General Tilghman A. Howard. The senior Beecher and Howard enjoyed talking with each other so much that it was arranged they should sleep in the same room so they could converse until drowsiness overcame them. Lyman Beecher thought Howard was a "sensible courteous man who has fallen into wrong company [the Democratic party]—& can feel the difference when he falls into the right Sort."[33]

From Rockville the Beechers traveled to Terre Haute. They arrived at noon on Friday, July 22, and spent a lazy afternoon reading

---

31. Mrs. Mason B. Thomas to Mrs. Kate M. Rabb, Crawfordsville, n.d., published in New York *Herald*, clipping, n.d., In.

32. *Ibid.*

33. Lyman Beecher to Lydia Jackson Beecher, Terre Haute, July 23, 1842, CtHS-D.

newspapers, talking, and sleeping. Lyman Beecher still felt unwell, and, as he wrote to his wife, he welcomed the opportunity to rest and to give a pill he had taken a chance to work.[34]

The Beechers were guests of Lucius H. Scott in the Vigo County seat. Scott had heard Lyman Beecher preach at Rockville and knew Henry from the latter's stay during the revival in Terre Haute. He liked the Beechers and was proud to entertain them.

Henry Ward Beecher preached to a large congregation at Jewett's church that evening, and his father was recovered enough to take the pulpit at the Saturday night service and again on Sunday morning. The younger Beecher then preached the afternoon and evening services. Whenever possible the men called attention to the needs of Wabash College. Lyman Beecher urged that measures be taken to arouse people to the plight of the struggling institution. To their host, he said that if it became necessary Henry would have to travel in behalf of the school. Neither Lyman Beecher nor Scott seemed to think it presumptuous that the former should so cavalierly offer his son's services. Scott believed that Henry would be more successful in such an enterprise than any other man as he was "popular & energetic & has the welfare of the institution much at heart."[35] The Beechers resumed their return journey to Indianapolis early the next morning.

An acquaintance of Henry Ward Beecher had taken up residence in Indianapolis some months earlier. Thomas Worthington Whittredge, scion of a prominent Ohio family, met Beecher who was six years his senior when the latter was a student at Lane. Whittredge achieved indifferent success as a painter of portraits and landscapes, and became interested in the Daguerre process. He decided to open a studio in Indianapolis where he thought he would encounter less competition than in Cincinnati. Arriving in the Hoosier capital with his equipment, he set up his business in a building between Illinois and Meridian streets on the south side of Washington Street. Customers were few, and Whittredge returned to painting to fill his time. The young bachelor who came from a good family, had an interesting profession, and could play the guitar with proficiency, enjoyed considerable popularity

34. *Ibid.*
35. L. H. Scott to Charles Hovey, Terre Haute, July 25, 1842, Hovey Letters #3, InCW.

in Indianapolis. He attended the Second Presbyterian Church and had been converted during the revival the past winter. Time passed agreeably, if not particularly profitably, for him.

Then the young man became ill. Hearing that Whittredge was very sick in his room at the Palmer House, Beecher procured a carriage and drove to the hotel where he got the painter and took him home to be nursed back to health. Whittredge remained in the Beecher home as a nonpaying guest for almost a year. Having no money and feeling a strong sense of gratitude and obligation to the Beechers, Whittredge painted their portraits. He could have found no better way to repay Beecher who was deeply interested in painting and who had a sentimental reason for wanting likenesses of his family. No picture existed of Beecher's mother to his knowledge, and this was a sorrow to him all his life. "My mother died when I was but a small child, and I do not remember to have ever seen her face. And as there was no pencil that could afford to limn her, I have never seen a likeness of her. Would to God that I could see some picture of my mother!"[36] In addition to the Beecher portraits Whittredge painted Tilghman A. Howard and some members of the legislature, but his commissions and his daguerreotype studio did not bring enough income to support him, and in May, 1843, after a sale of some paintings at Wiley's Auction Room he returned to Cincinnati.[37] He later studied in Europe and lived in the East, becoming one of the nation's leading landscape painters. Unfortunately the Beecher portraits have not been located.

While Beecher was in Madison attending Synod and later leading a revival, Mary Yandes married John Wheeler at her parents' home on September 8, 1842. Ordinarily Beecher might have expected to perform the ceremony, but the clergyman's disapproval of Wheeler, a Methodist, was known. Beecher's absence at the time of the wedding saved them all a certain amount of embarrassment.[38]

---

36. John R. Howard (ed.), *Patriotic Addresses in America and England, From 1850 to 1885*, p. 395.

37. Donald R. MacKenzie, "Early Ohio Painters: Cincinnati, 1830–1850," *Ohio History*, LXXIII (Spring, 1964), 112–14; Burnet, *Art and Artists of Indiana*, pp. 63–64, 68–69; Peat, *Pioneer Painters of Indiana*, pp. 159–60.

38. Julia D. Merrill to Samuel Merrill, Indianapolis, September 12, 1842, Samuel Merrill Papers, InHi; Robinson *et al.* (comps.), *Daniel Yandes and His Family*, pp. 1–10.

The Beechers' lives had fallen into a routine. Henry would rise early and work at his writing table until called for breakfast. Then depending upon the season he would work in his garden or return to his papers for two or three hours. The rest of the morning was devoted to making calls, attending to church business, or conducting a service. The noon meal might be eaten at home or, more rarely, he would dine at a friend's house. If he ate at home he would nap for an hour afterwards. More calling, meetings, and the like would take up the rest of the afternoon. His evening meal would be light or consist only of a cup or two of coffee if he were supposed to speak that night. After the evening's work was over Beecher would eat a simple supper and read in bed until he felt ready to sleep.

Eunice's life was limited almost entirely to domestic chores and obligations. Arising before her husband she lit the fires, prepared breakfast for all in the house, and tried to have the heavy work of washing, ironing, and housecleaning completed by mid-morning. For a short time she and her children might work with Henry in the garden. She enjoyed this, for it was one of the few times when she had her husband to herself. They were free to talk of matters of interest or concern to them alone until time for Eunice to return to the house to prepare the noon meal. She usually sewed in the afternoon, for most of the family's clothing was made by her hand. Only infrequently did Eunice pay visits or attend church services. A constant flow of visiting clergymen, acquaintances, and relatives passed through her sitting room, however, and she was expected to provide them meals and possibly a place to sleep. None could be turned away. After the evening meal had been prepared and served and the dishes washed, Eunice was free to do more sewing or to write letters. Along with her housework and other duties she had the constant care of small children, nursing of the ill, and the vexations of her own pregnancies to sap her energy. Henry and "Mother," as he called his wife, were usually in bed by ten o'clock.[39]

Work was made easier when they were able to employ a servant or

39. Mrs. Beecher, "Mr. Beecher as I Knew Him," *Ladies Home Journal*, December, 1891, p. 11; Stowe, "Sketches and Recollections of Dr. Lyman Beecher," *Congregational Quarterly*, VI, 234; Mrs. Henry Ward Beecher, Notes, n.d., CtY; Knox, *Life and Work of Henry Ward Beecher*, pp. 436–40; [Mrs. Beecher], *From Dawn to Daylight*, pp. 288–91.

two. Beecher engaged a man named Volz to assist him part-time in the garden. In periods of relative affluence or stress they had the help of Jim and Letitia, a Negro couple. Jim would accompany Beecher on his trips to distant revivals or church meetings. The two men would ride in a wagon along with their gear. The servant would do the driving leaving Beecher free to concentrate on his work. In Indianapolis Jim assisted with the livestock and the garden. When he was working for the Beechers, he did the milking; otherwise Beecher or Eunice did it. Letitia assisted Eunice with the housework and child care. It was her special responsibility to prepare Beecher's coffee on those evenings when he spoke in Indianapolis, and she took great pride in the quality of the beverage. The couple worked off and on for the Beechers until 1845.[40]

Henry Ward Beecher and his wife were included as a matter of course in the parties and gatherings which formed the social life of the members of the Second Presbyterian Church. Many of these took place during the day rather than at night because of the problems of lighting and transportation once darkness fell. A favorite social custom was for one family to invite other families to spend the day. Guests would begin to arrive in the late morning, and they would visit with each other until time for dinner while the children played and young couples courted. Dinner was served in the early afternoon and was a lavish meal which was consumed leisurely. Following the meal there would be more conversation and games.

Families would begin to leave in time to do the evening chores at home. After one such party at the Merrill home, however, this was not practicable. Mrs. Ketcham recalled, "The rain set in in torrents, till it was considered dangerous to go home. However, some did, though they said the little log bridge across Pogues-run rocked, and all that part was flooded. How they [her parents] accommodated those who stayed all night, I cannot remember. We had games and fun all day, but as the evening shades gathered the fun thickened."[41] Even staid John L. Ketcham joined in the merriment. Ketcham and Beecher treated the party

40. HWB met Jim and Letitia in Topeka, Kansas, in 1878. See James B. Pond, "Henry Ward Beecher" [address delivered before the Long Island Historical Society, March 8, 1897 in Long Island Historical Society Library] and Pond, *Eccentricities of Genius*, pp. 48–51; [Mrs. Beecher], *From Dawn to Daylight*, pp. 184–85; HWB, Misc. Papers, n.d., CtY.
41. "Reminiscences of Jane Merrill Ketcham," p. 71, In.

to "Dumb Orator." Ketcham did the reciting, and Beecher made faces and gestures. Later in the evening Henry and Eunice taught such games as "Hunting the Key Hole" and "Blow Out the Candle as the Jones Family Did." Their efforts were appreciated, particularly Eunice's, for it was not often she appeared to such good advantage in Indianapolis. "Mrs. B[eecher] was almost as good as his [HWB]. What actors they would have made," wrote Mrs. Ketcham. "The next gathering was at Mr. Bates; and so they went round; all delightful."[42]

Henry Clay stopped in Indianapolis on October 5, 1842, while on a tour of the states north of the Ohio River. The slender, gray-eyed former Senator was assessing his political strength and attempting to gain support as a potential candidate in the next presidential election. When a student at Amherst College Beecher had met Clay for he had been selected to present the politician with a Bible when he visited the school. More people welcomed Clay to Indianapolis than had appeared to greet Van Buren. An estimated thirty thousand saw or participated in a parade in his honor which contained military companies, fire companies, representatives of the various trades and professions, and bands from all over the state. Flanked by John J. Crittenden, Thomas Metcalfe, and Joseph L. White, the honored guest was escorted to ex-Governor Noah Noble's home east of Indianapolis where a giant barbecue was to be held on the grounds of the estate. While the aroma of barbecued meat hovered in the air, thousands of people milled around or stood to listen to Clay speak for about an hour. He appeared tired and bored, and his speech was "partisan, and a little egotistical."[43] Beecher thought Clay to be a dull fellow who "was not wound up, and had nobody to stick a pin in him."[44] As if that were not bad enough some of the food was ill-prepared. The next day's activities included a review of the military companies, another parade, and fireworks after dark. Clay then departed for Richmond, Indiana, where the Yearly Meeting of Friends was in session.[45]

On Sunday, October 16, the Beecher's son, Henry Barton Beecher,

42. "Reminiscences of Jane Merrill Ketcham," p. 71, In.
43. Holloway, *Indianapolis*, p. 75; Wallace, *An Autobiography*, I, 95–96.
44. Knox, *Life and Work of Henry Ward Beecher*, p. 210.
45. Holloway, *Indianapolis*, p. 75; Dunn, *Indiana and Indianans*, I, 513; Crocker, *Henry Ward Beecher's Speaking Art*, p. 48.

and six other children were baptized at the Second Presbyterian Church and Communion was celebrated. So important was the occasion that the Reverend Joseph Wilson made the long trip from Lafayette to deliver the sermon.[46]

Beecher was asked to officiate at the wedding of Thomas L. Sullivan to Laetitia Smith. It was a union of the offspring of two Hoosier giants, Judge Jeremiah Sullivan of Madison and United States Senator Oliver Hampton Smith. The senior Sullivan was born at Harrisonburg, Virginia, and was the son of an Irish Catholic. Smith was born near Trenton, New Jersey, and was of Quaker descent. The fathers were as disparate in temperament as were their backgrounds. Sullivan was a quiet man with gentle manners who preferred to express himself by means of satirical and humorous articles which he contributed to newspapers. Smith was forceful, fluent, and could be extremely sarcastic. The Smith family were members of the Second Presbyterian Church in Indianapolis.[47]

Though Smith was away from Indianapolis a great deal, he took a real interest in the affairs and services of the church. Thinking to honor the shaggy-browed Senator who was present at an evening service, Beecher asked him to lead the congregation in prayer. "[It] sounded more like an argument before a jury than a prayer," recalled John Bradshaw. "He [Smith] warmed up and continued it for almost half an hour; his argumentative powers got the better of him. The next day Beecher and Smith met on the street. Mr. Smith said: 'Mr. Beecher, never ask me to pray again.' 'No,' said Beecher, 'I don't think I ever will.' "[48]

Henry Ward Beecher no longer suffered from the self-doubt that had plagued his earliest years in the ministry. Continued observation of the life around him was leading him to believe that a man could control his own destiny. Something of this philosophy was implicit in a sermon

46. Records of the Second Presbyterian Church, InISPC.

47. Indianapolis *Indiana Journal*, November 23, 1842; Taylor, *Biographical Sketches and Review of the Bench and Bar of Indiana*, pp. 39–40, 63, 152–53; William W. Woollen, *Reminiscences of the Marion County Bar* (Indiana Historical Society Publications, VII, No. 3, Indianapolis, 1919), pp. 190–91.

48. John Bradshaw, Reminiscences, May 25, 1902, clipping in George S. Cottman's Indiana Scrapbook Collection, VIII, 44, In; *History of the United States and the State of Indiana*, pp. 251–52.

which he preached at the Second Presbyterian Church on Christmas morning, 1842. Beecher developed the theme that those who refused to heed and follow the law of God in their daily lives were self-condemned. He indicated that most people would enter that state of happiness or unhappiness which they had long been preparing for themselves through their thoughts and actions. Typically, he ended the sermon by admonishing those present to listen and to reform.[49]

49. HWB, Sermons, December 25, 1842, CtY.

XII

A Prayer for Present Help

THE NEW YEAR, 1843, OPENED WITH THE BEECHERS COMFORTABLY following their familiar schedule. They received word in February about the disposition of the estate of Eunice's father, Artemas Bullard, who had died as the result of a fall in his barn on May 6, 1842. His son-in-law, Ira M. Barton was his executor; and he wrote that the Beechers could expect to receive Eunice's share, approximately $400, in April if the rest of the heirs were satisfied with his arrangements. Eunice was to discuss the settlement carefully with her husband; in the meantime Barton would communicate with the other children.[1]

Eunice hoped that her mother would come to Indianapolis for a visit but Barton wrote that the excitement and fatigue of such a journey would be more than she could endure. Not liking to refuse Eunice, her mother mentioned the possibility of making the trip when a railroad reached Indianapolis.[2]

Following the successful revival in Lafayette in March, Beecher had returned to lead one at the Second Presbyterian Church which had gratifying results. Giving particular happiness to Beecher was the conversion of Charles Beecher. To their father he wrote,

1. Frost (comp.), *Ancestors of Henry Ward Beecher and His Wife Eunice White Bullard*, p. 15; Ira M. Barton to HWB and Mrs. Beecher, Worcester, Mass., February 15, 1843, CtY.

2. Ira M. Barton to HWB and Mrs. Beecher, Worcester, Mass., February 15, 1843, CtY.

171

God has been pleased to give. . . joy—Charles has been very deeply affected—has most heartily dedicated himself to *Christ* and tho' as yet he experiences no such *fulness* of intense personal love to Christ, or he seeks for his *Will* [he] is settled for Christ. . . . I thought it would be balm to your feelings to hear me say—what I never could say before—that on the whole, *I feel that Charles is safe.*[3]

The letter was brought to Lyman Beecher in his study where the clergyman was speaking to a student, and Beecher read it with growing emotion. Almost choking under the intensity of his excitement, he exclaimed, "His [Charles's] mother has been long in heaven, but she bound cords about her child's heart before she left which have drawn him back. He has never been able to break them."[4] For over a decade Lyman Beecher had struggled to remove Charles's doubt and to bring him to that degree of faith necessary for a true Christian. It was a great moment in his life when he learned that this son of his cherished Roxana's was saved.

The revival continued. Beecher was pleased, of course, when acquaintances and strangers heeded his call; but he was extremely elated at the number of relatives and friends who were numbered among the converts. After Charles came James, a younger half brother who was living in Indianapolis where he had been sent to benefit from Henry's influence. Almost as gratifying to Beecher was the conversion of the painter, Whittredge, who, as mentioned earlier, was living with the Beecher family. Whittredge possessed an easy-going disposition, and he was not inclined to be troubled by doubts. His experience was happy and joy-filled.[5]

Beecher had postponed a planned trip to Walnut Hills to see his father in order to conduct the revivals in Lafayette and Indianapolis. Lyman Beecher had been ill but since recovered, and it worried Henry that he had been unable to attend his father. "Nothing in my situation is so painful to me," he wrote, "as that I cannot come to you oftener. . . . Everyday, & more & more I look. . . to our meeting in Heaven. On earth it hardly seems possible, that we can be much together." That

3. HWB to Lyman Beecher, Indianapolis, March 18, 1843, MCR.

4. Charles Beecher (ed.), *Autobiography, Correspondence, Etc., of Lyman Beecher, D.D.,* II, 572.

5. HWB to Lyman Beecher, Indianapolis, March 18, 1843, MCR; List of Members, Records of the Second Presbyterian Church, InISPC.

Henry shared much of his father's philosophy about their mission in the West may be observed in his concluding statement, "Dear Father, may God strengthen you again to manifold labors, for not to labor is to die, without the blessings of litteral [*sic*] death. From the battlefield, I say farewell—hoping soon to see you face to face."[6]

Henry Ward Beecher presided at a meeting of Session on April 15, 1843, at which the perennial question was raised of the status of a member who had been excommunicated, but now wanted to return to the fellowship of the church. There was heated discussion as to whether or not the man should be reinstated. It was decided to give him another opportunity, however, and he was received by examination. That all members of the Session were not favorable to this action may be inferred from a brief note on the record stating that "some of Session, at least, were strongly attached" to him.[7] He was not to be considered a member in good standing but was placed temporarily under care of the Session.

Busy with his church and his garden the days passed uneventfully for Beecher. As the first of his vegetables ripened he began making the early morning trip to the market with them. Sometimes Hatty accompanied him. At five years of age she was of real assistance in the Beecher household and was proficient enough as a seamstress to do her share of the plain sewing.[8]

There was time to visit friends, and the number of invitations received by the Beechers increased as lawyers from all over the state began to arrive in Indianapolis for the term of the Supreme Court. The assembling of these men sparked a round of social events as residents of the city entertained acquaintances and political allies. On one such occasion were brought together "the Beechers, the Supreme Judges, strangers and all who were desirable it seemed to me," recalled Mrs. Ketcham. "Sperm candles adorned the parlors and hall; tallow ones must answer in the dining room. A warm . . . night, they all felt the heat, and one tallow candle began to bend towards the other. Mr.

6. HWB to Lyman Beecher, Indianapolis, March 18, 1843, MCR.
7. Records of the Second Presbyterian Church, pp. 47–48, 80, InISPC.
8. Mrs. Beecher, "Mr. Beecher as I Knew Him," *Ladies Home Journal*, January, 1892, p. 5; Annie B. Scoville, "Mrs. Harriet Beecher Scoville," *Plymouth Chimes* (1901), p. 56, CtY.

Beecher said to his neighbor, 'Don't you think that candle is about to succeed in his addresses?' "[9] Always observant of his surroundings and so aware of nuances that even a candle could imaginatively capture his attention, Beecher was sensitive to the opinions and actions of others. This would make it difficult for him to carry through his next major effort. He planned to preach an antislavery sermon from the pulpit of the Second Presbyterian Church.

Beecher was reluctant to deliver such a sermon in Indianapolis. Although Indiana's Constitution prohibited the introduction of slaves into the state there was strong proslavery sentiment present among an influential, aggressive, and vocal segment of the population. Acts of violence directed against Negroes or those suspected of having abolitionist views occurred frequently enough in the capital city to give any clergyman pause before he preached a sermon which might bring retribution upon himself and his family, and Beecher was cognizant of this fact. "It grew in me," stated the minister, "that [slavery] was a subject that ought to be preached upon; but I knew that just as sure as I preached an abolition sermon they would blow me up sky high, and my usefulness . . . would be gone."[10] Yet he was compelled morally by the action of the General Assembly, N.S., and by his Presbytery and Synod to speak out publicly against slavery. To hesitate longer would mark him as a coward among his fellow clergymen in the state who were avowed antislavery men. Three years earlier the Presbytery of Indianapolis had urged that its clergy give at least one such sermon each year, but Beecher had not yet complied. The *Indiana Democrat* had referred twice to the Presbytery's action, so that it was known among the members of Beecher's church. Beecher had given a sermon in 1842 on the political duties of Christians, but he sidestepped discussing the antislavery issue in depth.[11]

The hazards of taking such a stand against slavery or being suspected of such a position had been brought sharply home to him in the experiences of friends, family, and himself. A classmate at Lane Theo-

9. "Reminiscences of Jane Merrill Ketcham," pp. 75–76, In; Taylor, *Biographical Sketches and Review of the Bench and Bar of Indiana*, pp. 62, 152.

10. HWB, *Yale Lectures on Preaching*, I, 166–67.

11. Indianapolis *Indiana Democrat*, November 28, 1840 and March 5, 1841; HWB, Sermons, August [?], 1842, CtY; HWB, *Yale Lectures on Preaching*, I, 166–67.

logical Seminary named Amos Dresser had been whipped after a vigilante trial on July 18, 1835, in Nashville, Tennessee, for allegedly distributing abolitionist literature while selling Bibles in the South during vacation.[12] Beecher himself had been involved in the aftermath of a Cincinnati riot in 1836 which took place when infuriated pro-slavery advocates attacked and destroyed the printing press of *The Philanthropist*, an antislavery newspaper edited by James G. Birney. Beecher described his participation

> when the mob rose in Cincinnati and destroyed. . . [the newspaper], and once again the riotous spirit foamed over and they threatened to shoot down the colored people in Cincinnati, and had got to that point that the mayor called for special policemen to protect the city and the negro quarters, I was sworn in as a special policeman, and patrolled the streets for two nights armed to the teeth to defend the negroes.[13]

The Beecher family had feared for the safety of Lane Theological Seminary which rumor hailed as a place where runaway slaves were hidden. The family and faculty were grateful for the distance separating Walnut Hills from Cincinnati during the disturbance.[14]

Sometime in 1839 Calvin E. Stowe, who was thought by Lane students to be "a pretty good Abolitionist," and a man identified only as a brother-in-law of his made a harried journey of great personal risk in the dark of night to remove a servant employed in the Stowe household who, though technically free, was thought to be in danger of being kidnapped by agents of her former owner. The two men took the girl to a station of the Underground Railroad operated by a farmer named John Van Zandt where she would presumably be safer than she was feared to be in Walnut Hills. The girl was never captured.[15]

12. Annie B. Scoville, Notes, n.d., CtY; *The Narrative of Amos Dresser* (New York: Published by the American Anti-Slavery Society, 1836), pp. 5–15; W. Sherman Savage, *The Controversy Over the Distribution of Abolition Literature 1830–1860* (New York: Negro Universities Press, 1968), p. 34.

13. Knox, *Life and Work of Henry Ward Beecher*, p. 211.

14. Harlow, *The Serene Cincinnatians*, pp. 212–13.

15. Harriet Beecher Stowe, *The Key to Uncle Tom's Cabin* (London, n.d.), pp. 35–36. The identity of the Beecher who assisted Stowe is unknown. It may have been HWB, as Crow maintains, but it seems unlikely as no corroborative evidence has been located and HWB was seldom reticent in later life about his exploits. See Martha F. Crow, *Harriet Beecher Stowe* (New York: D. Appleton & Co., 1913), pp. 205–206; Gamaliel Bailey to James G. Birney, Cincinnati, October 28, 1838, quoted in Dumond (ed.), *Letters of James Gillespie Birney, 1831–1857*, I, 474.

More recently Van Zandt, a good friend of the Beecher family, had been almost ruined financially as the result of a judgment against him for aiding and abetting the attempted escape of nine runaway slaves in April of the preceding year. John Van Zandt, a resident of Hamilton County, Ohio, was a farmer who drove regularly to the Cincinnati market. On the night of April 23, 1842, he stayed with a Mr. Moore associated with Lane Theological Seminary in Walnut Hills, and at daybreak the farmer helped the escaping slaves into his covered wagon preparatory to transporting them to the next stage of the Underground Railroad in Springboro, Ohio. Van Zandt was stopped about thirteen miles north of Cincinnati by two men seeking the party which consisted of a man, his wife, their children, a mother-in-law, and others. Two of the Negroes fled, but the rest were returned to their owner in Kentucky. For his part in the episode Van Zandt was indicted and tried before the United States Circuit Court for the District of Ohio, found guilty, and fined $1,200.[16]

These incidents made Beecher understandably wary about preaching against slavery. Since he felt he must do so, however, he chose the time with care. The Supreme Court convened on Thursday, May 25, and Indianapolis was crowded. It was the custom for many of these visitors to attend the morning service at the Second Presbyterian Church to hear the renowned preacher. These people were, for the most part, representative of the sober and thoughtful elements in the state's citizenry. They would be apt to listen objectively and with little passion.

One of them, Alfred G. Riddle, accompanied a "small party of distinguished Indianians," to attend service at Beecher's church. He left a vivid account of the preacher and of the sermon which the clergyman feared might be inflammatory. "It was a lovely May morning," recalled Riddle.

> Very soon the quite spacious church was filled, and then packed, as were the galleries. When seemingly the latest had arrived, the pulpit. . . was

16. Van Zandt refused to pay on the advice of counsel, and the case was heard by the Supreme Court of the United States during the January, 1847, term. It was the opinion of the Court that the Fugitive Slave Act (1 Statutes at Large, 302), under which the action had been brought was not repugnant to the Constitution and the decision of the lower court was upheld. See Jones *v.* Van Zandt, U.S. Supreme Court Reports, 5 Howard 215–32; J. Winston Coleman, *Slavery Times in Kentucky* (Chapel Hill: The University of North Carolina Press, 1940), pp. 213–15.

still vacant. There was a minute of waiting, when there entered a rather heavy looking young man from the country—decidedly country—of a stout clumsy figure, and carelessly dressed. He came in hastily, paused just inside, as if surprised by the crowd. . . . No usher offered to care for him, and, as I thought, he moved timidly and awkwardly up the broad aisle, casting furtive glance on either side. . . . all turned their eyes on him and must have noted, as I did, the forlorn look on his face. . . . I fancied his step grew slower and his look more hopeless as he approached the . . . pulpit. Failing a seat elsewhere, he lifted his eyes. . . rushed up the steps and sat suddenly down, with a visible sense of relief at last.

Riddle watched the clergyman and expected little from a man wearing "heavy, coarse, soiled shoes, with baggy trowsers . . . too short—most decidedly so. Surely the man's reputation was overrated. When Beecher arose with a hymnal in his hand, Riddle noticed that the preacher's face was "full, heavy and flushed." The service began with a reading from Scripture, a hymn, and a prayer. Riddle was a little amused by the "gush of fervor in the prayer, especially for present help."

Henry Ward Beecher did not attempt to preach an abolitionist sermon, for he was not an abolitionist in 1843 and he was sure such a discourse would in any event be disastrous for him in its result. Such convictions as he possessed were similar to his father's in advocating antislavery without social upheaval. Beecher began his sermon, "The New Testament View of Slavery," slowly and chose his words with care. As he started to lose himself in his sermon he relaxed. Riddle continued,

A miracle had been wrought. The *exuviae* of the country boor had vanished. A man inspired, radiant, glorified, transfigured face aflame, eyes flashing, voice reverberating, stood instead. His notes a crushed crumple, in the vise of his right hand; were shaken aloft in the intense energy of free bold action. . . . I was transported to Galilee restored, saw its rugged yet lonely aspect. . . . That great audience there was so moved. I had glimpses of an expanse of faces, moving and swaying by a common impulse about me.

Scarcely aware of the passage of time, Riddle was surprised to learn that the sermon had lasted a full two hours.[17]

Henry Ward Beecher had prepared it meticulously. His notes cover sixty-four pages and attest to his patient study, analysis, and reasoning.

17. Alfred G. Riddle, "Discovery of Henry Ward Beecher," *Magazine of Western History*, V (April, 1887), 854–57.

It is probable that Beecher embellished and altered parts of the sermon as he delivered it, according to his custom, but its substance can be clearly discerned from his notes. In essence, Beecher declared slavery to be a moral evil whose "extinction is to be effected by the gradual action of those laws by which it is regulated."[18] Since men, bond and free, were equal in the sight of God, the enlightened among mankind should recognize a moral obligation to extend personal liberty to all. He spoke at length upon the premise that "there can be no free state of society . . . unless all individuals of that society are free." Beecher concluded: "It is right; it is true; one member cannot suffer & all not suffer. By the ties of patriotism, by the bonds of philanthropy; by the noble . . . unity of Christian faith, the several parts of this nation are knit together. These wrongs are our wrong; this peace is our peace; their degradation draws us down, their prosperity gilds our lot. When, then, the land is darkened with . . . evil, we only ask the right of Christians, to aid by all the wisdom that we have, by our sympathy, by our prayers & fervent exhortations our brothers, to rid themselves of this calamity."[19]

Primed to expect criticism or even physical danger, Henry Ward Beecher waited to learn what response his sermon would produce. Nothing happened. No rowdy fellow threatened him, no insults were hurled at him or his family, and discussion was desultory. Had Beecher attacked "Masters" and vilified them as individuals or glorified and sentimentalized "Slaves" as the equals of whites the reaction might have been more pronounced. As it was, he had declared that slavery was not forbidden by Scripture and that man had only a moral obligation to oppose it. Knowing that Beecher was tardily obeying an injunction of his denomination, those who might have made difficulties were not inclined to upset themselves over his strictures to use sympathy, prayer, and speeches to eliminate the institution. Christians had been resorting to these means for decades, and slavery was still solidly entrenched in the land.

18. Riddle's account of this sermon as having been heard in 1843 and the agreement of his recollection of the topic with HWB's notes indicate that the sermon was delivered that year. HWB's notation "May, 1846" on his outline was probably added by mistake later in reference to another sermon on slavery delivered in the latter year. See HWB, Sermons, May, 1846 [sic], CtY.

19. HWB, Sermons, May, 1846 [sic], CtY.

Beecher left Indianapolis almost immediately for Illinois, and on Sunday, June 4, 1843, he delivered a sermon in Springfield. It centered upon the values of the church and the importance of personal religion. To illustrate that those who were contemptuous of piety in others were showing their own ignorance he said:

> When I hear young men railing out against women—as being weak—easily tempted—and always less than they should be—I always understand him to be the corrupt one, not those of whom he speaks. If anyone has formed such a judgement of the Sex to wh[ich] his mother—his sisters belong—it is either because his vanity has wholly outgrown his sense, or. . . most usually— because he has known nothing of any other company—but the *doubtful*, or those. . . of whom there is no doubt at all. So it is with railing at. . . personal religion.[20]

Beecher's concern with the plight of the Negro and his championing of yet another part of society held in low esteem indicates his growing awareness and disapprobation of social inequities.

He made a second trip to Illinois within the month. This time his destination was Illinois College at Jacksonville where he had accepted an invitation to address the Rhetorical Society during commencement week.[21] He stayed on for the commencement ceremony on June 28, which was held in a small grove near the campus. Nearly one thousand people assembled to listen to the speeches, hear the music, and watch Professor Julian M. Sturtevant present diplomas to the ten graduates. This privilege would ordinarily have fallen to President Edward M. Beecher, but he was in the East.[22] The weather was pleasant, and most of the audience remained for the seven hours it took to complete the exercise. After visiting leisurely with friends and relatives, Beecher and his half brother Tom, who had accompanied him from Indianapolis,

20. HWB, Sermons, June 4, 1843, CtY.
21. HWB, *Address Delivered Before the Rhetorical Society of Illinois College. June, 1843, By Rev. Henry Beecher, of Indianapolis, Ia.* (Jacksonville, Ill., 1843).
22. Edward Beecher attended the General Assembly of the Presbyterian Church (New School) which convened in the latter part of May, 1843, in Philadelphia. It is probable he also attended meetings in New York City leading to the formation of the Society for the Promotion of Collegiate and Theological Education at the West on June 30, 1843. Edward Beecher had been a leading educator in promoting the establishment of such an organization. New York *Daily Tribune*, May 29, 1843.

started home by way of Terre Haute where they would be joined by Eunice and her children who were visiting acquaintances there.[23]

Just a few miles from the outskirts of Indianapolis the family party, joking and singing as they jolted along, met Daniel Yandes. "After shaking hands with us in his long-armed way," recalled Beecher, "he said, 'I suppose you have heard the news?' 'No,' said I, 'what is it?' 'Why, your brother George has killed himself!' We were all struck so dumb we could not ask a question. We started right off, and there wasn't one word spoke in the carriage all the way home."[24] It was appalling news to the Beechers. It was almost unbearable to Henry Ward Beecher that his best loved brother would have sinfully destroyed himself. Eunice years later would remember her husband's face which was "like marble," and she would not "forget the agony I saw there" during the remainder of the trip.[25] In Indianapolis they were told that George had not committed suicide as they had inferred from Yandes' statement but had died as a result of accidentally shooting himself. To Beecher the "relief was so great that it almost took away the sting of his [George's] death."[26]

Henry learned that on July 1, 1843, his brother had discovered that robins were eating the fruit of a favorite sweet cherry and had taken out his double-barrelled, muzzle-loading shotgun, intent upon shooting them. There were no witnesses to the accident, but it was thought that he had, as was his habit, blown the "smoke out of his gun, . . . hit the trigger and the gun discharged, the whole of the contents passing through his brain."[27] Blunt as was the way the news was communicated to Henry Ward Beecher, his father heard it even more abruptly and thoughtlessly. "A friend met me at a corner of the street," wrote Lyman

23. Thomas K. Beecher to Isabella Beecher Hooker, Jacksonville, March [?], 1843, CtHS-D; Charles H. Rammelkamp, *Illinois College, A Centennial History, 1829–1929* (New Haven: Published for Illinois College by Yale University Press, 1928), p. 54; Indianapolis *Indiana State Journal*, July 5, 1843; William D. Wood, "Illinois College at the Half Century," *Journal of the Illinois State Historical Society*, XVIII, No. 1 (April, 1925), p. 214; Julian M. Sturtevant, Jr. (ed.), *An Autobiography* (New York, 1896), pp. 253–54.

24. Derby, *Fifty Years Among Authors, Books and Publishers*, pp. 451–52.

25. Mrs. Beecher, "Mr. Beecher as I Knew Him," *Ladies Home Journal*, January, 1892, p. 5.

26. Derby, *Fifty Years Among Authors, Books and Publishers*, pp. 451–52.

27. *Ibid.*; Wilson, *Crusader in Crinoline*, p. 217.

Beecher, "and said, 'Have you heard the dreadful news which has come into the city this morning?' I said, 'No.' He said, 'Your son George is dead,' and handed me the paper containing the account. The shock was like that of a blow across my breast which almost suspended respiration, and left to me only the power of articulating at intervals, 'Oh! Oh! Oh!' Tears soon came to my relief."[28]

The death of George Beecher saddened the family, but of all his brothers and sisters it probably affected Henry the most. He could not bear to speak of it, and nearly thirty years later his sister Harriet called it one of the great sorrows of his life.[29] Beecher did not write to George's widow until more than a month after the accident, for he could not bring himself to do so earlier. To her he wrote, "For your sorrow—for *your* loneliness—for your Earthly deprivation—& heart poverty—I most deeply deplore George's translation to Heaven. For the work of Christ on Earth—I more deeply lament it." Speaking of his own anguish and bewilderment, Beecher continued, "Oh What can Christ mean—how can he *afford* to take only his Servants from the battle, in the very . . . heat of conflict. But oh me—how little we know! What *is* the Church above? Who knows what Ch[r]ist is doing & what he has for his servant to do in Heaven?" In keeping with his own faith, Beecher wrote consolingly to Sarah, "I do not know of any death to a Christian."[30] The Beecher family would continue to include George's widow and son in its letters, visits, and counsels as if he lived.

Still grieving over his brother's death, Henry Ward Beecher allowed himself to be drawn into a tangled controversy between Methodists and Presbyterians. As a trustee and supporter of Wabash College, Beecher was troubled by its precarious financial position. Since the onset of the Panic of 1837 the college had remained open only through the sacrifices and hard work of its faculty and friends. In 1839 the administration

---

28. Lyman Beecher to Sarah Buckingham Beecher [Summer], 1843, quoted in Charles Beecher (ed.), *Autobiography, Correspondence, Etc., of Lyman Beecher, D.D.,* II, 457.

29. Harriet Beecher Stowe to Mary B. Claflin, December 24, 1872, Claflin Papers, Hayes Memorial Library, Fremont, Ohio; [Mrs. Beecher], *From Dawn to Daylight,* pp. 299–300.

30. HWB to Sarah Buckingham Beecher, Walnut Hills, August 9, 1843, Beecher Family Papers. From the collections of the Cincinnati Historical Society Library, Cincinnati, Ohio.

building had burned, and it had been necessary to borrow money to replace it. The college officials secured a loan from the state of Indiana of $8,000 with interest to be paid in advance annually. This money was drawn from the state Sinking Fund which had been established to serve as a stabilizer for the State Bank. In 1842 the college could not maintain interest payments on the loan, and the decision was made to appeal to the state legislature for relief when it met in the winter of 1842–43.

To focus attention on the problems of education in Indiana and, indirectly, on those of Wabash College a convention on education was called by Samuel Merrill, James M. Ray, Henry Ward Beecher, and other Presbyterians, to meet on January 12. The day before the convention was to convene Merrill, Ray, and Beecher met privately and named themselves its principal officers at a meeting in the State Bank building. They had invited Governor Samuel Bigger, a Whig and a Presbyterian, to be the presiding officer at the convention; and Dr. Charles White, president of Wabash College, was scheduled to give the principal address.[31]

The Methodists residing in Indianapolis and throughout the state interpreted the convention as a frontal assault upon their interests. Aware of Presbyterian disdain for Methodist-sponsored institutions, the Methodist leaders were determined to counterattack. Learning of the hostile attitude toward the convention held by outstanding Methodists, the convention officers invited Matthew Simpson, president of Indiana Asbury University, to deliver an address. Simpson declined the invitation. The irritated Methodists construed the tardy request to Simpson as a public insult to the educator and to the denomination. The convention did fulfill the function of centering attention of many legislators on education. One result was that a suspension of further interest payments on the amount owed by Wabash College was effected until 1846.[32]

Henry Ward Beecher was a friend and ally of Governor Bigger who was opposed by James Whitcomb, a Democrat and a Methodist, in the

31. Calvin Fletcher Diary, January 12, 1843, InHi; Taylor, *Biographical Sketches and Review of the Bench and Bar of Indiana*, p. 71.

32. Clark, *The Life of Matthew Simpson*, p. 105 ff.; *Laws of Indiana*, 1842–43 (local), p. 185.

forthcoming gubernatorial election. It was assumed generally that most Methodists were Whigs, but as Bigger was thought to possess little respect for the Methodist Episcopal Church it was considered likely that many Methodist Whigs could be persuaded to vote for Whitcomb. Matthew Simpson had long disliked Bigger's partiality for Wabash College and the Presbyterian coterie, including Beecher, who had influence with the Governor. Simpson fomented discontent among his fellow Methodists, and news of it reached Bigger. Fearing Simpson might convince many Methodist Whigs to switch their votes to Whitcomb, the Governor decided to confront Simpson and to silence him if possible.

To effect such a meeting Bigger enlisted the aid of Lewis G. Thompson, a prominent Whig who was a physician in Fort Wayne. Thompson brought Simpson, the Democrat Edward R. Ames, who was a leading Methodist clergyman rivaling Simpson in denominational influence and an adviser of James Whitcomb, and Indiana Asbury's agent, S. C. Cooper, to Bigger's office. Simpson taxed the Governor with making anti-Methodist remarks. The Governor was also accused of using his official position to hinder the interests of Indiana Asbury University, of being personally disrespectful to Simpson, and of denigrating the character and professional ability of Methodist clergy and educators. The Governor explained away or denied the allegations. Simpson was not really appeased, but he appeared mollified and promised not to repeat the charges.[33]

Rumor reached Bigger and his supporters that Simpson was honoring the word of his pledge but not its spirit. Hoping to force Simpson to state whether Bigger was guilty or not of the accusations, James Stryker a Methodist minister who was a Whig sent Simpson a letter which adjured him that "if the charges are true, you are aware, that they will have an injurious influence upon the prospects of Gov. Bigger; if they are without foundation in fact, it is but an act of naked justice to that

33. Woollen, *Biographical and Historical Sketches of Early Indiana*, pp. 77–80; Clark, *Life of Matthew Simpson*, pp. 2, 135; Charles R. Poinsatte, *Fort Wayne, Indiana, During the Canal Era, 1828–1855* (*Indiana Historical Collections*, XLVI. Indianapolis: Indiana Historical Bureau, 1969), pp. 189–90; S. R. Ball to Matthew Simpson, Fort Wayne, Indiana, July 5, 1843, and James Stryker to Matthew Simpson, Brownstown, Indiana, June 10, 1843, Simpson Papers, DLC.

gentleman, that the public mind should be disabused, and that he should be exempted from the reproach, which, in consequence of the charges, have been inflicted upon him with no sparing hands."[34] Stryker's letter reached Greencastle while Simpson was away touring the southwestern part of Indiana in behalf of his college.

In the meantime the partisan newspapers of Indianapolis added more fuel to the fire by printing repeated charges and countercharges. Worried by the ill effect this might be having on his campaign, Bigger and his allies prevailed upon Noah Noble and others to prepare a statement designed to reassure Methodist Whigs that Bigger was not the ogre Simpson would have them believe. Noble attended the Methodist Episcopal Church, but he had many friends in the Presbyterian community and his daughter and son-in-law were members of the Second Presbyterian Church. The "Appeal to Methodists" which appeared over Noble's name in the *Indiana State Journal*, a Whig newspaper, on June 27, 1843, was a carefully worded account which hopefully would aid Bigger's cause. The editor of the *Indiana State Sentinel*, a Democratic paper, refused to be awed into silence, however, and in his reply which appeared a week later he reasserted Bigger's alleged bias against Methodists. The newspaper battle continued on into the month of July.

Simpson returned to Greencastle and found Stryker's letter awaiting him. In a reply dated July 5 the university president refused to discuss the political ramifications of his discontent with Governor Bigger, but he did write that "so far as my personal intercourse with Gov. Bigger is concerned I know of no improper treatment of any kind. I know of no effort which he has ever made to injure the Indiana Asbury University."[35] Simpson added that he had no political ambitions himself.

In view of Simpson's words and actions during the spring and summer of 1843 this was an incredible statement. While touring the state to raise money for his college he kept his promise not to attack Bigger by name but made remarks which could only be interpreted by the politically aware as slighting references to the Governor. These

34. James Stryker to Matthew Simpson, Brownstown, Indiana, June 10, 1843, Simpson Papers, DLC.

35. Matthew Simpson to James Stryker, Greencastle, July 5, 1843, Simpson Papers, DLC.

were carried to Indianapolis, and it was assumed there by Whigs and Democrats alike that Simpson's tour was a thinly disguised effort to discredit Governor Bigger.

Simpson maintained correspondence with key men in his denomination who informed him of interesting social, religious, and political news in their areas. His chief ally and informant in Indianapolis was Lucien W. Berry, pastor of Wesley Chapel and a trustee of Indiana Asbury University, who kept him fully aware of what was being said and done in the capital city. "The flame burns high yet in this place," reported Berry. "From every source we are getting information of your electioneering expedition. Ira Grover from Greensburg has just visited here and says in a speech which you made there you said the Methodist Church were fully competent to manage their own Educational interests though *those who are high in authority* contradict it etc. You cannot conceive the excitement which exists in this community."[36] Bigger, Merrill, Beecher, and others were almost beside themselves from what they regarded as Simpson's vindictiveness and perfidy.

Upset by Simpson's actions and distraught about George Beecher's death, Beecher left Indianapolis for Crawfordsville where he was to address the Society of Inquiry during the Wabash College commencement exercises. The heat was oppressive, many people had influenza, and some among those present were coming down with it. Professor William Twining gave the opening speech on Tuesday, July 18. Beecher spoke next to the Society of Inquiry, and in the evening the Euphronean Society heard a speech delivered by the Reverend Elipha White. Beecher's speech was reported in the friendly *Indiana State Journal* to have been delivered "in a manner apparently very gratifying to a large and intelligent audience."[37] So praised, it would presumably have passed into oblivion had not the preacher inserted a political reference to Matthew Simpson which electrified and enraged some of his audience.

Beecher had not resisted the temptation to promote Bigger's candidacy, so he thought, by relating the history of the education conven-

36. Lucien W. Berry to Matthew Simpson, Indianapolis, July 26, 1843, Simpson Papers, DLC; Cammack (ed.), "Cyrus Nutt Becomes A Hoosier," *Indiana Magazine of History*, LIII, 67–68.
37. Indianapolis *Indiana State Journal*, August 2, 1843.

tion the previous winter. He described events leading to calling the convention, the last minute invitation to Simpson and the latter's refusal. Beecher criticized Simpson severely for this action and subsequent conduct. For the sake of effect Beecher referred to the Greencastle man as P-r-e-s-i-d-e-n-t S-i-m-p-s-o-n as if the name were too obscene to be spoken aloud. The substance of Beecher's speech was reported in Indianapolis where it was discussed heatedly among Whigs and Democrats. Berry was delighted. To Simpson he wrote, "The [wrath] of the Whigs is descending fearfully on the head of Beecher for his Crawfordsville speech. Even the Members of his own Church are railing against him in the streets. This moment a leading Whig told me if Bigger was defeated it might—and would be ascribed to Beecher. I, of course, believing it to be a fact, have done my best to deepen the impression."[38]

It was recognized by the Whigs that Beecher had blundered badly. His attack on Simpson lent credence to statements made by Simpson about Bigger and his fellow Whigs. Knowing that Berry was close to Simpson the Whigs approached the minister and told him that Beecher had said if Berry "or any other *respectable* Methodist would visit him he would deny" what he allegedly had said at Crawfordsville in regard to Simpson. Berry told his visitors "that Mr. B[eecher] was either guilty of making an unprovoked attack on 'one professor Simpson and others' or he was not. If he was *and* his own Members who were present at the Commencement boldly declared *it* he must abide the consequences. If he did not then as a lie was published and reported involving his Character he alone was concerned to contradict it."[39] Berry refused to call upon Beecher. Berry's Whig visitors approached various Methodists hoping to gain the advantage by placing the Methodists in the inferior position of seeking a favor from Beecher, but Berry had warned his colleagues not to be taken in by the scheme.

"They [the Whigs] are in limbo, and I desire to see them kept there for awhile—especially Beecher," reported Berry to Simpson. "The indignation of the community never fell as heavily on any man as it does at the present on him. He is the most uneasy man you ever saw he is

38. Lucien W. Berry to Matthew Simpson, Indianapolis, July 26, 1843, Simpson Papers, DLC.
39. *Ibid.*

pacing from one place to another continually. He visited the Journal office several times yesterday; and I think it possible he intends to come out with a disclaimer."[40] Berry's conjecture was realized. In an ill-advised effort to negate the unfortunate effect of Beecher's Crawfordsville speech the editor of the Whig newspaper reprinted the offending report thereby giving it even wider circulation. To this tactical error he added: "We notice it . . . [the report], but merely to say that we have conversed with Mr. Beecher, who would not of course notice, in the least degree, an anonymous correspondent, but who pronounces the above false in every sense."[41] If the editor's conversation with Beecher were quoted accurately, and there is no reason to suppose it was not, it placed the clergyman in the position of being a liar. Too many people heard him castigate P-r-e-s-i-d-e-n-t S-i-m-p-s-o-n at Crawfordsville.

Berry was quite willing to exploit Beecher's rash speech and subsequent denial. Signing himself "Right of Conscience Man," the Methodist minister wrote an expose with Simpson cast as the maligned party. The actions and words of Beecher, Bigger, and others were construed in the worst possible light. Of it, Berry wrote, "It is severe though I think not rough or Unchristian."[42] Shortly after Berry's article appeared, Beecher took his family for a prolonged visit to Walnut Hills.

While there is a question as to what effect the controversy and Beecher's role in it had on the outcome of the election, James Whitcomb defeated Samuel Bigger by a margin of approximately two thousand votes for the first Democratic gubernatorial victory in the state for ten years. Contemporaries believed the outcome was determined by the Methodist Whig vote which supported Whitcomb in opposition to the allegedly anti-Methodist Bigger.[43]

Henry Ward Beecher spent little time in Indianapolis during the late summer and early fall of 1843. Tom wrote to sister Isabella in September that Henry was as "busy as ever—attending the revival meetings—which he *preaches up*—most every year—in different portions of

40. *Ibid.*

41. Indianapolis *Indiana State Journal,* August 2, 1843.

42. Lucien W. Berry to Matthew Simpson, July 26, 1843, Indianapolis, Simpson Papers, DLC; Indianapolis *Indiana State Sentinel,* August 1, 1843.

43. Clark, *The Life of Matthew Simpson,* pp. 105–108; Woollen, *Biographical and Historical Sketches of Early Indiana,* pp. 77–80.

the state."[44] The Merrill family remained loyal to him, and Catharine Merrill wrote that "our church seems deserted" without him.[45] The summer's unpleasantness faded away in men's minds, and Beecher gradually resumed his accustomed routine.

44. Thomas K. Beecher to Isabella Beecher Hooker, Indianapolis, September 9, 1843, CtHS-D.

45. Catharine E. Merrill to Samuel Merrill, Indianapolis, September [?], 1843, quoted in Graydon (comp.), *Catharine Merrill, Life and Letters*, pp. 59–60.

XIII

Author and Editor

BEECHER WAS ASKED INCREASINGLY TO OFFICIATE AT WEDDINGS IN Indianapolis and its environs. In the autumn of 1843 he presided at the wedding of nineteen-year-old Oliver Johnson to Pamelia Howland whose families lived near each other on farms adjacent to the capital city. Many years later Johnson recalled:

> The Howlands put on a nice weddin for us, eastern style. There was no licker or races for the bottle at our affair. I managed to buy a new coat that cost twelve dollars; my britches and boots and the rest of my gear was in purty good shape. I was so conscious of my backwoods ways I wasn't sure I could go through with the ceremony. Many of the guests was people from town, friends of the Howlands and strangers to me.
>
> The Reverend Henry Ward Beecher, a young preacher from Indianapolis, tied the knot. I well remember the advice he give us that evenin as he was leavin. To my new wife he said: "If you ever catch your husband comin in the house actin glum and out a fix, start singing the gayest tune you know and don't say a word to him." To me he said, "If you come in from work and find her with her sunbonnet pulled as far foreward as she can get it, whistle a soft tune and don't open your head to her." Parson Beecher was a lot diff'rent from most of the preachers at that time. He believed in mixin happiness and a good time with religion. He made a lot of friends with his style of preachin, especially with the young folks.[1]

1. Johnson, *A Home in the Woods, Oliver Johnson's Reminiscences of Early Marion County*, pp. 228–29; Mrs. Beecher, "Mr. Beecher as I Knew Him," *Ladies Home Journal*, June, 1892, p. 1.

Beecher was often called to "tie the knot" even for couples who did not attend his church.

A wedding which held especial significance for Henry Ward Beecher took place on the evening before Thanksgiving in 1843 when one of Samuel Merrill's daughters, tall and slender Priscilla, married Alexander Wilson. Priscilla Merrill was Beecher's favorite among all the Merrill daughters at this time, for she had captured his affection with her good sense and charm. He told her sister Catharine that "of all these young ladies [in Indianapolis] if I were a young man Priscilla Merrill would have been my choice."[2] Priscilla's new husband managed a paper mill in Lafayette for his cousin, Daniel Yandes, and the Merrills were grateful to Beecher for the introductions he gave the couple to residents of Lafayette.

Life in Indianapolis in the early winter of 1843 was enlivened by the arrival of a dancing master who also gave instruction in etiquette. Dressed in a frilled shirt, silk stockings, and pumps with silver buckles, the man was regarded as an oddity in the capital. One of his Hoosier pupils, sixteen-year-old Lew Wallace, would recall that the dancing master "also made his own music. *The Fisher's Hornpipe* with which he sped a quadrille was tearing enough to have quickened the bones of the unknown in a catacomb. He enrolled me a pupil of his academy; and, simple as the topic looks, I am bound to say there was never such a tempest of fun as when he called us out one by one to practice bowing, hat salutes, and posturing seated and standing."[3] The resultant foolery helped decide Beecher to launch a series of sermons designed to counteract the frivolous and pernicious influence of the wandering master's influence on the youth of Indianapolis, for Beecher thought "that throwing one's heels higher than their head a-dancing, is not exactly the way to teach virtue."[4]

The Devil was showing his hand in other ways as well, and the results were apparent among the members of the Second Presbyterian

2. "Reminiscences of Jane Merrill Ketcham," p. 74, In; Samuel Merrill to David Merrill, Indianapolis, January 17, 1844, Samuel Merrill Papers, InHi; Catharine Merrill, Journal, June 26, 1843, quoted in Graydon (comp.), *Catharine Merrill, Life and Letters*, pp. 48–51.

3. Wallace, *An Autobiography*, I, 91–92.

4. HWB, *Seven Lectures to Young Men* (Indianapolis: Thomas B. Cutler, 1844), p. 169.

Church. At an especially long meeting of Session on December 30, 1843, Beecher and the Elders Yandes, Bassett, Culley, and Ketcham considered a lengthy list of alleged misdeeds. The misconduct of two young people was evident in the person of their infant. They became parents only a few months after their marriage, and the size and appearance of the healthy infant pointed too clearly to the premarital intimacy of its parents. The mother was a member of a prominent Indianapolis family and a close friend of Catharine Merrill, so the scandal was especially grave. Session resolved unanimously to suspend the couple until they showed "sufficient evidence of harty [*sic*] repentance for said Sin;" and six other members of the church were notified to appear before Session in the lecture room of the church on January 13, 1844, to answer charges including Sabbath breaking, gambling, intemperance, use of profanity, and visiting a house of ill fame.[5] In truth, the Devil was busy in Beecher's domain!

Furnished a copy of the charge and the names of the witnesses against him as was customary, one of the men accused of neglect of public worship, intemperance, frequenting a brothel, gambling, and the use of profanity refused to wait until the thirteenth of January. The charges were extremely serious ones in a community which professed to find such alleged misconduct abhorrent. At a meeting of Session on January 4, 1844, the man admitted that he had been guilty of gambling and swearing, but he asserted his innocence on the other counts. Accepting his statement, the Session suspended him from privileges of the church until he could "give evidence of hearty repentance."[6] Less than two weeks later a second man was excommunicated. He had been one of the six charged with neglecting public worship and intemperance. Three days later, January 18, the members of Session examined the charge against a man and his wife. The couple allegedly neglected public worship and "countenanced houses of ill fame." The husband alone was charged with desecration of the Sabbath and intemperance. The Session decided none of the charges against the couple could be proved. Mortified and angered by the attention centered upon them, the couple along with two other accused men asked that their names be removed from

5. Records of the Second Presbyterian Church, InISPC; Graydon (comp.), *Catharine Merrill, Life and Letters*, p. 42.
6. Records of the Second Presbyterian Church, pp. 55–57, InISPC.

the list of church members. This request was granted on February 18, with a notation that it was done "for the good of the church."[7] With this the flurry of disciplinary measures directed against erring church members subsided.

While Beecher did not hesitate to discipline a wrongdoer he thought it more valuable to prevent the commission of immoral or foolish acts by those too young and inexperienced to realize the ill consequences they might incur. Incensed by the number of young men in Indianapolis who were engaging in such activities, Beecher set himself the task of preparing and delivering a series of lectures designed to persuade the community's youth to abstain from harmful diversions.[8]

Beecher could place himself mentally in the position of the person he wished to influence. "I never hear of the experience of others who are troubled," he said later, "or struggling, or groping their way, that their condition does not instantly present itself as a drama before my eyes and I do not *think* of it, but I *see* it."[9] Understanding how a temptation might appeal to a basically decent person, Beecher prepared each talk in a dramatic and appealing style to show the tempted that his was not a unique experience, what might happen to him if he yielded, and how to gird himself against giving in to temptation.

For seven weeks in the winter of 1843–44 Beecher delivered a lecture each Sunday evening which dealt with some form of immorality. His topics included: "Industry and Idleness," "Twelve Causes of Dishonesty," "Six Warnings [use and misuse of wealth]," "The Portrait-Gallery [excesses by the wit, humorist, cynic, libertine, politician, demagogue, and party man]," "Gamblers and Gambling," "The Strange Woman," and "Popular Amusements."

The lecture which was announced for December 24 entitled "The Strange Woman" evoked more comment than did any of the others. It was a daring topic to be discussed in an Indianapolis church in 1843. While prostitution was a fact of life in the city the respectable citizens

7. Records of the Second Presbyterian Church, pp. 55–59, InISPC.
8. Hudson, *The Great Tradition of the American Churches*, p. 188; Mrs. Beecher, "Mr. Beecher as I Knew Him," *Ladies Home Journal,* January, 1892, p. 5.
9. "Mr. Beecher as a Social Force," *Scribner's Monthly,* IV, 752–53; John R. Howard, *Henry Ward Beecher,* p. 24.

preferred to ignore its existence. Many church members were indignant with Beecher for broaching the sordid subject from the pulpit and warned that they would not attend if he persevered. Several families were noticeably absent when time for the lecture arrived, and many others were represented only by their adult males. The Second Presbyterian Church was crowded, however, with the curious from the city. Possessing faith in Beecher's good sense and discretion, Calvin Fletcher brought his wife to the controversial lecture. He was pleased with Beecher's presentation and wrote, "It was worthy of any ones attention or it was made so. I esteem these remarks [objecting to topic] by our citizens & the femals absence as false delicacy."[10]

Irked by the criticism he had received during the preceding week, Beecher inserted some sarcastic comments in regard to it in his address. Nowhere is this better expressed than in the footnote he appended to the printed lecture: "I await with some solicitude, the effect of this Lecture upon those whose exquisite sensibility has altogether out run the modesty of the Bible; —a book, proper, perhaps, for the coarseness of a former age, but it would seem, quite too indelicate for the refinement of this."[11] He began the lecture with pointed remarks about the nature of true innocence and virtue and continued that a subject which received so much attention in the Bible surely deserved recognition by Christians who hoped to protect their young.

Much of the lecture was devoted to the evil effects of literature, especially French, on the morals of readers. In the course of his address he commented on the works of Balsac [*sic*], Bulwer, Byron, Chaucer, Dickens, Dumas, Fielding, Ford, Godwin, Masson, Moore, George Sand, Shakespeare, Sterne, Eugene Sue, and Swift. Of them all, he thought the later plays of Shakespeare were the most suitable works to place in the hands of youth. The writers whose works he discussed show that Beecher's own tastes in literature were catholic. He neglected to discuss, however, why it was all right for him to be familiar with these works but not for others. The remainder of the lecture was devoted to a lurid depiction of the imagined pleasures of vice and its horrible conse-

10. Calvin Fletcher Diary, December 24, 1843, InHi; HWB, *Seven Lectures to Young Men*, p. 131.
11. HWB, *Seven Lectures to Young Men*, p. 131.

quences. Vividly worded, it must have excited the imaginations of its hearers.[12]

The other six lectures in the series were generally approved and drew large audiences. Beecher singled out specific sins, but he did not mention names of individuals in connection with them. There was a certain amount of speculation as to identities, nevertheless, and a few people expressed anger because they thought he referred to them.[13]

Thomas B. Cutler, Indianapolis printer and publisher, approached Beecher about publishing the lectures. The clergyman liked the idea and agreed, but it would be necessary first to enlarge his notes into essays. "When I first sat down to prepare them for the press," recalled Beecher,

> I took up the lecture on "Industry and Indolence." Said I to myself, "I have gone through these with my own ideas, now perhaps it might be well to see what others have written also; it might suggest something." I then took up a work containing two or three sermons on the same subject by Isaac Barrow, who was a great favorite of mine. Before I had read them half through, I found Barrow had said all I had, and had said it a great deal better. I then slung my manuscript under the bookcase and there I left it.[14]

Discouraged and dismayed, Beecher did not do any further work on the lectures for weeks. He was not permitted to forget them, however, as William Eckert with whom Beecher was friendly kept comparing them to similar essays he had read recently. The preacher secured a copy of the book mentioned by the harness maker and "After I had finished two of the lectures, I said, 'My goodness! If these lectures can be read with such ardor, I think my poor little book might as well come out from under the bookcase there.' So I went on and finished it."[15] This "poor little book" when published in 1844 under the title *Seven Lectures to Young Men* created a satisfactory stir and gave Henry Ward Beecher his first taste of national recognition.[16]

12. HWB, *Seven Lectures to Young Men*, pp. 136–66.
13. John R. Howard, *Henry Ward Beecher*, p. 49.
14. Derby, *Fifty Years Among Authors, Books and Publishers*, p. 466.
15. *Ibid.*, pp. 466–67; *Seventy-Fifth Anniversary. Second Presbyterian Church, Indianapolis, Indiana, 1838–1913*, p. 8.
16. An interesting analysis of the content and influence of *Seven Lectures to Young Men* may be read in Clifford Clark, Jr.'s, "The Changing Nature of Protestantism in Mid-Nineteenth Century America: Henry Ward Beecher's Seven Lectures to Young Men," *Journal of American History*, LVII, No. 4 (March, 1971), pp. 832–46.

Beecher's interest in horticulture intensified with the passing of time, and later in the year he was given the opportunity of combining his knowledge of it with his talents for writing and editing in a proposed periodical to be entitled the *Indiana Farmer and Gardener*. According to its prospectus it would be a semimonthly journal devoted to the garden, orchard, and farm. Single subscriptions would cost one dollar per year, and group subscriptions of four or more ordered together could be had for seventy-five cents each with payment to be made in advance. The *Indiana Farmer and Gardener* was a subsidiary of the Whig newspaper, the *Indiana State Journal*, and would be printed on the same press. Beecher would edit the agricultural paper; but technical aspects of its publication, financing, and distribution would be under the supervision of Samuel Vance B. Noel, publisher of the newspaper. As much of an issue's contents of the former as were wanted could be reprinted in the latter, but Beecher insisted upon acknowledgment of the source for he detested the prevailing practice of plagiarism.[17]

Contrary to Beecher's later recollection, the *Indiana Farmer and Gardener* was not the first periodical of its type to be published in the state. The *Indiana Aurora*, a weekly devoted to agriculture, education, and internal improvements, published by Moses M. Henkle, appeared from August, 1835, until early in 1836. Then, in March, 1836, under the sponsorship of the State Board of Agriculture the *Indiana Farmer* had begun publication with Henkle as editor, later succeeded by John W. Osborn and Jacob S. Willets. In 1837 it became the *Indiana Farmer and Stock Register*. Publication ceased in 1841. In January, 1844, a similar paper called the *Western Cultivator* under the editorship of W. Thompson Hatch had begun. Beecher knew Willets and Hatch who were active members of the Indiana Horticultural Society, and he must have been well acquainted with their periodicals.[18]

17. Indianapolis *Indiana State Journal*, January 15, 1845; HWB, *Plain and Pleasant Talk About Fruits, Flowers and Farming*, p. iii; "Fifty Years," *Indiana Farmer*, XXX, No. 48 (November 30, 1895), p. 1; James H. Butler, "Indiana Newspapers, 1829–1860," *Indiana Magazine of History*, XXII, No. 3 (September, 1926), p. 318; *Indiana Farmer and Gardener*, I, No. 13 (July 12, 1845), pp. 191–92.

18. John D. Barnhart and Donald F. Carmony, *Indiana. From Frontier to Industrial Commonwealth* (4 volumes. New York: Lewis Historical Publishing Co., 1954), II, 65; Donald F. Carmony, "Henry Ward Beecher and the Pioneer Agricultural Press," pp. 1–6, In; advertisement for *Indiana Farmer and Stock Register*, in Indian-

The issues of the *Indiana Farmer and Gardener* which appeared in 1845 were sprightly and informative. Beecher asked for contributions from readers and published those he considered worthwhile. A subscriber whose articles appeared frequently in its columns was John T. Plummer, a physician who lived in Richmond, Indiana. Plummer wrote about such diverse subjects as "Native Ornamental Shrubs," "Crops in Wayne County," and "Grasshoppers." Circulation of the periodical rose to seven hundred by the end of its first year of publication.[19]

Beecher did not receive a salary for his editorial work on the *Indiana Farmer and Gardener*. He did benefit indirectly, however, as he received sample seeds and nursery stock from firms which hoped he would comment favorably upon them in the paper. As a result, Beecher was able to plant an orchard composed of some rather rare and valuable fruit trees while his flower beds contained specimens unusual in Indiana. Beecher's love of flower growing was incomprehensible to some Indianapolis residents who considered it an unmanly pastime at worst and a useless one at best. When asked what benefit there was in it, Beecher replied, "What good! Why, make you happier & better everytime you look at them." He would continue, "Try it a year and you will never ask that question again."[20]

Henry Ward Beecher fitted his editorial work into the space between the time he arose and breakfast. He enjoyed it, and he seemed to relish the extra effort involved as he did that in tilling his garden. He may have had his work in connection with his gardening efforts in mind when he wrote on the flyleaf of a notebook that "it is my deliberate conviction that physical labor is indispensable to intellectual & moral health."[21] Out of his work on the *Indiana Farmer and Gardener* came what Eunice Beecher regarded as the "dearest compliment" he ever gave to her. An acquaintance reportedly said to Beecher, "With all the duties you have taken in hand, Mr. Beecher, we cannot understand how

apolis *Indiana Democrat*, August 2, 1837; Herbert H. Kellar (ed.), *Solon Robinson, Pioneer and Agriculturalist* (2 volumes. *Indiana Historical Collections*, XXI & XXII. Indianapolis: Indiana Historical Bureau, 1936), I, 213.

19. Bernhard Knollenberg, *Pioneer Sketches of the Upper Whitewater Valley* (Indiana Historical Society *Publications*, XV, No. 1, Indianapolis, 1945), p. 123; "Fifty Years," *Indiana Farmer*, November 30, 1895, p. 1.

20. Mrs. Henry Ward Beecher, Notes, n.d., CtY.

21. HWB, Notebook, January 10, 1845, CtY.

you can find time to edit the *Indiana Farmer*." Beecher replied, pointing to Eunice, "I could not, had not my wife taught me what I never knew till I married, the habit of early rising. Most of my work on the paper is done before my neighbors are up in the morning."[22] Eunice Beecher had been accustomed to waking early to begin her chores on her family's farm. When she married and moved to Lawrenceburgh, she continued to rise before daybreak and commence her housework. Perhaps Beecher was encouraged to follow her example by the inevitable noise which she must have made accidentally or purposefully in the habit of wives. The custom served him well in any event.

In his capacity as editor of the *Indiana Farmer and Gardener* Beecher spent much time examining material which he might use in its columns. He was exasperated by a basic shallowness which permeated writing on gardening and agricultural topics. Especially irritated by one sample, he penned a biting criticism:

> There is no writing so detestable as so called *fine writing*. It is painted emptiness. We especially detest fine writing about rural affairs—all the senseless gabble about dew, and zephyrs. . . . We always suspect a design upon our admiration, and take care not to admire. In short *geoponical cant, and pastoral cant, and rural cant* in their length and breadth are like, the whole long catalogue of cants, (not excepting the German Kant) intolerable.[23]

He made clearly evident that he eschewed fine writing by his own contribution in the next issue of the *Indiana Farmer and Gardener*.

Disgusted with the habits of many farmers and their families, Beecher selected several practices he found particularly offensive and described them under the title "Shiftless Tricks." A few are included:

> To raise your own frogs in your own yard; to permit, year after year, a dirty, stinking, mantled puddle to stand before your fence in the streets. . . . It is very shiftless to build your barnyard so that every rain shall *drain* it; to build your privy and dig your well close together; to build a privy of more than seven feet square—some in these parts have it of the size of the whole yard; to set it in the most exposed spot on the premises. . . . It is a dirty trick to make bread without washing one's hands after cleaning fish or chickens; . . . to use milk-pans alternately for wash-bowls and

22. Mrs. Henry Ward Beecher, Notes, n.d., CtY.
23. *Indiana Farmer and Gardener*, I, No. 19 (October 4, 1845), p. 294.

milk. To wash dishes and baby linen in the same tub, either alternately or together. . . .[24]

With such exceedingly plain writing did Beecher express his contempt for slovenly habits.

The officers of the Philomathean Society of Indiana University asked Beecher to address them on the evening of September 24, 1845, and an announcement was placed in the *Indiana State Journal* on September 3, inviting the public to attend. Beecher passed his time on the long ride to Bloomington by observing carefully the farms he passed and noting what practices were being followed. Although he rode through some of the most picturesque countryside in Indiana, he gave little thought to the scenery. Later, using the editorial "we," he wrote,

> We saw few houses or yards which were not in a bad condition. . . . All the slops from cooking, washing, &c., need not go down before the door; pigs need not range and litter and root up the yard. It is just as easy to have neatness in a log cabin as in a brick mansion. . . . We are quite sure that we have found out some of the places from which such unutterably dirty butter comes to this market [Indianapolis].[25]

Beecher was pleased with his reception at the state university, and he sustained his reputation as an eloquent speaker on the topic of "Intolerance." Unable to follow completely, however, his own pleas for tolerance, he was disturbed by aspects of his stay in Bloomington. He approved of the appearance and behavior of the students at the university, but, he wrote:

> we wish we could say as much for the mischevious [*sic*] urchins of the *town* of Bloomington. A ruder, noisier, and more saucy set, of unbewhipped chaps never blocked up the doors of a college; and with hooting and shrill whistling, made an addition to the commencement exercises not according to our notions. Cannot the trustees and faculty defend themselves from such juvenile imposition? But this was really the only draw back upon a day of great pleasure and profit.[26]

Despite such unpleasantness Beecher rode away from Bloomington

24. *Indiana Farmer and Gardener*, I, No. 20 (October 11, 1845), p. 306.
25. *Ibid.*, I, No. 19 (October 4, 1845), p. 290. In 1907, Selma N. Steele would observe similar conditions in her own search for butter while living in nearby Brown County. See Selma N. Steele, Theodore L. Steele, and Wilbur D. Peat, *The House of the Singing Winds* (Indianapolis: Indiana Historical Society, 1966), pp. 100–102.
26. *Indiana Farmer and Gardener*, I, No. 19 (October 4, 1845), pp. 290–91.

well satisfied. The editor of the local newspaper, the *Herald,* commended his speech in print and his words were reprinted in the *Indiana State Journal.* He wrote, "His reputation as a young man of learning and eloquence had preceded him [to Bloomington], and, he more than sustained himself. In *graphic description* and in *comparisons, of a most striking and peculiar character,* he is without an equal in the West. His satire was as sharp as a two-edged sword; and his denunciations overwhelming."[27] Heady praise for the clergyman!

Henry Ward Beecher prepared for a journey which would take him to the northern part of Indiana into a region which he had not as yet penetrated. Synod was meeting in Logansport, and he would stop to attend its sessions. Since he planned to be away from Indianapolis for two or three weeks, he secured a substitute preacher for his pulpit and prepared material for the succeeding two issues of the *Indiana Farmer and Gardener* which he put into the hands of its publisher.[28]

David V. Culley and Henry Ward Beecher left Indianapolis on October 7, 1845, to make the two-day ride to Logansport and arrived there in time for the opening of Synod. At Logansport Beecher was joined by his brother Charles. While dutifully attending the meetings Beecher also devoted time to sightseeing in the area. He visited the farm of a friend, W. Z. Stewart, and there enjoyed looking at the latter's Berkshires and Durhams. The noted nursery of Daniel Embree also attracted him with its impressive variety of fruit trees.[29]

When Synod adjourned Beecher turned his horse's head northward to La Porte, the farthest point of his trip. At first he thought the area through which he traveled was an old, long-settled country because of the number of open-fenced fields. Upon nearing the Kankakee River, however, the appearance of the countryside changed abruptly. He rode

> at a full trot across a raised road which lay through a wet prairie, [and came] to a long bridge. . . the Kankakee bridge. . . . For hundreds of yards, on each side of the river the water seemed to lie a foot or two deep,

27. Reprinted from the Bloomington *Herald* in the Indianapolis *Indiana State Journal,* October 1, 1845.

28. *Indiana Farmer and Gardener,* I, No. 21 (October 18, 1845), p. 321; Annie B. Scoville, Notes, n.d., CtY.

29. *Indiana Farmer and Gardener,* I, No. 23 (November 8, 1845), pp. 353–54; Records of the Synod of Indiana, I, 339–59, InHan; Dunn, *Indiana and Indianans,* II, 934.

and a strong, reedy grass, five or six feet in height, waved over it like an immense harvest white for the sickle; for the top of the grass was very white, and the river, with no perceptible current, lay in the midst. Flocks of small birds were flying about among the grassy forest; and what was much more exciting. . . flocks of wild duck were sporting on the open stream, or threading their way through the stems of grass and sedge.

Beecher arrived in La Porte on October 16. "Nothing more beautiful to a farmer's eye, can be conceived . . . ," he wrote. "It is a prairie country, but full of beautiful oak groves."[30] The city of La Porte was a thriving agricultural center with flour mills and small factories which catered to farmers' needs. So advanced was knowledge of farming among area residents that many were using the locomotive threshing machine, still a novelty elsewhere.

An agricultural fair began on the day Beecher arrived, but he spent much of his time resting and visiting with friends. Next morning, October 17, he began to "do" the fair. In the morning he watched a plowing contest, heard an address by G. Hathaway given at the Methodist Church, and then spoke briefly himself to the audience. "The extemporaneous remarks of Rev. H. W. Beecher . . . were listened to with the utmost attention," reported the La Porte *Tocsin*. "We do not recollect to have heard before so many apt, practical thoughts, communicated in so brief and able a manner."[31] Following the speech, he was a guest at a dinner sponsored by the La Porte Agricultural Society, and he ended the day by looking at the exhibits of domestic items which were displayed in the Courthouse. Soon he was headed home.

On January 1, 1846, the *Indiana Farmer and Gardener* merged with a Cincinnati publication begun in 1839 originally titled *The Western Farmer* and in 1840 renamed *The Western Farmer and Gardener*. Announcement of the consolidation appeared in the *Indiana State Journal* on January 14, 1846. Beecher and Edward J. Hooper of Cincinnati were listed as co-editors, but Beecher did most of the preparation and editing of the paper. In February a series of letters written by Thomas K. Beecher on a variety of subjects began to appear in the *Western Farmer and Gardener*. During the next six months ten letters

30. *Indiana Farmer and Gardener*, I, No. 23 (November 8, 1845), p. 354; Kellar (ed.), *Solon Robinson, Pioneer and Agriculturalist*, I, 321–23.
    31. Reprinted from the La Porte *Tocsin* in the Indianapolis *Indiana State Journal*, October 29, 1845.

were published on such diverse topics as the state buildings in Columbus, Ohio; the insane asylum in that city; descriptions of the cities of Louisville and Cincinnati; a general treatise on taxation; a travelogue describing points of interest between Cincinnati and Washington, D. C.; the government Patent Office; farm practices in New England; hydropathy; a discussion of capital and labor; and an essay on history. These letters were well written, but, for the most part, had little immediate relevance to agriculture. It was one way, however, of providing encouragement to Tom and also convenient filler for the periodical. Possibly the most popular issue of the year was the almanac for 1847 which Beecher inserted in a double number on October 19, 1846.[32]

The Western Farmer and Gardener contained the type of articles and features which Beecher had used in its predecessor. Though the content was interesting it lacked the sparkle which Beecher had imparted earlier when editing the paper was a novelty. Always workmanlike, however, *The Western Farmer and Gardener* would close the year 1846 with twelve hundred subscribers.[33] It ceased publication when Beecher left Indianapolis in 1847.

32. *Western Farmer and Gardener*, II, February 2-July 15, 1846; Thomas K. Beecher to Lyman Beecher, Philadelphia, August 11, 1846, CtHS-D; Indianapolis *Indiana State Journal,* January 14, 1846.

33. Dunn, *Greater Indianapolis*, I, 397; "Fifty Years," *Indiana Farmer*, November 30, 1895, p. 1; *Western Farmer and Gardener*, II, No. 1 (January 1, 1846), p. 16.

Thomas K.   William   Lyman   Edward   Mary   Charles   Henry Ward
Isabella   Catharine   Harriet

Lyman Beecher and His Children, ca. 1855

XIV

Beecher Aids a Brother

C HARLES BEECHER WAS A SOURCE OF CONCERN TO HENRY AND TO
their father. No sooner did he seem to be regaining his faith and
moving toward the ministry than he became involved in an unpleasant
episode with his eldest sister, Catharine E. Beecher. Although having the
proverbial heart of gold, Catharine's growing tendency to make tart
comments and give unasked advice had a grating effect on her family.
She was forgiven much because of her spinsterhood growing from the
tragic death of her fiance, the state of her health, and her kindnesses to
her relatives. Occasionally, though, she unintentionally wounded a
brother or sister too deeply. Lyman Beecher was ever on the alert to
prevent such a situation; but, if unsuccessful, he would attempt to
smooth over the difficulty.

Catharine irritated the sensitive Charles in some way, and he wrote
a sharp letter of rebuke to her which their father intercepted. If this
letter should "fall accidentally into her hands should wound too deep,"
wrote the father. "With her nervous incapacities she feels deeply any
appearance of light estimation on the part of her family friends or whom
she so sincerely loves. . . . But in her trying situation [aging spinster] it is
a happy knack of being always in the right demanding gratitude."[1]
Catharine was aware of Charles's displeasure with her but was spared
reading his angry letter by her father's action. When Henry learned of

1. Lyman Beecher to HWB, Walnut Hills, December 8, 1842, CtY.

the affair he sent her a pleasant letter and was probably responsible for Charles also mailing one. Lyman Beecher wrote that the letters had made her laugh, and the breach was mended.

Charles Beecher had the family weakness of going into debt. Although he had a wife and child to support, he had no profession or occupation in Indianapolis which furnished a steady source of income. There is no record that he received a salary for his work at the Second Presbyterian Church. He earned small fees for occasional tutoring and giving music lessons, but his teaching could not have produced a regular income on which to depend. Considering Henry's own financial situation, it is unlikely that Charles received any substantial monetary aid from him. The younger Beecher hoped to take John Wheeler's place as a teacher at the Franklin Institute when the Englishman left to become a professor at Indiana Asbury, but nothing came of it and the school soon closed.

When Lyman Beecher learned that Charles had accumulated debts in Indianapolis he wrote to Henry asking that the names of people to whom Charles owed money and the amounts due them be compiled and sent to him at Walnut Hills. The total must have been large for the father was not inclined to worry about small sums. The father was hopeful that some arrangement could be made by which he could pay part of the total and the creditors could be persuaded to accept Charles's promise to repay the rest in installments.

Lyman Beecher was even more worried about the health of Charles's wife. Sarah Coffin Beecher had not recovered satisfactorily from the birth of a son in 1841, and symptoms of anemia were present. The hardships of her life in New Orleans and Indianapolis and constant anxiety about money were taking their toll. Lyman Beecher was as concerned about her welfare as he would have been about one of his own daughter's; indeed, he never made a distinction between his children by birth or by marriage. They were all Beechers and all entitled to his love and aid. He wrote a letter to Sarah which he thought might encourage her and entrusted it to Henry to deliver if the latter thought it would comfort the young wife and mother.

Henry was rapidly becoming his father's mainstay in keeping the large Beecher family on an even keel. Largely through Henry's efforts

Charles was being spiritually reclaimed. Exposed to his personality and example young Tom had been encouraged to return to Illinois College to complete his senior year, and plans were made to bring James Beecher to Indianapolis for a season. Lyman Beecher wrote Henry that he had "great confidence in" his "wisdom & success."[2]

Once Charles Beecher made his fateful decision for Christ in 1843 his brother gave him little time to reconsider. Charles had preached and helped with the music during the revival. After it ended he gave a series of sermons from the pulpit of the Second Presbyterian Church based upon the life of Christ. Contrary to those usually prepared by his father and brothers, the sermons Charles Beecher favored were oriented toward historical narration with an admixture of mysticism. Jane Merrill Ketcham remembered long the "pathos and beauty beyond anything" in the sermons he delivered "on the Virgin and her Son."[3] When it was known Charles Beecher was to preach, the service would be well attended. In a journal entry dated April 23, 1843, for example, Catharine Merrill recorded: "Was at church from nine this morning until ten to-night and am too fatigued to write. The house was crowded to hear the lecture of Mr. Charles Beecher. He made clear the cause of the difference in the genealogies of Christ given by Matthew and by Luke."[4] Thus did Charles serve his apprenticeship in the ministry at brother Henry's church in Indianapolis.

A meeting of the Presbytery of Indianapolis which held special significance for the Beechers was convened at the Second Presbyterian Church on August 11, 1843, at eleven o'clock in the morning. If everything went well Charles Beecher would be accepted under the care of the Presbytery as a licentiate. First, he had to be examined by the three clergymen and three elders who were present. In accord with church practice he was assigned four themes: Popular Lecture, Romans 8:9; Sermon, Ephesians 6:12; Exegetical Exercise, John 5:17; and a Latin theme, *De Passionione Dei*. "After a full examination," the record shows, "all parts of the trial were sustained, and the candidate was

2. Lyman Beecher to HWB, Walnut Hills, December 8, 1842, CtY; Charles Beecher to Edward Beecher, Fort Wayne, September 7, 1847, CtY.

3. "Reminiscences of Jane Merrill Ketcham," p. 76, In.

4. Graydon (comp.), *Catharine Merrill, Life and Letters*, p. 45.

licensed to preach the Gospel within the bounds of this Pby [Presbytery]; or wherever God in his Providence might call him."[5]

Tom Beecher observed his brother Charles rather closely during this crucial period in the latter's life. He concluded that the neophyte clergyman was not as safe in the faith as their father and Henry hoped. [Charles's] "mind is not as yet," wrote Tom, "quite at rest upon all points—& I prophesy that it never will be. . . . He is however apparently happy & may become useful."[6] While waiting for Providence, in the form of Henry, his brother, to find him a church, Charles Beecher continued to supervise the music at the Second Presbyterian Church, teach a Bible Class, and preach occasionally.

Henry Ward Beecher was soon to commence one of the most laborious undertakings of his clerical career. He intended to organize a New School church in Fort Wayne and place his brother Charles in its pulpit as settled pastor. Fort Wayne was a prosperous community in northeastern Indiana with a population of about twenty-five hundred. Situated at the meeting of the Maumee, St. Marys, and St. Joseph rivers, it was the trading center for the surrounding region. The city had a relatively large Roman Catholic population, and the largest Protestant denominations represented by churches were the Lutheran, Methodist, and Presbyterian, O.S.

The First Presbyterian Church of Fort Wayne was considered to be the most important one in its Presbytery. In 1837 it had secured as its pastor Alexander T. Rankin and its services were held in a frame structure about forty feet square with a bell and steeple which was located between Barr and Lafayette streets. Rankin served the church from October, 1837, to September, 1843. During this period it retained its Old School connection, but an increasing sympathy for New School views became evident among some of its members. Samuel Merrill visited the city on a tour of the branch banks in October and became aware of this New School element. Learning that Rankin was no longer pastor and that the pulpit was vacant, Merrill thought an opportunity existed to place a New School man either at the helm of the existing church or else to organize a new church. He was convinced that the

5. Records of the Presbytery of Indianapolis, pp. 36–38, InHan.
6. Thomas K. Beecher to Isabella Beecher Hooker, Indianapolis, September 9, 1843, CtHS-D.

Presbyterians, N.S., "ought to [have] a first rate man here" but was also aware that "the people have not been in the habit of *paying* their pastor or contributing to religious purposes."[7] When Henry Ward Beecher was apprised of the situation, he reflected that a personal Beecher problem might be solved while a means was found to increase the strength of the New School in Indiana.

Beecher decided to make the long trip to Fort Wayne to assess the possibilities. As an opening move he offered to conduct meetings for its First Presbyterian Church, but its officers suspected his real motive and refused. Learning that the Indianapolis clergyman meant to come anyway, they communicated with Dr. William C. Anderson and implored him to come to Fort Wayne to block Beecher's efforts. Anderson was a respected professor of rhetoric and belles lettres at Old School-dominated Hanover College. So insistent was the plea from Fort Wayne that the forty-year-old Anderson started immediately, although it would prevent him from teaching his classes. He arrived in the northeastern Indiana city on April 14, 1844, and preached a sermon in the First Presbyterian Church that very day which, in effect, gave him control of the pulpit.

After riding and slogging through Indiana's horrendous spring mud for nearly three days, Beecher arrived in Fort Wayne. He went first to the home of acquaintances, Jesse L. Williams and his wife, Susan Creighton Williams, who were former residents of Indianapolis. Williams had been chief engineer of the Wabash and Erie Canal, but in recent years was engaged in operating a grist mill with Pliny Hoagland and Allen Hamilton. Mrs. Williams was a daughter of the William Creighton who was a Congressman during the War of 1812 and a granddaughter of David Meade who entertained the Marquis de Lafayette at the family estate of Chaumier du Prairie near Lexington, Kentucky. Beecher bluntly informed Susan Williams, a Presbyterian, that he had come to divide her church.[8] From the Williams home he went at once to another house where a group awaited him; and, in his travel-stained clothing, he conducted his first service in Fort Wayne.

7. Samuel Merrill to David Merrill, Fort Wayne, October 26, 1843, Samuel Merrill Papers, InHi.

8. Fort Wayne *Morning Gazette*, May 15, 1878; McCulloch, *Men and Measures of Half A Century*, p. 122.

As a tactical maneuver to emphasize his acceptance by the congregation of the First Presbyterian Church, Anderson invited Beecher to take a part in the next Sunday morning's service. Beecher did so, and the event ended amicably. The Indianapolis clergyman was not to be deterred, however, and that same afternoon preached a sermon at the Courthouse where he announced his intention to organize a New School church. For over two weeks Beecher and Anderson waged a holy battle for the allegiance of the Presbyterians in Fort Wayne. Beecher preached twice daily at the Courthouse and made visits to all he thought might be persuaded to join the proposed church. Anderson was just as busy in efforts to defeat Beecher's goal. The contest quickly became a topic of conversation in the community. The vigorous, magnetic Beecher opposed to the scholarly Anderson provided material for almost endless discussions as to their respective merits. Neither man weakened as the days passed.

The First Presbyterian Church claimed a membership of 139 people, and Henry Ward Beecher was able to woo just six away, five women and a man. It was a hard-fought campaign, and Beecher strove mightily to win this small group. Other New School churches had been founded with similar numbers. The Second Presbyterian Church of Indianapolis had only fifteen charter members in 1838, and the Presbyterian Church, N.S., in nearby Huntington, Indiana, was organized in 1843 with just nine members. The six in Fort Wayne asked for and received letters of dismissal from the First Presbyterian Church. Along with another six people who elected to join the new church, these twelve became the charter members of the Second Presbyterian Church (later Westminster Presbyterian Church) of Fort Wayne which was organized on May 5, 1844.

By June 4, 1844, Beecher saw both his goals realized when his brother Charles began serving as stated supply of the new church in Fort Wayne. Through sheer determination, Henry Ward Beecher had organized a church and placed in its pulpit the brother whose religious doubts had caused the family so much concern over the years. And he had done it, for all practical purposes, alone.[9]

9. George W. Allison, *Forest, Fort, and Faith. Historical Sketches of the Presbytery of Fort Wayne Organized January 2, 1845* (n.p., 1945), pp. 40–41; Fort Wayne *Morning Gazette*, May 15, 1878; *Centennial Celebration. First Presbyterian*

A few months later Henry Ward Beecher and John L. Ketcham rode north to Noblesville to attend a meeting of Presbytery on September 13, 1844, at which the former acted as moderator and the latter as clerk. Of particular interest to Beecher was news he received of his brother Charles. The younger Beecher requested permission to withdraw from the care of the Presbytery of Indianapolis in order to unite with the Presbytery of Logansport in which his church was located, and this was granted.

Disturbing to Henry, however, was the information that Charles was experiencing difficulties in his new post. During the return trip to Indianapolis the older brother mulled over what he had heard and inferred. Tired as he undoubtedly was from the rigors of the ride and the day's business, Beecher began writing a letter to Lyman Beecher as soon as he got home. So important was what he had to say that he wrote, *"Do not show this to any one but Mother & Harriet & then burn it."*[10] As Beecher analyzed the situation, his brother's troubles arose from the circumstance of being minister of a small new church and were increased by defects of personality. Most of the male members of the Second Presbyterian Church were newcomers to Fort Wayne. The older residents who included the influential and affluent of the city tended to belong to the Old School. Beecher had expected that Charles's church would draw new members from eastern families with Congregational backgrounds who would tend to be more sympathetic with New School ideas. He was worried about the effect of the Old School's contention expressed to newcomers that Charles's church was really Unitarian. "If the stream from the East *begins* to go wrong it will be difficult to check it," Beecher wrote to his father, "since strangers will be told, 'all who *have* come from Congregational Churches *have* gone with us.' We shall be cut off for supplies, defeated, & Charles, leaving with

Church (Fort Wayne, 1931); Huntington *Herald-Press,* November 3, 1943; Samuel Merrill to David Merrill, Fort Wayne, October 26, 1843, Samuel Merrill Papers, InHi; Poinsatte, *Fort Wayne During the Canal Era,* pp. 157–59; Bessie K. Roberts, "Reminiscences of Old Fort Wayne, Jesse L. Williams and J. R. Straughan," *The Old Fort News,* XVIII, No. I (March, 1955), pp. 3–6; Jesse L. Williams, *Historical Sketch of the First Presbyterian Church, Fort Wayne, Indiana* (Fort Wayne, [1860]), pp. 13–19.

10. HWB to Lyman Beecher, Indianapolis, September 13, 1844, MCR; Records of the Presbytery of Indianapolis, p. 45, InHan. Obviously the father did not burn the letter as instructed to do.

stigma of Unitarianism fastened upon him, will go away; find a resettle-
ment difficult; get sore. . . . It seems to me *that everything depends upon
his succeeding in this Enterprise."* Beecher assured his father that the
case was not hopeless, but that it was advisable that one of them go
immediately to Charles's aid. Henry hesitated to be first upon the scene.
He thought that his father could do more good as the elder man was
known as an opponent of Unitarianism and also possessed a wider
reputation as a clergyman.

Henry cited Eunice's approaching confinement as a reason for his
remaining temporarily in Indianapolis. So grave did the situation in
Fort Wayne appear to him, however, that he continued, "Nevertheless
if you cannot [go], I must. For I feel that some *leader* must be there
before Synod; & before they can get a successor to [William] Anderson.
Your age, reputation, experience, make you of all men the one to settle
Charles [*sic*] affairs for him." Then Beecher touched upon the core of
the matter. "Beside, (& subrosa) I am anxious that you should *com-
mune with Charles.* I do not believe that he is *tainted.* . . . All that I
think it worthwhile to attempt would be to repress . . . any new views,
& to urge, what he needs much to do, *practical preaching.* If you can
stand in the gap *once more,* I think you may dismiss all *care* of
C[harles] from your mind." With a reiteration that Charles's situation
was critical, Henry concluded that he would be looking for his father
to arrive in Indianapolis in a few days on his way north to Fort Wayne.[11]

Henry Ward Beecher also wrote an encouraging and admonishing
letter to Charles. "Preach little doctrine," he advised, "except what is
of mouldy orthodoxy; keep all your improved breeds, your short-
horned Durhams, your Berkshires, etc., away off to pasture. They will
get fatter, and nobody will be scared. Take hold of the most practical
subjects; popularize your sermons. I do not ask you to change yourself;
but, for a time, while captious critics are lurking, adapt your mode so as
to insure that you shall be rightly understood."[12]

In the meantime, Charles Beecher was preparing a quarterly report
to be sent to the executive secretary of the American Home Missionary

11. HWB to Lyman Beecher, Indianapolis, September 13, 1844, MCR.
12. HWB to Charles Beecher, [September, 1844], quoted in Charles Beecher
(ed.), *Autobiography, Correspondence, Etc., of Lyman Beecher, D.D.,* II, 476–77.

Society, Milton Badger. The report indicates that Henry Ward Beecher had not misunderstood or overstated the gravity of the situation to their father. Lengthy and minutely detailed, the report presented Charles Beecher's particular circumstances and also exhibits the problems facing a newly organized church in the West. Charles Beecher acknowledged that many of his difficulties arose from his own inexperience. The membership of his church currently numbered nineteen. Four of these lived out of the city and attended services infrequently. Of the remaining fifteen only three were males. One of these was too young to be of help, a second was an invalid, and the third was often away from Fort Wayne. Both Beecher and his wife were suffering from poor health. She could not visit members as a result, and his weakness had "limited greatly" his calling. The weather had been against success, since there had been an unprecedented rainy season followed by an excessively hot summer. Charles Beecher wrote of the absence of ordinary supplies. There were no hymnals, no provision for music, no lights for evening services, and no library for the use of the Sunday School.

The charge of Universalist tendencies leveled at him by Old School followers was mentioned. "This of course affords means of misrepresentation to the ill disposed," commented Charles. "These people [newcomers] have been thrown off by ultra high Calvinistic & Old School influences, & are becoming regular & attentive listeners. And as I have the misfortune to be at any rate rather original, I am of course represented as anything but sound in the faith." Charles Beecher emphasized the nature and quality of the opposition.

> By long maneuvering they [O.S.] Entrapped & bound hand & foot a decided New School majority. Kept away any N.S. Candidates, & have now more & more fortified their position. . . . The [O.S.] Session, rich, aristocratic, & formerly idle, are now. . . kept vigilant & active. Every new arrival visited, courted, told that they are N.S. in sentiment, & we Unitarian etc. Their patronage emplored, etc. & thus is fully organized & kept in action a most excellent system of opposition. I have no doubt it is their fixed resolve to cut off our Supplies, . . . dishearten us by neglect & Starve us out. They do nothing openly. . . . All is civil, polished.

Charles Beecher indicated how disheartened he was when he continued, "Now if I thought that New School were not worth something, If I thought it were not somehow dear to God, I would not stand a day longer."[13]

At this point in the composition of his report to Badger Charles received a letter from Henry which promised him material aid as well as furnishing him advice. As a result Charles reported that he had procured music books and had been enabled to purchase six lamps for fifteen dollars. He wrote that the Second Presbyterian Church of Indianapolis had given him a violin, and he thought it possible to organize a boys' singing school. Altogether the report ended in a much more optimistic vein than it had started which was probably due to the effect of his brother's letter.[14]

If Henry received an answer to his urgent letter to his father it has not been found. Meanwhile, he continued in his regular duties and pastimes. On October 4 and 5 he attended the annual fair of the Indiana Horticultural Society which was held in the State House. Flowers and vegetables were placed along the sides of the hall while fruit occupied tables for almost one hundred feet down its center. Beecher was appointed to the committee for judging fruit and also the one for judging flowers, the only man to serve on both. He limited his personal exhibit to a table of dahlias. On the afternoon of the second day he gave the principal address of the fair and spoke on general aspects of the cultivation of shrubs and flowers.[15]

Beecher was host to his father and brothers Charles and William who came to attend Synod at the Second Presbyterian Church in Indianapolis on October 10, 1844. Two items of business personally affected the Beechers. Charles's church was made the dominant one in his presbytery when ten northeastern counties, including the one containing Fort Wayne, were separated from the Presbytery of Logansport and formed into the new Presbytery of Fort Wayne. Henry Ward Beecher was honored when Synod commended his *Seven Lectures to Young Men* and recommended it to all.[16] Beecher enjoyed having his relatives with him, and he thought this Synod was one of the best he

---

13. Charles Beecher to Milton Badger, Fort Wayne, September 16, 1844, American Home Missionary Society Papers, microfilm, In.

14. *Ibid.*

15. Indianapolis *Indiana State Journal*, October 19, 1844.

16. Records of the Synod of Indiana, I, 325–38, InHan.

had attended. "We had a delightful Synod, full of the evidence of Christs presence," he wrote to Harriet. "It is amazing to me how men of . . . piety & multifarious experience—could have contrived to make ecclesiastical meetings so dry, dull & unholy, as they have hitherto usually been."[17] Henry Ward Beecher had little patience with those who thought pomposity and melancholy were appropriate attitudes for the Christian.

When traveling on one occasion with Hugh McCulloch, Beecher had entertained the banker by "mimick[ing] preachers who seemed to think that sanctimonious countenances and whining tones were the indications of zealous faith. To Mr. Beecher, religion was joyousness, Christianity the agency by which men were to be made not only better but happier," recalled McCulloch. " 'Some people,' said he, 'think that I am not solemn enough in the pulpit, nor staid or reverent enough out of it. I wonder what they would think if I should act just as I feel.' "[18] Beecher believed that he had been "born so that it is easy for me to be joyful. My mind rises into a joyful state spontaneously. It did before I knew anything about religion."[19] If the practice of religion and matters pertaining to religion were dull, Beecher believed, it was the fault of the practitioner and not of religion.

After talking with Charles at Synod and learning that he planned to request ordination when the newly constituted Presbytery of Fort Wayne met in November, Henry Ward Beecher and his father decided to wait and go to Fort Wayne at that time. The father arrived there first after a remarkable journey from Walnut Hills by way of canal boat to St. Mary's, Ohio. Setting out from the latter place on horseback at ten o'clock on Friday night, he rode for sixty-two miles over twisting, ill-defined roads and detours, reaching Fort Wayne at five o'clock on Saturday afternoon.[20] Once there he rode directly to the home of Hugh McCulloch whose guest he was to be during his stay in the city.

Bespattered with dust and mud the senior Beecher greeted the McCulloch family, told them something of his journey, and requested

17. HWB to Harriet Beecher Stowe, Indianapolis, October [?], 1844, CtY; Allison, *Forest, Fort, and Faith. Historical Sketches of the Presbytery of Fort Wayne Organized January 2, 1845,* p. 12.

18. McCulloch, *Men and Measures of Half A Century,* p. 144.

19. HWB, *Lecture-Room Talks,* pp. 156–57.

20. Indianapolis *Indiana State Journal,* April 16, 1845; HWB to Mrs. Henry Ward Beecher, Fort Wayne, November 11, 1844, CtY.

whiskey. Going almost at once to his room, he took a bath in cold water and followed it with a whiskey rubdown. He returned to the family "apparently as fresh as if he had been resting for hours," and stayed laughing and talking with them until nine o'clock when he went to bed. To McCulloch's question as to how he got through the awful ride, Beecher answered, "Comfortably enough, but I should not if my horse had not known more about roads than I did. I clung to the saddle, gave him the rein, and he brought me through all right." The next morning he awoke feeling rested and preached two sermons that day.[21]

Hugh McCulloch, cashier and manager of the Fort Wayne branch and also a director of the State Bank of Indiana, was a good friend of Henry Ward Beecher's whose church he frequently attended when in Indianapolis. Until Lyman Beecher's visit to Fort Wayne in 1844, however, the banker and the Ohio clergyman had not been well acquainted. McCulloch was charmed by Lyman Beecher who, he wrote, "proved to be one of the most social and agreeable of men. He spent a number of days at my house, and I became strongly attached to him. . . . he abounded in sympathy, in geniality, in good-will for everybody. He seemed to be happy in throwing off restraint and indulging his natural taste."[22] Lyman Beecher could have found few hosts in Fort Wayne more eager to welcome him. His comfort was assiduously provided for in the impressive story-and-a-half McCulloch house located between the Wabash and Erie Canal on the south of the St. Marys River on the north. Loving to hunt and noting a woods just across the river from McCulloch's home, Beecher borrowed a gun. On at least one occasion he bagged a rabbit and a pigeon for which he was duly admired by the McCulloch family. Most of the time, however, he attended to son Charles's interests in the city.

Henry Ward Beecher traveled to Fort Wayne on horseback, and it took him longer than on his previous trip in the spring as he was riding a different and slower horse. As he neared Fort Wayne he met Hugh McCulloch, and the men exchanged greetings and news. McCulloch was en route for Indianapolis, and the clergyman charged him to see Eunice and tell her that her husband had made his trip safely.[23] It

21. McCulloch, *Men and Measures of Half A Century*, pp. 148–49.
22. *Ibid.*
23. HWB to Mrs. Henry Ward Beecher, Fort Wayne, November 11, 1844, CtY.

was late afternoon when Beecher arrived in the city, but he was hurried to a meeting in a home where he met ten or fifteen men and women who might be persuaded to join the Second Presbyterian Church. Tired as he was, he "read a few passages from the New Testament, and made an address in language so beautiful and appropriate," recalled a listener, "in a voice so tender and affectionate, that all present were spellbound, and when he closed there was not a dry eye except his own in the room."[24]

Presbytery met as directed on Friday, November 8, 1844, with three ministers, one elder, and one licentiate present. Lyman Beecher delivered the sermon and some routine matters of business were acted upon. The Presbytery received Charles Beecher's application for ordination and considered it at once. He was examined as to the extent of his theological knowledge and his doctrinal beliefs. Following this, he gave a trial sermon with faith as its topic. Lyman Beecher showed evidence of emotional stress and "was repeatedly detected in the act of wiping his eyes."[25] The Presbytery declared its satisfaction with the examination, and candlelighting was set as the time for the ceremony of ordination.

In the evening before an assembly consisting of the members of Presbytery, Charles's family, members of the congregation, and other interested people the dignified service took place. Henry Ward Beecher preached a sermon based on a text from 1 Corinthians 22. His listeners were struck by what was assumed to be the coincidence that he should select the same text that Charles Beecher had chosen to use for his first sermon in Fort Wayne.

> Mr. [Thomas] Anderson from Huntington [Ind.] made the prayer after the right hand of fellowship and the Venerable Dr. [Lyman] Beecher gave the Charge. He commenced thus. "Twenty-eight years ago my dear son your mother now a saint in heaven committed you to my arms to bear you from her sight forever exclaiming what will become of you poor child. She gave you her blessing and consecrated you to God and said to me, I desire all my sons to be ministers of Christ." He then said, "one has gone to meet her there [George Beecher], the others are thanks

24. McCulloch, *Men and Measures of Half A Century*, pp. 141–42.
25. Charles Beecher (ed.), *Autobiography, Correspondence, Etc., of Lyman Beecher, D.D.*, II, 477–79; Allison, *Forest, Fort, and Faith. Historical Sketches of the Presbytery of Fort Wayne Organized January 2, 1845*, p. 12.

be to God ministers of him." You may well suppose [wrote Mrs. McCulloch] there was not a dry eye in the house.[26]

The Second Presbyterian Church of Fort Wayne had twenty-eight members at the time of Charles Beecher's ordination, an increase of sixteen since the spring, and plans were being made to acquire a church building in 1845. Subscriptions had started recently, and a total of $1,035 was pledged for the support of a pastor and building maintenance.[27] On the surface, at least, the new church seemed well on the way to success. Lyman Beecher did not underestimate the strength of the Old School opposition, however, nor did he close his eyes to the defects in Charles's character. He adjured his son to:

1. Be strong in thy determined purpose, for no ordinary decision will avail.
2. Count the cost, and give thyself *wholly* to thy work.
3. Preach the Gospel.
4. Take heed to thyself, to thy body, to thy mind.
5. Take heed to thy heart.
6. Take heed to thy doctrine.[28]

In a continuing effort to help Charles, his father and brother Henry worked together in conducting a protracted meeting lasting nearly three weeks. They drew sizable audiences, but it was difficult to gain commitments. Nine people joined the church and others expressed interest. The protracted meeting did result in Hugh McCulloch's admitting that he was beginning to feel there was "something in being a christian [*sic*]."[29] Reared in a Congregational church, McCulloch had not joined the Presbyterian fold to which his wife belonged.

Charles Beecher assisted with the services and organized activities which he thought might be beneficial to his church. He formed a Sabbath School class for young men, started a singing school, encouraged the establishment of a sewing society for the ladies, and assisted with

26. Susan Man McCulloch to Maria Man Halsey, Fort Wayne, [November [?], 1844], Hugh McCulloch Papers, InU.

27. *Ibid.*

28. Charles Beecher (ed.), *Autobiography, Correspondence, Etc., of Lyman Beecher, D.D.,* II, 477–79.

29. Susan Man McCulloch to Maria Man Halsey, Fort Wayne, [November [?], 1844], InU; William B. Schiltges, "Hugh McCulloch" (Paper read before the Indianapolis Literary Club, n.d.), InU.

plans for a concert and lecture. The weekly prayer meeting was his responsibility. So quickly had answer been made to his pleas for books and supplies that he was even able to share some surplus materials with poorer churches in the area.[30]

Henry Ward Beecher took time from his preaching and visiting to write notes to his two older children. "I hope you [Harriet Eliza] have been a very good girl since I left you. I have thought much about you—because I love you very much. I hope you try everyday to act so as to please Christ." He continued, "If you only try to please yourself that, is selfishness; if you try to make everybody about you happy is to act just as Christ did, when he was on earth." Making allowance for Henry Barton Beecher's tender age, the father wrote, "Papa gone away to Fort Wayne. Pretty soon pa get on his horse, & ride, ride, ride to see Henry. Henry go to the window—& see pa come & say Oh there's papa & pa run into the house and catch his little boy & kiss all to pieces."[31] The notes were enclosed in a letter to Eunice which expressed a curious mixture of affection and lack of consideration. "I hope you let the children go out in the *air* a good deal, & also the flower children;" wrote Beecher, "when it is even *cold* at morning & evening, then maybe an hour or two in the middle of the day." Giving her detailed directions to *"wet* the foliage thoroughly every day," he continued that if she had time she could get some green paint and cover "all the pots, for they, being porous evaporate the moisture & make a crack between the dirt & sides of pot, all around, painting will stop evaporation and occasion less waste of moisture." After similar instructions he ended, "I have no doubt they [flowers] will shew you to have been a very careful nurse."[32] It did not occur to him that a woman with small children and a household to care for had more pressing responsibilities than painting flower pots in November.

Between them, Lyman Beecher and Henry Ward Beecher had reinforced Charles's position in Fort Wayne; and when they returned to their homes they felt that he was safely ensconced in his position. For

---

30. Susan Man McCulloch to Maria Man Halsey, Fort Wayne, [November [?], 1844], InU.

31. HWB to Harriet Eliza Beecher and Henry Barton Beecher, Fort Wayne, November 11, 1844, CtY.

32. HWB to Mrs. Henry Ward Beecher, November 11, 1844, CtY.

the better part of a year everything seemed to be going reasonably well for him, but in September word reached Indianapolis that Charles was having difficulties. Julia Merrill, now a young woman, was visiting friends in Fort Wayne, and she wrote of the gossip circulating among the Presbyterian congregation. "Mr. [Charles] Beecher is pretty well liked here, though not so much as I expected," and more candidly,

> the truth is they find too much fault with him, some think he is conceited, that he knows & shows too often that he is *Dr. Beechers* son. Others say he preaches too plain, that no man ever did succeed that preached *The Bible*. He has not enough tact, etc etc. He seems to be common property & every [one] that pleases picks at him. He does not hear all that is said, or I should think he would become disheartened.[33]

Julia Merrill viewed Charles Beecher as a romantic figure, and her best friend, Elizabeth Bates, agreed with the sentiment. The two girls had been fascinated by the Beecher brothers, Henry and Charles, since they had come to know them. Julia had accompanied Henry and Eunice to Indianapolis in 1839 and ever afterwards took a proprietary interest in their fortunes. She and Elizabeth Bates were chaperoned by the clergyman to New England in 1841 and had returned with him and his family to the Hoosier capital that fall. When Charles arrived in Indianapolis the girls took a similar interest in him. They regarded the brothers, progressively, as heroes, religious mentors, and objects of romantic fancies. Julia adopted Henry as her special friend while Elizabeth was drawn more to Charles, or at least in view of her friendship with Julia found it prudent to seem fonder of Charles. It was in a letter to Elizabeth that Julia wrote, "Do you see Mr. [Henry] Beecher any now, if you do give him my love &c. Do you understand? I gave your message to Mr. Charles B. He laughed and said now he was a preacher he would try to do better."[34] Julia's letter to her mother gave no such instruction.

It was part of a pastor's duty to establish rapport with the young people of his church. Eunice Beecher had enjoyed Julia's company and aid at intervals during the girl's adolescence, and Elizabeth Bates was on

33. Julia D. Merrill to Jane Anderson Merrill, Fort Wayne, September 20, 1845, Samuel Merrill Papers, InHi.

34. Julia D. Merrill to Elizabeth Bates, Fort Wayne, September 21, 1845, Julia Merrill Moores Papers, InHi.

such good terms with Charles Beecher's wife that the latter sent her love to Elizabeth by way of Julia's letter. If the quality of the girls' affection for the brothers was changing subtly either the Beechers were unaware of it or did not take it seriously. There is no evidence that Henry Ward Beecher or Charles felt more than avuncular friendship and affection for these girls in 1845.

Beecher traveled to Terre Haute in October to attend Synod. He was elected moderator and was given the honor of preaching the missionary sermon on Sunday morning, October 11, 1846. Among the clergy in attendance was his brother Charles. The latter figured in a report laid before the body from the Presbytery of Fort Wayne.

Charles Beecher had offended members of his Presbytery who had attended the dedication of the Second Presbyterian Church in Fort Wayne with the contents of two sermons he delivered on the occasion. He was visited later by a committee who talked with him about the questionable views he expressed in the sermons. Charles Beecher defended himself "in a kind and brotherly manner," the committee reported, "and he wishes to remain in connection with the Presbytery if he may be permitted to do so."[35] The committee recommended that nothing further be done, but it stated that some of the minister's views were "subversive of all order in the house of God; . . . they are a total misapprehension of the views and practices of the Presbyterian Church with which he is connected."[36] The report was read, accepted, and laid on the table by the Presbytery of Fort Wayne. In October it was transmitted to the Synod at Terre Haute where it was read, approved, and signed by the moderator, Henry Ward Beecher, but no special attention was directed toward it by Synod.[37]

That the action directed against Charles Beecher was not more severe was probably due to the support which he received from influential members of his congregation and friends including Benjamin W. Oakley, John Hamilton, Royal W. Taylor, F. H. Tyler, and Hugh McCulloch. These men urged Charles Beecher to publish the sermons which, in their opinion, were "an able and fearless exposition of truths,

35. Allison, *Forest, Fort, and Faith. Historical Sketches of the Presbytery of Fort Wayne Organized January 2, 1845*, p. 13.
36. *Ibid.*
37. Records of the Synod of Indiana, III, 1–14, InHan.

which lie at the very foundation of Protestantism, and which seem for years to have been lost sight of by the great body of Protestant Christians." As a result appeared *The Bible, A Sufficient Creed; Being Two Discourses Delivered at the Dedication of the Second Presbyterian Church. Fort Wayne, Ia. February 22d, 1846* (Fort Wayne, 1846),[38] a book of thirty-three pages. Had Charles Beecher not received the support of these men and had the Presbytery been less concerned about the effect of weakening the new church in Fort Wayne, the outcome might have been different. From the standpoints of Presbytery and Synod, however, the remedy for Charles Beecher's heresy might be worse for the church politic than the illness. Henry Ward Beecher does not seem to have involved himself in the matter nor shown much interest in it. He had worked to convert Charles, to organize a church for him, and to establish him securely in the pulpit of that church. Charles Beecher need expect no more major efforts on his behalf from his elder brother in Indianapolis.

38. For the opinion expressed by Oakley and others see p. ii.

XV

Matters of Life and Death

THE BEECHER FAMILY HAD BEEN PLAGUED BY ILLNESS DURING MUCH of the fall and winter, and Eunice was so sick in the middle of January, 1844, it was thought she might die. The nature of her malady is not known, but as she conceived her fourth child about this time it is possible that her usual difficulties with pregnancy and a generally weakened condition produced alarming symptoms. Beecher's grasp on his church was firm, however, in spite of his domestic worries and problems. "The Congregation gradually increases," wrote Samuel Merrill, "and Mr. Beecher is still popular."[1]

Beecher's was not the only family troubled by sickness. A resident of the town much admired by the clergyman died at nine o'clock on the evening of February 7, 1844. While not everyone shared Beecher's regard for Noah Noble the latter was generally accorded respect. Calvin Fletcher considered the deceased to be "a man of gentlemanly bearing of very good sense but excessively fond of the good opinions & feelings of the world. He was balanced much between love of wealth & that of popularity. He was a man who stood fair before the world—was cut out to be one of natures masterpieces."[2] The business and professional men of Indianapolis assembled at Browning's hotel by nine o'clock on the

1. Samuel Merrill to David Merrill, Indianapolis, January 17, 1844, Samuel Merrill Papers, InHi.
2. Calvin Fletcher Diary, February 9, 1844, InHi.

morning of February 8, 1844, an intensely cold day, to plan the funeral to be held on the 11th. While the family of a public figure such as Noble would be consulted, it was considered a mark of respect for the funeral arrangements to be made by his peers. Nicholas McCarty, a merchant and real estate speculator, presided at the meeting. Forty-three men were appointed to a committee to make recommendations and attend to details. On the next day Samuel Merrill served as chairman at a meeting held in the Courthouse where resolutions of condolence were read, seconded, and forwarded to the Noble family. It was announced that all the men would attend the funeral and wear badges of mourning for thirty days to show respect for the dead man.

People arrived on foot and in carriages at the Noble home on the day of the funeral to view the corpse and say a few words of sympathy to the family. Snow fell steadily. Those who were to accompany the body to the church assembled at the house shortly after noon, and at one-thirty the procession formed. At its head were Calvin Fletcher, Oliver H. Smith, and James M. Ray. Immediately behind them walked Samuel Merrill, "Andy" Smith, and S. V. B. Noel. They were followed by the horse-drawn hearse, the Noble family and close friends, and members of the Masonic lodge to which the deceased had belonged. Others fell in behind the lodge members, and the lengthy procession proceeded slowly to Washington Street and thence to Meridian Street. Although the snow continued to fall heavily, the route was lined with spectators. Bells tolled.

Noble had joined the Methodist Episcopal Church, Wesley Chapel, of which Lucien W. Berry was then minister only a few days before his death, and it was to this church his body was borne in as much splendor as Indianapolis could provide. Berry was to conduct the funeral service. On the way to the church James M. Ray asked Calvin Fletcher, a Methodist, to request that Beecher and Phineas D. Gurley be permitted to participate in the service. Fletcher did so, Berry agreed, and Beecher and Gurley took places at the front of the church near the Methodist clergyman. The funeral began with a prayer by Gurley, Berry delivered the sermon, and the concluding prayer was offered by Beecher. Afterwards the coffin was taken to the new cemetery and committed to the earth. It was the largest funeral to take place in Indianapolis during Beecher's residence in the city. A week later the Presbyterian minister delivered his own memorial service for Noah Noble.[3]

Eunice's cousin, Julia Bullard, was still living with the Beechers in Indianapolis. She had become acquainted with the widower Stoughton A. Fletcher who was the father of two young daughters, and a friendship developed between the woman from Massachusetts and the banker. Attracted to Julia, Fletcher asked Beecher's permission as her nearest male relative to court her. Beecher had no objection, and Fletcher became a frequent caller at the Beecher home. Eunice Beecher liked him. "He was a man whom most would call eccentric," she wrote of his fictional counter-part, "and not very likely to be a general favorite; ... [he possessed] sterling traits of character ... his peculiarities (to friends) were sources of perpetual amusement, rather than any annoyance."[4] She encouraged the courtship.

Stoughton A. Fletcher was not a man to discuss his plans, and his brother Calvin learned of the proposed marriage between Stoughton and Julia Bullard less than a week before the wedding. Beecher performed the ceremony at the home of Elijah S. Alvord, a business associate of the groom's, on Tuesday evening, February 20, 1844. In keeping with Fletcher's widower status and Julia's circumstances the wedding was simple. A large number of family and friends were present to witness the ceremony, however, and share the wedding cake. The marriage of Fletcher and Julia Bullard formed the first family tie between the Beecher-Bullard families and a resident of Indianapolis.[5]

Life in the Beecher household was busy and rather gay in the summer of 1844. Charles and his family were settled in Fort Wayne, and there was a feeling of relief and gratification that he seemed to be on

3. Calvin Fletcher Diary, February 11, 1844, InHi; W. W. Hibben, *Rev. James Havens* (Indianapolis: Sentinel Co., 1872), p. 145; Woollen, *Biographical and Historical Sketches of Early Indiana*, pp. 66–67; Indianapolis *Indiana State Journal*, February 14, 1844; HWB, Sermons, February 18, 1844, CtY.

4. [Mrs. Beecher], *From Dawn to Daylight*, pp. 246–48; Sulgrove, *History of Indianapolis and Marion County, Indiana*, pp. 219–20; Dunn, *Indiana and Indianans*, III, 1236.

5. Calvin Fletcher Diary, February 17 and March 2, 1844, InHi; Indianapolis *Indiana State Journal*, February 28, 1844; [Mrs. Beecher], *From Dawn to Daylight*, pp. 273–74.

his way to usefulness in the family tradition. Harriet Beecher Stowe was a guest at Henry's for several weeks and basked in the freedom from household responsibility. "I enjoy myself very well here at Henry's. The cottage is still & quiet," she wrote to Calvin, "& I hear the clock tick with great satisfaction."[6] Eunice, heavy with another child, enjoyed Harriet's presence and companionship. A constant stream of callers passed through the Beecher doors. One of them who was especially welcome was the Reverend Darcia H. Allen, a faculty member at Lane, who stopped briefly on the morning of July 16 to leave two pocket handkerchiefs for Harriet and to tell her news of her family at home in Walnut Hills.

Always intrigued by the unusual, Beecher and his sister Harriet experimented with mesmerism, a forerunner of hypnotism which was a fad in both the United States and Europe. So widespread was interest in the phenomenon that a man named Keeley had lectured on it and given demonstrations in Indianapolis two years earlier. At about the time Henry Ward Beecher was trying to mesmerize his sister in Indiana a young man named William Ballantyne Hodgson was attempting the same feat on Mary Ann Evans (George Eliot) in England. Hodgson succeeded so well that Miss Evans "could not open her eyes, and begged him most piteously to do it for her, which he did immediately by passes."[7]

Possibly Beecher possessed more animal magnetism which was considered a prerequisite, for his sister's experience was even more intense than the English novelist's. She described it to her husband:

> The first session he succeeded in almost throwing me, into convulsions—spasms & shocks of heat & prickly sensation ran all over me my lungs were violently constricted & my heart in dreadful commotion & I was so frightened that I called out for quarter. The strange tempestuous effect was occasioned simply by our sitting opposite to each other with our eyes fixed & our thumbs in contact for about thirty minutes—& it was dissipated by making reverse passes which relieved first my head, then my lungs then my lower limbs & lastly my arms, tho the thumbs remained numb & prickly for some time after. You may be sure after

6. Harriet Beecher Stowe to Calvin E. Stowe, Indianapolis, July 16, 1844, MCR.

7. Mrs. Charles Bray to Mrs. Charles Christian Hennell, Coventry, England, July 28, 1844, quoted in Gordon S. Haight (ed.), *The George Eliot Letters* (7 volumes. New Haven: Yale University Press, 1954–1955), I, 180; Holloway, *Indianapolis*, p. 75.

being thus violently possessed with the demon of mesmerism, that I began to have rather reverend ideas of the same.

Fascinated by their success, Henry and Harriet made three more attempts and were rewarded with success each time. "The last time," penned Harriet, "I came nearer to the stupor & drowsiness described in books. The sensation was precisely the same and equal in amount to that produced by laudanum when I took 140 or 150 drops last spring—but the sleep was not consummated. Thus you see I have come to the verge of the spirit land." Harriet Beecher Stowe had thought she could not be mesmerized. She concluded her description of the odd experience to Calvin by writing, "Well but this is a strange business this human frame—I should be glad to know more of it."[8] Beecher departed for Crawfordsville to attend commencement, and their experiments were never resumed.

Late July was hot and sultry in Indianapolis with daytime temperatures ranging between 80 and 95 degrees, but the Beechers and their guest amused themselves in spite of the oppressive heat. Knowing of her interest in Negroes, Beecher took Harriet to visit Uncle Tom Magruder and his family who lived in a small house at the corner of Noble and Market streets in Indianapolis. Beecher was fond of the aged man who was thought to be about ninety-seven years old. Uncle Tom's household consisted of himself; his middle-aged children, Moses and Louisa; and another Negro named Peter who was about the age of Moses. Thomas Magruder had been the slave of Noah Noble's father; freed by Noah Noble, he and his family lived upon a pension which the ex-Governor had provided. Peter was a former slave of Judge Isaac Dunn, a resident of Lawrenceburgh. When Peter expressed loneliness, Judge Dunn arranged for him to live with the Magruder family whom he had known earlier in the river town. Henry Ward Beecher visited the Magruder cabin frequently, and his taking Harriet to see the family was not particularly noteworthy in itself. On at least one such visit she made notes of the conversation which occurred and described her surroundings.[9]

8. Harriet Beecher Stowe to Calvin E. Stowe, Indianapolis, July 16, 1844, MCR.
9. Indianapolis *Indiana State Journal*, February 26, 1857; Indianapolis *News*, September 2, 1911; Dunn, *Indiana and Indianans*, I, 506. Residents of Indianapolis believed Thomas Magruder and his family were prototypes for "Uncle Tom" and

Henry Ward Beecher ate supper one evening at the home of friends named Bradshaw who lived on a farm four miles north of the city. The minister enlivened table conversation with his wit, and everyone was in good spirits. Encouraged by his father's mellow mood, an adolescent son asked permission to attend a quarter race the next day. The running of such races was a popular sport with the young bloods of Indianapolis. The usual track was a lane lined on both sides by a fence not far from the Bradshaw land. The horses were, for the most part, ordinary animals whose owners were proud of their speed. Wagers of five dollars or more might be placed on the outcome of a race; and if foul play were suspected, a fight might follow. To watch or participate in a quarter race placed the person among the daring and worldly of Indianapolis. John Bradshaw doubted that his father would let him attend, but the senior Bradshaw never got a chance to state his opinion. Beecher listened to the boy and intervened quickly to say that he should not be permitted to go. The clergyman considered such races to be the resort of "all the idle, the dissipated, the rogues, . . . the worthless, [and] the refuse."[10] Beecher was appreciative of horses himself, and he understood the boy's disappointment but that did not outweigh the danger of attending a race.

Beecher happened to meet the lad in Indianapolis some time later, and he showed the youth a new horse he had purchased recently. Young Bradshaw spotted that Beecher's big bay horse was an old racer by a mark on its breast and agreed readily when the minister asked him to ride along to the Bradshaw farm. "As we were on the way," recalled John Bradshaw, "we came to a stretch of smooth, level road and before we passed the first milestone Mr. Beecher handed me his watch and let the horse out to speed. We fairly flew. I remember we made that mile in less than three minutes." At the supper table that evening the boy asked Beecher why it was all right to race the minister's horse but not to attend a quarter race. Beecher replied, "The Lord made that horse to run, and I let him."[11] Beecher's objection was not to racing but to the atmosphere surrounding it at the makeshift track.

certain other characters in Harriet Beecher Stowe's novel, *Uncle Tom's Cabin*. Mrs. Stowe did not cite such an origin in her book, *Key to Uncle Tom's Cabin*, pp. 37–50.

10. HWB, *Seven Lectures to Young Men*, pp. 187–88.

11. John Bradshaw, Reminiscences, May 25, 1902, clipping in George S.

Maria Bullard Barton and her nineteen-year-old son came to stay with the Beechers in the latter part of July. Young Barton had been a roommate of James Cooley Fletcher, eldest son of Calvin Fletcher, for a term at Brown University. The Fletcher boy had been a guest in the Barton home in Worcester, Massachusetts, where he had been kindly treated. Appreciative of the Bartons' courtesy to his son, Calvin Fletcher called on them at the Beecher home on July 25, and offered to show the young New Englander the points of interest in Indianapolis. They made plans for a sightseeing jaunt the next day. A hard rain fell during the night, and the day dawned pleasantly cool. Fletcher called for Barton in the afternoon and escorted him about the city. Afterwards they returned to the Beecher home where Fletcher remained to take tea with the Beechers, Harriet Beecher Stowe, the Bartons, and another brother of Eunice's, Talbut Bullard, who had recently arrived in Indianapolis. Fletcher invited the group to tea at his home the following day.[12]

Talbut Bullard was younger than Eunice Beecher. Just as her other brother, Artemas Bullard, had worked with Lyman Beecher in church affairs in the Cincinnati area, so Talbut Bullard and Charles Beecher had been associated in the operation of a school in New Orleans. When the school failed Talbut studied medicine in Cincinnati and arrived in Indianapolis on July 4, 1844, where he would later establish a practice. He brought with him his wife, Susan, and two children. To be included in the invitation to the Fletchers' party was a stroke of good fortune for the beginning physician as the Fletchers were a numerous and prosperous family.[13]

Since Beecher did not keep a carriage, Fletcher sent his sixteen-year-old son Miles in a rented vehicle to take the guests to the Fletcher residence. Fletcher could easily afford his own carriage, but it was typical of the man that he would not have one. Guests at the party included Stoughton and Julia Bullard Fletcher as well as the Beecher

Cottman's Indiana Scrapbook Collection, VIII, 44, In; Holloway, *Indianapolis,* p. 54; Abbott, "Henry Ward Beecher," *Atlantic Monthly,* XCII, 546–47; Mrs. Beecher, "Mr. Beecher as I Knew Him," *Ladies Home Journal,* March, 1892, p. 4.

12. Calvin Fletcher Diary, July 25 and 26, 1844, InHi.

13. Nowland, *Sketches of Prominent Citizens of 1876,* pp. 479–80; Annie Beecher Scoville, Notes, n.d., CtY; HWB to Lucy White Bullard, Indianapolis, October 30, 1844, CtY.

contingent. The gathering was a success, and Fletcher noted his satisfaction with it in his diary.[14]

Harriet's visit ended in August, and she returned to her home in Walnut Hills. "I have had such a delightful visit with Henry this summer," she wrote, "such warm full confiding outpouring of soul to soul— I love him so much."[15] It had been a good summer for Henry Ward Beecher. Perhaps his recognition of this was one reason why he delivered a sermon on gratitude on September 8, 1844. Selecting his text from Genesis, he elaborated on the theme to a crowded church.[16] Beecher's sense of well-being, unfortunately, was not destined to be with him long.

When he learned of Charles's difficulties with his church in Fort Wayne in the autumn of 1844, his family in Indianapolis was again unwell. Little Hatty was recovering from her third attack of malaria for the season, and baby Henry was convalescing from the same malady. The boy was improving rapidly, but Hatty needed constant care which Eunice could scarcely provide. Approaching the birth of her fourth child, Eunice was suffering from false labor pains. Beginning in late September the pains came intermittently with varying degrees of intensity. Her long wait ended on October 18, 1844, when she was delivered of "a fine, well formed & healthy boy—George Lyman—who eats & sleeps—and cries only by way of pepper & salt—a little only in a good while."[17] Beecher's letter announcing the child's birth to his anxious grandmother in Massachusetts was both brief and belated. Citing preoccupation with work for the twelve day delay, Beecher described the arrival of the infant in a paragraph and commented that Eunice had got along much better than she had anticipated. Eunice Beecher had endured a more difficult labor and delivery than her husband's letter indicated. The note which she included to her mother was written in a spidery handwriting which clearly proclaimed her weakness. "I am not well enough to write today. Will write soon. Henry is so hurried—with business just now," wrote Eunice, "that you must not scold him for a short

14. Calvin Fletcher Diary, July 27, 1844, InHi.

15. Harriet Beecher Stowe to Calvin E. Stowe, Walnut Hills, September 3, 1844, MCR.

16. Genesis 40:14–23; HWB, Sermons, September 8, 1844, CtY.

17. HWB to Lucy White Bullard, Indianapolis, October 30, 1844, CtY; HWB to Harriet Beecher Stowe, Indianapolis, October [?], 1844, CtY.

letter. He leaves for Fort Wayne on Monday to be gone 4 or 5 weeks."[18] Beecher's work in his brother's behalf kept him away nearer three weeks. It was during this absence from Indianapolis that Beecher wrote the letter quoted earlier, asking his wife, still weak from childbirth and with a new baby and two sick children to nurse, to paint his flower pots.

Henry Ward Beecher had the pleasure when he returned home to receive his good friend, Henry P. Coburn, as a member into the Second Presbyterian Church. Although a generation older than the minister, Coburn and he had become friends and shared a mutual love of gardening. Coburn resembled Beecher physically and was "a man of very extensive information, a great reader and a good talker; honest, independent and benevolent."[19] It is probable that the lawyer joined the church to please its pastor, for Coburn did not attach much importance to denominational differences.

The two men were frequently joined in conversation by Hiram Brown and Aaron Aldridge. Beecher had a special respect for the latter, a nurseryman, whom he came to know well.

> I like him because he loves flowers as I do, and I have a great admiration of him because he is one of the honestest men that I have ever met. I have made him a study. He is always what he appears to be—a perfectly upright man. Nothing would induce him to swerve from the truth, and yet he is an infidel, a disbeliever in the Bible and a future life. I wish that I and my church members were more like him.[20]

Another tie between Beecher and Coburn was their mutual love of books. In 1844 the Marion County Library was founded with Coburn as one of its trustees. It was he who selected the first books for the little collection which was located in a small room in the southwest corner of the Courthouse. The library soon had some two thousand volumes on its shelves; the number of subscribers ranged between seventy and one hundred. The first librarian was Henry P. Coburn's son, Augustus Coburn.[21]

---

18. Mrs. Henry Ward Beecher to Lucy White Bullard, Indianapolis, October 30, 1844, CtY.
19. Taylor, *Biographical Sketches and Review of the Bench and Bar of Indiana*, p. 77; List of Members, Records of the Second Presbyterian Church, InISPC.
20. McCulloch, *Men and Measures of Half A Century*, pp. 143–44.
21. Sulgrove, *History of Indianapolis and Marion County, Indiana*, p. 439.

Henry Ward Beecher was curious about the character of the men who settled Indianapolis. He read Calvin Fletcher's files of old city newspapers and even examined some of the early laws passed by the state legislature. Beecher told Fletcher on December 13, 1844, when he spent the evening at the latter's home, that he was thinking of preaching a sermon about the settlers. Fletcher told Beecher a great deal about the first inhabitants of Indianapolis and "the numerous candidates who ran for offices at the organization of the County in 1822. They were mostly Kentuckians who had failed in business & fled to this place for protection or to recussitate [sic] their fallen fortunes." Since Fletcher was one of the shrewdest men in the city his comments upon his contemporaries must have been enlightening. He told Beecher that another type of inhabitant were farmers "from White Water & Penn[sylvania] a few . . . Yankeys &c Composed the great body of the people."[22] In addition to gaining material for a sermon Beecher would have received insight into many of the men's actions on whom he depended for support. And the two friends must have enjoyed what came perilously close to being a good gossip.

In February, 1845, a fatal illness struck the young man who, with his wife, had been suspended by Session from the full privileges of church membership after the wife gave birth to a full-term baby less than five months after her wedding. The young man's situation posed a painful problem to Beecher. If the suspension were removed, would impressionable young people think the pastor and Session condoned fornication? To allow the young man to die without reinstatement seemed cruel to him and to his family. The decision was made to lift the suspension when it was generally accepted that he was dying. Death occurred on Wednesday, February 12, and his funeral service was preached by Beecher and J. C. Smith, a Methodist minister, at the morning service on Sunday, February 16, 1845, in the Second Presbyterian Church. Such a grave fault as the deceased had committed could not be overlooked, however, without incurring a misinterpretation of why his privileges as a church member had been returned. Calvin Fletcher was curious about the manner in which Beecher would tackle the problem

22. Calvin Fletcher Diary, December 14, 1844, InHi.

and was gratified when the clergyman "disposed of this delicate matter in a masterly manner, brief but excellent manner."[23]

Talbut Bullard and his wife were received into membership in the Second Presbyterian Church on March 30, 1845. Bullard had begun to practice medicine in Indianapolis as a partner of George W. Mears. He rapidly acquired a reputation as an articulate, intelligent, but quick-tempered man. His wife, a native of Marietta, Ohio, provided welcome feminine companionship for Eunice; and to some extent the Bullards filled the gap in family life left by the departure of Charles and Sarah for Fort Wayne.[24]

In April, Beecher was re-elected a trustee of Wabash College with Samuel Merrill, Samuel Lowrie, and Israel Williams. Some two months later, on June 29, 1845, his youngest child, George Lyman Beecher, was baptized.[25] But tranquility of the early summer would be shattered for Beecher a few days later.

The Fourth of July celebration was one of the important events of the year in Indianapolis, complete with a parade and patriotic speeches. As part of the festivities addresses were delivered at the Second Presbyterian Church by Edward Lander, later judge of the Court of Common Pleas, and by William Wallace, who represented the military companies. While decorum and oratory at the church engaged the attention of the audience, the lower orders of the city were celebrating boisterously on nearby Illinois Street, where liquor flowed freely. A young man, Nicholas Wood, became drunk and expressed it by an uneasy mixture of excessive joviality and quarrelsomeness. It chanced that a powerfully built Negro, John Tucker, who was a servant to James Blake, attempted to pass Wood on the street. Beginning by teasing Tucker, the drunken Wood ended by abusing him. The Negro tried to ease away quietly from Wood but was not permitted to do so. The noise of the encounter drew passers-by who added their own abusive comments. The angry Tucker hit Wood who fought back. The Negro's

23. *Ibid.*, February 16, 1845; Indianapolis *Indiana State Journal*, February 19, 1845.

24. Records of the Second Presbyterian Church, pp. 65–66, InISPC; Edson, *The Church God's Building*, pp. 16–17.

25. Ristine, *A Digest of the Minutes of the Board of Trustees of Wabash College, 1832–1922*, pp. 10–14; Records of the Second Presbyterian Church, p. 66, InISPC.

temerity in striking a white man aroused the growing crowd, and soon various objects were aimed at Tucker. The situation deteriorated. Tucker threw some of the missiles back, and a few men suffered minor injuries. The crowd turned into an angry mob with its rage directed against Tucker. Realizing his peril, the Negro turned and fled down Illinois Street. An operator of a grocery, William Ballenger, grabbed a club kept handy for emergencies and brained Tucker with it. Tucker fell dead.

Sound of the fray reached the occupants of the Second Presbyterian Church, and it was at its height when Tucker was mortally struck about a hundred yards from the church. According to Holloway, the congregation was "greatly disturbed" and the affair "nearly destroyed the meeting." Ballenger left the city and escaped punishment; the drunken Wood who had started the trouble, however, was made to stand trial and later imprisoned.[26]

The episode reopened the controversial question of relations between the races. It led to a conversation among Beecher, Calvin Fletcher, and an abolitionist newspaper editor, Henry W. Depuy in which they discussed the institution of slavery. They spoke frankly, and Fletcher and Beecher assumed that their views would be kept confidential. Depuy, editor of the *Indiana Freeman*, could not resist the opportunity to publish the opinions of the influential Fletcher and celebrated Beecher. Discomfited, Fletcher confided to his diary that the editor had "perverted many things. But is scarcly worthy of notice."[27] Prudent men did not speak openly about slavery, for no matter what their stance someone in the community would be offended. It could hurt a man's business or professional standing if not lead to violence against his person and property.

Henry Ward Beecher made plans to attend commencement at Wabash College. Once in Crawfordsville he succumbed to an attack of "chills and fever" which lasted for three days. Lyman Beecher learned of Henry's illness through a circuitous route. An acquaintance from Indianapolis of a neighbor of Lyman Beecher's arrived in Cincinnati on business and mentioned casually that Henry was ill. It worried Lyman

26. Holloway, *Indianapolis*, pp. 80–81; Meeker, *The Busy Life of Eighty-Five Years of Ezra Meeker*, pp. 11–12.
27. Calvin Fletcher Diary, July 30, 1845, InHi.

Beecher who hastened to make inquiries and was relieved to learn that Henry was all right again. "Alas a fever you know always strikes me with Dread when anybody has it but myself," wrote the concerned father. "What if he [HWB] should die. What a loss."[28] The father had a certain amount of justification for his worry as the season for malaria had arrived with July's high temperature.

A good friend of Henry Ward Beecher's, Stoughton A. Fletcher, became very ill in August, and for days on end Henry and Eunice helped nurse him. Stoughton and Julia had traveled earlier in the year to visit relatives in the East and, hopefully, to restore his poor health. Upon returning to Indianapolis two weeks previously Fletcher resumed work as he felt stronger than he had for months. In the hottest weather which Indianapolis could muster he went out into the heat of the day with a bare head on August 28. He felt the effects of this but instead of resting returned to work for the rest of the day. That evening he was increasingly unwell, and he permitted Julia to call her cousin Talbut to come and examine him the next day. Bullard advised Fletcher to discontinue work until he was stronger or until after the first frost.[29]

Growing weaker, Fletcher was examined by Bullard and George W. Mears on August 30. They diagnosed his malady as congestive fever and despaired privately of saving his life. Calvin Fletcher came and remained with his brother until noon. Stoughton spent another restless night and was obviously worse. His brother returned and began a vigil at Stoughton's bedside. The physicians told the family on Sunday evening that the ill man could not live. Mears and another physician, John L. Richmond, who had been called in as a consultant retired from the case; Bullard, more as a member of the family than in his professional capacity, remained with the ailing Fletcher. During the course of the day Stoughton was told that he was not expected to recover. It did not seem to disturb him, and he gave directions about his business and funeral. At times he was delirious and "Vented his prejudices & clung to early impressions & even language."[30]

---

28. Lyman Beecher to Lydia Jackson Beecher, Walnut Hills, August 9, 1845, CtHS-D.

29. Calvin Fletcher Diary, May 16 and August 16, 1845, InHi; Calvin Fletcher, Jr., to Sarah Hill Fletcher, Indianapolis, August 29, 1845, Fletcher Papers, InHi.

30. Calvin Fletcher Diary, August 31, 1845, InHi.

Stoughton was still living when morning came. He made known his last wishes, gave further instructions about his business, and selected six men to be his pallbearers. During the afternoon a group of men from the Second Presbyterian Church came to comfort him and his family with appropriate hymns and prayers in his presence as was customary when death was imminent. Stoughton grew weaker after their departure, and at two o'clock in the afternoon Bullard told the family he had tried every remedy he knew and could do no more. Another patient needed him, and he left. Only the Fletcher family and the Beechers remained with the sick man. Henry and Eunice had been at Stoughton's bedside together or singly since August 29 helping nurse him or attending to tasks in the afflicted household. Now, tired and distraught, Eunice was told by her husband that since no more could be done she should go home and rest. She started toward the Beecher house. About three o'clock Guy Leonard came and Calvin Fletcher, Sr., asked him to help lay out his brother. Beecher went to get a barber to come and shave Stoughton. The clergyman also had the task of preparing a funeral notice and taking it to the newspapers.

Stoughton A. Fletcher was just barely alive. Someone tried to find his pulse but could not; those in the bedroom thought he was dead. Just as death seemed a reality Eunice Beecher walked into the room. She had left her home a quarter of a mile away and returned. She felt Stoughton's pulse and said it was stronger, wet the sick man's mouth with a few drops of water, put cold cloths on his head, and told someone to go for Bullard.[31] The physician returned and was surprised to find Stoughton still alive. He cautioned the family not to be too hopeful for it was well known that the dying often exhibited a seeming burst of energy just before the end. Eunice would have none of it. In an attempt to rouse Stoughton from his coma cold water was poured twice over his head. Within two hours Fletcher roused enough to speak to those anxiously watching around his bed. It seemed to be a miracle.

Eunice stayed with Julia and a few friends to nurse Fletcher through the night. Calvin Fletcher, who had been almost constantly at his brother's side since August 29, was greatly impressed by the care shown Stoughton by Julia and Eunice. He conceived an admiration

31. Calvin Fletcher Diary, September 1, 1845, InHi.

234

and respect for Eunice Beecher whom he credited with saving his brother's life after everyone else had given him up. He had not been well acquainted with his brother's wife before Stoughton's illness. Possibly a little cool to their marriage, he had noted her kindness to Stoughton and her excellent housekeeping. In the future Calvin Fletcher had only good opinions of Julia Fletcher.[32]

Stoughton A. Fletcher lived, but another friend of Henry Ward Beecher's would not be so fortunate. Less than two months later news of the death of Priscilla Merrill Wilson was brought to the pastor as he was completing preparations for a prayer meeting to begin shortly in the lecture room of his church. It stunned him, for she had been a great favorite of his. As he would recall, "in her last sickness she called for me [HWB], and was anxious to have word sent to me that the views of Christ which I had taught her were sustaining her gloriously in that hour. I broke down as though a mountain had fallen on me. I cannot describe the strangeness of it. It was an inexpressible relief to me, so early in my ministry, to have such a testimony; but the thought that my views of the Saviour were sufficient, not only to live by, but to die by, quite overcame me. I tried to say something in that meeting about it, but it was very little that I could say then. And yet, that was enough."[33] Beecher told those who assembled for the prayer meeting of the twenty-two-year-old Priscilla's death. "No one there ever forgot Mr. Beecher's prayers and remarks," her sister wrote.[34]

Married in 1843 to Alexander Wilson, Priscilla had resided since her wedding in Lafayette where her husband was in business. In late October, 1845, she was expecting the birth of a baby, and she was visited by her sisters, Jane Merrill Ketcham and Julia Merrill, who were to stay with her through her confinement. Their invalid mother was visiting an uncle on his plantation in Louisiana and could not be with her. Priscilla was delivered of a son on a Sunday. The infant "moaned a little and died" five days later. The mother failed to regain her strength and visibly declined after the death of the child. Realizing she was dying,

32. *Ibid.*, September 3, 1845; Calvin Fletcher to Sarah Hill Fletcher, Indianapolis, August 31 and September 4, 1845, Fletcher Papers, InHi.

33. Ellinwood (ed.), *Autobiographical Reminiscences of Henry Ward Beecher*, p. 48.

34. "Reminiscences of Jane Merrill Ketcham," p. 77, In; Graydon, "A Pioneer Tale, The Life of Samuel Merrill," p. 18, In.

Priscilla selected the hymns to be sung at her funeral and also the text for the service, "Remember thy Creator in the days of thy youth."[35] Death came for her about midnight on the following Tuesday. Mrs. Ketcham recalled that "We had never seen such a triumphant death-bed. . . . But I was sorry for mother and father. She was gone and the heart-ache was left."[36] Priscilla Merrill Wilson was buried with her son in a Lafayette cemetery.[37]

Henry Ward Beecher grieved as sincerely and deeply for Priscilla as did her own family. "I never saw any one like Priscilla," he said, "how unfortunate that [there is] no picture of her."[38] This lack aggravated his sense of loss as it did in regard to his mother.

Beecher was informed shortly after that his father, stepmother, and a sister had been injured in an accident. The first report was that the injuries were serious, but a later one stated this was not the case. Although it meant that a donation party planned for Henry and Eunice by the congregation of the Second Presbyterian Church would have to be postponed, Beecher felt it necessary that he travel at once to Walnut Hills to find out for himself the extent of his family's injuries.[39] Beecher learned that the trio had been riding in a horse-drawn chaise on an especially dark night near Cincinnati. For some unknown reason the horse, chaise, and its occupants were thrown forty feet down a precipice, but only the vehicle was seriously damaged. Even in such a predicament Lyman Beecher's wit had not failed him. He called for help to some passing teamsters, and they inquired, "How shall we get down there?" "Easy enough," the senior Beecher supposedly replied, "Come as I did."[40] Henry Ward Beecher remained at Walnut Hills over Thanksgiving and no services were held at his church in Indianapolis. Many of his congregation, including the Merrill family, attended

35. Samuel Merrill to David Merrill, Madison, November 8, 1845, Samuel Merrill Papers, InHi; "Reminiscences of Jane Merrill Ketcham," p. 77, In.

36. "Reminiscences of Jane Merrill Ketcham," p. 77, In.

37. Graydon (comp.), *Catharine Merrill, Life and Letters*, p. 73.

38. "Reminiscences of Jane Merrill Ketcham," p. 77, In.

39. John L. Ketcham to Samuel Merrill, Indianapolis, November 21, 1845, Samuel Merrill Papers, InHi; Graydon (comp.), *Catharine Merrill, Life and Letters*, p. 69.

40. Stowe, "Sketches and Recollections of Dr. Lyman Beecher," *Congregational Quarterly*, VI, 234; John L. Ketcham to Samuel Merrill, Indianapolis, November 21, 1845, Samuel Merrill Papers, InHi.

service at the First Presbyterian Church whose pastor, Phineas D. Gurley, was Beecher's close friend.[41]

Beecher returned by steamer on the Ohio River as far as Madison, where he disembarked and then traveled north by rail to Edinburg where the track ended. He arrived in Edinburg at twilight on Saturday, ate some supper, and then continued his journey by coach to Indianapolis, for he was expected to preach at next morning's service. In the coach

> Mr. Beecher. . . took a seat inside the stage but after a short distance he pulled down the sash of the door and with much difficulty clambered up with the driver. There was a light snow, the road was slippery, and near Franklin the coach [skidded] while going down hill, going off at one side of a little bridge and overturning. After the passengers extricated themselves from the overturned coach, they found Mr. Beecher holding the reins of the four horses with one hand, while with the other he supported the driver, who had been badly injured.

After some delay the coach was righted, the driver left at a farm house, and a new driver found to take the coach on to Franklin, Indiana, which was reached at eleven o'clock.

> During the ride to Franklin [continued a fellow passenger] one of the passengers attributed the escape from serious injury to special providence, and another said he had a presentiment something would happen. Mr. Beecher showed some temper, saying there was no such thing as special providence, and illustrated it by remarking that if a wicked man and a child were taken to the top of a building and thrown off, the brains of the child were just as apt to be dashed out as those of the man.

Tired, upset, and worried that the slow coach might not get him to Indianapolis in time, Beecher left it at Franklin. He secured a buggy and hurried off alone. Next morning the passengers on the ill-fated stagecoach saw Beecher emerging from his church after the morning service just as their vehicle made its way through the city.[42]

The postponed donation party was held for the Beechers' benefit on Tuesday, December 2, 1845. At such events members of the congre-

41. Catharine Merrill, Journal, [November ?] 25, 18[45 ?], quoted in Graydon (comp.), *Catharine Merrill, Life and Letters*, p. 69.

42. Charles P. Ferguson, Reminiscences, Indianapolis *News*, September 7, 1901, clipping in George S. Cottman's Indiana Scrapbook Collection, VIII, 46, In.

gation planned the entertainment, provided a place of assembly and refreshments, and donated items of food, clothing, and household furnishings to the minister and his family. Elizabeth Bates wrote a description of it to Julia Merrill who was visiting her uncle in Louisiana. Julia replied, "I was very glad to hear that the Donation Party turned out so pleasantly. How much better you all feel than if you had not had it. I suppose Mrs. Beecher feels very happy. I hope it will continue to be practiced and that every year they will increase in pleasure."[43] For all her years of acquaintance with Eunice Beecher, Julia was much mistaken as to Mrs. Beecher's real feelings about donation parties. The minister's wife thought members of the church eased their consciences by fobbing off unwanted articles rather than providing the cash which the Beechers needed. Eunice Beecher enjoyed a party, but she deeply resented being made to feel that she and her family were objects of charity. She did not believe it wise to antagonize the congregation, however, and so she shammed more pleasure and gratitude than she felt.[44]

Henry Ward Beecher followed a grueling schedule of activities in 1845. He delivered two sermons each Sunday and preached elsewhere during the week; conducted a weekly prayer meeting; oversaw Sabbath School classes, the choir, and concerts; gave encouragement to the Ladies' Sewing Society; led revivals at the Second Presbyterian Church and away from Indianapolis; preached funeral sermons; performed weddings; visited the sick and wavering; presided at meetings of Session; was Stated Clerk of the Presbytery of Indianapolis; was prominent at Synod; and was in constant demand as a speaker on both religious and secular occasions. To this he added the care of a large garden and the editorship of the *Indiana Farmer and Gardener*. Beecher was increasingly active in civic organizations and social reforms which held statewide implications. His life was full, and he was successful.

43. Julia D. Merrill to Elizabeth Bates, Water Proof, Louisiana, December 31, 1845, Julia Merrill Moores Papers, InHi.
44. [Mrs. Beecher], *From Dawn to Daylight*, pp. 226–29.

XVI

Citizen

H ENRY WARD BEECHER PARTICIPATED ACTIVELY IN ALMOST EVERY civic organization in Indianapolis except a military company. One of the first which he joined was the Indiana Historical Society. Although ostensibly a state-wide organization, it was dominated by residents of the capital city. Established in 1830 the society had been moribund since 1835 when its last meeting was held. Wishing to instill life into the organization its president, Samuel Merrill, called a meeting for December 30, 1842, at which time officers for the upcoming year were selected. Merrill was re-elected president; Jeremiah Sullivan, Charles Dewey, and Isaac Blackford were chosen vice-presidents; and the Executive Committee consisted of Henry P. Coburn, James M. Ray, George H. Dunn, Douglass Maguire, and Henry Ward Beecher.

Toward the close of the meeting an election of honorary members to the society was held. These were to be distinguished men who had shown unusual interest in the West whether they had ever lived there or not. The following were chosen unanimously: George Bancroft, Lyman Beecher, John L. Blake, John B. Dillon, Daniel Drake, Salma Hale, John McLean, William H. Prescott, John L. Stephens, and Calvin E. Stowe. Beecher's father, brother-in-law, and former family physician, Daniel Drake of Cincinnati, were included in this select list.[1]

1. *Proceedings of the Indiana Historical Society, 1830–1886* (Indiana Historical

Beecher's interest in history was genuine. This was evident from an action of his earlier in 1842 when he presented a resolution to his Presbytery stating:

> Wher[e]as the Records of our churches will hereafter be of great value as materials for Church History & will be almost the only source of knowledge as to the labor, cares, & successes of the pioneers of the church in these early times, Resolved 1, That it be urged upon the clerk of every Session under our charge to make out as full a record of the history of the Church from year to year as is practicable.[2]

The Presbytery adopted it and authorized that copies be sent to each clerk of session within its bounds and also to the next meeting of Synod. It was a far-sighted and worthwhile goal. Beecher's continuing preoccupation with history during his residence in Indianapolis took the form frequently of long conversations with such men as Samuel Merrill and Calvin Fletcher who could give him firsthand accounts of past events in the city's and state's history. Thus, the minister was better versed in the subject than might have been expected in a relative newcomer.

Beecher belonged to a volunteer fire company. The company's meetings were important politically and socially. Agreements and understandings reached informally at them affected much that would later transpire in Indianapolis. Any man who aspired to any degree of civic prominence was a member of one or more fire companies. Beecher was enrolled; but, as a clergyman, he was not expected to fight fires. This did not suit his inclination, and he became noted "for fighting temporal fires with as much vigor as he did the eternal kind."[3] Upon the alarm being sounded Beecher would appear ready to take his part as a fire fighter under the direction of the "fireward" and an assistant who had to carry as a badge of office a pole five feet long and painted bright red. Beecher did not confine his fighting of fires to Indianapolis. When preaching in La Porte one Sunday he and the congregation were informed of a fire which had started near the church. Beecher rushed

Society *Publications*, I, No. 1, 1897), pp. 9–65; Christopher B. Coleman (ed.), *Centennial Handbook, Indiana Historical Society, 1830–1930* (Indiana Historical Society *Publications*, X, No. 1, 1930), pp. 5–6, 10, 13, 43–46.

2. Records of the Presbytery of Indianapolis, pp. 29–30, InHan.
3. Dunn, *Greater Indianapolis*, I, 170.

from the pulpit to go with the men and boys to fight the blaze. After it was extinguished he returned with dirt-streaked hands and clothing to the pulpit and finished his sermon.[4]

Largely as a result of his position as pastor of the Second Presbyterian Church, Beecher was one of eight men to be elected a vice-president of the Indianapolis Benevolent Society in 1842, and he was associated with the society until he left the city. Formally organized in 1835, the society sought to alleviate the suffering felt by extremely poor people who resided in Indianapolis. In the first years of its existence it did not solicit money from prosperous residents; instead, visitors would go in pairs—a man and woman—with baskets on their arms to request useful and needed items which would then be placed in the charge of a manager. Any person could approach this manager, a member of the society, and receive assistance if it were available. When someone did not have any items with which he wished to part, he might give money which would be kept in a fund to be spent for worthy purposes. The society met annually near the Thanksgiving holiday, since this was the period of the year when poverty was most felt.[5]

Indianapolis had its share of poor people who tended to reside in an area south of Washington Street. Many were recent Irish or German immigrants; others were free Negroes who arrived without means and could not find work. There were people who had been badly hurt by the effects of the depression and were almost destitute. These latter often succeeded by heroic measures to conceal their plight, but clergymen such as Beecher, Gurley, and Berry were in and out of homes of all classes and knew where real need existed. They were listened to carefully by the members of the Indianapolis Benevolent Society when they reported on conditions in the city.[6]

Henry Ward Beecher frequently offered the use of the lecture room of the Second Presbyterian Church to groups who needed the space for a meeting or program if he thought their purpose worthwhile. He might

4. *Ibid.*; John B. Donaldson, *Diamond Jubilee and Historical Sketch of the Presbyterian Church, La Porte, Indiana* (La Porte, Ind., n.d.), p. 3.

5. Thornbrough (ed.), *Diary of Calvin Fletcher*, I, 467n; Sulgrove, *History of Indianapolis and Marion County, Indiana*, p. 379; Holloway, *Indianapolis*, p. 50.

6. Indianapolis *Indiana Journal*, November 30, 1842; Stowe, *Men of Our Times*, p. 548; Rose, *The Circle*, p. 377; George S. Cottman, "Old-Time Slums of Indianapolis," *Indiana Magazine of History*, VII, No. 4 (December, 1911), p. 170.

or might not participate further. On one such occasion he helped organize a series of lectures to be given by himself and others under the sponsorship of the Union Literary Society. This organization had been established in 1835 in connection with the Marion County Seminary to serve primarily as a debate club. In November, 1846, it was suggested that the society institute a series of lectures such as were being well received in New England. To encourage attendance the lectures would be presented without charge, and prominent residents of Indianapolis such as Nicholas McCarty, Calvin Fletcher, Sr., James Blake, James M. Ray, and Austin W. Morris among others contributed money to meet expenses. Instead of relying upon a handbill to advertise the first lecture, the society had printed on note paper what were in essence invitations. The copy was submitted to Beecher as he was to be the initial speaker, and he took great pains that its appearance should be attractive.

Henry Ward Beecher delivered a lecture on "A view of social position as depending upon the degree of *intellect:* a law of nature" on Friday, December 11, 1846.[7] Immediately following his address the choir of the Second Presbyterian Church presented a short concert. Succeeding lectures in the series found the Honorable Godlove S. Orth speaking on "German Literature," the Reverend Samuel T. Gillett lecturing on "Naples and Mt. Vesuvius" and later on "Egypt," John B. Dillon discoursing about "China and the Chinese," and the Reverend Charles Axtell lecturing on "A life on the Ocean Waves," and "History" was presented by the Reverend S. L. Johnson. These lectures were the first of the genre to be presented in Indianapolis.[8]

Beecher supported attempts to secure the establishment of a state-supported school for the deaf and dumb. He was appointed to the Board of Trustees with Royal Mayhew, William Sheets, Phineas D. Gurley, Love H. Jameson, Livingston Dunlap, James Morrison, and James Whitcomb during the legislative session of 1843 to oversee such an institution. After becoming governor, James Whitcomb continued to advocate the project which was authorized by the legislature on January 15, 1844, under the title "Asylum for the Education of the Deaf and Dumb." Interest in creating the institution had been sparked in

7. HWB, Notes, December 10, 1846, CtY; Indianapolis *News*, October 12, 1878.
8. Holloway, *Indianapolis,* p. 50; Indianapolis *News*, October 12, 1878; Sulgrove, *History of Indianapolis and Marion County, Indiana,* pp. 261–62.

1842 when a deaf mute named James McLean opened a small school for the purpose in Parke County. McLean's school never had an enrollment of more than six pupils at a time and did not prosper. William Willard and his wife, also both deaf mutes, opened a similar private school in Indianapolis in the spring of 1843. By the end of its first year there were sixteen pupils enrolled, and the Board of Trustees for the proposed state institution contemplated using the Willard school as a nucleus. This was accomplished on October 1, 1844, when it was absorbed into the "Asylum for the Education of the Deaf and Dumb." Henry Ward Beecher and Matthew Simpson, so recently his antagonist, spoke in behalf of the school and assisted with the practical details involved in securing housing for the institution in a rented frame building at the corner of Illinois and Maryland streets.[9]

The efforts of James M. Ray and others to establish a school for the blind in Indiana similar to that already in existence in Kentucky likewise drew Beecher's interest. Ray was a leader in attempts to better the lot of the state's unfortunate citizens. He had helped organize the first Sabbath School in Indianapolis, been secretary of the first temperance society, and served as treasurer of the Indianapolis Benevolent Society. Beecher had known Ray, a Presbyterian, ever since coming to Indianapolis. They decided it would be a good time to focus attention on the plight of Indiana's sightless citizens when the state legislature convened in 1846. Ray brought a blind educator, William H. Churchman, and a group of the latter's pupils from the Kentucky School for the Blind to Indianapolis. Several lectures were delivered by Churchman and others on behalf of the blind at the Second Presbyterian Church. In addition to these speeches the legislators and public saw examples of the work of the blind pupils who demonstrated their accomplishments and, in general, proved that blind people could learn useful skills and care for themselves.

The lectures were well attended by the public. That the problems involved in teaching the blind were imperfectly understood, however, was made too clear in one instance when a member of the legislature

---

9. Logan N. Esarey, *A History of Indiana from Its Exploration to 1850* (2 volumes. Fort Wayne, Ind.: The Hoosier Press, 1924), I, 493; Dunn, *Indiana and Indianans*, II, 987–92; Amos Butler, *A Century of Progress: A Study of the Development of Public Charities and Correction, 1790–1915* (Jeffersonville, Ind., [1916]), p. 24.

attempted to help with a demonstration of the prowess of a blind pupil. To the amusement and embarrassment of the audience the lawmaker wrote a problem, held the paper before the sightless eyes of the pupil, and then with his own finger traced the problem while exhorting the pupil to solve it. The incident did not discredit the efforts of Ray; and may, indeed, have aided them by keeping the episode before the legislators as a subject for conversation. From this time until October 1, 1847, when Indiana opened its own School for the Blind on North Street in Indianapolis Henry Ward Beecher worked toward that goal.[10]

Possibly the cause of temperance was closest to Beecher's heart of all the reforms in the Hoosier capital during his residence there. Concurrently with his first revival in Indianapolis a wave of temperance feeling had swept his congregation. Beecher and many men from his church joined the temperance movement which reached Indianapolis in February with the arrival of a man known only as "Mr. Matthews," a reformed drunkard by his own account, who stayed long enough to form a local chapter of the Washingtonian Temperance Society. The first meeting was held on February 28, 1842, and by March 1 approximately 318 men had signed a pledge to abstain from liquor.[11]

Beecher had promoted temperance since his boyhood. Some sixteen years earlier his father had delivered six sermons on the subject in Litchfield, Connecticut, which received national attention. From these the younger Beecher had drawn inspiration for the temperance lectures he delivered during his student days. He had been active in the Dearborn County Temperance Society during his residence in Lawrenceburgh.[12] In Indianapolis Beecher came into contact with men again and again whose lives had been blighted by liquor. Hugh McCulloch recalled that

> One day Mr. Beecher was called upon unexpectedly to attend, at the wretched place where he died, the funeral of a man who had long been a drunkard. The deceased had no family, but he had a large number of friends, who had assembled to show their regard for him. . . . hard-faced

10. Dunn, *Greater Indianapolis*, I, 111; Dunn, *Indiana and Indianans,* II, 1002–1003; Esarey, *A History of Indiana from Its Exploration to 1850,* I, 493–94; Butler, *A Century of Progress: A Study of the Development of Public Charities and Correction, 1790–1915,* p. 25.

11. Indianapolis *Indiana Journal*, March 16, 1842.

12. Lawrenceburgh *Political Beacon*, February 16, 1839.

men were nearly all of them, such men as Mr. Beecher had never seen together; . . . but wretched and degraded as they had become, there was something of their better nature still left, and this was open to the warnings and appeals of the speaker. . . . They felt the justice of his rebukes, . . . All wept like children; two became temperate men.[13]

Beecher developed a detestation of the liquor industry and those associated with it.

The minister supported the work of the temperance society in the spring of 1842 when it purchased and disposed of a distillery in Indianapolis as a tangible means of reducing the amount of liquor available in the city. Beecher was unafraid of the rough men who were connected with the dispensing of liquor and from time to time tangled verbally with them. Usually, though, he limited himself to speaking out against liquor from the platform as when he opened "the winter campaign against King Alcohol" with a rousing speech to the temperance society in the lecture room of his church on Friday, November 11, 1842.[14]

His efforts to promote temperance continued unabated, and on January 7, 1845, he appeared at the Hall of Representatives to help organize the Indiana State Temperance Society and to give one of the speeches that evening. Aware that the wholesaler and distiller were at fault as well as the retailer of liquor he directed his remarks impartially at all of them. The former two were considered to be respectable and the latter was not, but Beecher made no such distinction. Later he used the columns of the *Indiana Farmer and Gardener* to report upon the visit of John Hawkins to Indianapolis and the latter's success in promoting temperance in the Hoosier capital. "An accession of 300 members," wrote Beecher, "in three days, must be regarded as a remarkable triumph."[15]

At this time in Indiana a place selling liquor might be referred to as a grocery or doggery. Relatively little beer was sold in it, and it relied chiefly on the sale of highly potent corn whiskey for a profit. Much of this liquor came from distilleries in Lawrenceburgh. Beecher learned that a new distillery capable of producing one hundred fifty barrels of

13. McCulloch, *Men and Measures of Half A Century*, p. 142; Dunn, *Indiana and Indianans*, II, 1038; Barrows, *Henry Ward Beecher, the Shakespeare of the Pulpit*, p. 98.

14. Dunn, *Indiana and Indianans*, II, 1038–39.

15. *Indiana Farmer and Gardener*, I, No. 2 (February 8, 1845), pp. 30–31.

whiskey a day was in operation there. He was furious. It was bad enough that an increased amount of this liquid poison would be available to the intemperate, but it was worse that this "latest fiendhouse was erected by a distinguished *temperance man,* and a *Christian!*"[16] The distiller, Cornelius G. W. Comegys, was an acquaintance of Beecher's who had been a merchant in Indianapolis until his purchase of the Miami Mills in Lawrenceburgh from E. D. John. Subsequently, Comegys added a distillery to the well-known flour mill. That a professing Christian such as Comegys should operate such an objectionable enterprise irritated Beecher, and he referred to it repeatedly.

Henry Ward Beecher's ire against Comegys increased in December when he learned that the latter had sued the editors of the Greensburg *Repository,* Jacob W. Mills and Orville Thomson, on an action of libel and asked damages of $5,000. "That's right. We know of no person on earth," wrote Beecher sarcastically, "who can so ill afford to lose his character as a Christian distiller. Five thousand dollars' worth of character lost, would make quite a hole in any distiller's character; but in a Christian distiller's not so bad a breach, we hope, as in an ungodly, impenitent distiller's case."[17] Quickly informed of Beecher's gratuitous insult, Comegys replied in an open letter addressed to the Citizens of Indianapolis. He stated "it cannot but be very painful for me to observe how very frequently the Rev. (?) H. W. Beecher attempts to hold me up to public derision and contempt. . . . His pulpit and his press have both been used, to gratify his petty malice, his unmanly and ungentlemanly attacks."[18] Comegys added further remarks about Beecher's behavior and motives which were not complimentary to the pastor.

Beecher replied in a lengthy open letter in which he began with a consideration of the question, "Can a consistent Christian and a tem-

16. *Ibid.,* pp. 31–32; Knox, *Life and Work of Henry Ward Beecher,* pp. 93–94; Indianapolis *Indiana State Journal,* January 29, 1845; *History of Dearborn, Ohio and Switzerland Counties, Indiana,* p. 283; Sulgrove, *History of Indianapolis and Marion County, Indiana,* p. 395.

17. *Western Farmer and Gardener,* II, No. 1 (January 1, 1846), p. 3. The court ruled for the defendants, and Comegys was ordered to reimburse Mills and Thomson for the costs and charges spent by them in their defense. See Cornelius G. W. Comegys v. Jacob W. Mills and Orville Thomson, Decatur County Circuit Court, Order Book, VI, 312, 323, 356, 375 (Fall term 1845).

18. C. G. W. Comegys to Citizens of Indianapolis, Lawrenceburgh, Indiana, December 31, 1845, Indianapolis *Indiana State Journal,* January 14, 1846.

perance man, conduct a whiskey-distillery and maintain his character?"
He denied any personal attack upon Comegys and referred to a threat
allegedly made by Comegys that the distiller would thrash Beecher.

> I think, indeed, that a Christian minister, soundly whipped by a Christian
> distiller [wrote Beecher] would be a spectacle of edification seldom
> vouchsafed to the church or the world. While, then, my unfeigned regard
> for his courage in thrashing a minister, will make me very prudent in
> my language, I must inform him, that if worst comes to worst, I shall
> engage a Quaker, and a woman to stand by, and fight for me in that
> disastrous hour; and if he vanquishes the three—a quaker, a preacher,
> and a woman, the scene shall be engraved, and, if I might suggest, it
> should go with the distiller's mark upon the head of each whiskey barrel,
> reminding every beholder, both of what the manufacturer has done,
> and what the contents of the barrel will enable others to do.[19]

Such insulting sarcasm further enraged the sensitive Comegys,
and he could not let Beecher's letter with its "spirit of calumniation
and malice" go unanswered.[20] He dropped all pretense of keeping the
dispute on a lofty plane and singled out three alleged offenses committed by Beecher for attack. The first was that the clergyman had
supposedly told an acquaintance that "he [HWB] had sacrificed great
advantages and prospects by becoming a preacher, as he might have
made a great deal more money, and distinguished himself like Mr.
[Henry] Clay if he had turned his attention to the law, instead of Theology!" Second, Comegys accused Beecher of deserting the church at
Lawrenceburgh just as he was becoming really useful there. Third,
Comegys charged Beecher with the immoral offense of owning and
reading works of fiction when in Lawrenceburgh which had filled the
preacher's "corrupt soul and imagination [with] their corrupt scenes."[21]
A week later another letter by Comegys was printed which was placa-
tory in tone, and Comegys contented himself with saying that "he
[HWB] is a man of talents and promise; but his zeal out-runs his discretion if not his knowledge. I meditate no violence upon the gentleman."[22]

19. HWB to C. G. W. Comegys, Indianapolis, January 14, 1846, Indianapolis
Indiana State Journal, January 14, 1846.
20. C. G. W. Comegys to Editor, Lawrenceburgh, Indianapolis *Indiana State
Journal*, January 28, 1846.
21. *Ibid.*
22. C. G. W. Comegys to Editor, Lawrenceburgh, January 20, 1846, Indianapolis *Indiana State Journal*, February 4, 1846.

Comegys included a premature promise that he was dropping the controversy.

The newspaper exchange was a source of much comment in Indianapolis, and word of it reached Julia Merrill who was visiting an uncle in Louisiana. Julia received the newspapers from Elizabeth Bates and wrote that she was "surprised with Mr. Beechers severity in the "Farmer,"—yet—when I saw Mr. Comegys reply it was merited. How well Mr. Beecher answers him. I should think he would sell his distillery at once or else burn it down."[23]

Sensing that Comegys was in a less contentious mood, Beecher wrote a mild reply and omitted the sarcasm which had permeated his previous letters. One of Comegys' charges had been that Beecher condoned the selling of grain to distillers when he resided in Lawrenceburgh. Beecher responded, "What if I did? It seems that I have learned to abhor, and Mr. C. to build distilleries. The only inconsistency that I can perceive is, that I have gone from a bad to a good ground."[24] Beecher concluded with a lengthy exposition on moral values versus monetary gain.

Comegys wrote a final letter to Beecher which was designed, figuratively, to draw blood:

> And if Mr. Beecher had used every argument that he has adopted, unconnected with my name, I should have offered no personal remarks upon himself; but I could not bear that a man of exceedingly censurable life, should, with a sanctimonious air, be continually flinging at me departures from Christain [sic] life. . . . His excuse is that he cannot hold still when some principle in religion is attacked. . . . Why is thy tongue still and thy pen idle, when the sentiments of thy brother and thy church on slavery are promulged? Thou idle boaster—where is thy vaunted boldness.[25]

With this the public controversy ended.

The distiller emerged in a better light from it than did Beecher.

---

23. Julia D. Merrill to Elizabeth Bates, Water Proof, Louisiana, January 28, 1846, Julia Merrill Moores Papers, InHi.

24. HWB to C. G. W. Comegys, Indianapolis, Indianapolis *Indiana State Journal*, February 11, 1846; Haweis, "Henry Ward Beecher," *Littell's Living Age*, CXIII, 205–206.

25. C. G. W. Comegys to Editor, Lawrenceburgh, February 16, 1846, Indianapolis *Indiana State Journal*, March 4, 1846.

Comegys' parting thrust in regard to the slavery issue was generally conceded to be just. Beecher had not spoken out against the evils of slavery as ordered by his denomination since the lukewarm sermon presented in 1843. The minister's harsh criticism of Comegys was also thought to be extreme in a community which accorded distillers respect. Even Julia Merrill felt that Beecher had gone too far in his remarks.[26]

Henry Ward Beecher would have greater success in his efforts to promote the cause of education in Indiana. Timed to appear when the state legislature was in session, Beecher had printed a lengthy article on education in the *Western Farmer and Gardener* on January 1, 1846. In it he recommended the establishment of common, or public, schools and minimum requirements for teachers. While Beecher never approached the zeal of his sister Catharine in advocating the cause of public education, he shared her concern enough to work for more and better schools in the Hoosier state. It has been estimated that one person in seven was illiterate in 1840 and by 1850 it would be one person out of five. Provision had been made for public education within Indiana since territorial days. The Land Ordinance of 1785 decreed that the funds derived from one section of land in each township should be used for the maintenance of a school. The Ordinance of 1787 gave encouragement to formal education. The Indiana Constitution of 1816 provided for township schools, county seminaries, and a state university to be supported by public funds. In 1843 the state treasurer, George H. Dunn, had become the ex-officio superintendent of common schools, and he was succeeded in office by Royal Mayhew in 1844. This combination of offices was considered sensible because the main task of the superintendent was accounting for the collection and expenditure of the school fund. Little or no matters of purely educational concern were involved.

Since its settlement the residents of Indianapolis had depended upon private tutors and schools to educate their children. Samuel Merrill had operated a school, for example, for his children and those of friends. Henry Ward Beecher taught a school for a short period himself. As the city grew in size teachers primarily from the East opened private schools including the Marion County Seminary for the children of those

26. Julia D. Merrill to Elizabeth Bates, Water Proof, Louisiana, March 10, 1846, Julia Merrill Moores Papers, InHi.

wealthy enough to afford the tuition. The children of the poor, with few exceptions, received no formal education.[27]

Beecher and his friends urged the establishment of a school system which would provide public-supported education for all children in the state. To achieve this they wished to see present laws implemented and available funds used more wisely than in the past. Additional legislation would be necessary to provide a more centralized framework for efficient administration.

The great difficulty was that many citizens of Indiana were apathetic or were opposed to such a plan. The opponents believed it was the responsibility of parents to provide the amount and quality of education for their children which would best fit them for adulthood. The skills which were learned in the classroom often had little relevance for children whose lives would presumably be confined to simple farming and household tasks. Why should the poor of the state be burdened with additional taxes to pay for the frills of formal education? Why should the childless and the aged be forced to pay more taxes to educate other people's children? Objections were raised to the specter of increased state control of education. Residents of Indiana were too close to the frontier with its exaggerated sense of freedom to accept readily the imposition of authority from an official in far-off Indianapolis. They resented that another might lawfully tell them how to raise their children. Sectional rivalry was also a factor. Many of the teachers in the state were originally from New England. Their Yankee ideas and accent grated upon those Hoosiers accustomed to southern ways and speech. Before the necessary enactments and local co-operation could be obtained, the advocates of the enlarged common school system had to overcome deeply ingrained prejudices.[28]

There had been agitation for educational reform for years, but it

27. Charles W. Moores, *Caleb Mills and the Indiana School System* (Indiana Historical Society *Publications*, III, No. 6, Indianapolis, 1905), p. 363; Holloway, *Indianapolis*, pp. 60, 163; Everett E. Jarboe, "The Development of the Public School System in Indiana From 1840 Through 1870" (Ph.D. dissertation, Indiana University, 1949), pp. 9, 44; Fassett A. Cotton, *Education in Indiana* (Indianapolis: Wm. B. Burford, 1904), p. 19.

28. Jarboe, "The Development of the Public School System in Indiana From 1840 Through 1870," pp. 46–50; Cotton, *Education in Indiana*, p. 10; Calvin Fletcher Diary, January 12, 1843, InHi.

began to gain momentum in the 1840s. Advocacy of it crossed political and denominational lines. Probably the outstanding educator in the state to advocate free public schools was Caleb Mills, a professor at Wabash College since 1833. In Indianapolis his goals were put before the public by himself and by Henry Ward Beecher through the medium of the newspaper, the *Western Farmer and Gardener*, and by speeches and sermons delivered at opportune times. When the legislature was in session there were usually several of the members at the Sunday evening service at the Second Presbyterian Church, and Beecher often tailored his sermon for that night to further his aims. He devoted his address on January 4, 1846, for example, to a discussion of public education.[29] On the day the legislature convened in December, 1846, an article by Caleb Mills, signed "One of the People," was published in the *Indiana State Journal*. It aroused much interest and comment in Indianapolis, and members of the House of Representatives were moved to pass a resolution on January 8, 1847, requesting the friends of education to call a convention for the following May for the purpose of discussing a system of common schools for the state.[30] Henry Ward Beecher was present at a meeting of interested citizens on January 25, and he was appointed chairman of a committee consisting of Edward R. Ames, John S. Bayless, James M. Ray, and Ovid Butler, charged with making preparations for the proposed convention. Beecher agreed to serve on the committee of correspondence which was responsible for making many of the plans and resolutions for the convention to be held from May 25 through May 27. At the planning session in January the chief speaker was William Slade, a former governor of Vermont and an associate of Catharine E. Beecher. It is probable that he came to speak at the Indianapolis meeting at the request of Henry Ward Beecher.[31]

Catharine E. Beecher was known nationally for her work in educa-

---

29. Charles Beecher to Eliza Butler Ogden, Indianapolis, January 4, 1846, quoted in G. L. Prentiss, *The Union Theological Seminary* (Asbury Park, N. J., 1899), pp. 454–56; *Western Farmer and Gardener*, II, No. 1 (January 1, 1846), pp. 7–8; Cotton, *Education in Indiana*, pp. 268–69; Knox, *Life and Work of Henry Ward Beecher*, pp. 456–57.

30. Moores, *Caleb Mills and the Indiana School System*, pp. 363–67.

31. Dunn, *Indiana and Indianans*, II, 891–93; Richard G. Boone, *A History of Education in Indiana* (New York: D. Appleton and Company, 1892; reprinted Indianapolis: Indiana Historical Bureau, 1941), pp. 95–96.

tion. Ranked with Emma Willard and Mary Lyon as one of the three leading female educators of the nineteenth century, she was highly intelligent, indomitable, and single-minded when working toward a goal. She was a fluent writer and "as willing as able" to pursue a conversation.[32] Prior to moving to Ohio with her father in 1832 she had established and operated a successful school for young women in Connecticut, and she opened another one in Cincinnati which prospered under her leadership. It was she who suggested that William McGuffey be offered the assignment of writing a series of readers when she had to refuse the task because of other commitments. Catharine E. Beecher was an extremely prolific writer. Two of her books which received much attention were *An Essay on the Education of Female Teachers* (New York, 1835) and *The Duty of American Women to Their Country* (New York, 1845). Her lectures and her writings constantly stressed the great need for public schools and competent teachers.[33]

Catharine E. Beecher's influence led to the formation of the Ladies' Society for the Promotion of Education at the West on February 4, 1846. Later in the year she helped found the Central Committee for Promoting National Education with her brother-in-law Calvin E. Stowe as its chairman. This led in a year to the establishment of the Board of National Popular Education under the direction of Governor William Slade. Its purpose was to find educated women in the East who would go to teach in new communities in the West. Miss Beecher provided much of the vision, inspiration, and practical support for these organizations. Although important in his own right, Slade was her figurehead for many years and delivered addresses which she prepared as it was still considered unwomanly and improper for a female to appear as a speaker before mixed audiences.[34]

Henry Ward Beecher's immediate interest in securing teachers for Indianapolis was spurred late in 1846 when two girls of the city were sent to be educated by the nuns of a Terre Haute convent when their parents could find no suitable teacher for them in the Hoosier capital.

---

32. Edward D. Mansfield, *Personal Memories Social, Political, and Literary With Sketches of Many Noted People, 1803–1843* (Cincinnati, 1879), pp. 265–66.

33. Ruggles, *The Story of the McGuffeys*, pp. 90–91.

34. Goodykoontz, *Home Missions on the American Frontier*, pp. 369–71; Dunn, *Indiana and Indianans*, I, 493–94.

Never as rabid an anti-Catholic as his father, Beecher was still aghast that innocent girls should be placed in such an environment.[35] He wrote to Harriet Beecher Stowe who quietly but effectually assisted her husband and Catharine in finding teachers for western communities. Harriet responded quickly. With Beecher relish for plucking good from evil, Harriet wrote,

> You [HWB] have received your first warning & who will educate the Indiana mothers if you do not. Meet these Jisuits [*sic*] by Yankee women—I'll risk the combat—one bright well trained free born Yankee girl is worth two dozen of your nuns who have grown up like potato sprouts in the shades of a convent & since you are a man for exigencies I rather rejoice that the Lord has put you up to an exertion even by taking two of your girls off to Terre Haute to a Catholic school.[36]

A second result of Beecher's letter to Harriet was that she and Catharine took pains to find and interest other young women in settling in Indiana as teachers. Fifty girls were being trained to be teachers who planned to emigrate westward when they completed their course of study in Albany, New York. Catharine E. Beecher thought she could persuade six or eight of them to go to Indiana. Miss Beecher was assisted by three other women and a Mr. Page, principal of the Normal School in Albany, in giving the prospective teachers a month's course in professional education. The latter consisted of:

1. Visiting the Normal School to witness methods of instruction.
2. A course of lectures by Mr. Page on the details of teaching the primary branches.
3. A course of lectures on History, with reference to its influence on the present character and condition of mankind.
4. A course of instruction on Physiology, with special reference to the preservation of the health of teachers.

35. The school in Terre Haute was St. Mary's Academy, a boarding school for young ladies which was opened in 1841 by the Sisters of Providence. It soon became known for its high standards of education and discipline. Indianapolis girls who attended there in 1845 and 1846 included Elvira and Flora Mayhew, daughters of Royal Mayhew, state treasurer, and Ruth and Almeria Drake, daughters of James P. Drake who raised and commanded the first Indiana company in the Mexican War and later served as state treasurer. Sister Mary Borromeo Brown, *The History of the Sisters of Providence of St. Mary-of-the-Woods* (New York: Benzier Brothers, 1949), pp. 518, 519, 523.

36. Harriet Beecher Stowe to HWB, Walnut Hills, January 29, 18[47 ?], CtY.

5. A course of instruction in Calisthenics.
6. Instruction on the best mode of teaching Composition, with exercises.
7. Lectures by Miss [Catharine E.] Beecher, in reference to the peculiarities of Western Society and modes of organizing and conducting different schools in different places.[37]

The friends of education in the Hoosier capital agreed to furnish board and room in their homes for such of these women who chose to go out to Indiana until permanent situations could be found for them. On June 15, 1847, nine young teachers sent forward by Catharine Beecher arrived in Indianapolis. Thus did Henry Ward Beecher through his own efforts and family connections aid the cause of common school education in Indiana.[38]

37. New York *Daily Tribune*, June 10, 1847.
38. Calvin Fletcher Diary, June 17, 1847. See also entries for May 12 and 14, and June 15 and 17, 1847, and Catharine E. Beecher to Fletcher, Brattleboro, Vt., June 7, 1847, Fletcher Papers, InHi.

XVII

Changing Circumstances

CALVIN FLETCHER WAS SO APPRECIATIVE OF EUNICE BEECHER'S efforts to save his brother's life the preceding autumn that he determined to present her with a memento of the occasion. A favorite gift was a set of silver tablespoons, and Fletcher ordered some for her engraved with a design of his choosing. To this was added Mrs. Beecher's initials, the date September 1, 1845, so crucial in Stoughton's recovery, and the word "pursue" taken from 1 Samuel 30:8. In a letter accompanying the gift Fletcher praised Eunice for her careful nursing, her unselfishness, and her faith that his brother would recover. He stated, "I trust that the inscription when explained to your children may not only encourage them to inquire but to follow your example."[1] It was a fine gift and attested to the regard he felt for Eunice Beecher who, in turn, had come to regard Calvin Fletcher like a brother since their shared vigil at Stoughton's bedside.[2]

Although Eunice had seemed to repulse death at Stoughton A. Fletcher's side, she could not stave it off when her son George was so threatened. Both Hatty and little Henry were seriously ill in late February, 1846. Soon the younger boy, Georgie, also sickened. The boy was the pet of the family and his mother's favorite. Worried and ex-

1. Calvin Fletcher to Mrs. Henry Ward Beecher [1846 ?], Fletcher Papers, InHi.
2. Calvin Fletcher, Jr., to Calvin Fletcher, Sr., Indianapolis, December 30, 1845, Fletcher Papers.

hausted by the older children's care and herself suffering the effects of early pregnancy, Eunice tried to nurse the three children. George Lyman Beecher lingered for eight days with an abnormally high fever and recurrent convulsions. "I shall not forget," recalled Henry Ward Beecher, "while I have conscious being, the look of grief and reproach which my little child gave me, in his anguish, when he was dying. He had always run to me for relief, and I had given it; but now, when mortal anguish was on him, why did I not help him? What could I say? What could I do, but stand by and tremble in agony?"[3] Hour after hour the anxious parents nursed the boy and watched him for signs of change.

When the father could stand it no more, he left the house and "at night, under a cold, brilliant, star-studded sky [he] raced and ran down the long street." There came a point when it seemed that the boy was better. "He seemed springing back to life, and was like a bird, fallen from the topmost branch of a tree, fluttering, and caught on the lowest branch, and seeming likely to hold on instead of going to the ground. Wide as heaven was," continued Beecher, "I filled it full of prayer and supplication. O, how I besought God, by every consideration which a soul can give to one that loves it, for the life of that child!"[4] The boy died. Eunice's grief was embittered by her feeling that neighbors and church members were indifferent to her family's loss. Too ill and distraught to realize that others were sick and had problems, she felt only that the people of Indianapolis were cold and unfeeling.[5]

Her bleak mood was deepened by the wintry chill which held the city in its grip and by the presence of over a foot of snow on the ground. The funeral service for George Lyman Beecher was held at the Beecher home at two o'clock on the afternoon of March 1, 1846, with Phineas D. Gurley, pastor of the First Presbyterian Church in charge. It was attended by the few relatives in Indianapolis and a handful of friends, including Calvin Fletcher, who braved the unusual cold to be present.[6]

3. Ellinwood (ed.), *Autobiographical Reminiscences of Henry Ward Beecher*, p. 118; [Mrs. Beecher], *From Dawn to Daylight*, pp. 308–15.

4. Ellinwood (ed.), *Autobiographical Reminiscences of Henry Ward Beecher*, pp. 114–15.

5. Mrs. Beecher, "Mr. Beecher as I Knew Him," *Ladies Home Journal*, January, 1892, p. 5; [Mrs. Beecher], *From Dawn to Daylight*, pp. 323–26.

6. Calvin Fletcher Diary, March 1, 1846, InHi.

After the service the mourners accompanied the body to the cemetery where it was interred. A heavy snow fell during the short trip. Beecher recalled:

> I got out of the carriage, and wading through snow took the little coffin in my arms, walked knee deep to the grave, and looking in I saw the winter to the very bottom of it, and laid his beautiful body in his cold, white grave. The snow-flakes followed and covered it, and then the earth hid it from the winter. . . . It seemed as if I had not only lost my child, but had buried him in eternal snow. It was very hard for faith or imagination to break through the physical aspect of things and find a brighter feeling.[7]

The burial of George Lyman Beecher occurred six years to the month after that of the infant boy stillborn to Eunice in 1840. The death of the latter had not touched his parents' emotions to any extent. Indeed, his death had seemed almost a relief for Eunice had been too ill to undertake his care. Georgie's death was far different. They had loved the child, watched him grow, and seen his tentative efforts to respond to the life about him.

Eunice Beecher was inconsolable, and Beecher was filled with sorrow and remorse. He tortured himself with remembering the times he scolded the dead boy for making so much noise the father could not concentrate upon his reading. He recalled the times he had felt put upon because he had to awaken at night to tend to the needs of the fretful child. Years later Beecher would recall seeing "the child's little shoe, and its little things that were put away in the drawer, how, in the anguish of your soul, you said, 'Oh! if it were a thousand times as much pain and care to me, would to God that I might have it back again!' "[8] For days Beecher struggled to comprehend and to understand why God had taken the little boy. "Yes, it is all for good," he could state finally. "It is bitter, and that is the reason it is sent. I need to take bitter, pain is good medicine, and it is best that I should take it." He believed he could yield only "dumb, unreasoning submission to the will of God."[9]

---

7. Mrs. Beecher, "Mr. Beecher as I Knew Him," *Ladies Home Journal*, January, 1892, p. 5.

8. Truman J. Ellinwood (reporter), *The Original Plymouth Pulpit* (4 volumes. Boston, 1897), I, 282–83.

9. Ellinwood (ed.), *Autobiographical Reminiscences of Henry Ward Beecher*, pp. 114–15.

C. G. W. Comegys' last letter attacking Beecher appeared three days after Georgie's burial, and the bereaved father had no heart to continue the controversy.

Possibly in an attempt to divert Eunice's attention from her loss Beecher began to talk about enlarging their tiny house. Beecher wrote to Ira M. Barton and asked for a loan of $500 to cover the remodeling and construction of an addition. Barton agreed to lend them the money, but he disapproved of using the sum to change the existing house. Before Barton's letter arrived in Indianapolis, however, Beecher had given that idea up as he learned the frame of the old house probably would not stand the strain of what he had proposed to do. Instead, he decided to build a new house on a lot he owned on East Ohio Street. He obtained a plan which he thought suitable and in good taste drawn by John Elder, one of the ablest architects in Indiana. Elder designed the courthouse in Clinton County; the finest hotel in Indianapolis, the Washington Hall; and the State Bank building in the capital city. It is possible that the plan he drew for Beecher is the only one for a house he ever drafted. For it Elder charged fifteen dollars.[10]

Beecher estimated cost of the new house to be $1,500. He hoped to obtain the additional $1,000 from the sale of his house on East Market Street. If that proved unfeasible he would add $205 he had received from selling a small house on one of the lots he had bought from Fletcher. This $705 should enable him to "put up & inclose the frame, & finish as much of it as the money will allow, & wait untill I can dispose of the [present] house & lot before completing it."[11] Barton would finally lend $700 toward building the new house.

Henry Ward Beecher was called frequently to assist with problems of people in the community. On one occasion, for example, he was asked to intervene with his friends the Hiram Bacons who were at odds with their church. Bacon and his wife, Mary Alice, had emigrated to

10. John Elder, Account Book, quoted in Lee Burns, *Early Architects and Builders of Indiana* (Indiana Historical Society *Publications*, XI, No. 3, Indianapolis, 1935), pp. 193–94; HWB to Ira M. Barton, Indianapolis, April 27, 1846, CtY; Kenneth Loucks, "John Elder: Pioneer Builder," *Indiana Magazine of History*, XXVI, No. 2 (March, 1930), pp. 31–33; Peat, *Indiana Houses of the Nineteenth Century*, p. 183.

11. HWB to Ira M. Barton, Indianapolis, April 27, 1846, CtY; Promissory note to Ira M. Barton from HWB, Indianapolis, May [?], 1846, CtY; Ira M. Barton to HWB [Worcester, Massachusetts?], June 15, 1846, CtY.

Indiana from Massachusetts and commenced farming in Washington Township near Indianapolis. They were charter members of the First Presbyterian Church of Washington Township when it was organized in 1830. The depression of the early 1840s hurt them financially, and Mary Alice Bacon began to make cheese which her husband sold in Indianapolis as a means of adding to their income. Since the milk given on Sunday morning had to be used or it would spoil, Mrs. Bacon habitually made cheese on that day as on any other. The Bacons were criticized severely for this practice by fellow church members who felt that they were violating the Biblical injunction to do no unnecessary work on the Sabbath. The Bacons were visited by the elders of the church who made impractical suggestions as to the disposition of the Sunday quota of milk, but Mrs. Bacon would not accept them or acknowledge herself in error. Saying that she got up at four o'clock in the morning to do the necessary work she was certain it did not interfere with her observance of the Sabbath. The Bacons continued to make and sell cheese, but the elders of the church were displeased and showed it.[12]

About the time of the cheese-making episode Bacon pledged a substantial amount toward the salary of the minister, but he subsequently refused to pay his pledge. For this he was disciplined by church officials, and he became even angrier. The matter dragged along for five years. A revival of interest in the affairs of the little church caused some of its members to seek a means of reconciling Bacon and encouraging him to pay what he had promised. They thought of Beecher's friendship with the farmer and asked him to intercede.

> I saw him [Bacon]. He admitted that he cut his name out of the subscription list, and said he would not pay the money. The excuse he gave was amusing. Said he, "The minister did not keep his agreement. He did not preach as I thought he was going to when I signed. Therefore the contract was not valid. As it was not kept on one side it was not binding on the other."

Hoping to appeal to Bacon's sense of justice and vanity, Beecher mentioned a competitor who sold cheese and continued,

12. Jacob P. Dunn, "Indiana's Part in the Making of the Story 'Uncle Tom's Cabin,'" *Indiana Magazine of History*, VII, No. 3 (September, 1911), pp. 114–15; Indianapolis *News*, September 2, 1911.

"Now, my friend, suppose So-and-So should make a contract in town to deliver five hundred weight of cheese, which he thought was good and merchantable, and he should deliver it; and the purchaser, on weighing it, should refuse to stand up to the contract and pay him his price, because it was not as good as your cheese? Do not you know," said I, "that to hold him to that test would be unfair, because it would be holding him to a test that he could not stand? For who, in this whole country does make as good cheese as you do!"[13]

Bacon saw the point of Beecher's example and agreed to pay the money. Later he became an elder in his church, and for the next few years had no more difficulties with his church officials or minister.

There was irony in Beecher's success in persuading Bacon to meet the latter's obligations to pay the amount promised towards the support of the minister of the First Presbyterian Church of Washington Township. The pastor of the Second Presbyterian Church was often short of cash himself because those who had promised to contribute toward his salary failed to do so on time. Though his salary was not paid regularly during the first six years of his pastorate in Indianapolis, he had been able to obtain enough of the money due him to meet immediate need. Toward the end of 1845 and in the early months of 1846, however, it was becoming ever more difficult to collect anything approaching the amount of his nominal salary. Since economic conditions were improving throughout the state and in Indianapolis, he interpreted this tardiness of payment as an indication of his congregation's dissatisfaction with him. This and other factors led him to question his position and prospects in Indianapolis. An indication of the direction his thoughts were taking may be inferred from his resignation of the position as Stated Clerk of the Presbytery of Indianapolis on April 3, 1846, at a meeting held in the Greenwood Presbyterian Church. The honor of holding the office was a considerable one, and his action implies that church preferment in Indiana held decreasing attraction or interest for ·him.[14]

He had an important decision to make: Should he speak out

13. Ellinwood (ed.), *Autobiographical Reminiscences of Henry Ward Beecher*, pp. 119–21; *Centennial Memorial. First Presbyterian Church. Indianapolis, Indiana*, pp. 49, 68–72.

14. HWB to Julia D. Merrill, Boston, June 5, 1847, Julia Merrill Moores Papers, InHi; Records of the Presbytery of Indianapolis, p. 71, InHan.

against slavery from his pulpit? The reasons against doing so were, if anything, more valid than they had been in 1843. If he did not preach such a sermon soon he would forfeit the respect of his clerical peers who were preponderantly antislavery in opinion. Since the beginning of the New School movement there had been repeated resolutions on Synod and Presbytery levels in Indiana encouraging the clergy to speak against slavery. The most recent injunction on the subject had been adopted by the Presbytery of Indianapolis at the meeting on April 3, 1846. Briefly, it said that the rapid disappearance of slavery was desirable, that it was neither always necessary nor desirable to exclude slave owners from Christian ordinances, that harsh slave owners should be disciplined as offenders against the Gospel, and that the General Assembly should give increased attention to problems brought on by slavery. The clergy were urged to inveigh publicly against slavery. With the exception of the examination of the New Testament view of slavery which he had preached at the Second Presbyterian Church in 1843 Beecher had not implemented his church's wish. It so happened that this action of Presbytery followed soon after Comegys' taunt about the preacher's failure to take a public stand.[15]

What effect the beginning of the Mexican War in May had on Beecher's decision to preach against slavery is conjectural. War was declared against Mexico on May 13, 1846. Three days later announcement was made that Indiana was requested to provide three regiments of infantry, and on the morning of May 22, Governor James Whitcomb issued a call for volunteers. The necessary financing was obtained when four branches of the State Bank of Indiana loaned a total of $35,000 for the purpose.[16] There was enthusiasm for the war among some Hoosiers who saw it as a means of securing additional land for the nation. There was also disapproval by antislavery men who believed it would spread slavery to new territories and add to the power of the slave states. As news of events leading to the conflict and the declaration of war trickled into Indianapolis, it triggered discussions and clashes between the two

15. Records of the Presbytery of Indianapolis, pp. 75–80, InHan; C. G. W. Comegys to Editor, Lawrenceburgh, February 16, 1846, Indianapolis *Indiana State Journal*, March 4, 1846; Newell D. Hillis (ed.), *Lectures and Orations by Henry Ward Beecher* (New York: Fleming H. Revell Co., 1913), pp. 194–95.

16. Dunn, *Indiana and Indianans*, I, 429.

factions. An unfortunate effect was that the Negro population of Indianapolis and known abolitionists frequently became the targets of
abuse of those whose passions became inflamed over the question. The
Mexican War did not affect Beecher personally. Only once in his surviving papers did he refer fleetingly to an event of the conflict. It is
unlikely, therefore, that it was a basic factor in the decision he had to
make.

Henry Ward Beecher had been so deeply shaken by the enmities
engendered by the controversy between Old School and New School
forces in the 1830s that it had become almost a fixed policy with him
never to place himself in the position of becoming involved in a dispute
remote from his immediate area of action. He had taken to heart Lyman
Beecher's belief that "true wisdom consists in advocating a cause *only
so far as the community will sustain the reformer*."[17] So long as the
agitation about slavery or its effects did not affect him personally or
obtrude offensively on his gaze, Beecher preferred to ignore the issue,
since he believed his entering into the controversy might result in ending
his usefulness as a clergyman in Indianapolis.

However, the time had come when he had to speak out. His church
would not let him forget its position. Comegys had reminded him
sharply and publicly of his duty. Most important, perhaps, events in
Indianapolis in which racial strife and related injustices occurred kept
coming to his attention. Henry W. DePuy who was editor of the *Indiana
Freeman* was repeatedly harassed because of his statements in the abolitionist newspaper. The sign from the front of the editorial office, for
example, was placed on a privy and the exterior of the office was
smeared with dirt and tar. The editor also received numerous threats
against his person.[18]

Beecher received his second offer of a thrashing for the year
through an incident growing out of a chance encounter with DePuy.
The editor was a timid, inoffensive man of the type that excites the mild
contempt of those who may even admire the person's convictions or
virtues. Walking down the street one day he was stopped by a bartender
who roundly cursed him in front of an audience who added their epi-

17. Lewis Tappan, *The Life of Arthur Tappan* (New York: Hurd & Houghton,
1870), p. 233.
18. Holloway, *Indianapolis*, p. 160; Dunn, *Greater Indianapolis*, I, 394.

thets and enjoyed themselves at the expense of the little man who could only stand and listen. Next day DePuy mentioned the humiliating experience to Beecher. The minister remarked, "Oh, why do you care for the abuse of this low fellow? No one whose esteem is worth having is influenced by him." Adding a few similar statements to cheer DePuy, Beecher edged away.

DePuy quoted verbatim what Beecher had said to him about the bartender in the next issue of the *Indiana Freeman*. Unaware of this the clergyman walked past the bartender's place of business on the day the paper was issued. The latter called, "Mr. Beecher, step in here. I want a word with you, Sir." Holding up the paper, he asked, "Did you say that?"

Beecher replied, "Yes, I did."

"If it were not for your cloth, Sir," raged the bartender, "I'd give you the damdest thrashing."

The minister threw his coat on the bar and said, "Never mind the cloth. You are not dealing with Mr. [DePuy] now but somebody that is willing to accommodate you."[19] The bartender backed down, and nothing more came of the incident.

Henry Ward Beecher's state of mind was not eased when he heard that an elder of the Second Presbyterian Church said, "If an Abolitionist comes here, I will head a mob and put him down."[20] The minister had had his fill of mobs years earlier in Cincinnati and more recently in Indianapolis. His patience was being severely tried, and as he later said, "Now, you know enough of me [HWB] to know that patience is not a natural gift. I have as much temper as anybody, and as much disposition to use it for rebuffing any aggressions upon my personal propriety and honor."[21]

The offer of another beating which Beecher received helped lessen his caution even more. It arose after Beecher expressed his outrage upon learning that a group of white men, including a constable, had beaten some Negroes and evicted them from their homes. He denounced publicly the actions and the men responsible for them. The

19. Ketcham, "Presbyterian (Marion County) History of 2nd Presbyterian Church of Indianapolis," pp. 18–20, In.
20. Barrows, *Henry Ward Beecher, the Shakespeare of the Pulpit*, pp. 95–96.
21. HWB, *Lecture-Room Talks*, p. 15.

constable heard what Beecher said and reportedly replied, "Beecher must take back what he has said about me, or I'll lick him within an inch of his life."

On the following day the minister took the dare and walked slowly past the constable's office. He was asked to step inside, and several passers-by who heard the invitation gathered outside to watch. The constable, a large muscular man, said, "I understand, Mr. Beecher, that you have said so and so about me," and he repeated the minister's comments. "Did you say that, sir?"

"I don't think I said exactly that, but it was about what I meant to say," responded Beecher.

"You're a d—d liar, sir, and if you were not a preacher I would lick you like a dog," was the retort.

"Dismiss all considerations of that kind," said Beecher, "I ask no favor on that score." The constable uttered some further threats and profanity. Beecher listened a few moments and turned to leave the office. "Good-bye, Mr. Constable, you will feel better when you cool off." Those who had gathered to listen to the exchange gave the victor's palm to Beecher and clapped for him as he reappeared on the street.[22]

Hugh McCulloch asked Beecher what would have been his response if the constable had struck him. "I should have warded off his blows," replied the minister, "and laid him upon his back in no time. I knew if I was not stronger that I was quicker and a better wrestler than he was . . . . I should have been sorry to have had a contest with such a fellow, but I could not stand and be whipped."[23] Such an incident, with all the others, convinced Beecher that he could no longer remain aloof from the controversy.

He fully expected, however, that he would be dismissed from his pastorate if he spoke out vigorously against slavery. It was a time when

the people of Indiana did not dare to say that their souls were their own, or that the negro's soul was his own. It seemed to me that my church would be shut up, and that I should be deprived of the means on which I depended for the support of my family. And I recollect that on a certain day, while reflecting upon the unhappy state of my affairs, I read this passage: "Let your conversation be without covetousness"—that is, Do

22. McCulloch, *Men and Measures of Half A Century*, pp. 144–46.
23. *Ibid.*

not borrow trouble about where your salary is coming from—"and be content with such things as ye have." "Why, yes," I thought, "I have not many things, but I will be content with them."[24]

Aware of his duty, sensitive to reproach, and angered by the threats against his person, Henry Ward Beecher decided to preach not one but two sermons denouncing slavery. As in 1843, Beecher planned to deliver them on a Sunday in May when the United States Circuit Court was sitting in Indianapolis. He anticipated that Judge John McLean would attend services at the Second Presbyterian Church as was the jurist's custom when in the city. McLean was well respected, and his presence should deter possible violence. His opinion was apt to be accepted, too, by men who held no firm convictions of their own. When Beecher announced his proposed topic for that day's services some of the elders tried to dissuade him from preaching upon such an inflammatory subject, but the preacher persisted.[25]

Beecher began his sermon by narrating the life of Moses and the bondage and deliverance of the children of Israel. He spoke bluntly about Pharaoh's tyranny. The analogy was clear, and the congregation was aware that the preacher was attacking the institution of slavery in the United States. No overt hostility was displayed to the sermon. At the day's second service Beecher's sermon dealt with slavery in America and the duty of the American Christian in regard to it. He did not bother to resort to the use of analogies but spoke pointedly against existing evils and abuses.[26] Beecher was interested in the reaction of Judge McLean to the sermons. He was told that someone had asked McLean what he thought of the antislavery discourses and, reportedly, the judge had replied, "I think if every minister in the United States would be as faithful it would be a great advance in settling this question."[27] McLean's colleagues took the cue and did not criticize Beecher for his stand.

Henry Ward Beecher was less than truthful when he stated later

24. HWB, *Sermons by Henry Ward Beecher. Plymouth Church. Brooklyn,* I, 193; Ellinwood (ed.), *Autobiographical Reminiscences of Henry Ward Beecher,* pp. 157-58.
25. Susan Man McCulloch to Hugh McCulloch, New York, June 16, 1846, InU.
26. Stowe, *Men of Our Times,* pp. 551-52; Knox, *Life and Work of Henry Ward Beecher,* pp. 214-15.
27. Knox, *Life and Work of Henry Ward Beecher,* pp. 214-15.

that there was no reaction to the sermons. He was not personally harmed or intimidated, but several members of the Second Presbyterian Church sought and received letters of dismissal to show their disapproval of the sermons.[28] Julia Merrill wrote to Susan McCulloch that the slavery sermons created great excitement in Indianapolis. Her father dismissed them more lightly. "Mr. Beecher gets along much as usual. He has lately," wrote Samuel Merrill, "as . . . [directed] by Synod preached two sermons on slavery. They did not suit the abolitionists nor the other extreme." The sermons created enough of a stir, however, to be printed in at least one eastern newspaper. A young boy living in Wisconsin was aware that an antislavery sermon by Beecher was printed in an eastern newspaper sent to his mother.[29]

To the sorrow and stress of the preceding months was now added the death of Susan Bullard, Talbut's wife. She had given birth some weeks earlier and lost strength continuously until her death in June. This was a blow to the Beechers, particularly since Eunice herself was expecting a baby late in the summer. Always apprehensive about childbirth and unusually weakened by grief and illness, Eunice had to wait the remaining weeks till her confinement with Susan's fate in her thoughts. Catharine Esther Beecher would be born without mishap, however, on August 1, 1846.[30]

Beecher was plagued that summer with a disciplinary matter. He heard repeatedly that Luke Munsell was drinking heavily, and he could ignore the reports no longer. At the meeting of Session on June 30, 1846, the task of questioning Munsell about his intemperance was assigned to David V. Culley. Munsell, a physician and civil engineer, had himself been clerk of the Session as late as April 15, 1843. It had been he who had gone with Beecher to bury the infant stillborn to Eunice in 1840. Culley talked with Munsell who denied the truth of the allegations. Since ten respectable men and women were witnesses against him his denial was not accepted, and the Session ordered that

28. Ibid.; Indianapolis Indiana State Journal, February 18, 1846.

29. Susan Man McCulloch to Hugh McCulloch, New York, June 16, 1846, InU; Samuel Merrill to David Merrill, Madison, May 31, 1846, Samuel Merrill Papers, InHi; Pond, Eccentricities of Genius, p. 39.

30. Ira M. Barton to HWB, Worcester, Massachusetts, June 15, 1846, CtY; Annie Beecher Scoville, Notes, n.d., CtY.

charges be preferred. The witnesses were William G. Wiley, A. M. Carnahan, James Blake, Mrs. William S. Hubbard, John L. Ketcham, Mrs. James Cooke, Dr. Ramsay, William Bradshaw, Dr. A. A. Ackley, and Davis Miller. Munsell was ordered to appear in the lecture room of the Second Presbyterian Church on July 15, 1846, to answer four counts of intemperance. Before then, however, Munsell met informally with Ketcham and Beecher to discuss the matter. Munsell admitted that the "habit of using brandy for the Rheumatism had unconsciously led him farther than he was aware." He was ordered to read a statement from the pulpit the following Sunday in which he would publicly regret his sin and promise to stop drinking liquor and join the Sons of Temperance. Munsell did so, and the Session ordered the case dropped.[31]

Henry Ward Beecher traveled to Terre Haute in October to attend Synod. He was elected moderator and was given the honor of preaching the missionary sermon on Sunday morning, October 11, 1846, before the assembly which included his brother Charles. The Indianapolis pastor had a bit of fun on his way home at the expense of a member of his church, Alexander Graydon. The latter entered the same stagecoach at Greencastle at night and as the interior was unlighted failed to recognize his fellow passenger. Beecher, altering his voice, inquired about Graydon's home, church, and pastor. Graydon spoke enthusiastically of Beecher and his work at the Second Presbyterian Church. The minister maintained his disguise until the next stop when he revealed his identity to the astonished Graydon who took the deception in good part.[32]

A windfall came to the Beechers on December 4, 1846, when Calvin Fletcher gave them a hog. Six of the twenty-four animals slaughtered that day by Fletcher were singled out to be distributed to clergymen in Indianapolis as tokens of Fletcher's esteem and as a practical contribution to their support.[33] It made a significant addition to the Beecher larder for it would provide meat for several months.

31. *The Second Presbyterian Church of Indianapolis. One Hundred Years, 1838–1938*, p. 130; Holloway, *Indianapolis*, p. 56; Records of the Second Presbyterian Church, pp. 70–72, InISPC.

32. Knox, *Life and Work of Henry Ward Beecher*, pp. 94–95; Mary Ellen Graydon, *A Family Retrospect* (Indianapolis: The Hollenbeck Press, 1909), pp. 48–49.

33. Calvin Fletcher Diary, December 4, 1846, InHi; Trask, "The Honorable Calvin Fletcher," *New-England Historical and Genealogical Register*, XXIII, 382.

Fletcher had contributed more handsomely to the minister than did many of the congregation of Beecher's church. The clergyman's salary was probably $800 yearly, but many of the pledges had not been paid and his salary was in arrears. "Eight hundred dollars does not seem to me to be an extravagant salary," wrote Beecher, "but I would gladly take six hundred dollars in lieu of it, if I could have it paid regularly."[34]

Beecher assisted with preparations for a Sabbath School convention in Roberts' Chapel on Wednesday, December 16, 1846. The first session was attended mainly by clergymen with a disappointingly small number of laymen present. Matthew Simpson gave a "very good very convincing" address that evening. Next day the question was discussed whether or not lawyers should go to court on Sunday. Fletcher, Beecher, and Simpson were asked to speak at the evening meeting, but the two former did not have an opportunity to do so because the Methodist educator used up all the allotted time. Calvin Fletcher was piqued.[35]

Simpson's and Beecher's paths crossed again a few weeks later in connection with Wabash College affairs. The college faced the end of the period of grace which had been extended in regard to payment of a loan made from Indiana's Sinking Fund. Indebtedness to the state amounted to $10,600, and the college did not have the money to meet its obligation. Friends of the institution in the state legislature prepared a bill which would permit the college in lieu of payment to surrender basically worthless bonds and give free tuition for five years to approximately one hundred men who would then become common school teachers. The scheme was distasteful to Methodists who found the prospect of Wabash College educating and inflicting this large number of Presbyterian teachers on the suggestible youngsters of Indiana too much for contemplation. John S. Bayless, a Methodist minister, shared his colleagues' suspicion of Beecher and Wabash College, and he hurriedly urged Matthew Simpson to come to Indianapolis and combat the bill.[36]

Simpson and Edward R. Ames arrived in the capital to work for the bill's defeat. Ames allegedly had great influence with Governor

34. HWB to William T. Cutler, Indianapolis, December 15, 1846, CtY.

35. Calvin Fletcher Diary, December 16 and 17, 1846, InHi.

36. John S. Bayless to Matthew Simpson, Indianapolis, December 20, 1846, Matthew Simpson Papers, DLC.

James Whitcomb and supposedly could persuade him to veto the bill should it pass the legislature. Rumor and intrigue swirled along the corridors and in the meeting places of the city as both Presbyterians and Methodists girded for another battle. Beecher was quietly active in urging passage of the bill. Whitcomb did not approve the bill but permitted it to become a law without his signature, thus giving Wabash College more breathing space in its constant struggle for survival.[37] Beecher had been shrewd enough this time not to be drawn into open controversy.

As the end of the year approached Beecher answered a letter of his sister Harriet's in which he chided her for asking him to write of his convictions "as if a man could spread his soul on paper just as he spreads butter on bread." As if in amends for his ill-natured remark he urged that she recover from an illness and hoped in the spring to see her "plump & fair as Hebe." He continued, "I am in labour over-measure. It seems to me that I never before this year really felt what I owed to this state—to its necessities. 'As thy day is so shall thy strength be'—therefore I work on—and am cheered by unquestionable token of a better day—of an upward tendency throughout the State."[38]

It was Eunice, however, who told Harriet the realities of their existence in Indianapolis. Of her husband she wrote that

> if there ever was a man who had *no* liesure [*sic*]—whose time was constantly occupied from five in the morning—till eleven at night it is this same brother of yours. . . . We have had more sickness than ever before in one year (he has himself had more 'ill spells' than he has had since we married)—& that has brought more home cares upon him—then he has looked after every stick of timber that has gone into our new house—thus—& is still obliged to keep constant watch over these Hoosier carpenters. Then he has had more public duties devolving upon him than usual—aside from those strictly belonging to him in his church & among his people. His paper—& horticultural matters in general—lots & lots of other things.[39]

37. A. W. Harrison to Matthew Simpson, Indianapolis, January 14 and 15, 1847, Matthew Simpson Papers, DLC; Clark, *The Life of Matthew Simpson*, pp. 110–11; Indiana *Senate Journal*, 1846–47, pp. 449–55; Osborne and Gronert, *Wabash College, The First Hundred Years, 1832–1932*, pp. 61–62.

38. HWB to Harriet Beecher Stowe, Indianapolis, December 27, 1846, CtY.

39. Mrs. Henry Ward Beecher to Harriet Beecher Stowe, Indianapolis, December 27, 1846, CtY.

The Beecher Home on East Ohio Street, Indianapolis

Then Eunice confided to Harriet that "my heart is almost broken by this years trials & excepting when my kind husband is near me I hardly know myself—so full of wretchedness & anguish is every thought & feeling." Her thoughts were still centered on her dead baby:

> Dear little Georgie! how much pleasure I used to anticipate in showing him to you & father. . . . 'I miss his small step by my chair I miss him at the morning prayer I miss him *all day everywhere*! & I have the wildest longings to *look into his grave & see* if he is, indeed there—or if this be not a horrible dream—from which I may one day wake to find our *house* once more made happy by his merry music & affectionate carresses.

The Beechers' new house was supposed to be completed by June, and Eunice wrote Harriet that it "will be large enough to be a place of meeting for the whole [Beecher] tribe—if they will consider it such." Eunice believed that her peace of mind would improve when they moved into it and away from the house in which she saw constant reminders of "Georgie."

To Harriet who was her sympathetic contemporary Eunice wrote starkly that if Harriet "were to step in I think you would have some trouble to recognnise [*sic*] your sister in the thin faced—grey headed—toothless old woman you would find here."[40] For Henry Ward Beecher and his wife the year had brought contention, grief, and illness. To Eunice it also brought full realization that her youth was gone. It was a bitter, bitter time.

---

40. Mrs. Henry Ward Beecher to Harriet Beecher Stowe, Indianapolis, December 27, 1846, CtY.

XVIII

A New Consideration

THE JANUARY THAW SET IN EARLY IN 1847, THERE WAS A "GREAT
freshet," and by the 7th of the month the highest point of the
resulting flood waters was reached. In the surrounding countryside
damage was heavy. Many cattle were swept away by the high waters,
fences were destroyed, and buildings on low ground suffered. Several
houses in the western part of Indianapolis were isolated by high water,
some were swept from their foundations, and the banks of Pogue's Run
and Fall Creek began to give way in places. Streets were inundated, and
little ponds appeared in unaccustomed places.[1]

The Merrill family, bored with cold weather and inactivity, hoped
to take advantage of the relatively warmer weather to entertain their
friends. Young Samuel Merrill was entrusted with the family carriage
to deliver the invitations in style, but he was unaware of the family
dog perched under the vehicle. As the boy approached Market Street
he drove into standing water, since he estimated correctly he could get
through it and remain dry. The dog Ben under the carriage was not as
fortunate. He was swept away, but he managed to reach a portion of a
board fence sticking above the water and climbed upon it. The driver

---

1. Holloway, *Indianapolis*, pp. 83–84; Logan Esarey (ed.), *The Pioneers of
Morgan County, Memoirs of Noah J. Major* (Indiana Historical Society *Publications*,
V, No. 5, Indianapolis, 1915), p. 268.

of the carriage was unaware of his pet's plight and continued on his way. Ben began to howl when he realized he had been deserted.

Beecher who lived nearby heard the dog's clamor, investigated, and saw his predicament. The minister returned to his home where he got a wash tub, carried it as close to the dog as he could, and then pushed it toward Ben with a long pole. It was Beecher's hope that the dog would jump into the tub, and then the dog and tub could be maneuvered out of the deep water. Ben refused to jump. Beecher got another tub, bored holes in both, and then fastened the two together with a clothesline. He pushed this contraption toward the dog, but again Ben would not co-operate. Not to be deterred, Beecher built a crude raft on which the dog deigned to ride to safety. The dog "ever after showed his gratitude when Mr. Beecher came," recalled Mrs. Ketcham, "by placing his paws on Mr. Beecher's shoulders and wagging his stump of a tail vigorously."[2] What Eunice Beecher thought of having her wash tubs and clothesline so abused for the sake of a Merrill dog can be surmised.

Henry Ward Beecher was called to assist with a revival in progress at the Second Presbyterian Church in Madison, by its pastor, the Reverend Harvey Curtis. He was unable to leave Indianapolis at once, however, because of Eunice's illness. As soon as she was better he started on horseback for the bustling Ohio River city. It took him four and a half hours over rough roads to reach Franklin, where he spent the evening with Daniel Yandes, and they attended a service at a Baptist church. Next day Beecher rode to the point reached by the Madison & Indianapolis Railroad, one of Samuel Merrill's enterprises, where he gave his horse Charley into the care of a friend to await his return and then took the train south to Madison.[3]

More imposing than Indianapolis in 1847, Madison had graded streets and paved sidewalks. It was a thriving industrial center with four pork-packing plants, one of which was reputedly the largest in

2. Jane Merrill Ketcham erroneously attributed this incident to the year 1845. See Indianapolis *News*, April 22, 1908.

3. Woollen, *Biographical and Historical Sketches of Early Indiana*, p. 514; Julia D. Merrill to Elizabeth Bates, Madison, February 11, 1847, Julia Merrill Moores Papers, InHi; HWB to Mrs. Henry Ward Beecher, Madison, February [16 ?], 1847, CtY.

the nation; a starch factory, a glue factory, flour mills, iron foundries, and similar works. There was a chamber of commerce, a public library, and numerous retail stores. The wharves along the Ohio River were crowded with men and goods arriving and departing on the daily steam packets plying the river between Cincinnati and Louisville. Much of the merchandise brought into Indiana crossed these wharves and passed through one of the six or more wholesale houses in the city. Beautiful and stately homes lined the principal residential streets attesting to the wealth and taste possessed by Madisonians. The city was important and exciting.[4]

When Henry Ward Beecher reached Madison he learned that Samuel Merrill and Julia Merrill had preceded him. Merrill was in the city on railroad business and recovering from an illness. Beecher saw the banker and reported that the latter "sat up all the day that I arrived, goes about the house like other folks & eats like *ten* common people." Julia was glad to see him, Beecher wrote to Eunice, and teasingly took from him a "Daguerotype [*sic*], . . . would keep it if I did not *make* her give it up." Beecher continued, "I shall call a Council *you* [Eunice Beecher], *Betty* [Elizabeth Bates] etc & have the matter adjudicated," and termed it "a clear case of *petit larceny*."[5] Shortly after Beecher's arrival in Madison Julia Merrill left the city to make a visit to her namesake, Great Aunt Julia Dumont, who lived in nearby Vevay, Indiana.[6]

Beecher found that religious fervor had penetrated the consciousness of residents of the community with the Presbyterian and Methodist churches receiving most of the resultant attention.[7] Assessing the state of feeling in the Second Presbyterian Church, he estimated that he should remain to preach for eight or ten days. Beecher spent the first day or two quietly as he did "not yet feel a *liberty* of preaching, as I have not got fully into the sympathy & interest of the work."[8] By the middle of the following week he was preaching, visiting, and conducting inquiry meetings. Within a few days the revival so affected several

4. Woollen, *Biographical and Historical Sketches of Early Indiana*, pp. 513, 536–37.

5. HWB to Mrs. Henry Ward Beecher, Madison, February [16 ?], 1847, CtY.

6. Graydon, "A Pioneer Tale, The Life of Samuel Merrill," pp. 5–6, In.

7. Samuel Merrill to Hazen Merrill, Madison, February 14, 1847, Samuel Merrill Papers, InHi.

8. HWB to Mrs. Henry Ward Beecher, Madison, February [?], 1847, CtY.

young men that they showed promise of becoming Christians. Beecher was gratified by his success with them and thought he might remain longer in Madison than he had planned to do.[9]

The clergyman was in excellent humor. To his wife he wrote long letters filled with expressions of tenderness for her, details of his work, and bits of gossip. "And now my dear wife," he wrote shortly after his arrival, "be of good cheer; do not drown me or murder me, or maim or wound me, lay aside your usual ferocious propensities which are so active when I am away. The first thing I thought when I awoke this morning was whether you were thinking of me, what you were probably doing."[10] He took time to do some shopping. For the children he bought trinkets and for Eunice he purchased oranges. Mailing the gifts to his family, he wrote to Eunice that the oranges, a rare treat in February, were specifically for her enjoyment. For himself, he had purchased a

> pair of beautiful boots, had a present of a pair of superfine cloth pantaloons, which are beautiful, I bought for $3.50 another pair which are quite genteel and will wear like iron for common use, and I have a splended [sic] coat making the whole cost of cloth and making to be $20. But the gentleman put the cloth and materials at cost, (six dollar broadcloth) and he says that the coat at $20 is five less than anyone could get it for in Cincinnati, so when I get a *vest* I shall be fitted out fully.[11]

Madison's tailors were thought to be more skillful and fashionable than those in Indianapolis.

Beecher was giving a great deal of thought to Eunice, their children, and his position in Indianapolis. "I am hardly away from home an hour's ride before I begin to review our life together," he wrote to his wife, "the greatness of your love to me, the degree of self-sacrifice you have endured, your willingness to labor, to suffer, to wear out, without complaint, and your unhesitating acquiescence in my remaining when your health seems to be sacrificed."[12] They had discussed the possibility of returning East to reside permanently at various times but

9. Julia D. Merrill to Catharine Merrill and Mary Jane Merrill, Madison, February 21, 1847, Samuel Merrill Papers, InHi.

10. HWB to Mrs. Henry Ward Beecher, Madison, February [16 ?], 1847, CtY.

11. HWB to Mrs. Henry Ward Beecher, Madison, February [?], 1847, CtY.

12. *Ibid.*

had not acted upon it. During the past autumn, however, Beecher had held long conversations with a visitor to Indianapolis in which the subject had been pursued. Formerly a partner of James Cooke who was a member of the Second Presbyterian Church in Indianapolis, William T. Cutler was a New York merchant and an acquaintance of Beecher who spent several days in the Hoosier capital attending to some business and sightseeing. Cutler had met Beecher first when the latter was about eleven-years-old and Cutler attended Lyman Beecher's church. He heard Henry Ward Beecher preach several times in the fall of 1846 in Indianapolis, learned of his interests and achievements, and spent much time talking with him. He liked Beecher and thought the minister might be suited to fill the pastorate of a proposed Congregational church in Brooklyn. Their conversations led Cutler to think that Beecher could be persuaded to accept such a position. Beecher had not told his wife immediately of the intriguing possibility, however, and apparently did not do so until after the beginning of the new year.[13]

Henry Ward Beecher believed that his father would object to such a move, and he left Cutler with the impression that the elder clergyman's opinion carried great weight with his son. Deciding to assess for himself the opposition which Henry might face from his formidable father, Cutler stopped in Walnut Hills on his return journey to talk with Lyman Beecher. The latter "set his face like a flint against it, enquired who he could send to in your state to carry out his plans? I told him," continued Cutler to Henry Ward Beecher, "you could do *here* [New York] somethin[g] like the work he accomplished in Boston. Still he felt that you could do more for the King of Kings in the West than here."[14] The ministerial dynasty of Beechers which it had been Lyman Beecher's dream to erect in the West would crumble if Henry should leave and return to live in the East. George Beecher was dead. Edward Beecher had returned to Boston in 1844 to become pastor of the Salem Street Church. William Beecher was a minister, but he was too weak a reed for Father Lyman's purpose; it was all the family could do to keep William in a pulpit for he had a regrettable tendency

13. Mrs. Henry Ward Beecher to Harriet Beecher Stowe, Indianapolis, December 27, 1846, CtY; Knox, *Life and Work of Henry Ward Beecher*, pp. 88–89.
14. William T. Cutler to HWB, New York, December 8, 1846, CtY.

to irritate the members of his congregation. Charles was pastor of the Second Presbyterian Church in Fort Wayne, but not particularly secure in the position. Tom and James had doubts about entering the ministry. Only Henry, the son most like his father, could shore up the tottering edifice which Lyman Beecher had worked for nearly two decades to build.

Regardless of his father's expressed disapproval of the idea, Beecher answered Cutler's letter promptly. Without committing himself, the Indianapolis pastor wrote at length of his willingness to be considered for a pastorate in New York. The gist of what he said may be read in such sentiments as "A man should work just where he is until he is clearly called somewhere else. . . . I have no plan for staying here, or for going to the West, or for going to the East. . . . I do not care in whose hands truth may be found, or in what communion; I will thankfully take it of any." In other words, Beecher was available if circumstances were favorable, and he had no objections to breaking his connection with the Presbyterian Church and heading a Congregational one. As Cutler was "at the fountain of news," Beecher asked him to write of "things in the great world."[15]

An unexpected benefit from Cutler's overt interest in Beecher was that it prompted payment of a portion of the latter's salary from the Second Presbyterian Church. It had been surmised that Beecher might be considering leaving the Indianapolis pastorate from the numerous times he was seen deep in conversation with the merchant. It chanced that Edwin J. Peck, a wealthy member of Beecher's church, was Cutler's traveling companion on the boat from Madison to Cincinnati. Peck urged Cutler not to woo Beecher away from the Second Presbyterian Church and told the latter that "he would rather build your [HWB's] house & pay you $100 a year than have you leave."[16] Four friends of Beecher, unnamed in his accounts, did contribute fifty dollars each to the minister to supplement his income in 1846 and would do so again in 1847.[17]

15. HWB to William T. Cutler, Indianapolis, December 15, 1846, CtY.
16. *Ibid.*, December 8, 1846.
17. Knox, *Life and Work of Henry Ward Beecher*, p. 455; [Mrs. Beecher], *From Dawn to Daylight*, pp. 280–86.

As a result, Henry Ward Beecher had gone to Madison in better spirits than he had been able to muster for months, splurged on gifts and clothes, and felt warmed by the knowledge that his prospects seemed brighter. The revival was proceeding smoothly and successfully, and he had good friends to share his recreation. Even Julia Merrill returned to Madison in time to hear him preach on the Sunday before he planned to return to Indianapolis. Eunice had written earlier that she envied the young woman her presence in Madison, and Beecher had replied that she need not do so. He had concluded, "Give my love to Elizabeth [Bates] and a good warm kiss, as the kiss for Julia is on hand."[18]

It is conjectural what, if anything, occurred between Henry Ward Beecher and Julia Merrill shortly afterwards in Madison. Perhaps Beecher bestowed the promised kiss on Julia to discover that the child he had known was now a woman. What is certain is that the quality of the relationship between Julia Merrill and Beecher changed sometime in the short interval between the latter's letter to his wife and his return to Indianapolis. Never again did he display his former paternal attitude toward Julia, and she made little effort to hide her deepening feelings for Beecher from him or her family and friends.

The tie between the Merrill and the Beecher families might have become even stronger than one of friendship if Talbut Bullard had his way. Since his wife's death Bullard had resumed going about socially and was known to be seeking a replacement for the dead Susan. Of all the young women in Indianapolis he was drawn particularly to the unmarried Merrill daughters and called frequently at their home. Twenty-three-year-old Catharine observed cynically his efforts at courtship and did not regard them with favor. While Julia was in Madison her older sister wrote to her that "Dr. Bullard now and then pays her [their mother] a friendly *filial* visit, gives her a good deal of advice and seems to take a warm interest in her recovery." What especially irritated Catharine Merrill were the physician's continual references to her father as "Pa."[19] For a time another sister, Jane Merrill Ketcham, appeared to favor Bullard as a suitor for one of her sisters; and this, too,

18. HWB to Mrs. Henry Ward Beecher, Madison, February [?], 1846, CtY.
19. Catharine Merrill to Julia D. Merrill, Indianapolis, February 21, 1847, Julia Merrill Moores Papers, InHi; Dunn, *Indiana and Indianans*, III, 1440.

irkcd Catharine. At thirty-two, the widower Bullard held little appeal for the most eligible young ladies of Indianapolis.[20]

Even while Henry Ward Beecher was busy with the revival in Madison events were occurring in New York of which Cutler kept him informed. The proposed church was becoming a fact. Impetus for organizing a society to form a second Congregational Church in Brooklyn came largely from John Tasker Howard, Seth Hunt, and Henry C. Bowen. Another who was greatly interested in the project was David Hale who was associated with the Broadway Tabernacle in New York. Brooklyn was thought to be growing rapidly enough to be well able to support another Congregational Church in addition to the Church of the Pilgrims which had been established there in 1844.

When Beecher returned to Indianapolis from Madison, he found waiting a letter from the New York merchant which mentioned the strong support being given Beecher by influential clergymen in New York for the post of pastor of the proposed church. Cutler told him that a call would be extended to him and that Beecher could expect to command a salary of $2,000 per year. As an inducement to leave Indianapolis, Cutler wrote,

> You can probably do as much or more for the West by living here, you could *publish* much to benefit the world. Your influence would be felt *beyond* the *Atlantic* as well as *West* of the *Alleghenys*. You would have a *world* of people here to listen to your *preaching*, you would have much to stimulate to study and action—other minds here to *vie* with, to see who should *best* sow Christ and build up his Kingdom. Suppose you were to come and stay 5 years, then return to the West you would be *eminently better fited* [*sic*] *to be a General in the Army opposed* to Satan![21]

It was a passage calculated to fire the imagination of any preacher with a spark of ambition in his soul.

Henry Ward Beecher was invited to speak at a meeting of the American Home Missionary Society to be held in the Broadway Tabernacle during the May Anniversary Week, a time when religiously oriented organizations convened in New York for a series of separate

20. Catharine Merrill to Julia D. Merrill, Indianapolis, February 21, 1847, Julia Merrill Moores Papers, InHi; Edson, *The Church God's Building. A Historical Discourse Delivered December 22, 1867*, pp. 16–17.
21. William T. Cutler to HWB [New York], February 13, 18[47], CtY.

and combined meetings designed to recharge delegates' spiritual batteries and provide a common ground where business could be transacted formally and informally. The promoters of the planned church could evaluate Beecher's ability as a preacher and try to determine if his personality would be suited for the venture in Brooklyn. He could assess the potential for himself professionally and for the welfare of his family. Beecher accepted the invitation, and in a letter to David Hale wrote that he might accept the pastorate in Brooklyn if it were offered him.[22]

Henry C. Bowen assumed the lead in negotiating with Beecher to leave Indianapolis and move to Brooklyn. Bowen was more familiar with Beecher's history than were the other promoters with the exception of Cutler. A distant cousin of Bowen's, Joseph K. Sharpe, was a member of Beecher's church in Indianapolis; and Bowen's wife, the former Lucy Maria Tappan, was a daughter of Lewis Tappan whose brother, Arthur Tappan, had sponsored Lyman Beecher at the inception of Lane Theological Seminary. Bowen sent a cordial letter to Beecher which stated that the clergyman could "do a *vast* amount of good here [Brooklyn] no man can doubt and good too that no other man *can* do." Bowen urged Beecher to give his answer before May 1, 1847, if he planned to make the change. Sale of pews occurred on that date which provided much of a church's revenue for the following year. He also said that it would not be necessary for Beecher to move at once so long as he promised to take the Brooklyn pulpit.[23] What Bowen did not do, and could not, was send an authorized call to Beecher extending an invitation to become pastor of an existing church. In accordance with the laws of New York State such a call was impossible until a society was organized prior to the formation of a church.

News that Henry Ward Beecher might become pastor of the new church was circulated. Bowen was a brilliant publicist who managed to capture the imagination of the public which he encouraged to view Beecher as the romantic missionary serving among rough backwoodsmen. Such a background was just the novelty needed to stimulate

22. Henry C. Bowen to HWB, New York, March 26, 1847, CtY.

23. Henry C. Bowen to HWB, New York, March 26 and September 6, 1847, CtY; Dunn, *Indiana and Indianans*, III, 1432–33; Foote, *The Schools of Cincinnati, and Its Vicinity*, p. 214.

interest in the clergyman and the new church in Brooklyn. Beecher's talents and exploits, real and imaginary, were magnified; and the clergyman's name was on the lips of those people who derive vicarious satisfaction from such publicity.

Actually, Henry Ward Beecher was well qualified for the proposed pastorate. Although most of his work had taken place within the confines of a western state, his reputation was nationally known. First, he was a son of the renowned Lyman Beecher and brother to George Beecher who had been a power in the Presbyterian Church and a brother to Edward Beecher who was pastor of a prominent Boston church; second, he was the author of *Seven Lectures to Young Men* which had been successful enough to bring attention to him as a talented Beecher; third, visitors from the East traveling through Indiana had heard him preach; fourth, Beecher had delivered sermons at churches in Massachusetts and New York when he visited members of his family; and fifth, he had kept abreast of clerical developments in Presbyterian and Congregational circles in the East. Because of his family connections and the favorable impression of his preaching ability held by influential Easterners, Henry Ward Beecher was a logical choice for the post.[24]

While Beecher's name was being bruited about in clerical and lay circles in the East he was in the midst of an election campaign which found the temperance men of Indianapolis pitted against the "Grog drinking" men. So close was the outcome expected to be that men such as Beecher and Calvin Fletcher went into the streets to distribute literature and try to persuade men to vote for the temperance candidates. "I never felt more mortified at a thing of the Kind than that I had to go into the Streets & solicit votes for any cause & so incurred the odium of the wicked," wrote Fletcher, and "they expressed their resentment by voting for me Ketcham & Beecher for fence viewer."[25] The temperance candidates won, so their work was not in vain.

In addition to obtaining a substitute preacher and otherwise preparing to leave for the East Beecher had the work of preparing

---

24. Charles Butler to Eliza Ogden Butler, Indianapolis, February 8, 1846, quoted in Prentiss, *The Union Theological Seminary*, pp. 497–98; HWB, Journal, February 28, 1840, CtY.

25. Calvin Fletcher Diary, April 10, 1847, InHi.

material for issues of the *Western Farmer and Gardener* which would appear during the six or eight weeks he planned to be gone. In his capacity as editor he selected or wrote the principal features and left enough space for inclusion of usable letters which might be received from readers. The publisher had been vexed by failure to receive sufficient newsprint to get the issues out on time, but in April a new contract was signed which should alleviate the chronic shortage. Beecher informed his readers that they could expect to receive the periodical on schedule.[26]

Henry Ward Beecher planned to take Eunice and their children with him. His wife had been ill for months, and he hoped the journey would restore her health. Before they could leave Indianapolis, however, there was much work to be done. Promised that the new house on East Ohio Street would be ready for occupancy by their return in June, they sold the small house in which they had been living and stored their household goods. Arrangements were made for the care of their domestic animals and garden. Beecher had purchased new clothes in Madison, but Eunice had to contrive suitable and sufficient garments for herself and the children to wear on the extended trip. So eager was she to go, however, that somehow she accomplished all the work.[27] Their journey to New York was marred for Eunice Beecher by an embarrassing incident. When the train on which the Beechers were riding stopped at a station, Beecher got off to get an item for his wife's comfort. An elderly woman who was seated nearby noticed his consideration and said, "Cheer up, my dear madam, cheer up. Surely whatever may be your trial, you have cause for great thankfulness to God who has given you such a kind and attentive son."[28] Eunice Beecher was only too aware that she looked older than her husband, and the incident upset her. The Beecher family arrived in New York without further ado.

26. Indianapolis *Indiana State Journal*, May 11, 1847; Butler, "Indiana Newspapers, 1829–1860," *Indiana Magazine of History*, XXII, 305; John L. Ketcham to HWB, Indianapolis, June 1, 1847, John L. Ketcham Papers, InHi.

27. Joseph Howard, Jr., *Life of Henry Ward Beecher*, pp. 125–27; Mrs. Beecher, "Mr. Beecher as I Knew Him," *Ladies Home Journal*, January, 1892, p. 5.

28. Barrows mistakenly places this incident in October, 1847, at which time Eunice Beecher was already in Massachusetts. See Barrows, *Henry Ward Beecher, the Shakespeare of the Pulpit*, p. 109; Joseph Howard, Jr., *Life of Henry Ward Beecher*, pp. 58, 127.

The American Home Missionary Society was celebrating its twenty-first anniversary when Beecher arose to address it on May 12, 1847, in the Broadway Tabernacle. The audience thought him youthful with his long, thick hair, beardless chin, and large blue eyes. "His nose was straight, full and prominent. His mouth formed a perfect bow," recalled Howard, "and when the well-developed lips parted they disclosed the regular, well-set teeth. There was nothing clerical in his face, figure, dress or bearing."[29] Indeed, some thought a country bumpkin had mistakenly taken a seat upon the dais. The other clergymen were resplendent in white cravats, but Beecher "wore a black bombazine stock, and that stock had got twisted around so that the buckle was under one ear and in plain sight, while his clothes were rusty and ill-fitting."[30]

People were curious to see and hear this western preacher who had received so much comment. Sensing this mood and feeling their willingness to accept him, Beecher began, "I am going to tell you something about the devil's colporteurs. I have been watching them for years on the Western steamboats. I can go among them as you, brethren, could not; for you see that nobody would ever suspect me of being a preacher."[31] The sophisticated audience looked at him and at his peers, understood that Beecher was unabashed by his unfashionable appearance, and began to laugh with, not at, the man so newly arrived from the West. "That opening sentence," wrote a biographer, "established his reputation, and he held his audiences spellbound from that time on."[32] Beecher spoke at length and with great earnestness of the need for missionaries in the West, the conditions of life which they faced, and the necessity for supporting them in the field. So favorably did he impress his listeners that he received invitations to speak at subsequent meetings of other societies.[33]

Beecher was asked to preach at the first services of the new Congregational church on Cranberry Street in Brooklyn. Formerly the site

---

29. Joseph Howard, Jr., *Life of Henry Ward Beecher*, pp. 128, 133–34.
30. Knox, *Life and Work of Henry Ward Beecher*, p. 458.
31. *Ibid.*
32. *Ibid.*
33. New York *Daily Tribune*, May 13, 1847; John R. Howard, *Remembrance of Things Past* (New York: Thomas Y. Crowell Co., 1925), pp. 39–40; John R. Howard, *Henry Ward Beecher*, pp. 55–56.

of the First Presbyterian Church, the land and building had been purchased for the sum of $20,000 when the Presbyterians sold it after
moving to a new location on Henry Street. The Congregational church,
still unnamed, was situated on a plot comprising seven lots each of
which measured 100′ x 25′ and surrounded by large shade trees.[34]
There was a sizable audience at the morning service on Sunday, May
16, 1847, but it was surpassed in the evening when nearly eight hundred
people crowded into the building to hear Beecher speak on "Man's Ac-
countability to God." Taking his text from Romans 14:12, Beecher
elaborated upon the theme that each person must explain the way in
which he spent his time, the use and abuse of his imagination, how well
he performed his duties, and to what extent he did his duty to God and
received the salvation offered by Christ. His listeners were visibly
moved. It was not one of his better presentations, for he was nervous
and at times spoke too rapidly. The New York *Daily Tribune* thought
well enough of the sermon, however, to print it in its entirety centered
on the front page. Beecher was invited to preach again at Cranberry
Street with the understanding he should receive his board and lodging
plus twenty dollars a Sunday.[35]

As a result of his successful reception in New York during Anniversary Week he was invited to speak at meetings held in Boston during
its sister Anniversary Week. He gave an address at a meeting of the
Massachusetts Home Missionary Society in Boston on Tuesday, May
25, 1847, and another to the American Temperance Union meeting that
evening at the Winter Street Church. On Wednesday, May 26, he spoke
at a gathering of the Massachusetts (Orthodox) Sabbath School Society
held in Boston's Tremont Temple. Thursday evening found him ad-
dressing the American Board of Commissioners for Foreign Missions in
the same building. Speeches to the societies were interspersed with

---

34. John R. Howard, *Remembrance of Things Past*, pp. 38–39; *A Church in
History* (Brooklyn: Plymouth Church of the Pilgrims, 1949), pp. 3–4; Joseph Howard,
Jr., *Life of Henry Ward Beecher*, pp. 128–30; William T. Cutler to HWB, [New York],
February 13, [1847], CtY; Griswold, *Sixty Years with Plymouth Church*, pp. 23–24.

35. Brooklyn *Daily Eagle*, May 11 and 15, 1847; New York *Daily Tribune*,
May 18, 1847; *A Church in History*, p. 4; Joseph Howard, Jr., *Life of Henry Ward
Beecher*, p. 128; Henry C. Bowen to HWB, New York, May 24, 1847, CtY; Knox,
Life and Work of Henry Ward Beecher, pp. 99–100.

sermons delivered by Beecher in Boston's churches.[36] Word of Beecher's popularity in Boston reached Bowen and the other promoters in New York, and they became almost frantic for fear that this missionary preacher they had publicized and brought eastward might be persuaded to accept another pastorate. They bombarded him with letters urging him to become the minister of the new church. In one, Bowen described the first prayer meeting held in the church less than a week after Beecher's first sermon there, and said that Beecher "was spoken of as the man of our choice—'our first love' the desire of our hearts."[37] At the conclusion of the prayer meeting a committee of five men had been appointed to make arrangements for the formation of the proposed society and church. Beecher was invited to return to Brooklyn and preach on the Sunday the church would be organized.

Eastern acquaintances of the Beechers had been genuinely shocked by Eunice's appearance and state of health. "Who knows but that God has *providentially* laid the hand of sickness upon your wife in order to *furnish* a *clear* reason," wrote Bowen, "for you to come to us."[38] A clergyman named Spalding told Cutler that he thought Beecher would take the Brooklyn post because of Eunice's condition. The former said that when she was a guest in his home she was so weak she could scarcely walk upstairs without assistance. Milton Badger expressed the opinion that "if the sickness of a missionaries wife will justify his return to his native land, it will most assuredly justify a removal from one part of the land to the other!"[39] Eunice Beecher's health was discussed at an informal gathering of some members of the American Home Missionary Society when someone said Beecher might be criticized for leaving the missionary field in the West. It was the consensus, though, "that not a word can be said against your [HWB] coming to Brooklyn if your wifes health is in the condition represented," reported Bowen.[40] The promoter referred again and again to Eunice's health as a reason why Beecher should resign his Indianapolis pastorate and settle in Brooklyn.

36. New York *Daily Tribune*, May 28 and 31, 1847.
37. Henry C. Bowen to HWB, Brooklyn, May 20, 1847, CtY.
38. *Ibid.*
39. William T. Cutler to HWB, New York, May 22, 1847, CtY.
40. Henry C. Bowen to HWB, New York, May 24, 1847, CtY.

Another factor which the promoters thought might be keeping Beecher from giving them a definite acceptance was his father's negative attitude. Bowen was not unsympathetic with Lyman Beecher's position, but he felt the elder clergyman was misguided in insisting that Henry remain in Indiana. Bowen wrote to Lyman Beecher setting forth much the same arguments that he directed toward Henry Ward Beecher. In connection with this, Bowen held a long conversation with Dr. Nathaniel Taylor of New Haven, Connecticut. Taylor and the elder Beecher knew each other well. Taylor had opposed his friend's leaving the East to take up residence in Ohio, so it is unlikely that he was free from prejudice. He told Bowen that Henry's place was in the East, and he ended the talk saying he would write to Lyman Beecher advocating the son's return.[41] In spite of this and similar pressures Lyman Beecher remained adamant against his son's leaving the West. His attitude may be observed in a letter to John Tasker Howard in which he stated that Henry was "settled in Indianapolis, . . . at a point of great influence, where he could do great good, and it would be folly to remove him." The good Doctor said also to some friends that "in Indianapolis Henry would make a mark, but in the vicinity of New York he would simply sink out of sight among the greater men, and have no especial influence, except in a very limited sphere."[42] The unknown element, of course, was to what extent Henry Ward Beecher would be influenced by his father in making his decision to remain in Indianapolis or to remove eastward.

In conversations with clergymen, laymen, and reporters Bowen spoke of his admiration for Henry Ward Beecher's abilities and, in general, performed a superb piece of promotion. References to Beecher and the question of whether or not he would move to Brooklyn continued to appear in newspapers and periodicals. The clergyman was displeased with some of the publicity about his affairs, though, and he wrote a rather sharp letter of protest to Bowen about the unjustified "blowing of trumpets." It irritated the clergyman that some of the articles in the papers gave the impression that he was contemptuous of the abilities of his peers in New York. "What you see in the papers,"

41. Henry C. Bowen to HWB, New York, May 24, 1847, CtY.
42. Joseph Howard, Jr., *Life of Henry Ward Beecher*, p. 131; Barrows, *Henry Ward Beecher, the Shakespeare of the Pulpit*, p. 104.

replied Bowen, "is an *omen for good,* it shows that the public mind is not scared." He continued, "The fact is it is impossible for a man to do any good work, at the present day, without *all sorts of demonstrations,* even shoutings sometimes from the Devil himself."[43] David Hale, a proprietor of the *Journal of Commerce,* also wrote a letter of reply which was much stiffer in tone and was not as fawning as was Bowen's. "We have a right," Hale stated, "to adopt what we deem the best plan and be industrious as Christians in building up the interests in which we are connected."[44] It was a remonstrance and a warning that Hale was not as infatuated with Beecher as was Bowen who seems to have convinced himself that the clergyman's presence was essential to the success of the new church.

Henry Ward Beecher had another reason for not wanting statements in the New York press which implied that he was committed to the Brooklyn pastorate. The excitement created by his success had been communicated to the congregation of the prestigious Park Street Church in Boston. Invited to preach in its pulpit where his father and brother Edward had been favorably received in their time and where he had preached on his wedding trip, he delivered a sermon there on June 6, 1847. The congregation was so pleased with Beecher's sermon and personality that its officers discussed offering him the post of associate pastor. The pastor of the church, Silas Aiken, wrote to Beecher that he "would rejoice in having you as an associate. Though I must say with John the Baptist 'He must increase & I must decrease.' . . . You may rest assured of *my hearty cooperation.*" Aiken stressed the plentifulness of work for two men, that he thought Beecher could serve the West well in Boston, that the health of the latter's family should be better there, that he would have access to good libraries, and, after all, that he would be living in *"the heart of New England."* Knowing a little of Beecher's interest in horticulture, the Boston pastor mentioned it would be possible for Beecher to reside in the country if he were so inclined.[45]

43. Henry C. Bowen to HWB, New York, May 28, 1847, CtY; Brooklyn *Daily Eagle,* May 11, 1847; Henry C. Bowen to HWB, Brooklyn, May 20 and 24, 1847, CtY; William T. Cutler to HWB, New York, May 22, 1847, CtY.

44. [David Hale?] to W. H. [*sic*] Beecher, New York, June 1, 1847, CtY.

45. Silas Aiken to HWB, Boston, June 10 and 11, 1847, CtY.

Beecher did not write to anyone in the Hoosier capital for the first few weeks he was in the East. After receiving a letter containing a bank draft from Julia Merrill and Elizabeth Bates he was prompted to write and acknowledge it. "Although . . . out of means, & . . . either obliged to borrow, or to receive payment for preaching each Sabbath, . . . Still the draft was not half so welcome as was the feeling that you," he wrote to Julia, "thought of me & mine, & thought so much as to Enter into our probable wants, and to make provision for them, when such provision was, as I very well know, not easy for you."[46] Averring his personal wish to return to Indianapolis, Beecher gave "the State of my wife's health, & the disposition of my own people" as the two factors upon which his decision would be based. The latter referred to the difficulty he had been having for almost a year in securing payment of his salary. After writing of his activities Beecher concluded, "And now dear Julia, you may well imagine how much more I think & feel than I can write. So you must call upon your *imagination* to interpret an ampler meaning than these hasty lines can give."[47] Within a few days of Beecher's receiving the money from Julia and Elizabeth, John L. Ketcham wrote to the pastor that a draft for $100 was being sent to him as part of his salary from the Second Presbyterian Church.[48]

After preaching to the congregation of the Park Street Church in Boston, Beecher had gone to his brother-in-law's home in Worcester. A delegation from the Park Street Church traveled there on June 10 to see if Beecher would accept a call to be associate pastor of their church should the position be offered him, only to find that they had missed him. Events in Brooklyn were proceeding so rapidly that Beecher had thought it wise to leave Massachusetts earlier than he had planned and return to New York. The proposed church on Cranberry Street now had a name. Seeking to relate it to the Church of the Pilgrims, the wife of one of the promoters suggested that an appropriate name might be the Plymouth Brethren. Mulling this over, those at the meeting changed it slightly to Plymouth Church and so it would be known.

46. HWB to Julia D. Merrill, Boston, June 5, 1847, Julia Merrill Moores Papers, InHi.

47. *Ibid.*

48. John L. Ketcham to HWB, Indianapolis, June 1, 1847, John L. Ketcham Papers, InHi.

Plymouth Church was formally organized on Sunday, June 13, 1847, with the Reverend Richard L. Storrs, pastor of the sister Church of the Pilgrims as the main speaker. Twenty-one people were recognized as charter members.[49]

At a meeting held the next evening Beecher was called unanimously to become pastor of Plymouth Church at a salary of $1,500 per year. He did not commit himself but temporized with now familiar allusions to doubts about where his duty lay. The promoters were aware that the Park Street Church had made overtures to Beecher, for he had said to Bowen and Howard that "I don't want to go there [Park Street Church]. I don't want to build on another's foundation, and I must confess that I find myself very strongly attracted to your enterprise, because here I could start my own church my own way, and build it from the ground as I think it ought to be."[50] He left them with the impression that he was favorably disposed to accept their call, but that he had to consider the possibility of accepting an invitation to Boston should that be more advantageous. When they pleaded with him to become pastor of the Cranberry Street church he replied that he felt it right to give life in the West one more chance before making a decision and said nothing about waiting to learn what offer he would receive from Boston.

Henry Ward Beecher returned to Indianapolis with the heady knowledge that a promising future awaited him in his native East if he desired it.

49. Charter members of Plymouth Church included Henry C. Bowen, Lucy Maria Bowen, Eli C. Blake, Benjamin Burgess, Mary Burgess, Mary Cannon, David Griffin, Richard Hale, Julia Hale, John Tasker Howard, Rachael Knight, John F. Morse, Rebecca Morse, John Payne, Eliza Payne, Charles Rowland, Maria Rowland, Alpheus R. Turner, Louisa Turner, John Webb, and Martha Webb. See John R. Howard, *Henry Ward Beecher*, pp. 55–56; John R. Howard, *Remembrance of Things Past*, pp. 39–40; *A Church in History*, p. 187; Silas Aiken to HWB, Boston, June 11, 1847, CtY; Brooklyn *Daily Eagle*, June 14, 1847.

50. Joseph Howard, Jr., *Life of Henry Ward Beecher*, pp. 130–31; Mrs. Beecher, "Mr. Beecher as I Knew Him," *Ladies Home Journal*, January, 1892, p. 5.

XIX

Homeward Bound

DISAPPOINTMENT AND ILLNESS AWAITED THE BEECHERS IN INDI-
anapolis. They had been assured that the house being built for
them at 327 E. Ohio Street would be ready for occupancy upon their
return from the East. It was not; and having no acceptable alternative,
they moved into it. In an effort to hasten completion of work on the
structure Beecher and Talbut Bullard painted its exterior in the long
summer evenings while Eunice held a lantern so they could continue
work by its light. One after another parents and children succumbed
to illness. Within six weeks all were or had been sick, and Eunice
was experiencing alarming symptoms related to her heart.[1]

Immersed in such domestic problems, Beecher did not write to
anyone in a position of authority at the Park Street Church or Plymouth
Church. He received letter after letter from members of the latter be-
seeching him to become their pastor. Repeatedly was emphasized the
benefit Eunice's health should receive if he returned her to her native
place, the good that Beecher could accomplish in Brooklyn and its
sphere, and the valuable service he could perform there as an ambas-
sador and fund raiser for the West.[2] Those from Bowen became in-

1. Mrs. Henry Ward Beecher, Notes, n.d., CtY; Indianapolis *Sunday Star,*
December 23, 1928, and July 7, 1929; Mrs. Beecher, "Mr. Beecher as I Knew Him,"
Ladies Home Journal, January, 1892, p. 5; HWB, Reminiscences, n.d., CtY.

2. For an example of such a letter see John Payne to HWB, Brooklyn, July 12,
1847, CtY.

creasingly passionate in urging the clergyman to accept the call to Brooklyn. Apparently upset by a rumor that Beecher was going to move to Boston, Bowen wrote "the truth is we are *willing* to do more for you than you ever *dreamed* of we are in the condition of . . . any loving wife like yours or mine, willing to do just what, 'you say,' for you have 'stolen our hearts.' . . . We want you; come! you must come!"[3]

Bowen's letters also provided Beecher with an extremely practical incentive to accept the call to Plymouth Church. Cutler had written earlier that the new church might offer $2,000 per year to Beecher, and the church in fact had promised him a salary of $1,500 annually with assurance of later increases. Fearing that Beecher might be lured to Boston, however, Bowen and the other promoters conceived the idea in July of raising a subscription as an added inducement which would be used to pay the clergyman's debts in Indiana and defray his expenses of moving eastward. They secured pledges totaling $800 for the purpose by July 11, with many people still likely to contribute. Later Bowen wrote that $1,000 had been raised which Beecher would not be expected to repay. "One thing I wish to say, we are 'keeping still' the fact of our raising the money to pay your debts," the merchant stated to Beecher, "only those who feel interested in your coming have been called upon. The public know nothing of this matter." Recalling Beecher's earlier expressed dislike of personal publicity, Bowen did not want to antagonize him. Beecher did not reply to any of Bowen's letters, and finally the latter could no longer endure the suspense. He asked the minister to write to him as he did not even know if the Beecher family had arrived safely in Indianapolis.[4]

In the meantime, Silas Aiken was also writing regularly to Beecher. The pastor of the Park Street Church explained that because of the legal necessity to give advance public notice of a meeting of the society it had been impossible for church officials to extend a call to Beecher before his return to Indiana. He reassured Beecher that a call would follow shortly, as it did, and that "a good spirit prevails among us. You would be," wrote Aiken, "received with open hand & heart."[5] Aiken's letters

3. Henry C. Bowen to HWB, New York, July 21, 1847, CtY.
4. Henry C. Bowen to HWB, New York, July 14, 21, and 30, 1847, CtY.
5. Silas Aiken to HWB, Boston, July 13, 1847, CtY; Silas Aiken *et al.* to HWB, Boston, July 15, 1847, CtY.

were more restrained than Bowen's but no less cordial. The call to become associate pastor of the Boston church did not mention the amount of the attached salary. Beecher replied that he could not make a decision until he knew what he could expect to receive. Somewhat affronted, Aiken responded, "I am sure it is the purpose of this people [Park Street Church] to give you an adequate & generous support; and if the salary they may propose, should prove insufficient, I have no doubt, more would be forthcoming."[6] He told Beecher that his own salary had always been promptly paid and that it was the congregation's intention to give Beecher any aid he might require in leaving the West. While waiting for a salary commitment from Boston, Beecher resumed writing to Bowen in New York.

Bowen was becoming impatient and was irked at Beecher's tactics of delay. "If you settle the *question now Not* to come," wrote Bowen to Beecher, "it is in my view *practically* settled for *life*. The *meridian* of your usefulness will soon pass, your views & feelings will settle and—fasten you where you are. Do you *always* expect to remain in your *present position?*"[7] This bluntness and threat jolted Beecher into action. Not even waiting to learn what salary he might be offered by the Boston church, Beecher submitted a letter of resignation on August 12, 1847, to the elders of the Second Presbyterian Church of Indianapolis. He gave the state of his wife's health as his reason for doing so in "the firm belief that in removing temporarily to the sea-coast I should save the life & restore the health of my wife."[8] Beecher made no mention of his dissatisfaction with the nonpayment of his salary. Some of the congregation were aware, though, that this was a factor in his decision. "I suppose it is always hard to raise ministers' salaries," commented Jane Merrill Ketcham. "Notwithstanding he loved us and would never have left of his own accord."[9]

Soon Beecher received a letter from Isaac Parker, chairman of the Park Street Church's Prudential Committee. Parker in behalf of the committee offered $1,500 to Beecher if he resided in the country or $1,800 annually if the clergyman elected to live in Boston. In addition

6. Silas Aiken to HWB, Boston, August 3, 1847, CtY.
7. Henry C. Bowen to HWB, August 6, 1847, CtY.
8. Records of the Second Presbyterian Church, pp. 83–84, InISPC.
9. "Reminiscences of Jane Merrill Ketcham," p. 79, In.

the church would provide an unspecified sum to assist with Beecher's moving expenses.[10] The letter was courteous but must have seemed cold after Bowen's unrestrained pleas. In Brooklyn Beecher would receive a salary of $1,500 the first year with assurance of later increases and a sum exceeding $1,000 to pay his debts and expenses in moving. He would be the sole pastor of a new church in an area particularly appealing to him. At the Park Street Church in Boston he could receive either $1,500 or $1,800 with no promise of an increase in the near future, he would be an associate pastor, and he would be expected to fit himself into the confines of an established church with its defined policies and traditions. Beecher made his decision and sent his acceptance in an envelope closed by a picture seal showing a gate ajar and bearing the legend, "I'm all unhinged."[11]

Scarcely less unhinged was Henry C. Bowen when he opened Beecher's informal acceptance of the call to be pastor of the Plymouth Church. The letter was shared with John Tasker Howard who would recall that it affected them so much they were "in each other's arms, crying and laughing and capering about like a couple of school-boys."[12] Bowen wrote immediately to Beecher with expressions of delight and added, "You are at liberty to draw at sight on Bowen & McNamee for any sum not exceeding one thousand dollars at your pleasure which draft or drafts will be duly honored."[13] Beecher had anticipated this permission and had already drawn $500 of it of which he paid $200 to Calvin Fletcher on the mortgage on the Ohio Street lots.[14] Even with this money from the people of Plymouth Church and with what he could collect of his overdue salary in Indianapolis there would not be enough to pay all Beecher's debts. He decided to pay as many of them as he could and give notes for the rest.

Henry Ward Beecher's formal letter of acceptance of the call to Plymouth Church, dated August 19, 1847, was addressed to Howard,

10. Isaac Parker to HWB, Boston, August 11, 1847, CtY.
11. Joseph Howard, Jr., *Life of Henry Ward Beecher*, pp. 131–32.
12. *Ibid.*
13. Henry C. Bowen to HWB, New York, August 17, 1847, CtY.
14. John L. Ketcham to David Merrill, Indianapolis, August 18, 1847, Samuel Merrill Papers, InHi; Calvin Fletcher Diary, August 18, 1847, InHi; HWB to Mrs. Henry Ward Beecher, Indianapolis, September 5, 1847, CtY; Henry C. Bowen to HWB, New York, September 6, 1847, CtY.

Bowen, Charles Rowland, and other officials. It accepted the call, mentioned his diffidence in assuming the responsibility, and stated that he hoped to move to Brooklyn in late October.[15] The suspense was over. Beecher would become the first pastor of the Plymouth Church in Brooklyn. That it was Congregational instead of Presbyterian was of no consequence to him. He would receive almost twice as much salary his first year there as he was supposedly being paid in Indianapolis plus the additional money subscribed to pay his debts and defray his traveling expenses.

The Beechers lost little time in making preparations to leave Indianapolis. Hastening to quit the detested Hoosier capital, Eunice Beecher's only regret was that the "little green graves" must be left. She and her children left the city for Walnut Hills escorted by Beecher and Talbut Bullard. Beecher remained there with them for a few days to visit with his family and then returned to Indianapolis while Bullard escorted Eunice and the children to Massachusetts where they would remain until Beecher came to take them to Brooklyn.[16]

Eunice Beecher's departure was not mourned by the people of Indianapolis. Beecher had given his wife's poor health as his reason for leaving the West, but some in and out of his church diagnosed the nature of her illness to suit themselves. Beecher had "returned from the East fully set to remain with us," wrote John L. Ketcham, *"if his wife could live* in the West. But if it became manifest that he should, by remaining loose [*sic*] her, he told me he should at once, without any noise, or consultation, go to the East for a time. And sure enough," continued Ketcham, "Mrs. Beecher has already had another attack of her disease—palpitation of the heart." Not only was Ketcham skeptical of the seriousness of Eunice Beecher's illness he also had little regard for her character. "Mrs. B[eecher] has not, I really believe," he wrote, "a real friend in the Church. Full of large tales, and enormous exaggerations, no one believes a word she says. And I believe the opinion is

15. HWB to John T. Howard, Henry C. Bowen *et al.*, Indianapolis, August 19, 1847, quoted in Knox, *Life and Work of Henry Ward Beecher*, pp. 128–29.

16. Margaret [Jackson ?] to Lydia Jackson Beecher, Walnut Hills, August 21, 1847, CtHS-D; Mrs. Beecher, "Mr. Beecher as I Knew Him," *Ladies Home Journal*, January, 1892, p. 5; [Mrs. Beecher], *From Dawn to Daylight*, p. 338; HWB, Sermons, August 22, 1847, CtY.

Julia Merrill

EMILY B. MOORES

general that her recent sickness was *for the occasion.*"[17] Henry Ward Beecher professed to take his wife's symptoms seriously and wrote to Harriet that Eunice had lately had spasms from which she had almost perished.[18]

Despite their personal regard for Henry Ward Beecher the Merrill family had continued to hope that David Merrill could one day be persuaded to come and settle in Indianapolis. On the same day that Beecher's resignation was accepted Ketcham wrote to David Merrill,

17. John L. Ketcham to David Merrill, Indianapolis, August 12 and 18, 1847, Samuel Merrill Papers, InHi.

18. Margaret [Jackson ?] to Lydia Jackson Beecher, Walnut Hills, August 21, 1847, CtHS-D.

his wife's uncle, offering him the pastorate of the Second Presbyterian Church.[19] Merrill was not interested and once again refused the post. A month later two men were considered for the position. One was a young graduate, name now unknown, of the New York Theological Seminary and the other was the Reverend Shubert Granby Spees of Cincinnati with whom Beecher was acquainted and who would succeed the latter as pastor of the Second Presbyterian Church in Indianapolis.[20]

News of Beecher's resignation evoked little real regret among the members of his church. "We have liked him as a preacher but many of the Ch[urch] as I now learn," commented Samuel Merrill, "complain much of him as a Pastor."[21] Eight years as minister of the Indianapolis church had not helped Beecher erase the faults for which he had been censured in Lawrenceburgh. It was the opinion of Ketcham, a shrewd observer, that Beecher was "a great man in the pulpit—but wofully deficient in every other respect. Often he has failed to attend prayer meeting without any excuse. Never has been in Sabbath School more than thrice in his residence here of seven years. Visits almost none among his people. Makes appointments for meetings of Session, & half the time forgets them. Always funny & often frivolous."[22] After a serious illness or other crisis Beecher habitually vowed to perform his pastoral duties more conscientiously, but it was never long until he had resumed his accustomed pattern of attending to his interests and inclinations and putting off unpleasant duties until a more convenient season.

Just as in Lawrenceburgh he had been credited as an able preacher so, continued Ketcham, Beecher had "the admiration of every body—and I should think that he has been off on preaching and other excursions at least one quarter of his time since he has been our Pastor. Well, he always made a noise wherever he went and we were flatered by it & held on." Few people really regretted Beecher's resignation, though.

19. John L. Ketcham to David Merrill, Indianapolis, August 12, 1847, Samuel Merrill Papers, InHi.

20. HWB to Mrs. Henry Ward Beecher, Indianapolis, September 12, 1847, CtY; Moore, *History of the Presbytery of Indianapolis*, p. 54.

21. Samuel Merrill to David Merrill, Indianapolis, September 5, 1847, Samuel Merrill Papers, InHi.

22. John L. Ketcham to David Merrill, Indianapolis, August 18, 1847, Samuel Merrill Papers, InHi; John R. Howard, *Henry Ward Beecher*, p. 146.

"The truth is, we, as a *town,* feel that we are loosing a valuable citizen; but he has never endeared himself as a pastor to his church—he has not been a Pastor at al—only a brilliant preacher—and brilliant he is."[23]

Although the male members of her family could speak calmly of Beecher's impending departure, Julia Merrill was very upset by the prospect. She had known for months that the clergyman might accept a pastorate in the East, so she was not surprised by his resignation. Wishing to be with him as much as she could before he would leave for good, Julia found out when he was expected to return from Walnut Hills where he had taken Eunice and the children. It was her plan to take Elizabeth Bates and meet Beecher at Greenwood south of Indianapolis and have the pleasure of riding with him in a buggy to the capital city. Julia Merrill's mother was sick, however, and decided to leave immediately to consult physicians in Cincinnati. The mortally ill and extremely weak Mrs. Merrill insisted that Julia accompany her on the arduous journey. As a result, Julia had to give up her scheme to meet Beecher at Greenwood. She wrote sadly to Elizabeth Bates how much she "had hoped to see Mr. Beecher again—but—I could not." Of the journey as far as Madison she continued, "I rode silently along for miles, . . . and thought over for the thousandth time all those happy days which are *gone.*"[24] Her mother's illness did not distract her from this private grief.

Julia's woes might have been magnified if she had known that her affairs were being discussed publicly in Indianapolis. Sometime earlier in the summer Talbut Bullard had proposed marriage to her and been refused. His haste to marry after his wife's death the previous year was thought unseemly, and he became almost a figure of fun to the young women of Indianapolis. News of Julia's refusal leaked out. It was assumed that it was she who had told, and she was widely criticized for her supposed lack of tact and sympathy. Beecher heard of it, of course, and did what he could to set the matter aright. At tea one afternoon where it was being discussed Beecher "cleared Julia of all

23. John L. Ketcham to David Merrill, Indianapolis, September 29, 1847, Samuel Merrill Papers, InHi; John L. Ketcham to HWB, Indianapolis, June 1, 1847, John L. Ketcham Papers, InHi.

24. Julia D. Merrill to Elizabeth Bates, Madison, September [?], 1847, Julia Merrill Moores Papers, InHi; HWB to Mrs. Henry Ward Beecher, Indianapolis, September 5, 1847, CtY.

blame. Told her [his hostess] that it got out through Ketcham and Merril [*sic*] & not by any fault of Julia's." Beecher was of the opinion that it would not injure either Bullard or Julia Merrill permanently in the eyes of the community.[25]

Unaware of the gossip about her at home, Julia arrived in Cincinnati with her ailing mother. She had little sympathy for the sick woman, and to Catharine Merrill she complained, "Oh Kate what am I to do? you know how badly I want to get home to see Mr. Beecher before he goes—I must—as long as there was any necessity on Ma's part . . . I could stay very willingly—but if I am to be detained here for no earthly reason Why—I shall almost rebel. . . . You know if I should miss seeing him altogether how many long years may elapse before I see him again."[26] Julia urged her sister to come and stay with their mother, so that she could return to Indianapolis to see Beecher. However, Mrs. Merrill was growing steadily worse and realized that she must leave for Indianapolis at once if she hoped to have strength to reach her home and family. She and Julia were met by Catharine at Columbus, and the trio proceeded slowly to the capital which they reached on Friday evening, September 24. "Mrs. Merrill is very low & sinking fast. It would be miraculous," commented Beecher to his wife, "if she lived many weeks."[27] Jane Anderson Merrill died on October 6, 1847.[28]

Henry Ward Beecher spent his last month in Indianapolis settling his financial affairs and making preparation to move eastward. Bowen had offered to help him find living quarters in Brooklyn, promised to care for any of the clergyman's plants which might be shipped East, and repeatedly expressed pleasure at the clergyman's expected arrival. Bowen thought it advisable to insert a gentle remonstrance in one letter which included some cancelled bills of Beecher's, and he stated

> if you [HWB] have *any more bills unpaid* in those parts please let us know & if it is not *too much* we will cancel them. We want you to be able to look every man in the face 'square & fair' & say (to yourself)

25. HWB to Mrs. Henry Ward Beecher, Indianapolis, September 12, 1847, CtY.
26. Julia D. Merrill to Catharine Merrill, Cincinnati, September 16, 1847, Samuel Merrill Papers, InHi.
27. HWB to Mrs. Henry Ward Beecher, Indianapolis, September 27, 1847, CtY.
28. For an account of her death see a letter written by Samuel Merrill to David Merrill, Indianapolis, October 6, 1847, Samuel Merrill Papers, InHi.

I owe you nothing. If you get into debt when you get here you must 'look
out for yourself' as I am afraid my agency or the agency of your friends
will not be quite so *promptly* responded to a second time for the same
thing.[29]

Beecher's furniture was not considered valuable enough to warrant the
expense of shipping it to Brooklyn, so he sold it. He planned to take
only his clothes, a few keepsakes, his papers, and his books to his new
home. Since he had acquired scores of books, there was much work
entailed in packing them properly for shipment. Beecher found the task
irksome and spread it over a period of days between other chores and
diversions. He lived alone in the house on East Ohio Street, for it was
"the pleasantest place, after all, that I can find."[30]

He missed his wife. "Oh how glad I shall be to hold you once more
in my arms! To kiss you & love you & talk of a thousand things. . . . I
never knew how necessary you are to my comfort and happiness untill
you are separated from me." Nearly two weeks later he wrote in the
same vein, "Oh how I long to see you. To stay much longer here would
dry me up. When I get on the journey the excitement & the feeling of
progress toward you will make it easier to bear." He was lingering in
Indianapolis mainly to attend the wedding of Talbut Bullard to Catherine Phalan. "I really feel," stated Beecher,

> a little hurt. . . that Rev. Mr. [Samuel Lee] Johnson [rector of Christ
> Church] is to perform the ceremony. . . . But it seemed to me that rela-
> tionship on his [Talbut Bullard's] part should have been of more account
> with Cate, than the not particularly important relation wh[ich] Mr.
> Johnson sustains to her. Although I very much like Cate, yet the other
> influences under which Talbut will be left are not such as I could desire,
> & his weakness on the side of flattery is so great that I have little hope of
> any remedy. It is one of those cases about which we must make up our
> minds to hope for the best, & let it alone.

Talbut Bullard and Catherine Phalan married without Beecher's professional aid on September 30, 1847, and in time became the parents of
six children. Bullard practiced medicine in Indianapolis until his death
in 1863.[31]

29. Henry C. Bowen to HWB, New York, September 1 and 16, 1847, CtY.

30. HWB to Mrs. Henry Ward Beecher, Indianapolis, September 5 and 12,
1847, CtY.

31. HWB to Mrs. Henry Ward Beecher, September 5, 12, and 24, 1847, CtY;
Dunn, *Greater Indianapolis*, I, 129, 611.

Henry Ward Beecher delivered his farewell sermon at the Second Presbyterian Church of Indianapolis on Sunday morning, September 26, 1847. He gave as his reason for leaving the West the necessity of taking Eunice to a healthier climate, and he did not mention his difficulty in collecting his full salary. Beecher could derive satisfaction that the church was united and prosperous. In the eight years he served as its pastor its membership had climbed to over two hundred seventy people. This time he could not be accused of abandoning a faltering church. In the evening he spoke to the young men of the community. He was pleased that they had raised a subscription among themselves to purchase a gold watch which they presented to him. "Such tokens of kindness," Beecher wrote, "especially when I have not turned aside from ever a painful fidelity, is especially comforting."[32] His years of work in Indianapolis for the Second Presbyterian Church, the city, and the state received no other tangible recognition.

Three days later he held an auction at which he sold such of his plants and trees as he could. What remained were divided among a few of his friends. "On Friday morning, I shall start for *home, happiness* & you! May God preserve us to a happy meeting," he wrote to Eunice.[33]

Beecher's departure from Indianapolis was overshadowed by the arrival of the first train ever to puff its way into the city. First projected in 1834, construction of the Madison and Indianapolis Railroad was completed in 1847 at an average cost of $800 per mile of track. In recent years Samuel Merrill had been a leading promoter of the enterprise.[34] When the train's arrival was announced for the first week in October visitors began to pour into Indianapolis to witness the event.

32. HWB to Mrs. Henry Ward Beecher, Indianapolis, September 27, 1847, CtY; Stowe, *Saints, Sinners and Beechers*, pp. 271–72; [Mrs. Beecher], *From Dawn to Daylight*, p. 326; Edson, *The Church God's Building*, p. 7.

33. Mrs. Beecher, "Mr. Beecher as I Knew Him," *Ladies Home Journal*, January, 1892, p. 5; Knox, *Life and Work of Henry Ward Beecher*, p. 95; HWB to Mrs. Henry Ward Beecher, Indianapolis, September 27, 1847, CtY; [Mrs. Beecher], *From Dawn to Daylight*, pp. 331–32.

34. Merrill purportedly proposed HWB's name as a candidate to be a superintendent on the Madison and Indianapolis Railroad but the latter was defeated by one vote. No substantiation for this could be located in either Beecher or Merrill papers. See Joseph Howard, Jr., *Life of Henry Ward Beecher*, p. 61; Dunn, *Indiana and Indianans*, I, 393, 400; Calvin Fletcher Diary, October [?], 1847, InHi; Graydon, "A Pioneer Tale, The Life of Samuel Merrill," pp. 14–15, In.

Putting on steam at Greenwood the train came tearing into the city on October 1, at a speed of twelve miles per hour and came to a stop at its terminal on South Street. Beecher planned to leave aboard it when it made the return trip to Madison.

Beecher ate his last breakfast in Indianapolis at the table of Samuel Merrill. Julia walked with him to the terminal and waited with him until the train pulled away an hour and a half late. No one else came to say goodbye to him. When he boarded the train, he found what passed for a seat. Beecher observed that "the car was no car at all, a mere extempore wood box, used sometimes without seats for hogs, but with seats for men; of which class I (oh! me miserable!) happened to be one."[35] His discomfort was shared by other passengers, including his seat mate William H. Wishard. Wishard, two years younger than Beecher, was a Presbyterian and physician who had studied at the Ohio Medical College in Cincinnati, and the men had mutual acquaintances and interests. Beecher was not proud of being a passenger on the first train ever to go from Indianapolis to Madison for there was little glory and less comfort in it. The tiresome journey ended when the train arrived in Madison at eleven o'clock at night, and Beecher learned that all the taverns were full.[36]

In preparing to leave Indianapolis Beecher had of necessity and choice severed most of his ties with its residents. What business affairs remained would be dispatched by mail or by Talbut Bullard acting as his agent. Only the problem presented by Julia Merrill's attachment for him and her distress at his departure caused him concern and occupied his thoughts next morning as he waited for the boat which would carry him to Cincinnati. "From me you have probably received more ideas," he wrote to her, "more influences going to form opinion, & character than from all others." He reminisced about their long acquaintanceship and indicated the changing nature of their relationship. In an uncharacteristically obscure style he continued,

> As I sat upon the wharf-boat & looked upon the water I thought of the passage of life, ... Who knows the fate of that half wilted flower that is flowing past? At what point. . . will it sink? Who that sees these

35. HWB to Julia D. Merrill, Madison, October 3, 1847, Julia Merrill Moores Papers, InHi.
36. *Ibid.*; Dunn, *Indiana and Indianans*, IV, 1627–29.

passing objects can have one idea of their destiny, except that they will be wafted down, *no one can tell when*. And who can look down that darker strand on which *we* lie; or tell its events—or presume our history. . . . Those who best know themselves—how longingly do they desire shadows to depart, and the reality to come. The number is few; few sit waiting for hope of glory; yet there are *some*; some who awaken to sing at the approaching dawn as birds do in the twilight of morning. And when such find each other out, it seems hard that they should be parted. But of this too God knows best.[37]

Was the half-wilted flower a euphemism for Eunice Beecher? Was he making a guarded promise to Julia? If this were true, it would seem to be a highly personal letter, yet he wrote that Julia might care to share it with Elizabeth Bates. Perhaps he was simply attempting to ease Julia's pain at their parting by intimating that it might not be for long. His solution to this temptation, his other problems, and his dissatisfaction with life in Indianapolis was clear. He boarded a packet at Madison on October 3, 1847, which would take him to Cincinnati and, ultimately, "home, happiness" and Eunice. A destiny awaited him that would find him at his death forty years later considered by his contemporaries as one of the most famous and influential Americans of the nineteenth century.

37. HWB to Julia D. Merrill, Madison, October 3, 1847, Julia Merrill Moores Papers, InHi. Julia Merrill married Charles W. Moores on December 25, 1854.

Bibliographical Note

AFTER BEECHER'S DEATH IN 1887 THERE APPEARED NUMEROUS BIOG-
raphies devoting a few chapters to his residence in Indiana. The best is
A Biography of Henry Ward Beecher (New York, 1888) by his son,
William C. Beecher, and son-in-law, Samuel Scoville. This family biog-
raphy contains facts and reminiscences not available elsewhere and
has been drawn upon heavily by succeeding biographers. Thomas W.
Knox's *Life and Work of Henry Ward Beecher* (Chicago, 1887) presents
additional information about the clergyman's career. Joseph Howard,
Jr.'s *Life of Henry Ward Beecher* (Philadelphia, 1887) and John R.
Howard's *Henry Ward Beecher* (New York, 1891) are most valuable
for the information they include about the events which culminated in
Beecher's leaving Indianapolis to become minister of Plymouth Church
in Brooklyn. John H. Barrow's *Henry Ward Beecher, the Shakespeare
of the Pulpit* (New York, 1893) and other biographies owe much to
the preceding works. The pertinent chapters in Paxton Hibben's *Henry
Ward Beecher: An American Portrait* (New York, 1927) are not reliable. Annie Beecher Scoville, Beecher's granddaughter, has left a critical
commentary among her papers in the Yale University Library which
clearly defines the inadequacies of Hibben's work. Additional errors in
Hibben's biography of Beecher were found in the preparation of this
study. Lyman B. Stowe's *Saints, Sinners and Beechers* (Indianapolis,
1934) contains facts about the family not published previously.

Henry Ward Beecher's published sermons, lectures, and essays are extremely readable and contain useful biographical data in anecdotes and illustrations. An informative and useful book is a semi-fictional narrative written by Mrs. Henry Ward Beecher under the pseudonym "A Minister's Wife." Entitled *From Dawn to Daylight* (New York, 1859), it is an account of her domestic life and attitudes while living in Indiana. Mrs. Beecher did stray from fact when she enlarged the extent of her good deeds; changed the order of some events, for example, the date of an individual's death; and exaggerated the motives and actions, real or suspected, of acquaintances. In referring to passages in *From Dawn to Daylight* care has been taken to verify the accuracy of their content with other sources.

A recent thesis by Clifford Clark, Jr., entitled "Henry Ward Beecher: Revivalist and Antislavery Leader, 1813–1867" (Unpublished Ph.D. thesis, Harvard University, 1968) is of interest for some insights it gives into Beecher's character.

There are relatively few articles which deal extensively with Beecher's life in Indiana. Possibly the most valuable is "Mr. Beecher as I Knew Him" written by Mrs. Henry Ward Beecher and published in ten installments in *Ladies Home Journal* (October, 1891–August, 1892). Much of the material is based on family letters and reminiscences. Reference has been made only to those events noted in the articles about which other proof exists.

The largest collection of Beecher letters, diaries, journals, sermons, and miscellaneous papers which are relevant is located in the Beecher Family Papers at Yale University Library. Less extensive collections are housed in the Library of Congress and in the library of The Stowe-Day Foundation. Useful items were discovered in the Beecher-Stowe Family Papers in the Schlesinger Library, Radcliffe College, and in the Beecher Family Misc. MSS. at the Hayes Memorial Library in Fremont, Ohio. Scattered letters of value are located elsewhere. A loss of magnitude occurred when many letters written during Beecher's years in Indiana were destroyed when he left Indianapolis in 1847 (see Mrs. Henry Ward Beecher, "Mr. Beecher as I Knew Him," *Ladies Home Journal,* October, 1891, p. 3).

Church records are a fruitful source of information. The pertinent

Session records of the First Presbyterian Church (later Independent Presbyterian Church) at Lawrenceburgh, Indiana, were destroyed unfortunately by the effects of flood and mutilation (see John H. Thomas, *An Historical Sketch of the Presbyterian Church of Lawrenceburgh, Indiana* [Lawrenceburgh, Ind., 1887], pp. i, 11). The American Home Missionary Society Papers (microfilm copy, Indiana Division, Indiana State Library) contain information pertinent to Henry Ward Beecher and aspects of missionary work in Indiana. Records of the Presbytery of Indianapolis and Records of the Synod of Indiana located in the Archives at the Hanover College Library are helpful in reconstructing Beecher's participation in denominational affairs, as are records relating to his interest in Wabash College in the Archives at the Wabash College Library. The Records of the Second Presbyterian Church, Indianapolis, Indiana, are invaluable as a source of detailed information about Beecher's pastorate. In cases where Beecher initiated or participated in disciplinary actions against members of a church the members' names have not been included when they figured in no other incident in Beecher's career and when no valid purpose could be served historically.

References to Henry Ward Beecher and his life in Indianapolis abound in the Samuel Merrill Papers, Julia Merrill Moores Papers, and the Calvin Fletcher Papers housed in the Indiana Historical Society Library. In the Indiana Division, Indiana State Library, are unpublished reminiscences about Beecher or containing reference to him. These include Katharine Merrill Graydon's "A Pioneer Tale, The Life of Samuel Merrill," Jane Merrill Ketcham's "Presbyterian (Marion County) History of 2nd Presbyterian Church of Indianapolis," and her "Reminiscences of Jane Merrill Ketcham," and Margaret M. Scott's "Local Woman Tells of Early Indianapolis and of Mr. McGuffy's [*sic*] 'Select School' for Young Ladies in Ky." Of these, Mrs. Ketcham's are the most useful. Although her time sense was occasionally distorted, her memories of events were generally accurate when compared with other evidence. A service of the Indiana State Library which is helpful is its Indiana Biographical Series, consisting of indexed newspaper clippings of obituaries and reminiscences about prominent figures in Indiana history.

Newspapers are excellent sources of information about Beecher's activities in Indiana. The Lawrenceburgh *Political Beacon*, Indianapolis newspapers, the *Indiana Farmer and Gardener* and its successor, the *Western Farmer and Gardener* were especially valuable.

Indeed, one cannot fail to be impressed by the abundance of surviving material about this supposedly obscure portion of Henry Ward Beecher's life. Other references of secondary importance have been cited in the notes.

Index